Language for Life

GLENCOE SPANISH

1A & 1B

ALL NEW LANGUAGE ADVENTURES

STUDENT EDITION

DESIGNED WITH YOUNGER STUDENTS IN MIND

STEP-BY-STEP: LOGICAL LANGUAGE SEQUENCING

Junior High and Intermediate students get an early start in building practical skills, step-by-step, through the real-life contexts that are the heart of this program. Logical language sequencing provides a solid foundation for language learning and retention.

GLENCOE SPANISH Level 1A is composed of the first eight chapters of the **Bienvenidos Level 1** text. **Level 1B** includes an introductory **Repaso** and the remaining eight chapters of the **Level 1** program.

OBJECTIVES FOR SUCCESS

Set the scene . . . and the pace

As soon as they begin each chapter, students know what skills they are expected to master. Introduced by colorful photographs, chapter openers:

- ★ clearly list objectives
- ★ set the chapter theme
- ★ give students a glimpse of the Spanish-speaking world
- ★ promote curiosity and interest in building skills

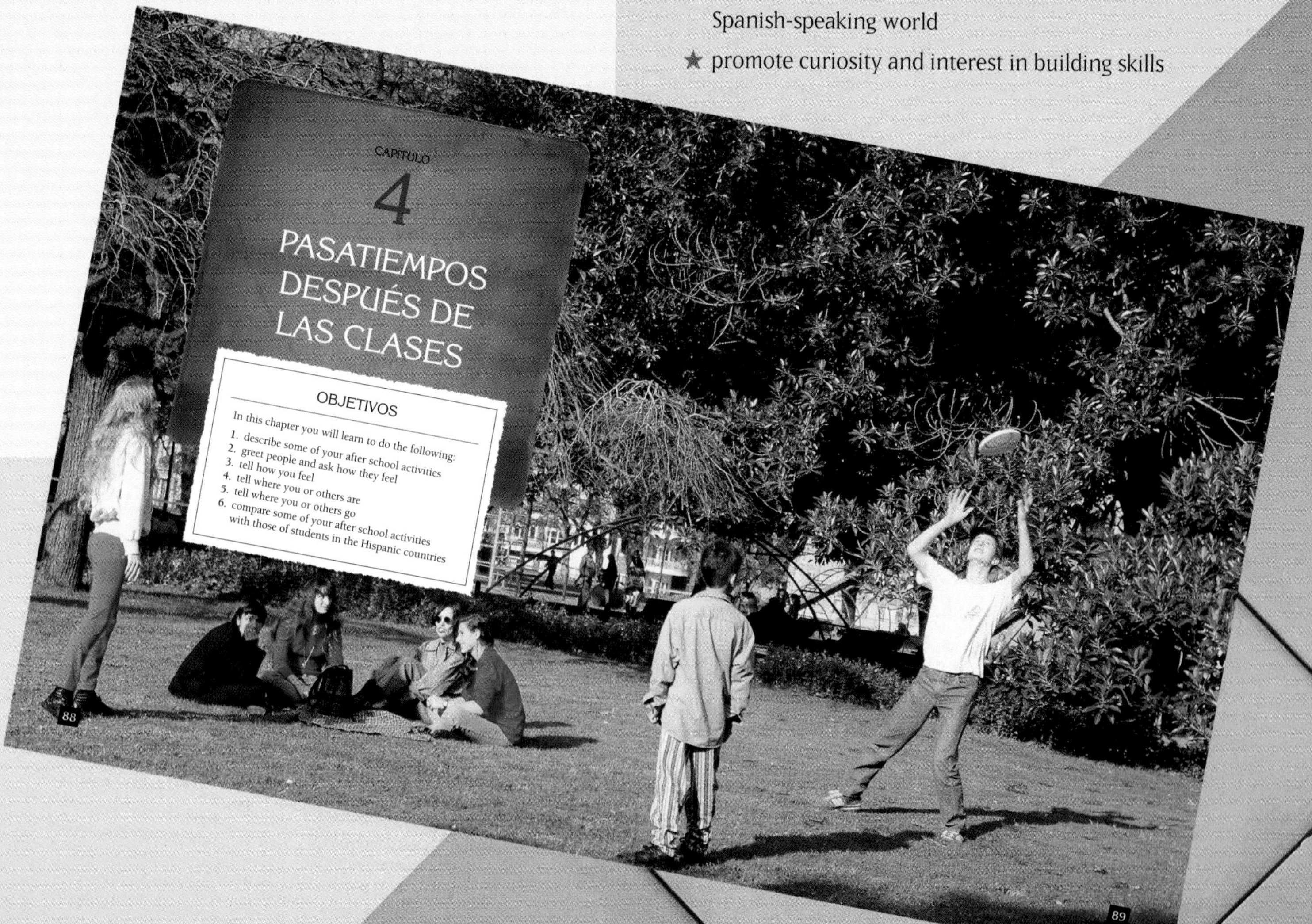

CAPÍTULO
4
PASATIEMPOS DESPUÉS DE LAS CLASES
OBJETIVOS
In this chapter you will learn to do the following:
1. describe some of your after school activities
2. greet people and ask how they feel
3. tell how you feel
4. tell where you or others are
5. tell where you or others go
6. compare some of your after school activities with those of students in the Hispanic countries
88
89

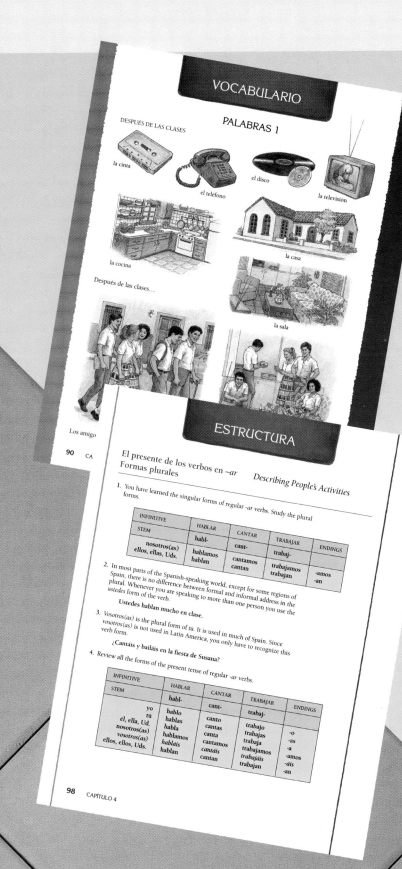

VOCABULARIO

PALABRAS 1

DESPUÉS DE LAS CLASES

la cinta

el teléfono

el disco

la televisión

la cocina

la casa

Después de las clases…

la sala

Los amigo

90   CA

ESTRUCTURA

El presente de los verbos en –ar
Formas plurales   *Describing People's Activities*

1. You have learned the singular forms of regular -ar verbs. Study the plural forms.

INFINITIVE	HABLAR	CANTAR	TRABAJAR	
STEM	habl-	cant-	trabaj-	ENDINGS
nosotros(as)	hablamos	cantamos	trabajamos	-amos
ellos, ellas, Uds.	hablan	cantan	trabajan	-an

2. In most parts of the Spanish-speaking world, except for some regions of Spain, there is no difference between formal and informal address in the plural. Whenever you are speaking to more than one person you use the *ustedes* form of the verb.

  Ustedes hablan mucho en clase.

3. *Vosotros(as)* is the plural form of *tú*. It is used in much of Spain. Since *vosotros(as)* is not used in Latin America, you only have to recognize this verb form.

  ¿Cantáis y bailáis en la fiesta de Susana?

4. Review all the forms of the present tense of regular -ar verbs.

INFINITIVE	HABLAR	CANTAR	TRABAJAR	
STEM	habl-	cant-	trabaj-	ENDINGS
yo	hablo	canto	trabajo	-o
tú	hablas	cantas	trabajas	-as
él, ella, Ud.	habla	canta	trabaja	-a
nosotros(as)	hablamos	cantamos	trabajamos	-amos
vosotros(as)	habláis	cantáis	trabajáis	-áis
ellos, ellos, Uds.	hablan	cantan	trabajan	-an

98   CAPÍTULO 4

VOCABULARIO

useful, thematic vocabulary enables students to communicate in real-life situations

With **GLENCOE SPANISH,** the difference is in the presentation. Vocabulary is always introduced under the umbrella of an overall theme. These themes are of high interest to younger students and cover such topics as sports, eating in a restaurant, leisure activities, plane travel and many more. New words are presented both individually and in context and are followed by Ejercicios and interactive Comunicación activities. This logical, culturally integrated vocabulary presentation ensures that your students will quickly be able to use these words in realistic situations.

ESTRUCTURA

clear explanations with concrete results

Students start with clear, concise structure explanations, then practice new grammar in carefully controlled exercises. Students build confidence by practicing these contextualized exercises before trying the open-ended Comunicación activities that follow. Your students will be challenged, yet comfortable, learning their new language.

COMUNICACIÓN

Students have numerous opportunities to use what they have learned in real-life communicative situations.

CONVERSACIÓN

A conversation is presented **after** the students have practiced the vocabulary and structure, enabling them to use these elements in a real-life situation.

ACTIVIDADES DE COMUNICACIÓN

These occur **3 times** in every chapter. Students practice the language they have learned in a variety of formats. Student-centered, lively activities encourage creative interactive participation. Some written communicative activities are presented.

LECTURA

skill building—with every reading

Through these engaging reading selections (all in Spanish), students can apply new grammar skills, study the proper usage of new vocabulary words and develop their critical-thinking skills—**all at the same time.**

REALIDADES

cultural insights complete the connection

Spectacular photographs and realia give students visual insight into the Spanish-speaking world—providing opportunities for discussions on the similarities and differences that exist between these cultures and Hispanic cultures in the United States.

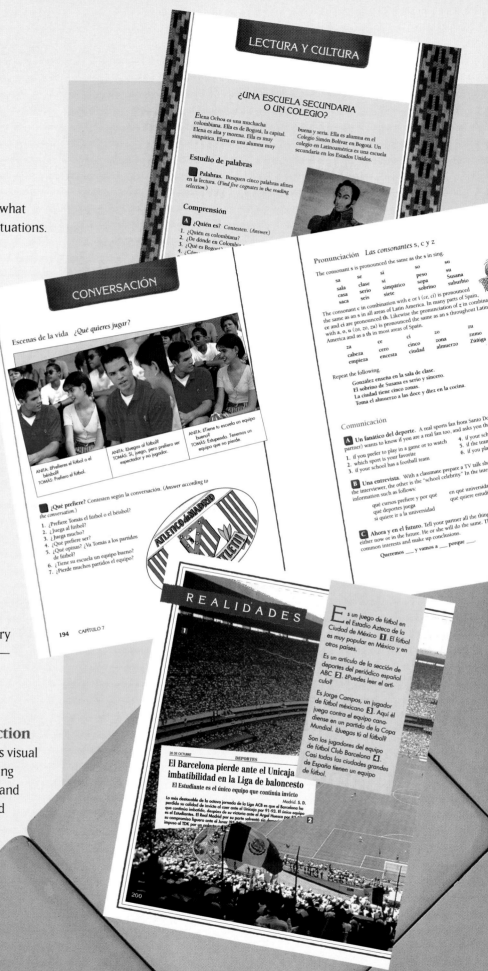

CULMINACIÓN

**integrates and evaluates
one chapter at a time**

Oral and written activities at the end of
each chapter require students to integrate
and evaluate the language and cultural
concepts they've just learned. The
Reintegración exercises help students build
skills incrementally by recalling important
words, expressions and structures from
current—and previous—chapters.

FONDO ACADÉMICO

**explores other disciplines
without leaving the language**

Through interdisciplinary readings in the natural sciences,
social sciences, and the arts and humanities, your
students are encouraged to stretch their Spanish reading
skills and gain meaningful insight into Hispanic cultures.

NUESTRO MUNDO

"hands-on" realia

Even more reading, culture and realia are provided in
Nuestro Mundo...no other program gives you more.

REPASO

recycling and review

Every fourth chapter is followed by **Repaso** sections that
recycle main vocabulary and structure points. New,
stimulating exercises, activities and dialogues help
students expand language skills.

YOUR ONE-SOURCE ONE-STOP TEACHING TOOL

NEW!
INTERLEAF SECTIONS FOR TEACHERS

Preceding every chapter, they contain additional teacher material such as Print and Multimedia Resources, Scope and Sequence and information about various program components.

TEACHER'S WRAPAROUND EDITION

Our comprehensive **Teacher's Wraparound Edition** gives you everything you need to introduce, explain and expand lessons—all in one place and all at a glance—so you're always flexible and always prepared.

The **Teacher's Wraparound Edition,** with pages identical to the student edition, plus teaching suggestions and techniques, enriches and expands every page. Activities encourage students to participate and communicate in pairs or cooperative learning groups.

VOCABULARIO
PALABRAS 1

Vocabulary Teaching Resources

1. Vocabulary Transparencies, 6.1 (A & B)
2. Audio Cassette 4B
3. Student Tape Manual, pages 212–213
4. Workbook, pages 55–56
5. Communication Activities Masters, pages 29-30, A & B
6. Chapter Quizzes, page 25 Palabras 1

Bell Ringer Review
Write the following on the board or use BRR Blackline Master 6-1: Complete.
1. La familia come en ___.
2. La familia prepara la comida en ___.
3. La familia mira la televisión en ___.
4. Hay siete ___ en la familia.
5. La casa está en la ___ Mayor.

VOCABULARIO

PALABRAS 1

LA FAMILIA

el abuelo   los abuelos   la abuela

los padres   los hijos

el padre   la madre   la hija   el hijo

el esposo   el marido   la esposa   la mujer   la tía   el tío

los tíos

los nietos

el nieto   el primo   la nieta   la sobrina   la prima   el sobrino

el gato   el perro

154   CAPÍTULO 6

TOTAL PHYSICAL RESPONSE

(following the Vocabulary presentation)

Getting Ready
For TPR 1 draw a family tree on the board. Write in the name of each family member.

TPR 1
___, levántate, por favor.
Ve a la pizarra.

Mira el árbol genealógico.
Toma la regla.
Enséñame, (indícame) Pepe.
Enséñame el padre de Pepe.
Y la tía de ___.
Enséñame su hermana.
Enséñame su tío.
Enséñame el primo de ___.
Enséñame a sus abuelos.
Gracias, ___. Regresa a tu asiento, por favor.

154

Es la familia Galdós.
El señor y la señora Galdós tienen dos hijos.
Tienen un hijo y una hija.
Los Galdós tienen un perro.
No tienen un gato.

¿Cuántos años tienen los hijos?
Pepe, el hijo, tiene dieciséis años.
Celia, la hija, tiene catorce años.
Son jóvenes. No son viejos.

CAPÍTULO 6   **155**

For TPR 2 dramatize the meaning of *escribe*.

TPR 2
Si tienen un hermano, levántense.
Y ahora siéntense.
Si tienen una hermana, levanten la mano.
___, ¿tú tienes una hermana, no? Levántate, por favor.
Ven acá.
Ve a la pizarra.
Toma la tiza.

Escribe el nombre de tu hermana en la pizarra.
¿Cuántos años tiene? Escribe su edad.
¿Ella va a qué escuela? Escribe el nombre de su escuela.
Gracias, ___. Pon la tiza aquí, por favor.
Y ahora, regresa a tu asiento y siéntate.

155

PRESENTATION
(pages 154–155)

A. Have students close their books. Using Vocabulary Transparencies 6.1 (A & B), have students repeat the names of the Galdós family after you or the recording on Cassette 4B. Be sure that they pronounce as carefully as possible.

B. Ask the following questions as students look at the transparencies: *¿Es la familia Galdós? ¿Es la familia Galdós o Marechal? ¿Qué familia es? ¿Tienen el señor y la señora Galdós dos hijos? ¿Tienen un hijo? ¿Tienen una hija? ¿Tienen dos o tres hijos? ¿Cuántos hijos tienen los Galdós? ¿Tienen un perro? ¿Tienen un gato? ¿Qué animalito tienen?*

C. Now have students open their books to pages 154–155 and read the words and sentences for additional reinforcement.

Vocabulary Expansion

You may wish to give students the following additional words:
una mascota
un cachorro
hijo único
hija única
gemelos

ABOUT THE LANGUAGE

1. Explain to students that in Spanish no *s* is added to the family name to include all the members: *los García, las Dávila, los Marechal, los Álvarez.*

2. The suffix *-astro(a)* means "step": *el padrastro, la madrasta, el hijastro, la hijastra.* In many areas its meaning is almost pejorative and it is not used. Depending on the degree of intimacy and if the biological parent is deceased, one may say *mi madre* for a stepmother. If the biological mother is alive, one would say, *la esposa de mi padre.* Instead of *hermanastro(a),* one would say either *hermano(a)* or *el/la hijo(a) de la esposa de mi padre.*

KEY TOPICS INCLUDE:

★ Chapter Resources
★ Bell Ringer Reviews
★ For the Younger Student
★ Geography Connection
★ Vocabulary Expansion
★ Cognate Recognition
★ Informal Assessment
★ Learning from Photos and Realia
★ Reteaching
★ Additional Practice
★ Independent Practice
★ Art/History Connection
★ Total Physical Response
★ Cooperative Learning
★ Did You Know?
★ Critical-Thinking Activities
★ For the Native Speaker
★ Chapter Projects

MORE THINGS TO DO . . .
AND MORE WAYS TO DO THEM

TEACHER'S
CLASSROOM RESOURCES

Evaluation, reinforcement and extra practice are all easy to access...and integrate...with the comprehensive resources found in **GLENCOE SPANISH Teacher's Classroom Resources.**

The **Writing Activities Workbook and Student Tape Manual** is a two-part workbook that offers:

★ **Additional writing practice** to reinforce the vocabulary and structure topics in each chapter.

★ **Activity sheets** for students to use when listening to the audio cassette recordings.

Additional resources include:

★ **Bell Ringer Reviews** serve as short warm-ups that recycle vocabulary and grammar from previous chapters.

★ **Communication Activities Masters** provide further opportunities for students to practice their communication skills in Spanish.

★ **Situation Cards** are sets of guided conversational situations correlated to each chapter.

★ **Overhead Transparencies Binder** includes five categories of colorful transparencies: **Vocabulary, Grammar/ Pronunciation, Communication, Maps and Fine Art.**

NEW! LESSON PLAN BOOKLET

Detailed plans for every chapter help teachers choose effective lesson formats.

NEW! PERFORMANCE ASSESSMENT

Task-based tests provide an alternative approach to measure student learning.

★ **Chapter Quizzes** are designed to help both students and teachers evaluate students' mastery of a specific vocabulary section or structure topic.

★ The Testing Program consists of three different types of tests: **discrete point tests, chapter proficiency tests** on blackline masters and the Computer Software Practice and Test Generator Program. The software component allows teachers to print out ready-made tests or to customize tests.

★ The **Video Cassette** and Videodisc Programs capture the flavor of Hispanic culture in the student text while reinforcing vocabulary and structure chapter-by-chapter. The video is accompanied by a **Video Activities Booklet.**

★ The Audio Cassette Program includes recorded material for each chapter of **GLENCOE SPANISH.** Also available in CD format.

★ **CD-ROM Programs** enhance and expand upon what is in the textbook. They can be used for makeup, practice, reward or as a full-class presentation. Students receive immediate confirmation of their responses, written and oral.

GLENCOE SPANISH . . .
THE DIFFERENCE BETWEEN ORDINARY AND EXTRAORDINARY!

UNLOCK STUDENT POTENTIAL WITH THE POWER OF GLENCOE SPANISH.

LEVEL 1: PART A

0-02-641011-7	Student Edition 1A
0-02-641012-5	Teacher's Wraparound Edition 1A
0-02-641015-X	Writing Activities Workbook & Student Tape Manual 1A, SE
0-02-641004-4	Writing Activities Workbook, TAE
0-02-641017-6	Student Tape Manual, TE
0-02-641026-5	Transparency Binder

LEVEL 1: PART B

0-02-641013-3	Student Edition 1B
0-02-641014-1	Teacher's Wraparound Edition 1B
0-02-641016-8	Writing Activities Workbook & Student Tape Manual 1B, SE
0-02-641004-4	Writing Activities Workbook, TAE
0-02-641017-6	Student Tape Manual, TE
0-02-641024-9	Teacher's Classroom Resources (Parts A & B Combined)

LEVEL 1 (A & B COMBINED)

0-02-641001-X	Student Edition
0-02-641002-8	Teacher's Wraparound Edition
0-02-641003-6	Writing Activities Workbook & Student Tape Manual, SE

RESOURCES

0-02-641008-7	Audio Cassette Program with Student Tape Manual, TE
0-02-641009-5	Audio Compact Disc Program with Student Tape Manual, TE
0-02-641031-1	Bell Ringer Reviews
0-02-641022-2	Communication Activities Masters
0-02-641023-0	Situation Cards
0-02-641005-2	Chapter Quizzes with Answer Key
0-02-641007-9	Testing Program with Test Cassettes Binder
0-02-641006-0	Testing Program Booklet with Answer Key
0-02-641018-4	Video Cassette Program with Video Activities Booklet
0-02-641019-2	Videodisc Program with Video Activities Booklet
0-02-641021-4	VideoActivities Booklet with Video Script
	Practice & Test Generator
0-02-641027-3	IBM
0-02-641028-1	Apple
0-02-641029-X	Macintosh
0-02-641032-X	Spanish for Spanish Speakers
0-02-641033-8	Spanish for Spanish Speakers, TAE
0-02-641053-2	Performance Assessment Tests
0-02-641054-0	Lesson Plans
0-02-646102-1	CD-ROM (Class Disk Package)

GLENCOE
McGraw-Hill

FOR MORE INFORMATION, CONTACT YOUR NEAREST REGIONAL OFFICE OR CALL

1-800-334-7344

FL 91270-9

1. Northeast Region
Glencoe/McGraw-Hill
15 Trafalgar Square #201
Nashua, NH 03063-1968
Phone: 603-880-4701
Phone: 800-424-3451
Fax: 603-595-0204

2. Mid-Atlantic Region
Glencoe/McGraw-Hill
P.O. Box 458
Hightstown, NJ 08520-0458
Phone: 609-426-5560
Phone: 800-553-7515
Fax: 609-426-7063

3. Atlantic-Southeast Region
Glencoe/McGraw-Hill
Brookside Park
One Harbison Way, Suite 101
Columbia, SC 29212
Phone: 803-732-2365
Phone: 800-731-2365
Fax: 803-732-4582

4. Southeast Region
Glencoe/McGraw-Hill
6510 Jimmy Carter Boulevard
Norcross, GA 30071
Phone: 770-446-7493
Phone: 800-982-3992
Fax: 770-446-2356

5. Mid-America Region
Glencoe/McGraw-Hill
936 Eastwind Drive
Westerville, OH 43081
Phone: 614-890-1111
Phone: 800-848-1567
Fax: 614-899-4905

6. Great Lakes Region
Glencoe/McGraw-Hill
846 East Algonquin Road
Schaumburg, IL 60173
Phone: 708-397-8448
Phone: 800-762-4876
Fax: 708-397-9472

7. Mid-Continent Region
Glencoe/McGraw-Hill
846 East Algonquin Road
Schaumburg, IL 60173
Phone: 708-397-8448
Phone: 800-762-4876
Fax: 708-397-9472

8. Southwest Region
Glencoe/McGraw-Hill
320 Westway Place, Suite 550
Arlington, TX 76018
Phone: 817-784-2113
Phone: 800-828-5096
Fax: 817-784-2116

9. Texas Region
Glencoe/McGraw-Hill
320 Westway Place, Suite 550
Arlington, TX 76018
Phone: 817-784-2100
Phone: 800-828-5096
Fax: 817-784-2116

10. Western Region
Glencoe/McGraw-Hill
709 E. Riverpark Lane, Suite 150
Boise, ID 83706
Phone: 208-368-0300
Phone: 800-452-6126
Fax: 208-368-0303
Includes Alaska

11. California Region
Glencoe/McGraw-Hill
15319 Chatsworth Street
P. O. Box 9609
Mission Hills, CA 91346
Phone: 818-898-1391
Phone: 800-423-9534
Fax: 818-898-3864
Includes Hawaii

Glencoe Catholic School Region
Glencoe/McGraw-Hill
25 Crescent Street, 1st Floor
Stamford, CT 06906
Phone: 203-964-9109
Phone: 800-551-8766
Fax: 203-967-3108

Canada
McGraw-Hill Ryerson Ltd.
300 Water Street
Whitby, Ontario
L1N 9B6, Canada
Phone: 905-430-5088
Fax: 905-430-5194

International
The McGraw-Hill Companies
International Marketing
1221 Avenue of the Americas
28th Floor
New York, NY 10020
Phone: 212-512-3641
Fax: 212-512-2186

DoDDS and Pacific Territories
McGraw-Hill School
Publishing Company
600 Delran Parkway
Delran, NJ 08075
Phone: 609-764-4586
Fax: 609-764-4587

Bienvenidos

ABOUT THE AUTHORS

Conrad J. Schmitt

Conrad J. Schmitt received his B.A. degree magna cum laude from Montclair State College, Upper Montclair, NJ. He received his M.A. from Middlebury College, Middlebury, VT. He did additional graduate work at Seton Hall University and New York University.

Mr. Schmitt has taught Spanish and French at the elementary, junior, and senior high school levels. He was Coordinator of Foreign Languages for Hackensack, New Jersey, Public Schools. He also taught Spanish at Upsala College, East Orange, NJ; Spanish at Montclair State College; and Methods of Teaching a Foreign Language at the Graduate School of Education, Rutgers University, New Brunswick, NJ. He was editor-in-chief of Foreign Languages and Bilingual Education for McGraw-Hill Book Company and Director of English language Materials for McGraw-Hill International Book Company.

Mr. Schmitt has authored or co-authored more than eighty books, all published by Glencoe, a division of Macmillan/McGraw-Hill, or by McGraw-Hill. He has addressed teacher groups and given workshops in all states of the U.S. and has lectured and presented seminars throughout the Far East, Europe, Latin America, and Canada. In addition, Mr. Schmitt has travelled extensively throughout Spain, Central and South America, and the Caribbean.

Protase E. Woodford

Protase "Woody" Woodford has taught Spanish at all levels from elementary school through graduate school. At the Educational Testing Service in Princeton, NJ, he was Director of Test Development, Director of Language Programs, Director of International Testing Programs and Director of the Puerto Rico Office. He was appointed "Distinguished Linguist" at the U.S. Naval Academy in 1988. He is the author of over two dozen Spanish and English language textbooks for schools and colleges. He has served as a consultant to the American Council on the Teaching of Foreign Languages (ACTFL), the National Assessment of Educational Progress, the College Board, the United Nations Secretariat, UNESCO, the Organization of American States, the U.S. Office of Education, the United States Agency for International Development (AID), the World Bank, the Japanese Ministry of International Trade and Industry, and many ministries of education in Asia, Latin America, and the Middle East. In 1994 he was invited to chair the National Advisory Council on Standards in Foreign Language Education.

GLENCOE SPANISH 1

Bienvenidos

Conrad J. Schmitt

Protase E. Woodford

GLENCOE

McGraw-Hill

New York, New York   Columbus, Ohio   Mission Hills, California   Peoria, Illinois

Glencoe/McGraw-Hill

A Division of The **McGraw·Hill** *Companies*

Copyright ©1997 by the Glencoe/McGraw-Hill School Publishing
Company. All rights reserved. Except as permitted under the United
States Copyright Act, no part of this publication may be reproduced or
distributed in any form or by any means, or stored in a database of
retrieval system, without prior permission of the publisher.

Printed in the United States of America

Send all inquiries to:

Glencoe/McGraw-Hill
15319 Chatsworth Street
P.O. Box 9609
Mission Hills, CA 91346-9609

ISBN 0-02-641002-8 (Teacher's Wraparound National Edition)
ISBN 0-02-641012-5 (Teacher's Wraparound Part A National Edition)
ISBN 0-02-641014-1 (Teacher's Wraparound Part B National Edition)

1 2 3 4 5 6 7 8 9   AGH   02 01 00 99 98 97 96

CONTENTS

INTRODUCTION

Welcome to **Glencoe Spanish**, the junior high and high school Spanish series from the Glencoe Division of Macmillan/McGraw-Hill School Publishing Company. Every element in this series has been designed to help you create an atmosphere of challenge, variety, cooperation and enjoyment for your students. From the moment you begin to use **Glencoe Spanish**, you will notice that not only is it packed with exciting, practical materials and features designed to stimulate young people to work together towards language proficiency, but that it goes beyond by urging students to use their new skills in other areas of the curriculum.

Glencoe Spanish uses an integrated approach to language learning. The introduction and presentation of new material, reinforcement of previously learned material, evaluation, review, exercises and activities in **Glencoe Spanish** are designed to span all four language skills. Another characteristic of this series is that students use and reinforce these new skills while developing a realistic, up-to-date awareness of the Hispanic culture. **Glencoe Spanish** incorporates a new feature unique to this series. Spanish is used as the medium of instruction for a series of interdisciplinary presentations in the areas of natural sciences, social sciences, and the arts and humanities.

The Teacher's Wraparound Edition you are reading has been developed based on the advice of experienced foreign language educators throughout the United States in order to meet your needs as a teacher both in and out of the foreign language classroom. Here are some of the features and benefits which make **Glencoe Spanish** a powerful set of teaching tools:

- flexible format
- student-centered instruction
- balance among all four language skills
- contextualized vocabulary
- thorough, contextual presentation of grammar
- an integrated approach to culture

FEATURES AND BENEFITS

Flexible Format While we have taken every opportunity to use the latest in pedagogical developments in order to create a learning atmosphere of variety, vitality, communication and challenge, we have also made every effort to make the **Glencoe Spanish** series "teacher-friendly."

Although the Student Textbook and the Teacher's Wraparound Edition provide an instructional method, every minute of every class period is not laid out. Plenty of room for flexibility has been built in to allow you to draw on your own education, experience and personality in order to tailor a language program that is suitable and rewarding for each individual class.

A closer look at the most basic component, the Student Textbook, serves as an example of this flexibility. Each chapter opens with two sections of vocabulary (*Vocabulario*: *Palabras* 1 and *Palabras* 2) each with its own set of exercises. *Vocabulario* is followed by *Estructura*, consisting of a series of grammar points, each with accompanying exercises. But there is nothing which says that the material must be presented in this order. The items of vocabulary and grammar are so well integrated that you will find it easy, and perhaps preferable, to move back and forth between them. You may also wish to select from the third and fourth sections of each chapter (the *Conversación* and *Lectura y Cultura* sections) at an earlier point than that in which they are presented, as a means of challenging students to identify or use the chapter vocabulary and grammar to which they have already been introduced.

These options are left to you. The only requirement for moving successfully through the Student Textbook is that the vocabulary and grammar of each chapter be presented in their entirety, since each succeeding chapter builds on what has come before.

In the Student Textbook, there is a marked difference between learning exercises (*Ejercicios*) and communication-based activities (*Comunicación*), both of which are provided in each chapter. The former serve as their name implies, as exercises for the acquisition and practice of new vocabulary and structures; while the latter are designed to get students communicating in open-ended contexts using the Spanish they have learned. You can be selective among these, depending on the needs of your students.

The abundance of suggestions for techniques, strategies, additional practice, chapter projects, independent (homework) assignments, informal assessment, and more, which are provided in this Teacher's Wraparound Edition—as well as the veritable banquet of resources available in the wide array of ancillary materials provided in the series—are what make **Glencoe Spanish** truly flexible and "teacher-friendly." They provide ideas and teaching tools from which to pick and choose in order to create an outstanding course.

Student-Centered Instruction Today's classroom is comprised of students who have different learning styles, special needs, and represent different cultural backgrounds. The emphasis on student-centered instruction provided by

Glencoe Spanish allows the teacher to capitalize on and deal positively with such diversity and encourage students to become involved in their own learning.

Glencoe Spanish anticipates the requirements of today's classroom by offering ideas for setting up a cooperative learning environment for students. Useful suggestions to this end accompany each chapter, under the heading Cooperative Learning, in the bottom margin of the Teacher's Wraparound Edition. Additional paired and group activities occur in the Student Textbook (*Comunicación*), and in other headings such as Additional Practice in the Teacher's Wraparound Edition. Besides cooperative learning strategies, **Glencoe Spanish** contains many other student-centered elements that allow students to expand their learning experiences. Here are some examples: suggestions are offered in the Teacher's Wraparound Edition for out-of-class chapter projects on topics related to the chapter theme and "For the Younger Student," activities aimed primarily at the middle school/junior-high student.

In the Student Textbook, new grammatical material is divided into "bite-sized" lessons, so as not to be intimidating. The Writing Activities Workbook provides a self-test after every fourth chapter, so that students can prepare alone or in study groups for teacher-administered quizzes and tests. The Audio Cassette Program allows students to work at their own pace, stopping the tape whenever necessary to make directed changes in the language or to refer to their activity sheets in the Student Tape Manual. The Computer Software element consists of not only a Test Generator for the teacher, but a Practice Generator for students, with which they can practice vocabulary and grammar items at their own pace.

These and other features discussed elsewhere in this Teacher's Manual have been designed with the student in mind. They assure that each individual, regardless of learning style, special need, background, or age, will have the necessary resources for becoming proficient in Spanish.

Balance Among All Four Language Skills

Glencoe Spanish provides a balanced focus on the listening, speaking, reading, and writing skills throughout all phases of instruction. It gives you leeway if you wish to adjust the integration of these skills to the needs of a particular individual, group or class. Several features of the series lend themselves to this: the overall flexibility of format, the abundance of suggested optional and additional activities and the design of the individual activities themselves. Let's look at some sections of a typical chapter as examples of the other two characteristics mentioned.

If the suggested presentation is followed, students are introduced to new words and phrases in *Vocabulario* by the teacher, and/or by the audio cassette presentation. The focus is on listening and speaking through modeling and repetition. The *Ejercicios* which accompany the *Vocabulario* section can be done with books either closed (accentuating listening and speaking) or open (accentuating reading, listening and speaking). However, these *Ejercicios* can just as well be assigned or reassigned as written work if the teacher wishes to have the whole class or individuals begin to concentrate on reading and writing. Throughout the *Vocabulario* section, optional and additional reinforcement activities are suggested in the Teacher's Wraparound Edition. These suggestions address all four language skills. Later in each chapter, students are asked to combine the material learned in *Vocabulario* with material from the grammar section (*Estructura*) using a combination of listening, reading, writing and speaking skills in the process.

Reading and writing activities are brought into play early in the **Glencoe Spanish** series. The authors realize that communication in Spanish includes the use of reading and writing skills and that these skills are indispensable for the assimilation and retention of new language and the organization of thought. Students are launched into writing, for example, as early as Chapter 1, through the use of brief assignments such as lists, labeled diagrams, note taking or short answers. Longer writing activities are added in later chapters. These textbook activities are further reinforced in the Writing Activities Workbook.

Let's take a closer look at how each of the four skills is woven into the Student Textbook, the Teacher's Wraparound Edition and the ancillary materials.

Listening You the teacher are the primary source for listening, as you model new vocabulary, dialogues, structure and pronunciation, share your knowledge of Spanish culture, history and geography, talk to students about their lives and your own, or engage in culturally oriented activities and projects. As always, it is your ability to use Spanish as much as possible with your students, both in and outside of the classroom, which determines how relevant and dynamic their learning experience will be.

Glencoe Spanish offers numerous ways in which to develop the listening skill. There are teacher-focused activities, which provide the consistent modeling that students need. Teachers who use the Audio Cassette Program will find that these recordings help students become accustomed to a variety of voices, as well as rates of speed. Activities in which students interact with each other develop listening spontaneity and acuity.

In the Student Textbook, new vocabulary will be modeled by the teacher. Students' attention on the sounds of the new words can be maximized by presenting this material with books closed and using the Vocabulary Transparencies to convey meaning. Following each *Palabras* segment are several *Ejercicios* for practicing the new vocabulary. These can also be done with books closed. After the two *Palabras* segments comes *Comunicación*, in which students may work in pairs or groups and must listen to each other in order to find information, take notes or report to others on what was said in their group. In *Estructura*, students listen as the teacher models new grammatical material and then are given a chance to practice each Structure in several *Ejercicios*. Once again, closing the book will provide increased focus on the listening skill. The next section of each chapter is *Conversación*, in which a real-life dialogue is modeled either by the teacher or by playing the recorded version from the Audio Cassette Program. The dialogue is followed by several communication-based activities, where students must listen to and interact with their peers. In *Bienvenidos* (Level 1), *Conversación* also contains a *Pronunciación* segment, covering an aspect of pronunciation related to the chapter material. Here again, students will be listening either to teacher or recorded models. The last section of each chap-

ter, *Culminación*, offers more listening-intensive activities (*Comunicación oral*) where students must be able to understand what their partners say in order to play out their role.

In addition to the Student Textbook, the Teacher's Wraparound Edition offers several other listening-based activities correlated to the chapters. Some of these listening activities are "Total Physical Response" (Level 1) and "Pantomime" (Level 2). Here students must perform an action after listening to a spoken command. There are other listening-based activities suggested under the heading "Cooperative Learning" and often under "Additional Practice," both of which appear in the bottom margins in each Teacher's Wraparound Edition chapter.

The Audio Cassette Program has two main listening components. The first is practice-oriented, wherein students further reinforce vocabulary and grammar, following directions and making changes in speech. They can self-check their work by listening to the correctly modeled utterances, which are supplied after a pause.

The second part of the program places more attention on the receptive listening skills. Students listen to language in the form of dialogues, announcements, or advertisements—language delivered at a faster pace and in greater volume—and then are asked to demonstrate their understanding of the main ideas and important details in what they have heard. The Student Tape Manual contains activity sheets for doing this work. The Teacher's Edition contains the complete transcript of all audio materials to assist you in preparing listening tasks for your class.

More listening practice is offered through the Video Cassette Program. This material corresponds to and enriches that in the Student Textbook, and gives students a chance to hear variations of the language elements they have been practicing, as spoken by a variety of native speakers from different parts of Latin America and Spain. Students' listening comprehension can be checked and augmented by using the corresponding print activities in the Video Activities Booklet.

Speaking Most of the areas of the Student Textbook and the Teacher's Wraparound Edition mentioned above simultaneously develop the speaking skill. After hearing a model in the *Vocabulario* or *Estructura* sections, students will repeat it, either as a whole class, in small groups, or individually. From these models, they will progress to visual ones, supplied by the Vocabulary Transparencies or the photos and graphics in the textbook. The real thrust in the *Ejercicios* accompanying these two sections is to get students to produce this new material actively. Then, in *Comunicación*, students have the opportunity to adapt what they have learned by asking for and giving information to their classmates on a given topic. Here, and in the *Conversación* sections, students are engaged in meaningful, interesting sessions of sharing information, all designed to make them want to speak and experiment with the language. The suggestions in the "About the Language" section in the Teacher's Wraparound Edition enrich speaking skills by offering variants of expressions and speech mannerisms currently popular in Hispanic culture, especially among teenagers, so that from the start your students will be accustomed to speaking in a way that is accurate and reflective of contemporary Spanish. In Chapter 1, for example, this feature discusses the variations of *muchacho(a)* /*chico(a)*, the difference between *bolígrafo* and *pluma*, and provides information on the use and formation of nicknames, among other things. Previously presented material is constantly recycled in the communication-based activities, so that students' speaking vocabularies and knowledge of structure are always increasing. For this purpose, each *Culminación* section contains a *Reintegración* segment. The length of utterances is increased over time, so that when students complete Level 1 (*Bienvenidos*) they will have acquired an appreciation of the intonation and inflection of longer streams of language. To assist you in fine-tuning your students' speech patterns, the *Pronunciación* section is presented in each chapter of Level 1.

The speaking skill is stressed in the first part of each recorded chapter of the Audio Cassette Program, where pauses are provided for the student to produce directed, spoken changes in the language. This is an excellent opportunity for those students who are self-conscious about speaking out in class to practice speaking. The Audio Cassette Program gives these students a chance to work in isolation. The format of making a change in the language, uttering the change and then listening for the correct model improves the speaking skill. The Audio Cassette Program can serve as a confidence-builder for self-conscious students, allowing them to work their way gradually into more spontaneous speech with their classmates.

The packet of Situation Cards provides students with yet another opportunity to produce spoken Spanish. They place the student into a contextualized, real-world situation. Students must ask and/or answer questions in order to perform successfully.

Reading Each chapter of the Student Textbook has readings based on the chapter theme. The first reading, *Lectura y Cultura* is accompanied by a comprehension check and an exercise called *Estudio de palabras*, which focuses on useful strategies for vocabulary-building and recognizing word relationships, which students can carry over into other readings. The second reading, *Descubrimiento Cultural*, is optional and is to be read for more specific and detailed information about the theme of the chapter and as a stimulus for discussion on this theme. In the next section of each chapter, *Realidades*, students again use their reading skills albeit to a lesser degree. While the *Realidades* section is primarily visual in nature, students nevertheless are referred to numbered captions to learn more about the photographs shown in this two-page spread.

After every four chapters of the Student Textbook, **Glencoe Spanish** provides a unique section called *Fondo Académico*. This presentation is designed to use reading to bridge the gap between Spanish and other areas of the curriculum. Three separate readings are offered, one in each of three areas: natural sciences, social sciences and arts and humanities. Here students have a chance to stretch their reading abilities in Spanish by reading basic information they may have already learned in other academic subjects. Although the material has been carefully written to include themes (as well as words and structures) which students have learned in previous chapters, it contains the most challenging readings. The *Fondo Académico* sections are optional.

The Writing Activities Workbook offers

additional readings under the heading *Un Poco Más*. These selections and the accompanying exercises focus on reading strategies such as cognate recognition, related word forms and the use of context clues. In addition to the reading development above, students are constantly presented with authentic Spanish texts such as announcements from periodicals, telephone listings, transportation schedules, labeled diagrams, floor plans, travel brochures, school progress reports and many others, as sources of information. Sometimes these documents serve as the bases for language activities, and other times they appear in order to round out a cultural presentation, but, in varying degrees, they all require students to apply their reading skills.

Writing Written work is interwoven throughout the language learning process in **Glencoe Spanish**. The exercises, which occur throughout the *Vocabulario* and *Estructura* sections of each chapter in the Student Textbook are designed in such a way that they can be completed in written form as well as orally. Frequently, you may wish to reassign exercises which you have gone through orally in class as written homework. The Teacher's Wraparound Edition makes special note of this under the topic "Independent Practice". At the end of each chapter of the Student Textbook, direct focus is placed on writing in the *Culminación* section, under the heading *Comunicación escrita*. Here there are one or more activities that encourage students to use the new vocabulary and structure they have learned in the chapter to create their own writing samples. These are short and may be descriptive, narrative, argumentative, analytical or in the form of dialogues or interviews. Often a context is set up and then students are asked to develop an appropriate written response.

The Writing Activities Workbook is the component in which writing skills receive the most overt attention. All of the exercises in it require writing. They vary in length from one-word answers to short compositions. They are designed to focus on the same vocabulary and grammar presented in the corresponding chapter of the Student Textbook, but they are all new and all contextualized around fresh visual material or situational vignettes. Since they often have students making lists, adding to

charts and labeling, they provide an excellent means for students to organize the chapter material in their minds and make associations which will help them retain it. As students' knowledge of Spanish increases, longer written pieces are required of them. One workbook section entitled *Mi Autobiografía* has students write installments of their own autobiographies. This is an effective way of stretching student writing skills. It also challenges students to personalize the Spanish they have been studying.

Students are also asked to make implicit use of writing almost everywhere in the series. They are constantly taking notes, listing, categorizing, labeling, summarizing, comparing or contrasting on paper. Even the Audio Cassette Program and the Video Cassette Program involve students in writing through the use of activity sheets. By choosing among these options, you can be sure that your students will receive the practice they need to develop their writing skills successfully.

Contextualized Vocabulary

From the moment students see new words at the beginning of each chapter in **Glencoe Spanish**, they see them within an identifiable context. From the start, students learn to group words by association, thereby enhancing their ability to assimilate and store vocabulary for long-term retention. This contextualization remains consistent throughout the practice, testing and recycling phases of learning.

In the *Vocabulario* section, each of the *Palabras* segments contains a short exchange or a few lead-in sentences or phrases which, together with colorful visuals, establish the context of the topic. Other vocabulary items which occur naturally within this topic are laid out among additional visuals, often as labels. The result is that students see at a glance the new language set into a real-life situation which provides "something to talk about"—a reason for using the language. The accompanying exercises enrich the context of the language. Each *ejercicio* practice item is related to the others within the set, so that when taken together they form a meaningful vignette or story. In other sections of the chapter, these words and phrases are reintroduced frequently.

Moreover, future chapters build on vocabulary and grammar from previous ones. Chapter themes introduced in Level 1 are reintroduced in Level 2 along with additional related vocabulary. Special attention has been given to vocabulary in the reading sections of the series as well. For example, in *Lectura y Cultura*, students are encouraged to stretch their vocabularies in order to get as much meaning as possible from the selections. In addition to glossed words and frequent use of cognate recognition, the corresponding *Estudio de palabras* is there to help them with this. Another example is the *Fondo Académico* section after every four chapters. The selections here include glossaries of the most important new vocabulary items. The accompanying activities put implicit understanding of vocabulary to the test.

Thorough, Contextual Presentation of Grammar

A quick look through the chapters of *Bienvenidos* (Level 1) and *A Bordo* (Level 2) will show the role grammar plays in the overall approach of the **Glencoe Spanish** series. Although grammar is by no means the driving force behind the series, it is indeed an important aspect. In **Glencoe Spanish**, grammar is presented as one of seven sections in each chapter. What makes this series particularly effective is that, as well as being thorough, the presentation of grammar runs concurrent with, and is embedded in, the chapter-long situational themes. Students are presented with Spanish structure both directly, as grammar, and also as a set of useful functions. These will aid in communicating, expanding and improving their Spanish across the four skills, and learning about Hispanic culture as well as other areas of the school curriculum. Another important series characteristic is that the presentation of grammar has been divided into short, coherent "doses," which prevent grammar from becoming overwhelming to the student.

Throughout this series you will see that as you teach the various grammar topics, student interest remains high because each exercise relates to a communicative topic and the format always varies. As is the case with the vocabulary exercises, the individual practice

items in the grammar section are related to each other contextually, in order to heighten student interest.

You will find that it is easy to move in and out of the teaching of grammar, dipping into the other sections of a chapter or other components as you see fit. The grammar segments are short and intelligently divided. Each one provides a good sense of closure; they are taught in one section, are included as much as possible in the others; and have a coherent contextual theme.

Aside from the Student Textbook and Teacher's Wraparound Edition, with their focus on grammar in the *Estructura* section of each chapter and in the *Repaso* after every four chapters, **Glencoe Spanish** offers students opportunities to practice grammar in other components as well. Chapter by chapter, the Writing Activities Workbook provides ample tasks in which students must put to writing the new structures on which they have been working in class. The Audio Cassette Program includes recorded sections in every chapter of the Student Tape Manual which correspond directly to *Estructura* in the Student Textbook. The Computer Software Program's Practice Generator contains additional grammar-based exercises. Students' knowledge of grammar is evaluated in the Chapter Quizzes and in the Testing Program. Each grammatical structure is practiced in other components, such as the Communication Activities Masters, Situation Cards and Video Cassette Program.

An Integrated Approach to Culture

True competence in a foreign language cannot be attained without simultaneous development of an awareness of the culture in which the language is spoken. That is why **Glencoe Spanish** places such great importance on culture. Accurate, up-to-date information on Hispanic culture is presented either implicitly or explicitly throughout every phase of language learning and in every component of the series.

The presentation of Spanish in each chapter of the Student Textbook is embedded in running contextual themes. These themes richly reflect the varied cultures of Latin America, Spain and Hispanic communities in the U.S. Even in chapter sections which focus primarily on vocabulary or grammar, the presence of culture comes through in the language used as examples or items in exercises, as well as in the content of the accompanying illustrations, photographs, charts, diagrams, maps or other reproductions of authentic documents in Spanish. This constant, implicit inclusion of cultural information creates a format which not only aids in the learning of new words and structures, but piques student interest, invites questions and stimulates discussion of the people behind the language.

Many culturally oriented questions raised by students may be answered in the sections devoted to culture: *Lectura y Cultura, Descubrimiento Cultural,* and *Realidades.* Through readings, captioned visuals and guided activities, these sections provide fundamental knowledge about such topics as family life, school, restaurants, markets, sports, transportation, food, hotels, offices and hospitals, among many others. This information is presented with the idea that culture is a product of people—their attitudes, desires, preferences, differences, similarities, strengths and weaknesses—and that it is ever changing. Students are always encouraged to compare or contrast what they learn about Hispanic culture with

their own, thereby learning to think critically and progress towards a more mature vision of the world. For more information on this unique feature, read the section immediately following, and also the section entitled ORGANIZATION OF THE STUDENT TEXTBOOK.

All of the cultural material described in the Student Textbook can be augmented by following a variety of suggestions in the Teacher's Wraparound Edition. There are guidelines for culturally rich instruction and activities, as well as useful, interesting facts for the teacher, under headings such as Chapter Projects, Geography Connection, History Connection, Critical Thinking Activity, Did You Know? and others.

Throughout the TWE there are sections entitled About the Language. In each of these sections, teachers are given regional differences for lexical items such as *el carril, las pista, la vía, la banda, el canal* for lane of a highway, or *el autobús, la guagua, el camión, el micro* for a bus. In addition to lexical regionalisms, explanations are given for structural variations: *contestar* vs. *contestar a; jugar* vs. *jugar a.*

INTERDISCIPLINARY READINGS:
FONDO ACADÉMICO

This distinctive feature of **Glencoe Spanish** allows students to use their Spanish skills to expand their knowledge in other areas of the school curriculum. The interdisciplinary readings, called *Fondo Académico*, occur in the Student Textbook after chapters 4, 8, 12, and 16. They consist of three different readings on topics chosen from the natural sciences, the social sciences and the arts and humanities. Each reading topic is accompanied by pre- and post-reading activities. In the *Fondo Académico* sections, students may read about the metric system, for example: the history of its development, the values of its respective units and how it compares to the English system. They may read and talk about great Spanish painters, such as Velázquez and Goya, (Level 1, pages 124, 240, and 241) and learn details which help to put the work of these artists in perspective *vis à vis* other major events in world history. Or they may learn about the great Inca civilization of the past and the evidence of it which can still be found today. Aside from providing basic information about the above topics—*Diego Velázquez es un importante pintor clásico*, for example— the readings have a Hispanic perspective. They include insights that students might not receive if they were reading about the same topic in an American textbook. In the selection about Velázquez, for example,

we read: *En el siglo XVII Flandes es parte del imperio español*. By using these interdisciplinary *Fondo Académico* readings, you can open up two-way avenues of exchange between the Spanish classroom and other subject areas in the school curriculum. These readings will also allow your students to exercise critical thinking skills, draw conclusions, and begin to interrelate in a mature way the knowledge coming to them from fields which they formerly considered unrelated to Spanish. Perhaps the social studies, art, or science teachers in your school will have the pleasure of hearing from your students, "I learned in Spanish class that..." or conversely, students will have outside knowledge about a topic to bring to discussions in your class.

It is hoped that these readings with interdisciplinary content will make this kind of cognitive connection more common in the overall learning process. Of course, students are building their Spanish language skills while learning about the other subject areas. The selections in *Fondo Académico* recycle as much as possible the structures and vocabulary from previous chapters. Glossed words contribute to vocabulary-building, while the accompanying activities encourage discussion in Spanish around the topic.

SERIES COMPONENTS

In order to take full advantage of the student-centered, "teacher-friendly" curriculum offered by **Glencoe Spanish**, you may want to refer to this section to familiarize yourself with the various resources the series has to offer. Both Levels 1 and 2 of **Glencoe Spanish** contain the following components:

- Student Edition
- Teacher's Wraparound Edition
- Writing Activities Workbook & Student Tape Manual, Student Edition
- Writing Activities Workbook, Teacher's Annotated Edition
- Student Tape Manual, Teacher's Edition (tapescript)
- Audio Program (Cassette or Compact Disc)
- Overhead Transparencies
- Video Program (Videocassette or Videodisc)
- Video Activities Booklet
- Computer Software: Practice and Test Generator
- Communication Activities Masters
- Bell Ringer Review Blackline Masters
- Situation Cards
- Lesson Plans
- Chapter Quizzes with Answer Key
- Testing Program with Answer Key
- Performance Assessment
- CD-ROM Interactive Textbook
- Nosotros y nuestro mundo

LEVEL 1 *BIENVENIDOS* IN TWO VOLUMES

At the junior high and intermediate school levels, where the material in **Bienvenidos** is normally presented in two years, a two-volume edition is available, consisting of **Bienvenidos Part A** and **Bienvenidos Part B**. This two-volume edition may also be more suitable for other types of language programs where students are studying Spanish for limited periods of time, where student aptitude varies from the norm or for those programs where the teacher chooses to modify the pacing for other reasons. In addition to the **Bienvenidos** Student Edition, the components of Level 1 which are also available in two volumes are the Teacher's Wraparound Edition, the Writing Activities Workbook and Student Tape Manual, Student Edition. All other Level 1 components are completely compatible with this "split" edition of **Bienvenidos**.

   Bienvenidos Part A consists of Chapters 1 through 8. **Bienvenidos Part B** opens with 33 pages of *Repaso*, a review section containing new activities designed to reenter the material in **Part A**. It then continues with Chapters 9 through 16.

ORGANIZATION OF THE STUDENT TEXTBOOK

***Bienvenidos* Preliminary Lessons** Chapter 1
of the Level 1 textbook (***Bienvenidos***) is pre-
ceded by a group of eight preliminary lessons
which bear the same title as the Level 1 textbook. These short lessons, A through H, will
help orient your students to some of the routines of the foreign language classroom at the
beginning of the term. They prime students
with a few essential question words and get
them using high-frequency Spanish phrases for
greetings and leave-takings, moving about the
classroom, and identifying basic classroom
objects. Each preliminary lesson contains exercises and activities to help students retain this
introductory material. If you guide them
through all of the preliminary lessons in the
Bienvenidos section before beginning Chapter
1, your students will be able to make a smooth
transition into the regular chapter material,
and you will be able to conduct more of the
classroom activities, including giving directions in Spanish.

Following the eight preliminary lessons,
each chapter of ***Bienvenidos*** is divided into the
following sections:

- *Vocabulario (Palabras 1 & Palabras 2)*
- *Estructura*
- *Conversación*
- *Lectura y Cultura*
- *Descubrimiento Cultural*
- *Realidades*
- *Culminación*

After every fourth chapter, the following
special sections appear:

- *Nuestro Mundo*
- *Repaso*
- *Fondo Académico* (interdisciplinary readings)

Vocabulario The new vocabulary is laid out
in two segments, *Palabras 1* and *Palabras 2*.
Each of these presents new words in a cultural
context in keeping with the theme of the chapter. Ample use is made of labeled illustrations
to convey meaning and to provide an interesting introduction to the new vocabulary. The
contextual vignettes into which the vocabulary
items are embedded make use of the same
grammatical structures which will be formally
addressed in the chapter, and recycle words
and structures from previous chapters. Accompanying each *Palabras* segment is a series of
Ejercicios requiring students to use the new
words in context. These *Ejercicios* employ
techniques such as short answer, matching,
multiple choice and labeling. They are always
contextual, forming coherent vignettes. They
lend themselves well to any variations you
might wish to apply to their delivery (books
open, books closed, done as a class, in groups
or pairs, written for homework). Wrapping up
the *Vocabulario* section is *Comunicación*, a segment consisting of communicative-based activities which combine the new words from both
Palabras sections. These are more open-ended
activities, requiring students to personalize the
new language by performing such tasks as
gathering information from classmates, interviewing, taking notes, making charts or report-
ing to the class.

Estructura   This is the grammar section of each chapter. It is conveniently and logically divided into two to four segments to aid in student assimilation of the material. Each segment provides a step-by-step description in English of how the new grammatical structure is used in Spanish, accompanied by examples, tables and other visuals. Each segment's presentation is followed by a series of flexible *Ejercicios*, designed along the same lines as those which accompany the *Vocabulario* section, and focusing on the grammar point. As in *Vocabulario*, the presentation of the new structures and the subsequent exercises are contextualized. The examples as well as the items in the exercises are never separate and unrelated, but always fit together in vignettes to enhance meaning. These vignettes are directly related to the overall chapter theme or a theme from a previous chapter. The *Estructura* section makes regular use of the new vocabulary from *Palabras 1* and *Palabras 2*, allowing for free interplay between these two sections of the chapter. This thorough yet manageable layout allows you to adapt the teaching of grammar to your students' needs and to your own teaching style.

Conversación   Now that students have had a chance to see and practice the new items of vocabulary and grammar for the chapter, this section provides a recombined version of the new language in the form of an authentic, culturally rich dialogue under the heading *Escenas de la vida*. This can be handled in a variety of ways, depending on the teacher and the class and as suggested by accompanying notes in the Teacher's Wraparound Edition. Teacher modeling, modeling from the recorded version, class or individual repetitions, reading aloud by students, role-playing or adaptation through substitution are some of the strategies suggested. The dialogue is accompanied by one or more exercises which check comprehension and allow for some personalization of the material. Then students are invited once again to recombine and use all the new language in a variety of group and paired activities in the *Communicación* section. New vocabulary and expressions are sometimes offered here, but only for the sake of richness and variation, and not for testing purposes. Every chapter in Level 1 also contains a *Pronunciación* segment which appears after the *Conversación*. It provides a

guide to the pronunciation of one or more Spanish phonemes, a series of words and phrases containing the key sound(s), and an illustration which cues a key word containing the sound(s). These pronunciation illustrations are part of the Overhead Transparency package accompanying the series. *Pronunciación* can serve both as a tool for practice as students perform the chapter tasks, and as a handy speaking-skills reference to be used at any time.

Lectura y Cultura   This is a reading about people and places from Latin America and Spain, offering further cultural input to the theme of the chapter and providing yet another recombination of the chapter vocabulary and grammar. As is always the case with **Glencoe Spanish**, material from previous chapters is recycled. Following the reading and based on it is *Estudio de palabras*—an exercise that gives students a chance to experiment with and expand their Spanish vocabularies by using strategies such as searching for synonyms, identifying cognates, completing cloze exercises, matching and others. Next comes a series of comprehension exercises based on the reading (*Comprensión*), and finally the *Descubrimiento Cultural*, where more cultural information is offered. The *Descubrimiento Cultural* is optional in each chapter.

Realidades   These pages are intended as brief but enjoyable visual insights into the Spanish-speaking world. The two pages of this section are filled with photographs of scenes that are pertinent to the chapter theme. Each photograph is identified with a caption, thereby providing additional reading practice. Students are encouraged to formulate questions about what they see, and to compare and contrast elements of Hispanic culture with their own. The *Realidades* section is optional in each chapter.

Culminación   This wrap-up section requires students to consolidate material from the present as well as previous chapters in order to complete the tasks successfully. *Culminación* provides an opportunity for students to assess themselves on their own and to spend time on areas in which they are weak. You the teacher can pick and choose from these activities as you see fit. The first segment of *Culminación* consists of *Comunicación oral*, where students must use the Spanish they have learned to talk about various aspects of themselves: likes, dislikes, favorite activities, hobbies or areas of expertise, among others. This is followed by *Comunicación escrita*, which encourages students to apply their knowledge of Spanish in written form. The *Reintegración* segment recalls selected items of vocabulary and grammar from previous chapters. It is short and not meant as a comprehensive review, but rather as a quick reminder of important words, expressions and structures. Finally, the vocabulary words and expressions taught in the current chapter are listed categorically under the heading *Vocabulario*, serving as a handy reference resource for both the student and the teacher.

Nuestro Mundo This feature occurs after chapters 4, 8, 12 and 16 in the Student Textbook. *Nuestro Mundo* presents students with bits of "hands on" realia taken from Hispanic newspapers, magazines and documents. Each piece of realia is accompanied by a variety of activities designed so that students use their Spanish skills in order to understand what they see. In the *Nuestro Mundo* feature after Chapter 4 for example, students are presented with an actual report card from a school in Chile. The accompanying activities have students answer direct questions about it, use critical thinking skills to talk about how the school might be organized and use context clues to guess at the meaning of some of the Spanish the report card contains.

Repaso This review section, designed to coincide with the more comprehensive Unit Tests in the Testing Program, occurs after chapters 4, 8, 12, and 16 in the Student Textbook. In each *Repaso*, the main vocabulary and grammar points from the previous four chapters are recycled through a variety of new exercises, activities and dialogues. While in the individual chapters new grammar was divided into smaller, "bite-sized" portions to aid in the planning of daily lessons and help students assimilate it, now it is reviewed in a more consolidated format. This allows students to see different grammatical points side by side for the first time, to make new connections between the different points, and to progress toward a generative, "whole grammar." For example, in the *Repaso* following Chapter 4 of

Bienvenidos, many of the salient nouns and adjectives from the first four chapters are reviewed together in the form of a reading about an Argentine family, followed by questions. In similar fashion this same *Repaso* presents all forms of *-ar* verbs and those of *ir, dar* and *estar* together on one page for the first time, accompanied by exercises, so that students can make final associations between each subject pronoun and its correct verb form. A similar consolidation is done for the definite and indefinite articles, singular and plural. This material was previously spread out among the first four chapters. Every possible combination of vocabulary and grammar does not reappear in the *Repaso* but by carefully going through these exercises and activities and referring to the preceding chapters, students will be encouraged to make necessary connections and extrapolations themselves and therefore develop a true, working knowledge of the Spanish they have studied. The *Repaso* is designed to be used by students studying alone, in study groups or as a whole class with teacher guidance.

Fondo Académico This is a unique, interdisciplinary feature of **Glencoe Spanish** which allows students to use and expand upon the Spanish language skills they have been studying, while at the same time applying them to useful topics in the areas of the natural sciences, social studies and the arts and humanities. This material is presented in the form of three readings, one from each of the above areas, accompanied by photos and illustrations. To stimulate discussion and aid in comprehension, there are pre-reading and post-reading activities. The reading selections are more vocabulary intensive than those in the regular chapters. A Spanish-English glossary is provided for each one. The focus here is on the interdisciplinary content rather than the language itself. By engaging your students in some or all of these readings, you will encourage them to stretch their Spanish reading skills in order to obtain useful, interesting information which will be of great service to them in their other academic courses. You will be giving students the opportunity to judge for themselves the added insight that the study of Spanish offers to their overall education.

SUGGESTIONS FOR TEACHING
THE STUDENT TEXTBOOK

Teaching the Preliminary Lessons A through H in *Bienvenidos* (Level 1)

The first day of class, teachers may wish to give students a pep-talk concerning the importance of the language they have chosen to study. Some suggestions are:

- Show students a map (the maps located in the back of the Student Textbook can be used) to remind them of the extent of the Spanish-speaking world.
- Have students discuss the areas within North America in which there are a high percentage of Spanish speakers. Ask them to name local Spanish-speaking sources including any individuals or groups they may know in their community.
- Make a list of place names such as San Francisco, Los Angeles, El Paso, Las Vegas, or names in your locality that are of Spanish origin.
- Explain to students the possibility of using Spanish in numerous careers such as: government, teaching, business, (banking, import/export), tourism, translating.
- The first day teachers will also want to give each student a Hispanic name. Teachers may want to give Hispanic nicknames to students with names like Kevin or Candy.

The short Preliminary Lessons A through H in *Bienvenidos* are designed to give students useful, everyday expressions that they can use immediately. Each lesson is designed to take one day. The topics present students with easily learned expressions such as *Hola, Buenos días, ¿Qué tal?, Adiós* etc., but do not confuse the students by expecting them to make structural changes such as the manipulation of verb endings. Formal grammar begins with Chapter 1. No grammar is taught in the *Bienvenidos* Preliminary Lessons.

Teaching Various Sections of the Chapter

One of the major objectives of the **Glencoe Spanish** series is to enable teachers to adapt the material to their own philosophy, teaching style, and students' needs. As a result, a variety of suggestions are offered here for teaching each section of the chapter.

Vocabulario

The *Vocabulario* section always contains some words in isolation, accompanied by an illustration that depicts the meaning of the new word. In addition, new words are used in contextualized sentences. These contextualized sentences appear in the following formats: 1) one to three sentences accompanying an illustration, 2) a short conversation, 3) a short narrative or paragraph. In addition to teaching the new vocabulary, these contextualized sentences introduce, but do not teach, the new structure point of the chapter.

A vocabulary list appears at the end of each chapter in the Student Textbook.

General Techniques

- The Vocabulary Transparencies contain all

illustrations necessary to teach the new words and phrases. With an overhead projector, they can easily be projected as large visuals in the classroom for those teachers who prefer to introduce the vocabulary with books closed. The Vocabulary Transparencies contain no printed words.

■ All the vocabulary in each chapter (*Palabras 1* and *Palabras 2*) is recorded on the Audio Cassette Program. Students are asked to repeat the isolated words after the model.

Specific Techniques

Option 1 Option 1 for the presentation of vocabulary best meets the needs of those teachers who consider the development of oral skills a prime objective.

■ While students have their books closed, project the Vocabulary Transparencies. Point to the item being taught and have students repeat the word after you or the audio cassette several times. After you have presented several words in this manner, project the transparencies again and ask questions such as:

¿Es una mesa?
¿Qué es?
¿Es el mesero?
¿Quién es? (Level 1, Chapter 15)

■ To teach the contextualized segments in the *Palabras*, project the Vocabulary Transparency in the same way. Point to the part of the illustration that depicts the meaning of any new word in the sentence, be it an isolated sentence or a sentence from a conversation or narrative. Immediately ask questions about the sentence. For example, the following sentences appear in Level 1, Chapter 5:

La familia Castillo vive en un apartamento.
Ellos viven en el quinto piso.

Questions to ask are:

¿La familia Castillo vive en una casa o en un apartamento?
¿Quién vive en un apartamento?
¿La familia Castillo vive en el quinto piso o en el cuarto piso?
¿En qué piso vive la familia Castillo?

■ Dramatizations by the teacher, in addition to the illustrations, can also help convey the meaning of many words such as *cantar*, *bailar*, etc.

■ After this basic presentation of the *Palabras* vocabulary, have students open their books and read the *Palabras* section for additional reinforcement.

■ Go over the exercises in the *Palabras* section orally.

■ Assign the exercises in the *Palabras* section for homework. Also assign the corresponding vocabulary exercises in the Writing Activities Workbook. If the *Palabras* section should take more than one day, assign only those exercises that correspond to the material you have presented.

■ The following day, go over the exercises that were assigned for homework.

Option 2 Option 2 will meet the needs of those teachers who wish to teach the oral skills but consider reading and writing equally important.

■ Project the Vocabulary Transparencies and have students repeat each word once or twice after you or the audio cassette.

■ Have students repeat the contextualized sentences after you or the audio cassette as they look at the illustration.

■ Ask students to open their books. Have them read the *Palabras* section. Correct pronunciation errors as they are made.

■ Go over the exercises in each *Palabras* section.

■ Assign the exercises of the *Palabras* section for homework. Also assign the vocabulary exercises in the Writing Activities Workbook.

■ The following day, go over the exercises that were assigned for homework.

Option 3 Option 3 will meet the needs of those teachers who consider the reading and writing skills of utmost importance.

■ Have students open their books and read the *Palabras* items as they look at the illustrations.

■ Give students several minutes to look at the *Palabras* words and vocabulary exercises. Then go over the exercises.

■ Go over the exercises the following day.

Expansion Activities

Teachers may use any of the following activities occasionally. These can be done in conjunction with the options previously outlined.

- After the vocabulary has been presented, project the Vocabulary Transparencies or have students open their books and make up as many original sentences as they can, using the new words. This can be done orally or in writing.
- Have students work in pairs or small groups. As they look at the illustrations in the textbook, have them make up as many questions as they can. They can direct their questions to their peers. It is often fun to make this a competitive activity. Individuals or teams can compete to make up the most questions in three minutes. This activity provides the students with an excellent opportunity to use interrogative words.
- Call on one student to read to the class one of the vocabulary exercises that tells a story. Then call on a more able student to retell the story in his/her own words.
- With slower groups you can have one student go to the front of the room. Have him or her think of one of the new words. Let classmates give the student the new words from the *Palabras* until they guess the word the student in the front of the room has in mind. This is a very easy way to have the students recall the words they have just learned.

Estructura

The *Estructura* section of the chapter opens with a grammatical explanation in English. Each grammatical explanation is accompanied by many examples. Verbs are given with complete paradigms. In the case of other grammar concepts such as the object pronouns, many examples are given with noun versus pronoun objects. Irregular patterns are grouped together to make them appear more regular. For example, *ir, dar,* and *estar* are taught together in Chapter 4, as are *hacer, poner, traer, salir* and *venir* in Chapter 8. Whenever the contrast between English and Spanish poses problems for students in the learning process, a contrasting analysis between the two languages is made. Two examples of this are the reflexive construction in Level 1 and the subjunctive in Level 2. Certain structure points are taught more effectively in their entirety and others are more easily acquired if they are taught in segments. An example of the latter is the presentation of the preterite of irregular verbs. In Level

1, Chapter 10, the object pronouns *me, te, nos* are presented immediately followed by *lo, la, los, las* in Chapter 11, and *le, les* in Chapter 12.

Learning Exercises

The exercises that follow the grammatical explanation are presented from simple to more complex. In the case of verbs with an irregular form, for example, emphasis is placed on the irregular form, since it is the one students will most often confuse or forget. In all cases, students are given one or more exercises that force them to use all forms at random. The first few exercises that follow the grammatical explanation are considered **learning exercises** because they assist the students in grasping and internalizing the new grammar concept. These learning exercises are immediately followed by test exercises—exercises that make students use all aspects of the grammatical point they have just learned. This format greatly assists teachers in meeting the needs of the various ability levels of students in their classes. Every effort has been made to make the grammatical explanations as succinct and as complete as possible. We have purposely avoided extremely technical grammatical or linguistic terminology that most students would not understand. Nevertheless, it is necessary to use certain basic grammatical terms.

Certain grammar exercises from the Student Textbook are recorded on the Audio Cassette Program. Whenever an exercise is recorded, it is noted with an appropriate icon in the Teacher's Wraparound Edition.

The exercises in the Writing Activities Workbook also parallel the order of presentation in the Student Textbook. The Resource boxes and the Independent Practice topics in the Teacher's Wraparound Edition indicate when certain exercises from the Writing Activities Workbook can be assigned.

Specific Techniques for Presenting Grammar

Option 1 Some teachers prefer the deductive approach to the teaching of grammar. When this is the preferred method, teachers can begin the *Estructura* section of the chapter by presenting the grammatical rule to students or by having them read the rule in their textbooks.

After they have gone over the rule, have them read the examples in their textbooks or write the examples on the chalkboard. Then proceed with the exercises that follow the grammatical explanation.

Option 2 Other teachers prefer the inductive approach to the teaching of grammar. If this is the case, begin the *Estructura* section by writing the examples that accompany the rule on the chalkboard or by having students read them in their textbooks. Let us take, for example, the direct object pronouns *lo, la, los* and *las*. The examples the students have in their books are:

Elena compró *el boleto*.	Elena *lo* compró.
Compró *los boletos* en la ventanilla.	*Los* compró en la ventanilla.
Elena pone *la crema* en la maleta.	Elena *la* pone en la la en maleta.
Pone *las toallas* en la maleta.	*Las* pone en la maleta.
Elena conoce *al muchacho*.	Elena *lo* conoce.
Conoce a *los muchachos*.	*Los* conoce.
Roberto conoce a *Elena*.	Roberto *la* conoce.
Conoce a *sus amigas*.	*Las* conoce.

In order to teach this concept inductively, teachers can ask students to do or answer the following:

- Have students find the object of each sentence in the first column. Say it or underline the object if it is written on the board.
- Have students notice that the nouns disappeared in the sentences in the second column. Have students give (or underline) the word that represents the noun.
- Ask students what word replaced *el boleto, los boletos, la crema*, etc.
- Ask: What do we call a word that replaces a noun?
- Ask: What direct object replaces a masculine noun? A feminine noun, etc.?
- Have students look again. Ask: What word replaces *el boleto, Elena?*
- Ask: Can *lo* and *la* be used to replace either a person or a thing?
- Ask: Where do the direct object pronouns *lo, la, los, las* go, before or after the verb?

By answering these questions, students have induced, on their own, the rule from the examples. To further reinforce the rule, have students read the grammatical explanation and then continue with the grammar exercises that follow. Further suggestions for the inductive presentation of the grammatical points are given in the Teacher's Wraparound Edition.

Specific Techniques for Teaching Grammar Exercises

In the development of the **Glencoe Spanish** series, we have purposely provided a wide variety of exercises in the *Estructura* section so that students can proceed from one exercise to another without becoming bored. The types of exercises they will encounter are: short conversations, answering questions, conducting or taking part in an interview, making up questions, describing an illustration, filling in the blanks, multiple choice, completing a conversation, completing a narrative, etc. In going over the exercises with students, teachers may want to conduct the exercises themselves or they may want students to work in pairs. The *Estructura* exercises can be done in class before they are assigned for homework or they may be assigned before they are done. Many teachers may want to vary their approach.

All the *Ejercicios* and *Comunicación* activities in the Student Textbook can be done with books open. Many of the exercises such as question-answer, interview, and transformation can also be done with books closed.

Types of Exercises

Question Exercises The answers to many question exercises build to tell a complete story. Once you have gone over the exercise by calling on several students (Student 1 answers items numbered 1,2,3; Student 2 answers items numbered 4,5,6 etc.), you can call on one student to give the answers to the entire exercise. Now the entire class has heard an uninterrupted story. Students can ask one another questions about the story, give an oral synopsis of the story in their own words, or write a short paragraph about the story.

Personal Questions or Interview Exercises Students can easily work in pairs or teachers can call a student moderator to the front of the room to ask questions of various class members. Two students can come to the front of the room and the exercise can be performed as follows—one student takes the role of the interviewer and the other takes the role of the interviewee.

Completion of a Conversation See Chapter 8, *Ejercicio E*, page 217 as an example. After students complete the exercise, they can be given time either in class or as an outside assignment to prepare a skit for the class based on the conversation.

Conversación

Specific Techniques Teachers may wish to vary the presentation of the *Conversación* from one chapter to another. In some chapters, the dialogue can be presented thoroughly and in others it may be presented quickly as a reading exercise. Some possible options are:

- Have the class repeat the dialogue after you twice. Then have students work in pairs and present the dialogue to the class. The dialogue does not have to be memorized. If students change it a bit, all the better.
- Have students read the dialogue several times on their own. Then have them work in pairs and read the dialogue as a skit. Try to encourage them to be animated and to use proper intonation. This is a very important aspect of the *Conversación* section of the chapter.
- Rather than read the dialogue, students can work in pairs, having one make up as many questions as possible related to the topic of the dialogue. The other students can answer his/her questions.
- Once students can complete the exercise(s) that accompany the dialogue with relative ease, they know the dialogue sufficiently well without having to memorize it.
- Students can tell or write a synopsis of the dialogue.

Pronunciación

Specific Techniques Have students read on their own or go over with them the short explanation in the book concerning the particular sound that is being presented. For the more difficult sounds such as *rr, ll, j, g, d, t,* etc., teachers may wish to demonstrate the

tongue and lip positions. Have students repeat the words after you or the model speaker on the audio cassette recording.

Comunicación

Specific Techniques The *Comunicación* section presents activities that assist students in working with the language on their own. All *Comunicación* sections are optional. In some cases, teachers may want the whole class to do all the activities. In other cases, teachers can decide which activities the whole class will do. Another possibility is to break the class into groups and have each one work on a different activity.

Lectura y Cultura

Specific Techniques: Option 1 Just as the presentation of the dialogue can vary from one chapter to the next, the same is true of *Lectura y Cultura*. In some chapters, teachers may want students to go over the reading selection very thoroughly. In this case all or any combination of the following techniques can be used.

- Give students a brief synopsis of the reading selection in Spanish.
- Ask questions about the brief synopsis.
- Have students open their books and repeat several sentences after you or call on individuals to read.
- Ask questions about what was just read.
- Have students read the story at home and write the answers to the exercises that accompany *Lectura y Cultura*.
- Go over the *Estudio de palabras* and *Comprensión* in class the next day.
- Call on a student to give a review of the story in his/her own words. Guide them to make up an oral review. Ask five or six questions to review the salient points of the reading selection.
- After the oral review, the more able students can write a synopsis of *Lectura y Cultura* in their own words.

It should take less than one class period to present *Lectura y Cultura* in the early chapters. Later. you may wish to spend two days on those selections you want students to know thoroughly.

Option 2 When teachers wish to present *Lectura y Cultura* less thoroughly, the following techniques may be used:

- Call on an individual to read a paragraph.
- Ask questions about the paragraph read.
- Assign *Lectura y Cultura* to be read at home. Have students write the exercises that accompany the *Lectura*.
- Go over the *Estudio de palabras* and the *Comprensión* the following day.

Option 3 With some reading selections, teachers may wish merely to assign them to be read at home and then go over the exercises the following day. This is possible since the only new material in *Lectura y Cultura* consists of a few new vocabulary items that are always footnoted.

Descubrimiento Cultural

The optional *Descubrimiento Cultural* is a reading selection designed to give students an in-depth knowledge of many areas of the Spanish-speaking world. You can omit any or all of this reading or they may choose certain selections that you would like the whole class to read. The same suggestions given for the *Lectura y Cultura* section of each chapter can be

followed. Teachers may also assign the reading selections to different groups. Students can read the selection outside of class and prepare a report for those students who did not read that particular selection. This activity is very beneficial for slower students. Although they may not read the selection, they learn the material by listening to what their peers say about it. The *Descubrimiento Cultural* can also be done by students on a voluntary basis for extra credit.

Realidades

Specific Techniques The purpose of the *Realidades* section is to permit students to look at highly appealing photographs from the Spanish-speaking world and to acquaint them with the many areas where Spanish is spoken. The *Realidades* section contains no exercises. The purpose is for students to enjoy the material as if they were browsing through pages of a magazine. Items the students can think about are embedded in the commentary that accompanies the photographs. Teachers can either have students read the captions in class or students can read the captions on their own.

ORGANIZATION OF THE TEACHER'S WRAPAROUND EDITION

One important component, which is definitive of **Glencoe Spanish** and adds to the series' flexible, "teacher-friendly" nature, is the Teacher's Wraparound Edition (TWE), of which this Teacher's Manual is a part. Each two-page spread of the TWE "wraps around" a slightly reduced reproduction of the corresponding pages of the Student Textbook and offers in the expanded margins a variety of specific, helpful suggestions for every phase in the learning process. A complete method for the presentation of all the material in the Student Textbook is provided—basically, a complete set of lesson plans—as well as techniques for background-building, additional reinforcement of new language skills, creative and communicative recycling of material from previous chapters and a host of other alternatives from which to choose. This banquet of ideas has been developed and conveniently laid out in order to save valuable teacher preparation time and to aid you in designing the richest, most varied language experience possible for you and your students. A closer look at the kinds of support in the TWE, and their locations, will help you decide which ones are right for your pace and style of teaching and for each of your classes.

The notes in the Teacher's Wraparound Edition can be divided into two basic categories:
1. Core notes, appearing in the left- and right-hand margins, are those which most directly correspond to the material in the accompanying two-page spread of the Student Textbook.
2. Enrichment notes, in the bottom margin,

are meant to be complimentary to the material in the Student Textbook. They offer a wide range of options aimed at getting students to practice and use the Spanish they are learning in diverse ways, individually and with their classmates, in the classroom and for homework. The enrichment notes also include tips to the teacher on clarifying and interconnecting elements in Spanish language, Hispanic culture, geography and history—ideas that have proved useful to other teachers and which are offered for your consideration.

Description of Core Notes in the Teacher's Wraparound Edition

Chapter Overview At the beginning of each chapter a brief description is given of the language functions which students will be able to perform by chapter's end. Mention is made of any closely associated functions presented in other chapters. This allows for effective articulation between chapters and serves as a guide for more successful teaching.

Chapter Objectives This guide immediately follows the Chapter Overview and is closely related to it. Here the emphasis is on the lexical and structural objectives of the chapter.

Chapter Resources The beginning of each chapter includes a reference list of all the ancillary components of the series that are applicable to what is being taught in the chapter, including the Writing Activities Workbook and Student Tape Manual, Audio Cassette Program,

Overhead Transparencies, Communication Activities Masters, Video Cassette Program, Computer Software: Practice and Test Generator, Situation Cards, Chapter Quizzes and Test Booklets. A more precise version of this resource list will be repeated at the beginning of each section within the chapter, so that you always have a handy guide to the specific resources available to you for each and every point in the teaching process. Using these chapter and section resource references will make it easier for you to plan varied, stimulating lessons throughout the year.

Bell Ringer Reviews These short activities recycle vocabulary and grammar from previous chapters and sections. They serve as effective warm-ups, urging students to begin thinking in Spanish, and helping them make the transition from their previous class to Spanish. Minimal direction is required to get the Bell Ringer Review activity started, so students can begin meaningful, independent work in Spanish as soon as the class hour begins, rather than wait for the teacher to finish administrative tasks, such as attendance, etc. Bell Ringer Reviews occur consistently throughout each chapter of Levels 1, 2, and 3.

Presentation Step-by-step suggestions for the presentation of the material in all segments of the six main section headings in each chapter— *Vocabulario, Estructura, Conversación, Lectura y Cultura, Realidades,* and *Culminación* are presented in the left- and right-hand margins. They offer the teacher suggestions on what to say, whether to have books open or closed, whether to perform tasks individually, in pairs or in small groups, expand the material, reteach, and assign homework. These are indeed suggestions. You may wish to follow them as written or choose a more eclectic approach to suit time constraints, personal teaching style and class "chemistry". Please note however, that the central vocabulary and grammar included in each chapter's *Vocabulario* and *Estructura* sections is intended to be taught in their entirety, since this material will appear in succeeding chapters. In addition, answers for all the *Ejercicios* in each segment are conveniently located near that exercise in the Student Textbook.

Because the answers will vary in *Comuni-*

cación activities, they are usually not provided. However, the presentation notes do suggest tips for modeling correctness in student responses to these activities. Besides this running presentation, the teacher notes offer other topics for enrichment, expansion and assessment. A brief discussion of these may help you incorporate them into your lesson plans.

About the Language Since Spanish is such a growing, living language, spoken in so many different places of the world by people of different cultures and classes, the usage and connotation of words can vary greatly. In this section, information is offered on the differences. The most important feature of this section is the presentation of regionalism. In the student text itself, we present those words that are most universally understood. The many regional variants are given in this About the Language section.

Vocabulary Expansion These notes provide the teacher handy access to vocabulary items which are thematically related to those presented within the Student Textbook. They are offered to enrich classroom conversations, allowing students more varied and meaningful responses when talking about themselves, their classmates or the topic in question. Note that none of these items, or for that matter any information in the Teacher's Wraparound Edition, is included in the Chapter Quizzes, or in the Testing Program accompanying **Glencoe Spanish**.

Cognate Recognition Since the lexical relationship between Spanish and English is so rich, these notes have been provided to help you take full advantage of the vocabulary-building strategy of isolating them. The suggestions occur in the *Vocabulario* section of each chapter and are particularly frequent in Level 1 in order to train students from the very beginning in the valuable strategy of recognizing cognates. Various methods of pointing out cognates are used, involving all four language skills, and the activities frequently encourage students to personalize the new words by using them to talk about things and people they know. Pronunciation differences are stressed between the two languages. The teacher notes also call attention to false cognates when they occur in other chapter sections.

Informal Assessment Ideas are offered for making quick checks on how well students are assimilating new material. These checks are done in a variety of ways and provide a means whereby both teacher and students can monitor daily progress. By using the Informal Assessment topic, you will be able to ascertain as you go along the areas in which students are having trouble, and adjust your pace accordingly or provide extra help for individuals, either by making use of other activities offered in the Teacher's Wraparound Edition or devising your own. The assessment strategies are simple and designed to help you elicit from students the vocabulary word, grammatical structure, or other information you wish to check. Because they occur on the same page as the material to which they correspond you may want to come back to them again when it is time to prepare students for tests or quizzes.

Reteaching These suggestions provide yet another approach to teaching a specific topic in the chapter. In the event some students were not successful in the initial presentation of the material a reteaching activity offers an alternate strategy. At the same time, it provides successful students another chance to further consolidate their learning.

History Connection Following these suggestions can be seen as a very effective springboard from the Spanish classroom into the history and social studies areas of the curriculum. Students are asked to focus their attention on the current world map, or historical ones, then they are invited to discuss the cultural, economic and political forces which shape the world with an eye on Hispanic influence. The notes will assist you in providing this type of information yourself or in creating projects in which students do their own research, perhaps with the aid of a history teacher. By making the history connection, students are encouraged to either import or export learning between the Spanish classroom and the history or social studies realms.

Geography Connection These suggestions encourage students to use the maps provided in the Student Textbook as well as refer them to outside sources in order to familiarize them with the geography of Hispanic America and the Spain. These optional activities are another

way in which **Glencoe Spanish** crosses boundaries into other areas of the curriculum. Their use will instill in students the awareness that Spanish class is not just a study of language but an investigation into a powerful culture that has directly or indirectly affected the lives of millions of people all over the globe. By studying geography, students will be urged to trace the presence of Hispanic culture throughout Europe and the Americas. The notes also supply you the teacher with diverse bits of geographical and historical information which you may decide to pass on to your students.

Description of Enrichment Notes in the Teacher's Wraparound Edition

The notes in the bottom margin of the Teacher's Wraparound Edition enrich students' learning experiences by providing additional activities to those in the Student Textbook. These activities will be helpful in meeting each chapter's objectives, as well as in providing students with an atmosphere of variety, cooperation and enjoyment.

Chapter Projects Specific suggestions are given at the start of each chapter for launching individual students or groups into a research project related to the chapter theme. Students are encouraged to gather information by using resources in school and public libraries, visiting local Hispanic institutions or interviewing Spanish-speaking people or other persons knowledgeable in the area of Hispanic culture whom they may know. In Chapter 1, for example, they are asked to compare their own educational system with one from a Spanish-speaking country. These projects may serve as another excellent means for students to make connections between their learning in the Spanish classroom and other areas of the curriculum.

Learning from Photos and Realia Each chapter of **Glencoe Spanish** contains, many colorful photographs and reproductions of authentic Spanish documents, filled with valuable cultural information. In order to help you take advantage of this rich source of learning, notes have been provided in the way of additional, interesting information to assist you in highlighting the special features of these up-to-date realia. The questions that appear under this topic have been designed to enhance learners' reading and critical thinking skills.

Total Physical Response (Level 1) At least one Total Physical Response (TPR) activity is provided with each *Palabras* segment that makes up the *Vocabulario* section of the chapter. Students must focus their attention on commands spoken by the teacher (or classmates) and demonstrate their comprehension by performing the task as requested. This strategy has proven highly successful for concentrating on the listening skill and assimilating new vocabulary. Students are relieved momentarily of the need to speak—by which some may be intimidated—and yet challenged to show that they understand spoken Spanish. The physical nature of these activities is another of their benefits, providing a favorable change of pace for students, who must move about the room and perhaps handle some props in order to perform the tasks. In addition, Total Physical Response is in keeping with cooperative learning principles, since many of the commands require students to interact and assist each other in accomplishing them.

Cooperative Learning Several cooperative learning activities are included in each chapter. These activities include guidelines both on the size of groups to be organized and on the tasks the groups will perform. They reflect two basic principles of cooperative learning: (a) that students work together, being responsible for their own learning, and (b) that they do so in an atmosphere of mutual respect and support, where the contributions of each peer are valued. For more information on this topic, please see the section in this Teacher's Manual entitled Cooperative Learning.

Additional Practice There are a variety of Additional Practice activities to complement and follow up the presentation of material in the Student Textbook. Frequently the additional practice focuses on personalization of the new material and employs more than one language skill. Examples of Additional Practice activities include having students give oral or written descriptions of themselves or their classmates; asking students to conduct interviews around a topic and then report their

findings to the class. The additional practice will equip you with an ample, organized repertoire from which to pick and choose should you need extra practice beyond that in the Student Textbook.

Independent Practice Many of the exercises in each chapter lend themselves well to assignment or reassignment as homework. In addition to providing extra practice, reassigning on paper exercises that were performed orally in class makes use of additional language skills and aids in informal assessment. The suggestions under the Independent Practice heading in the bottom margin of the TWE will call your attention to exercises that are particularly suited to this. In addition to reassigning exercises in the Student Textbook as independent practice, additional sources are suggested from the various ancillary components, specifically the Writing Activities Workbook and the Communication Activities Masters.

Critical Thinking Activities To broaden the scope of the foreign language classroom, suggestions are given that will encourage students to make inferences and organize their learning into a coherent "big picture" of today's world. These and other topics offered in the enrichment notes provide dynamic content areas to which students can apply their Spanish language skills and their growing knowledge of Hispanic culture. The guided discussions suggested derived from the chapter themes invite students to make connections between what they learn in the Spanish program and other areas of the curriculum.

Did You Know? This is a teacher resource topic where you will find additional details relevant to the chapter theme. You might wish to add the information given under this topic to your own knowledge and share it with your students to spur their interest in research projects, enliven class discussions and round out their awareness of Hispanic culture, history or geography.

For the Younger Student Because Level 1 (*Bienvenidos*) is designed for use at the junior high and intermediate level as well as the high school level, this topic pays special attention to the needs of younger students. Each chapter contains suggestions for meaningful language activities and tips to the teacher that cater to the physical and emotional needs of these youngsters. There are ideas for hands-on student projects, such as creating booklets or bringing and using their own props, as well as suggestions for devising games based on speed, using pantomime, show and tell, performing skits and more.

For the Native Speaker This feature has been provided with the realization that the modern Spanish-as-a-second-language class in the U.S. often includes students whose first language is Spanish. These students can provide the class, including the teacher, with valuable information about Hispanic culture as well as the living Spanish language they use in their everyday lives. For the Native Speaker invites them to share this information in an atmosphere of respect and trust. There are often lexical and structural variations in the parlance of native speakers from different areas of the Spanish-speaking world. For the Native Speaker points out, or asks the native speakers to point out, many of these variations. When such variations are caused by the interference of English—for example, the inclusion of the indefinite article with professions and nationalities (*Juan es un médico*)—the interference is pointed out, and native speakers are guided in practicing the corrected structure. Such correction is handled with sensitivity. The idea is more to inform native speakers that borrowed words and structures are not used in all situations, rather than to make value judgments as to which usage is right and which is wrong.

ADDITIONAL ANCILLARY COMPONENTS

All ancillary components are supplementary to the Student Textbook. Any or all parts of the following ancillaries can be used at the discretion of the teacher.

The Writing Activities Workbook and Student Tape Manual

The Writing Activities Workbook and Student Tape Manual is divided into two parts: all chapters of the Writing Activities Workbook appear in the first half of this ancillary component, followed by all chapters of the Student Tape Manual.

Writing Activities Workbook The consumable workbook offers additional writing practice to reinforce the vocabulary and grammatical structures in each chapter of the Student Textbook. The workbook exercises are presented in the same order as the material in the Student Textbook. The exercises are contextualized, often centering around line art illustrations. Workbook activities employ a variety of elicitation techniques, ranging from short answers, matching and answering personalized questions, to writing paragraphs and brief compositions. To encourage personalized writing, there is a special section in each chapter entitled *Mi Autobiografía*. The workbook provides further reading skills development with the *Un Poco Más* section, where students are introduced to a number of reading strategies such as scanning for information, distinguishing fact from opinion, drawing inferences and reaching conclusions, for the purpose of improving their reading comprehension and

expanding their vocabulary. The *Un Poco Más* section also extends the cultural themes presented in the corresponding Student Textbook chapter. The Writing Activities Workbook includes a Self Test after Chapters 4, 8, 12 and 16. The Writing Activities Workbook, Teacher Annotated Edition provides the teacher with all the material in the student edition of the Writing Activities Workbook plus the answers—wherever possible—to the activities.

Student Tape Manual The Student Tape Manual contains the activity sheets which students will use when listening to the audio cassette recordings. The Teacher's Edition of the Student Tape Manual contains the answers to the recorded activities, plus the complete tapescript of all recorded material.

The Audio Program (Cassette or CD)

The recorded material for each chapter of **Glencoe Spanish**, Levels 1 and 2 is divided into two parts — *Primera parte* and *Segunda parte*. The *Primera parte* consists of listening and speaking practice for the *Vocabulario* (*Palabras 1 & 2*) and the *Estructura* sections of each chapter. There is also a dramatization of the *Conversación* dialogue from the Student Textbook, and a pronunciation section.

The *Segunda parte* contains a series of activities designed to further stretch students' receptive listening skills in more open-ended, real-life situations. Students indicate their understanding of brief conversations, advertisements, announcements, etc., by making the appropriate response on their activity sheets located in the Student Tape Manual.

Overhead Transparencies

There are five categories in the package of Overhead Transparencies accompanying **Glencoe Spanish**, Level 1. Each category of transparencies has its special purpose. Following is a description:

Vocabulary Transparencies These are full-color transparencies reproduced from each of the *Palabras* presentations in the Student Textbook. In converting the *Palabras* vocabulary pages to transparency format, all accompanying words and phrases on the *Palabras* pages have been deleted to allow for greater flexibility in their use. The Vocabulary Transparencies can be used for the initial presentation of new words and phrases in each chapter. They can also be used to review or reteach vocabulary during the course of teaching the chapter, or as a tool for giving quick vocabulary quizzes.

    With more able groups, teachers can show the Vocabulary Transparencies from previous chapters and have students make up original sentences using a particular word. These sentences can be given orally or in writing.

Pronunciation Transparencies In the *Pronunciación* section of each chapter of *Bienvenidos* (Level 1), an illustration has been included to visually cue the key word or phrase containing the sound(s) being taught, e.g., Chapter 3, page 79. Each of these illustrations has been converted to transparency format. These Pronunciation Transparencies may be used to present the key sound(s) for a given chapter, or for periodic pronunciation reviews where several transparencies can be shown to the class in rapid order. Some teachers may wish to convert these Pronunciation Transparencies to black and white paper visuals by making a photocopy of each one.

Communication Transparencies For each chapter in Levels 1 and 2 of the series there is one original composite illustration which visually summarizes and reviews the vocabulary and grammar presented in that chapter. These transparencies may be used as cues for additional communicative practice in both oral and written formats. There are 16 Communication Transparencies for Level 1, and 16 for Level 2.

Map Transparencies The full-color maps located at the back of the Student Textbook have been converted to transparency format for the teacher's convenience. These transparencies can be used when there is a reference to them in the Student Textbook, or when there is a history or geography map reference in the Teacher's Wraparound Edition. The Map Transparencies can also be used for quiz purposes, or they may be photocopied in order to provide individual students with a black and white version for use with special projects.

Fine Art Transparencies These are full-color reproductions of works by well known Spanish-speaking artists including Velázquez, Goya, and others. Teachers may use these transparencies to reinforce specific culture topics in both the *Realidades* sections, as well as the optional *Fondo Académico* sections of the Student Textbook.

The Video Program (Cassette or Videodisc)

The video component for each level of **Glencoe Spanish** consists of one hour-long video and an accompanying Video Activities Booklet. Together, they are designed to reinforce the vocabulary, structures, and cultural themes presented in the corresponding Student Textbook. The **Glencoe Spanish** Video Program encourages students to be active listeners and viewers by asking them to respond to each video *Escena* through a variety of previewing, viewing and post-viewing activities. Students are asked to view the same video segment multiple times as they are led, via the activities in their Video Activities Booklet, to look and listen for more detailed information in the video segment they are viewing. The Video for each level of **Glencoe Spanish** begins with an Introduction explaining why listening to natural, spoken Spanish can be a difficult task and therefore why multiple viewings of each video *Escena* are required. The Introduction also points out the importance of using the print activities located in the Video Activities Booklet in order to use the Video Program successfully.

Video Activities Booklet

The Video Activities Booklet is the vital companion piece to the hour-long video.

It consists of a series of pre-viewing, viewing, and post-viewing activities on Blackline Masters. These activities include specific instructions to students on what to watch and listen for as they view a given *Escena* in the video. The Video Activities Booklet also contains a Teacher's Manual, Culture Notes, and a complete Transcript of the video soundtrack.

Computer Software: Practice and Test Generator

Available for Apple II, Macintosh and IBM-compatible machines, this software program provides materials for both students and teacher. The Practice Generator provides students with new, additional practice items for the vocabulary, grammar and culture topics in each chapter of the Student Textbook. All practice items are offered in a multiple choice format. The computer program includes a randomizer, so that each time a student calls up a set of exercises, the items are presented in a different order, thereby discouraging rote memorization of answers. Immediate feedback is given, along with the percent of correct answers, so that with repeated practice, students can track their performance. For vocabulary practice, illustrations from the *Vocabulario* section of the Student Textbook have been scanned into the software to make practice more interesting and versatile.

The Test Generator allows the teacher to print out ready-made chapter tests, or customize a ready-made test by adding or deleting test items. The computer software comes with a Teacher's Manual as well as a printed transcript of all practice and test items.

Communication Activities Masters with Answer Key

This is a series of Blackline Masters which provide further opportunities for students to practice their communication skills using the Spanish they have learned. The contextualized, open-ended situations are designed to encourage students to communicate on a given topic, using specific vocabulary and grammatical structures from the corresponding chapter of the Student Textbook. The use of visual cues and interesting contexts will encourage

students to ask questions and experiment with personalized responses. In the case of the paired communication activities, students actively work together as they share information provided on each partner's activity sheet. Answers to all activities are given in an Answer Key at the back of the Communication Activities Masters booklet.

Situation Cards

This is another component of **Glencoe Spanish** aimed at developing listening and speaking skills through guided conversation. For each chapter of the Student Textbook, there is a corresponding set of guided conversational situations printed on hand-held cards. Working in pairs, students use appropriate vocabulary and grammar from the chapter to converse on the suggested topics. Although they are designed primarily for use in paired activities, the Situation Cards may also be used in preparation for the speaking portion of the Testing Program or for informal assessment. Additional uses for the Situation Cards are described in the Situation Cards package, along with specific instructions and tips for their duplication and incorporation into your teaching plans. The cards are in Blackline Master form for easy duplication.

Bell Ringer Reviews on Blackline Masters

These are identical to the Bell Ringer Reviews found in each chapter of the Teacher's Wraparound Edition. For the teacher's convenience, they have been converted to this (optional) Blackline Master format. They may be either photocopied for distribution to students, or the teacher may convert them to overhead transparencies. The latter is accomplished by placing a blank acetate in the paper tray of your photocopy machine, then proceeding to make a copy of your Blackline Master (as though you were making a paper copy).

Lesson Plans and Block Scheduling

Flexible lesson plans have been developed to meet a variety of class schedules, including block scheduling. The various support materials are incorporated into these lesson plans at their most logical point of use, depending on the nature of the presentation material on a given day. For example the Vocabulary Transparencies and the Audio (Cassette or Compact Disc) Program can be used most effectively when presenting the chapter vocabulary. On the other hand, the Chapter Quizzes are recommended for use one or two days after the initial presentation of vocabulary, or following a specific chapter grammar topic. Because student needs and teacher preferences vary, space has been provided on each lesson plan page for the teacher to write additional notes and comments adjusting the day's activities as required.

Block Scheduling This type of scheduling differs from traditional scheduling in that fewer class sessions are scheduled for larger blocks of time over fewer days. For example, a course might meet for 90 minutes a day for 90 days, or half a school year. While there are a number of different block scheduling configurations in use, the 90 minute time block is most common.

For schools themselves, the greatest advantage of block scheduling is that there is a better use of resources. No additional teachers or classrooms may be needed, and more efficient use is made of those presently available in the school system. The need for summer school is greatly reduced because the students that do not pass a course one term can take it the next term. These advantages are accompanied by an increase in the quality of teacher instruction and student's time on-task.

There are many advantages for teachers who are in schools that use block scheduling. For example, teacher-student relationships are improved. With block scheduling, teachers have responsibility for a smaller number of students at a time, so students and teachers get to know each other better. With more time, teachers are better able to meet the individual needs of their students. Teachers can also be more focused on what they are teaching. Block scheduling may also result in changes in teaching approaches, classrooms that are more student centered, improved teacher morale, increased teacher effectiveness, and decreased burn-out. Teachers feel free to venture away from discussion and lecture to use more productive models of teaching.

Block scheduling cuts the time needed for introducing and closing classes in half. It also eliminates half of the time needed for class changes, which results in fewer discipline problems. Flexibility is increased because less complex teaching schedules create more opportunities for cooperative teaching strategies such as team teaching and interdisciplinary studies.

Chapter Quizzes with Answer Key

This component consists of short (5 to 10 minute) quizzes, designed to help both students and teachers evaluate quickly how well a specific vocabulary section or grammar topic has been mastered. For both Levels 1 and 2, there is a quiz for each *Palabras* section (vocabulary) and one quiz for each grammar topic in the *Estructura* section. The quizzes are on Blackline Masters. All answers are provided in an Answer Key at the end of the Chapter Quizzes booklet.

Testing Program with Answer Key

The Testing Program consists of three different types of Chapter Tests, two of which are bound into a testing booklet on Blackline Masters. The third type of test is available as part of the computer software component for **Glencoe Spanish**.

1. The first type of test is discrete-point in nature, and uses evaluation techniques such as fill-in-the-blank, completion, short answers, true/false, matching, and multiple choice. Illustrations are frequently used as visual cues. The discrete-point tests measure vocabulary and grammar concepts via listening, speaking, reading, and writing formats. (As an option to the teacher, the listening section of each test has been recorded on cassette by native Spanish speakers.) For the teacher's convenience, the speaking portion of the tests has been physically separated from the listening, reading, and writing portions, and placed at the back of the testing booklet. These chapter tests can be administered upon the completion of each chapter. The Unit Tests can be administered upon the completion of each Repaso (after every four chapters).

2. The Blackline Master testing booklet also contains a second type of test, namely the Chapter proficiency tests. These measure students' mastery of each chapter's vocabulary and grammar on a more global, whole-language level. For both types of tests above, there is an Answer Key at the back of the testing booklet.

3. A third type of test is part of the Computer Software: Practice and Test Generator Program (Macintosh; IBM; Apple versions). With this software, teachers have the option of simply printing out ready-made chapter tests, or customizing a ready-made test by selecting certain items, and/or adding original test items.

Performance Assessment

In addition to the tests described earlier, the Performance Assessment tasks provide an alternate approach to measuring student learning, compared to the more traditional paper and pencil tests. The performance assessment tasks include teacher-student interviews, individual and small-group research tasks with follow-up presentations, and skits that students perform for the class. The Performance Assessment tasks can be administered after every fourth chapter in the textbook. They appear in conjunction with the *Repaso* following Chapters 4, 8, 12, and 16.

COOPERATIVE LEARNING

Cooperative learning provides a structured, natural environment for student communication that is both motivating and meaningful. When students develop friendly relationships in their cooperative groups and become accustomed to the multiple opportunities to hear and rehearse new communicative tasks, the filter that prevents many students from daring to risk a wrong answer when called upon to speak in front of a whole class can be minimized. The goal of cooperative learning is to provide opportunities for learning in an environment where students contribute freely and responsibly to the success of the group. The key is to strike a balance between group goals and individual accountability. Group (team) members plan how to divide the activity among themselves, then each member of the group carries out his or her part of the assignment. Cooperative learning provides each student with a "safe," low-risk environment rather than a whole-class atmosphere. As you implement cooperative learning in your classroom, we urge you to take time to explain to students what will be expected of every group member—listening, participating, and respecting other opinions.

In the Teacher's Wraparound Edition, cooperative learning activities have been written to accompany each chapter of the Student Textbook. These activities have been created to assist both the teacher who wants to include cooperative learning for the first time, and the experienced practitioner of cooperative learning.

Classroom Management: Implementing Cooperative Learning Activities

Many of the suggested cooperative learning activities are based on a four-member team structure in the classroom. Teams of four are recommended because there is a wide variety of possible interactions. At the same time the group is small enough that students can take turns quickly within the group. Pairs of students as teams may be too limited in terms of possible interactions, and trios frequently work out to be a pair with the third student left out. Teams of five may be unwieldy in that students begin to feel that no one will notice if they don't really participate.

If students sit in rows on a daily basis, desks can be pushed together to form teams of four. Teams of students who work together need to be balanced according to as many variables as possible: academic achievement in the course, personality, ethnicity, gender, attitude, etc. Teams that are as heterogeneous as possible will ensure that the class progresses quickly through the curriculum.

Following are descriptions of some of the most important cooperative learning structures, adapted from Spencer Kagan's Structural Approach to Cooperative Learning, as they apply to the content of *Bienvenidos*.

Round-robin Each member of the team answers in turn a question, or shares an idea with teammates. Responses should be brief so that students do not have to wait long for their turn.

Example from *Bienvenidos*, Preliminary Lesson H, Days of the week:

Teams recite the days of the week in a roundrobin fashion. Different students begin additional rounds so that everyone ends up needing to know the names of all the days. Variations include starting the list with a different day or using a race format, i.e., teams recite the list three times in a row and raise their hands when they have finished.

Roundtable Each student in turn writes his or her contribution to the group activity on a piece of paper that is passed around the team. If the individual student responses are longer than one or two words, there can be four pieces of paper with each student contributing to each paper as it is passed around the team.

A to Z Roundtable Using vocabulary from *Bienvenidos*, Chapters 8 and 14, students take turns adding one word at a time to a list of words associated with plane or train travel in A to Z order. Students may help each other with what to write, and correct spelling. Encourage creativity when it comes to the few letters of the alphabet that don't begin a specific travel word from their chapter lists. Teams can compete in several ways: first to finish all 28 letters; longest word; shortest word; most creative response.

Numbered Heads Together Numbered Heads Together is a structure for review and practice of high consensus information. There are four steps:

Step 1: Students number off in their teams from 1 to 4.

Step 2: The teacher asks a question and gives the teams some time to make sure that everyone on the team knows the answer.

Step 3: The teacher calls a number.

Step 4: The appropriate student from each team is responsible to report the group response.

Answers can be reported simultaneously, i.e., all students with the appropriate number either stand by their seats and recite the answer together, or they go to the chalkboard and write the answer at the same time. Answers can also be reported sequentially. Call on the first student to raise his or her hand or have all the students with the appropriate

number stand. Select one student to give the answer. If the other students agree, they sit down, if not they remain standing and offer a different response.

Example from *Bienvenidos*, Chapter 2, Telling time

Step 1: Using a blank clock face on the overhead transparency, or the chalkboard, the teacher adjusts the hand on the clock.

Step 2: Students put their heads together and answer the question: *¿Qué hora es?*

Step 3: The teacher calls a number

Step 4: The appropriate student from each team is responsible to report the group response.

Pantomimes

Give each team one card. Have each team decide together how to pantomime for the class the action identified on the card. Each team presents the pantomime for ten seconds while the rest of the teams watch without talking. Then each of the other teams tries to guess the phrase and writes down their choice on a piece of paper. (This is a good way to accommodate kinesthetic learning styles as well as vary classroom activities.)

Example from *Bienvenidos*, Chapter 4 vocabulary

The teacher writes the following sentences on slips of paper and places them in an envelope:

1. *Hablan.*
2. *Hablan por teléfono.*
3. *Estudian en la biblioteca.*
4. *Escuchan discos.*
5. *Miran la televisión.*
6. *Preparan una merienda.*
7. *Toman un refresco.*
8. *Bailan.*
9. *Cantan.*
10. *Llegan a una fiesta.*

Each team will draw one slip of paper from the envelope and decide together how to pantomime the action for the class. As one team pantomimes their action for 30 seconds, the other teams are silent. Then the students within each team discuss among themselves what sentence was acted out for them. When they have decided on the sentence, each team sends one person to write it on the chalkboard.

Inside/Outside Circle Students form two concentric circles of equal number by counting off 1–2, 1–2 in their teams. The "ones "form a circle shoulder to shoulder and facing out. The "twos" form a circle outside the "ones" to make pairs. With an odd number of students, there can be one threesome. Students take turns sharing information, quizzing each other, or taking parts of a dialogue. After students finish with their first partners, rotate the inside circle to the left so that the students repeat the process with new partners. For following rounds alternate rotating the inside and outside circles so that students get to repeat the identified tasks, but with new partners. This is an excellent way to structure 100% student participation combined with extensive practice of communication tasks.

Other suggested activities are similarly easy to follow and to implement in the classroom. Student enthusiasm for cooperative learning activities will reward the enterprising teacher. Teachers who are new to these concepts may want to refer to Dr. Spencer Kagan's book, *Cooperative Learning,* published by Resources for Teachers, Inc., Paseo Espada, Suite 622, San Juan Capistrano, CA 92675.

SUGGESTIONS FOR CORRECTING HOMEWORK

Correcting homework, or any tasks students have done on an independent basis, should be a positive learning experience rather than mechanical "busywork". Following are some suggestions for correcting homework. These ideas may be adapted as the teacher sees fit.

1. Put the answers on an overhead transparency. Have students correct their own answers.

2. Ask one or more of your better students to write their homework answers on the chalkboard at the beginning of the class hour. While the answers are being put on the chalkboard, the teacher involves the rest of the class in a non-related activity. At some point in the class hour, take a few minutes to go over the homework answers that have been written on the board, asking students to check their own work. You may then wish to have students hand in their homework so that they know this independent work is important.

3. Go over the homework assignment quickly in class. Write the key word(s) for each answer on the chalkboard so students can see the correct answer.

4. When there is no correct answer, i.e., "Answers Will Vary", give one or two of the most likely answers. Don't allow students to inquire about all other possibilities however.

5. Have all students hand in their homework. After class, correct every other (every third, fourth, fifth, etc.) homework paper. Over several days, you will have checked every student's homework at least once.

6. Compile a list of the most common student errors. Then create a worksheet that explains the underlying problem areas, providing additional practice in those areas.

STUDENT PORTFOLIOS

The use of student portfolios to represent long-term individual accomplishments in learning Spanish offers several benefits. With portfolios, students can keep a written record of their best work and thereby document their own progress as learners. For teachers, portfolios enable us to include our students in our evaluation and measurement process. For example, the content of any student's portfolio may offer an alternative to the standardized test as a way of measuring student writing achievement. Assessing the contents of a student's portfolio can be an option to testing the writing skill via the traditional writing section on the chapter or unit test.

There are as many kinds of portfolios as there are teachers working with them. Perhaps the most convenient as well as permanent portfolio consists of a three-ring binder which each student will add to over the school year and in which the student will place his or her best written work. In the **Glencoe Spanish** series, selections for the portfolio may come from the Writing Activities Workbook; Communication Activities Masters; the more open-ended activities in the Student Tape Manual and the Video Activities Booklet, as well as from written assignments in the Student Textbook, including the *Comunicación escrita* sections. The teacher is encouraged to refer actively to students' portfolios so that they are regarded as more than just a storage device. For example, over the course of the school year, the student may be asked to go back to earlier entries in his or her portfolio in order to revise certain assignments, or to develop an assignment further by writing in a new tense, e.g., the *pretérito*. In this way the student can appreciate the amount of learning that has occurred over several months time.

Portfolios offer students a multidimensional look at themselves. A "best" paper might be the one with the least errors or one in which the student reached and synthesized a new idea, or went beyond the teacher's assignment. The Student Portfolio topic is included in each chapter of the Teacher's Wraparound Edition as a reminder that this is yet another approach the teacher may wish to use in the Spanish classroom.

PACING

Sample Lesson Plans

Level 1 (*Bienvenidos*) has been developed so that it may be completed in one school year. However, it is up to the individual teacher to decide how many chapters will be covered. Although completion of the textbook by the end of the year is recommended, it is not necessary. Most of the important structures of Level 1 are reviewed in a different context in Level 2 (*A bordo*). The establishment of lesson plans helps the teacher visualize how a chapter can be presented. By emphasizing certain aspects of the program and de-emphasizing others, the teacher can change the focus and the approach of a chapter to meet students' needs and to suit his or her own teaching style and techniques. Sample lesson plans are provided below. They include some of the suggestions and techniques that have been described earlier in this Teacher's Manual.

STANDARD PACING		
	Days	**Total Days**
(Preliminary Lessons A–H)	5 days	5
Capítulos 1–16	8–9 days per chapter	144
Testing	1 day per test	16
Repaso (4)	2 days each	8
Nuestro Mundo, Fondo Académico (4 [optional])	2 days each	8

	Class	**Homework**
Day 1	*Palabras 1* (with transparencies) exercises (Student Textbook)	*Palabras* Exercises (written) Writing Activities Workbook: *Palabras 1*
Day 2	*Palabras 2* (with transparencies) exercises (Student Textbook)	*Palabras* Exercises (written) exercises from Student Textbook (written) prepare *Comunicación* Writing Activities Workbook: *Palabras 2*
Day 3	present *Comunicación* one *Estructura* topic exercises (Student Textbook)	exercises from Student Textbook (written) Writing Activities Workbook (written)

Day 4	two *Estructura* topics exercises (Student Textbook)	exercises from Student Textbook (written) Student Tape Manual exercises
Day 5	one *Estructura* topic exercises (Student Textbook)	exercises from Student Textbook (written) Writing Activities Workbook (written)
Day 6	*Conversación* (pronunciation) *Comunicación* Audio Cassette Program	read *Lectura y Cultura* *Estudio de palabras*
Day 7	review *Lectura y Cultura* *Comprensión* questions Video Program	read *Descubrimiento Cultural* and *Realidades*
Day 8	review homework *Comunicación oral* Situation Cards	*Comunicación escrita*
Day 9	Communication Activities Masters Communication transparency	review for test
Day 10	Test	after Chapters 4, 8, 12, 16:

Repaso (review), *Nuestro Mundo*, and *Fondo Académico* (optional) sections

Day 1	grammar review	exercises in Student Textbook and Workbook
Day 2	correct homework *Comunicación*	review for Test
Day 3	Unit Test	pre-read *Nuestro Mundo*, *Fondo Académico*, first selection (optional)
Day 4	*Fondo Académico*, first selection (optional)	*Fondo Académico*, second selection (optional)
Day 5	*Fondo Académico*, third selection (optional)	*Fondo Académico*, second selection in-depth (optional)

ACCELERATED PACING

	Days	Total Days
(Preliminary Chapters A–H)	5 days	5
Chapters 1–8	8 days per chapter	64*
Chapters 9–16	7 days per chapter	64
Test	1 day per test	16
Repaso (4)	2 days each	8
Fondo Académico (4 [optional])	2 days each	8

	Class	Homework
Day 1	*Palabras 1* (with transparencies) exercises (Student Textbook)	*Palabras* exercises (written) Writing Activities Workbook: *Palabras 1*
Day 2	*Palabras 2* (with transparencies) exercises (Student Textbook)	*Palabras* exercises (written) Exercises from Student Textbook (written) prepare *Comunicación* Writing Activities Workbook: *Palabras 2*
Day 3	present *Comunicación* two *Estructura* topics	exercises from Student Textbook (written) Writing Activities Workbook (written)
Day 4	two *Estructura* topics	exercises from Student Textbook (written) Writing Activities Workbook (written)
Day 5	*Conversación* present *Comunicación* Audio Cassette Program	read *Lectura y Cultura* *Estudio de palabras* and *Comprensión*
Day 6	*Descubrimiento cultural* (optional) *Realidades* (optional) Video Cassette Program Communication Activities Masters	*Culminación*
Day 7	review *Culminación* Situation Cards Communication transparency	review for test
Day 8	Test	After Chapters 4, 8, 12, 16: *Repaso*

*Note: After Chapter 8, the teacher may choose among the *Culminación* activites on days 6 and 7, thereby eliminating one day, or the teacher omits Chapter 16.

Repaso (review) *Nuestro Mundo*, and *Fondo Académico* (optional) sections

Day 1	*Repaso* exercises	review for Test
Day 2	Unit Test	
Day 3	*Nuestro Mundo, Fondo Académico*, first selection (optional)	*Fondo Académico*, second selection (optional)
Day 4	*Fondo Académico*, third selection (optional)	

USEFUL CLASSROOM WORDS AND EXPRESSIONS

Below is a list of the most frequently used words and expressions needed in conducting a Spanish class.

Words

el papel	paper
la hoja de papel	sheet of paper
el cuaderno	notebook
el cuaderno de ejercicios	workbook
la pluma	pen
el bolígrafo	ballpoint pen
el lápiz	pencil
la goma	(pencil) eraser
la tiza	chalk
la pizarra	chalkboard
el pizzarón	chalkboard
el borrador	chalkboard eraser
el cesto de papeles	wastebasket
el pupitre	desk
la fila	row
la silla	chair
la pantalla	screen
el proyector	projector
la cinta	cassette
el libro	book
la regla	ruler

Commands

Both the singular (*tú*) and the plural (*ustedes*) command forms are provided.

Ven.	Vengan.	Come.
Ve.	Vayan.	Go.
Pasa. (Entra.)	Pasen. (Entren.)	Enter.
Espera.	Esperen.	Wait.
Pon.	Pongan.	Put.

Dame.	Denme.	Give me.
Dime.	Díganme.	Tell me.
Tráeme.	Tráiganme.	Bring me.
Repite.	Repitan.	Repeat.
Practica.	Pratiquen.	Practice.
Estudia.	Estudien.	Study.
Contesta.	Contesten.	Answer.
Aprende.	Aprendan.	Learn.
Escoge.	Escojan.	Choose.
Prepara.	Preparen.	Prepare.
Mira.	Miren.	Look at.
Describe.	Describan.	Describe.
Empieza.	Empiecen.	Begin.
Pronuncia.	Pronuncien.	Pronounce.
Escucha.	Escuchen.	Listen
Habla.	Hablen.	Speak.
Lee.	Lean.	Read.
Escribe.	Escriban.	Write.
Pregunta.	Pregunten.	Ask.
Sigue el modelo.	Sigan el modelo.	Follow the model.
Haz el papel de…	Hagan el papel de…	Take the part of…
Toma.	Tomen.	Take.
Abre.	Abran.	Open.
Cierra.	Cierren.	Close.
Da vuelta a la página…	Den vuelta a la página…	Turn the page.
Borra.	Borren.	Erase.
Continúa.	Continúen.	Continue.
Siéntate.	Siéntense.	Sit down.
Párate.	Párense.	Stand up.
Levanta la mano.	Levanten la mano.	Raise your hand.
Cállate.	Cállense.	Be quiet.
Pon atención.	Pongan atención	Pay attention.
Presta atención.	Presten atención.	Pay attention.
Atiende.	Atiendan.	Attention.
Atención, por favor.		Your attention, please.
Silencio.		Silence.
Cuidado.		Careful.
Otra vez.		Again.
Uno por uno.		One at a time.
Todos juntos.		All together.
En voz alta.		Out loud.
Más fuerte, por favor.		Louder, please.
En español.		In Spanish.
En inglés.		In English.

GLENCOE SPANISH 1 CD-ROM INTERACTIVE TEXTBOOK

The *Glencoe Spanish 1 CD-ROM Interactive Textbook* is a complete curriculum and instructional system for high school Spanish students. The four-disk CD-ROM program contains all elements of the textbook plus photographs, videos, animations, and games to enhance and deepen students' understanding of the Spanish language and culture. Although especially suited for individual or small-group use, it can be connected to a large monitor or LCD panel for whole-class instruction. With this flexible, interactive system, you can introduce, reinforce, or remediate any part of the Spanish 1 curriculum at any time.

The CD-ROM program has three major components—Contents, Games, and References. The Contents contain all the components of the Spanish 1 *Bienvenidos* textbook. These components have been enhanced with photographs, live video, animations, and audio. In addition, there are readings and activities specifically for native speakers, as well as self-tests. These latter elements are unique to the CD-ROM program.

The Contents Menu

The following selections can be found in the Contents menu.

Vocabulario Vocabulary is introduced in thematic contexts. New words are introduced, and communication activities based on real-life situations are presented.

Estructura Students are given explanations of Spanish structures. They then practice through contextualized exercises. One of the grammar points in each chapter is enhanced with an electronic comic strip with which students can interact.

Conversación Interactive video enhances this feature comprised of real-life dialogues. Students may listen to and watch a conversation and then choose to participate as a character as they record their part of the dialogue.

Lectura y cultura Readings give students the opportunity to gain insight into Hispanic culture. They are also able to hear the readings in Spanish. The similarities and differences between Hispanic and U.S. culture are emphasized.

Hispanoparlantes This activity is intended to help native speakers formally learn more about the structual and grammatical aspects of their primary language. It has been added exclusively to the CD-ROM program to challenge and inspire native speakers.

Realidades In *Realidades*, students discover the similarities and differences that exist among various cultural groups in the Spanish-speaking world, including Hispanic cultures in the United States. The narration for each photograph and live-video segment is done by a native speaker from the part of the Hispanic world featured. This gives students insight into the variations in the Spanish language.

Culminación Chapter-end activities require students to integrate the concepts they have learned. There are oral and written activities as well as activities aimed at building skills, and a vocabulary review linked to the glossary.

Prueba The self-test provides a means for students to evaluate their own progress.

At the end of each four chapters are three features—Nuestro Mundo, Repaso, and Fondo Académico. These selections may also be found in the Contents menu.

Nuestro Mundo This activity provides students with additional readings centered around Hispanic cultures and real-life situations.

Repaso In the *Repaso* section, students participate in a variety of review activities.

Fondo Académico These activities enable students to practice their Spanish reading skills through interdisciplinary readings that provide insights into Hispanic cultures.

The Game Menu

The Game menu gives users access to *¿Quién Sabe Más?* (Discs 1 and 3) and *El Laberinto del Lenguaje* (Discs 2 and 4). Each game reviews the vocabulary, grammar and culture topics that have been presented in the four chapters contained on that particular CD-ROM disc.

The Reference Menu

Maps, verb charts, and the Spanish-English/English-Spanish glossaries can be selected from this menu. The maps include Spain and North Africa, South America, and Central America.

For more information, see the User's Guide accompanying the *Glencoe Spanish 1 CD-ROM Interactive Textbook.*

Spanish for Spanish Speakers: Nosotros y nuestro mundo

This two-level series has been designed for the teaching of Spanish at the secondary school level to native speakers of Spanish residing in the United States. Each of the sixteen chapters takes into account the diversified background of these students—many of whom have a very strong command of the Spanish language and others who have a somewhat limited knowledge of the Spanish language. The textbook also attempts to take into account the specific problems facing the teacher of classes with native Spanish speakers. In some cases, the native-speaking students are placed in separate courses and in other cases, they are in classes with English-speaking students learning Spanish as a foreign language. For these reasons, *Nosotros y nuestro mundo* can be used as a basal textbook in courses for native speakers, or it can be used as an adjunct to the **Glencoe Spanish** series in classes that have both native speakers of Spanish and English. In the latter case, it is presumed that teachers will have less time with their students and a fair amount of the material will need to be acquired by students through independent study or cooperative group work.

Organization

Each of the sixteen chapters is divided into six parts:

- *Nuestro conocimiento académico*
- *Nuestro idioma*
- *Nuestra cultura*
- *Nuestra literatura*
- *Nuestra creatividad*
- *Nuestra diversiones*

Nuestro conocimiento académico This section of each lesson serves several purposes. It exposes students to important information that is presented in other disciplines of the school curriculum. In some cases, it may contain material that students have learned in another course, or it may present information that for one reason or another, they have not previously studied. In addition to the reading topic itself, this section also introduces students to higher level vocabulary that they seldom encounter in Spanish when taking other courses in English.

Many native Spanish-speaking students have an extensive vocabulary on topics related to home, school, family, and everyday activities. Many of these same students, however, possess a limited vocabulary on topics such as geography, economics, finance, medicine, literature, art, music, etc. This is particularly true for students who have lived in the United States for many years and who have been educated in English. It is also true for students who are recent arrivals to the United States and who, for one reason or another, have received little formal education in their native country.

Nuestro idioma It is a known fact that native

speakers of Spanish do not need the same type of grammatical/structural or syntactical information about their language as do individuals who are acquiring Spanish as a foreign language. The native speaker has no difficulty responding with *Hablo...* in reply to a question with *¿Hablas...?* The English speaker, on the other hand, needs a great deal of practice before he/she will be able to respond using a proper verb form.

The material in the *Nuestro idioma* section deals with linguistic principles and problems specific to the native speaker. *Nuestro idioma* deals with all the following areas: grammar/structure, spelling, pronunciation, morphology, etc.

In this section we have taken into account the regional differences in the Spanish spoken by the many native-speaking groups in the U.S. Particular attention has been paid to the Spanish spoken by Mexicans, Mexican-Americans, and of those groups from the Caribbean basin. The Spanish of other areas is also dealt with.

Much attention is given to linguistic problems that arise from living in a bilingual environment—the superimposition of English, for example. In the units that deal with these specific problems, we have been extremely careful to differentiate between *regionalismos* and *vulgarismos* while taking into account that one of the most fascinating aspects of language is that it is forever changing and while many changes are completely acceptable, others are less so.

Nuestra cultura   The *Nuestra cultura* section is an extremely important part of each chapter. It serves to introduce students to the tremendous cultural wealth of the Spanish-speaking world both within and outside of the United States.

In this section the word *hispano(a)* is used frequently. Although the word *hispano(a)* can have political overtones and some prefer the use of the word *latino(a)*, we use *hispano(a)* to refer to anyone whose mother tongue is Spanish. In addition, each native speaker of Spanish has his or her own cultural identity: Mexican-American, Mexican, Puerto Rican, Cuban, Nicaraguan, Spaniard, etc.

Nuestra literatura   The *Nuestra literatura* section of each lesson introduces students to the literature of the entire Spanish-speaking world. Most selections are of famous authors throughout history as well as contemporary writers. (The works of some lesser-known writers are also represented if we felt the topic would be of particular interest to your students.) In this section, there are examples of the various literary genres: poetry, fable, prose, short story, novel, legend, etc.

Nuesta creatividad   The *Nuestra creatividad* section provides students with much opportunity to brainstorm. Many of the activities start with very simple tasks and progress to having students add more information until they finally produce a story, essay or speech on their own. The activities themselves are quite self-explanatory. Some have the students working in groups, others have them working independently. The creative activities deal with both oral and written expression. Students are given the opportunity to write paragraphs, to develop short stories, and to write poetry on their own. They will also give different types of speeches: expository, persuasive, etc.

Nuestras diversiones   The *Nuestra diversiones* section of each chapter is something to be enjoyed by both students and teachers alike. Here we include magazine and newspaper articles from periodicals that are available in Spanish in the United States. Students are given the opportunity to sit back, read, and enjoy the material. Hopefully this type of reading activity will develop the desire for students to read on their own—now and in the future.

You can decide how thoroughly you wish to cover a particular article. You may just have students read it once on their own, or you may wish to ask comprehension questions about it. You may also have students retell what they read in their own words. They may do this either orally or in writing.

About the Cover

Long before the Spaniards arrived in the New World in 1492, the Mayan Civilization had developed to a very advanced stage. The city of Chichen-Itzá, located on the Yucatán peninsula of present-day Mexico, is one of the many sites where we can still see evidence of the beauty and balanced proportions of Mayan architecture. This is a view of the pyramid of "El Castillo," one of the most famous Mayan constructions.

GLENCOE SPANISH 1B

Bienvenidos

Conrad J. Schmitt

Protase E. Woodford

GLENCOE

McGraw-Hill

New York, New York   Columbus, Ohio   Mission Hills, California   Peoria, Illinois

Printed in the United States of America.

Send all inquiries to:
Glencoe/McGraw-Hill
15319 Chatsworth Street
P.O. Box 9609
Mission Hills, CA 91346-9609

ISBN 0-02-641013-3 (Student Edition)
ISBN 0-02-641014-1 (Teacher's Wraparound Edition)

1 2 3 4 5 6 7 8 9   AGH   01 00 99 98 97 96

Acknowledgments

We wish to express our deep appreciation to the numerous individuals throughout the United States who have advised us in the development of these teaching materials. Special thanks are extended to the people whose names appear here.

Kristine Aarhus
Northshore School District
Bothell, Washington

Kathy Babula
Charlotte Country Day School
Charlotte, North Carolina

Veronica Dewey
Brother Rice High School
Birmingham, Michigan

Anneliese H. Foerster
Oak Hill Academy
Mouth of Wilson, Virginia

Sharon Gordon-Link
Antelope Valley Unified High School
Lancaster, California

Leslie Lumpkin
Prince George's County Public Schools
Prince George's County, Maryland

Loretta Mizeski
Columbia School
Berkeley Heights, New Jersey

Robert Robison
Columbus Public Schools
Columbus, Ohio

Rhona Zaid
Los Angeles, California

Bienvenidos

CONTENIDO

REPASO

CAPÍTULO 9

DEPORTES Y ACTIVIDADES DE INVIERNO

CAPÍTULO 10

LA SALUD Y EL MÉDICO

CAPÍTULO 11

ACTIVIDADES DE VERANO

CAPÍTULO 12

ACTIVIDADES CULTURALES

MUSEO DIOCESANO   Nº 0339

ENTRADA

CUENCA

CAPÍTULO 13

LA ROPA Y LA MODA

xi

CAPÍTULO 14

UN VIAJE EN TREN

CAPÍTULO 15

EN EL RESTAURANTE

CAPÍTULO 16

EL CAMPING

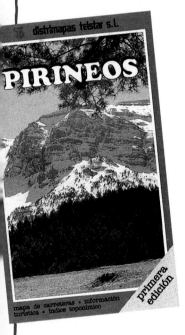

APÉNDICES

xiii

OVERVIEW

Repasos A–C cover the key grammatical points and vocabulary topics presented in *Bienvenidos*, **Part A**. Additional review work can be found in the *Reintegración* section of each chapter and in the review chapters following each four chapters of *Bienvenidos*.

Repaso A reviews vocabulary needed to describe a school, as well as school and after-school activities. The regular *-ar* verbs and the verbs *ir, dar,* and *estar* are reviewed.

Pacing

This chapter should take three to four days depending on the length of the class, the age of the students, and student aptitude.

REPASO

A

LOS AMIGOS Y LOS CURSOS

xiv

R–1

LEARNING FROM PHOTOS

1. Have students say as much as they can about the photo on pages xiv–1 in their own words. Or you may wish to ask students the following questions about the photograph: *¿Están en la escuela los amigos? ¿Dónde están? ¿Cuántos muchachos hay? ¿Cuántas muchachas hay? ¿Es moderno el café?*

2. Have students tell what they think each student ordered at the café.

VOCABULARIO

Vocabulary Teaching Resources

1. Workbook, *Repaso A*
2. Bell Ringer Review Blackline Masters

Bell Ringer Review

Write the following on the board or use BRR Blackline Master R-1: Make a list of expressions that you remember from last year that can be used to describe some school activities.

Los alumnos

PRESENTATION (*page 2*)

Have students repeat each line after you with books open.

Ejercicio A

PRESENTATION

Before going over Exercise A, you may wish to ask more detailed questions about each sentence. For example: *¿Quiénes van a la escuela? ¿Adónde van? ¿Cómo van?*

ANSWERS

Ejercicio A

1. Los alumnos van en el bus escolar.
2. Ellos llegan a las ocho menos cinco de la mañana.
3. Los alumnos hablan con su profesor.
4. El profesor enseña.
5. Los alumnos están en la sala de clases en la escuela.
6. Los alumnos van al café.
7. Toman una merienda.

Los alumnos

Los alumnos van a la escuela en el bus escolar.
Ellos llegan a la escuela.
Un alumno habla con el profesor.
El profesor enseña.
Los alumnos estudian.
Están en la sala de clase.
Después de las clases, los alumnos van a un café.
Toman una merienda en el café.
Toman un refresco.

A En la escuela. Contesten.

1. ¿Cómo van los alumnos a la escuela? ¿Van a pie, en carro o en el bus escolar?
2. ¿A qué hora llegan a la escuela, a las ocho menos cinco de la mañana o a las ocho menos cinco de la tarde?
3. ¿Con quién hablan los alumnos en la escuela, con su profesor o con sus parientes?
4. ¿Quién enseña, el alumno o el profesor?
5. ¿Dónde están los alumnos ahora? ¿Están en la sala de clase en la escuela o están en casa?
6. ¿Adónde van los alumnos después de las clases? ¿Van a la escuela, a la tienda de discos o al café?
7. ¿Qué toman en el café? ¿Toman una merienda o un refresco?

Cafeterías GG Pastelerías

Doñana

ESPECIAL DESAYUNOS Y MERIENDAS
CHURROS, PORRAS, LABOR PROPIA
Pl. Jacinto Benavente, 2 .... 467 0834
Frente al teatro Calderón

R–2 REPASO

LEARNING FROM PHOTOS AND REALIA

1. You may wish to ask the following questions about the photograph on page 2: *¿Quién enseña? ¿Cuántos alumnos hay en el grupo? ¿Son alumnos serios? ¿Es interesante o aburrida la clase? ¿Qué opinas?*

2. With regard to the realia on page 2, ask students: *¿Cuál es el nombre de la cafetería? ¿En qué calle está? ¿Cuál es el número de teléfono? ¿Cuáles son las especialidades de estas cafeterías?*

B **¿Qué hacen?** Escojan.

1. ¿Cómo van los alumnos?
   a. a la escuela   b. a las ocho   c. a pie
2. ¿Quién enseña?
   a. el profesor   b. en la escuela   c. español
3. ¿Quiénes hablan?
   a. por teléfono   b. los alumnos   c. el profesor
4. ¿Cuándo llegan?
   a. en el bus   b. con sus amigos   c. a las ocho
5. ¿Qué estudian?
   a. en la escuela   b. mucho   c. álgebra
6. ¿Adónde van?
   a. en casa   b. al café   c. hoy

REPASO   **R–3**

Vocabulary Expansion

You may wish to point out to students that *churros* are a type of deep-fried Spanish doughnut. They are narrow and twirled. A *porra* is also a fried doughnut, but it is larger and thicker than a *churro*.

PRESENTATION *(page 3)*
Expansion of *Ejercicio B*
You may wish to have students make up questions about the answer choices. For example: *¿Adónde van los alumnos? ¿Cuándo van? ¿A qué hora van?*

ANSWERS
Ejercicio B
1. c
2. a
3. b
4. c
5. c
6. b

GEOGRAPHY CONNECTION

El Bosque de Chapultepec es un parque famoso en la Ciudad de México. Los domingos por la tarde los capitalinos van al parque donde dan un paseo o toman una merienda. En el parque hay un castillo famoso, el Castillo de Chapultepec. En el siglo XIX sirve de residencia para el emperador Maximiliano.

HISTORY CONNECTION

The grounds of Chapultepec Park were once (in the early 1500s) the favorite gardens of the Aztec emperor Montezuma.

LEARNING FROM PHOTOS AND REALIA

1. You may wish to ask the following questions about the photograph on page 3: *¿Es grande la escuela? ¿Es bonita? ¿Llevan uniforme los alumnos? ¿Llevan sus libros en una mochila? ¿Es una escuela mixta? ¿Están llegando los alumnos a la escuela o están saliendo de la escuela?*

2. Regarding the ad on page 3, ask students: *¿Cuál es el nombre del café? ¿En qué ciudad está? ¿Cuántas líneas telefónicas tiene? ¿Es necesario tener una reservación para ir al Café Chapultepec?*

3

ESTRUCTURA

Bell Ringer Review

Write the following on the board or use BRR Blackline Master R-2: Make a list of after-school activities.

Structure Teaching Resources

1. Workbook, *Repaso A*
2. Bell Ringer Review Blackline Masters

Los verbos en -ar

PRESENTATION *(page 4)*

A. Write the three infinitives from page 4 on the board and underline the endings. Write the forms for just one verb *(hablar)* and have students provide the endings for the other verbs. Have the class repeat each form in unison.

B. Read each of the explanations in steps 2–5 and call on an individual to read the sentences that illustrate the point.

Los verbos en *-ar*

1. Review the forms of regular *-ar* verbs in Spanish.

INFINITIVE	HABLAR	TOMAR	CANTAR
ROOT	habl-	tom-	cant-
yo	hablo	tomo	canto
tú	hablas	tomas	cantas
él, ella, Ud.	habla	toma	canta
nosotros(as)	hablamos	tomamos	cantamos
vosotros(as)	*habláis*	*tomáis*	*cantáis*
ellos, ellas, Uds.	hablan	toman	cantan

2. Remember that the subject pronouns can be omitted in Spanish.

> (Yo) Hablo español.
> (Tú) Hablas inglés.
> (Nosotros) Estudiamos mucho.

3. To make a sentence negative, put *no* before the verb.

> El profesor enseña. Los alumnos no enseñan.
> Los alumnos toman exámenes. Los profesores no toman exámenes.

4. You use *tú* when speaking to a friend, a family member, or any person who is the same age as yourself.

> Antonio, (tú) hablas español, ¿no?

5. You use *Ud.* when speaking to an older person, someone you do not know well, or anyone to whom you wish to show respect.

> ¿Habla Ud. inglés, señor López?

R–4 REPASO

LEARNING FROM REALIA

Ask students to say all they can about the advertisement on page 4.

C En la escuela. Contesten.

1. ¿A qué hora llegan los alumnos a la escuela?
2. ¿Cuántas asignaturas toman?
3. ¿Sacan notas buenas o malas?
4. ¿Estudian mucho o poco?
5. Y tú, ¿a qué hora llegas a la escuela?
6. ¿En qué llevas tus libros?
7. ¿Qué asignaturas estudias?
8. ¿Qué notas sacas?

REPASO   **R–5**

PRESENTATION (page 5)
Ejercicio C
   Do Exercise C first with books closed. You may then wish to have students read it for additional reinforcement.

ANSWERS
Ejercicio C
   Answers will vary.
1. Los alumnos llegan a la escuela a las…
2. Los alumnos toman… asignaturas.
3. Ellos sacan notas buenas (malas).
4. Estudian mucho (poco).
5. Yo llego a la escuela a las…
6. Yo llevo mis libros en…
7. Estudio…
8. Saco… notas.

COOPERATIVE LEARNING

1. Have students work in pairs. One makes up a question about the illustration on page 5 and the other one answers. They can then reverse roles.
2. Have students work in pairs to write a paragraph about the illustration. They can each volunteer some words and expressions that will be put into sentences to form a paragraph. As a final step, they will edit the paragraph to find any errors. You may wish to give students the word *casco* (helmet).

PRESENTATION (page 6)

Ejercicio D

A. Do Exercise D with books open.

B. Call on individuals to supply the correct verb form.

C. Then have two students read the conversation aloud with as much expression as possible.

Ejercicio E

Note If students ask about *fotos instantáneas,* explain to them that *las fotos* is a shortened form of *las fotografías.*

Ejercicio F

After having individuals provide the correct verb forms, you may call on one or two students to read the entire exercise aloud.

Expansion of *Ejercicio F*

Call on one student to retell the information in Exercise F in his/her own words.

ANSWERS

Ejercicio D

1. hablas
2. hablo
3. hablas
4. estudio
5. hablamos
6. escuchamos

Ejercicio E

1. bailamos
2. toca
3. toca, cantan
4. Preparan
5. Tomas
6. miramos

Ejercicio F

1. estudia
2. trabaja
3. estudia
4. hablan
5. cantan
6. estudio
7. trabajo
8. saco
9. hablamos
10. cantamos
11. tocamos
12. toman
13. miramos
14. miramos
15. escuchamos
16. hablamos

D ¿Qué lenguas hablas? Completen.

—Oye, Paco. Tú ___ (hablar) español, ¿no?
  ₁

—Sí, (yo) ___ (hablar) español. Y tú también ___ (hablar) español, ¿no?
  ₂   ₃

—Sí, pero no muy bien. Yo ___ (estudiar) español en la escuela. En la clase de
  ₄

español nosotros ___ (hablar) y ___ (escuchar) cintas.
  ₅   ₆

E En la fiesta. Completen.

1. Durante la fiesta nosotros ___. (bailar)
2. José ___ el piano. (tocar)
3. Mientras él ___ el piano, Sandra y Manolo ___. (tocar, cantar)
4. ¿ ___ Uds. refrescos para la fiesta? (preparar)
5. ¿ ___ tú fotos instantáneas durante la fiesta? (tomar)
6. Sí, y todos nosotros ___ las fotografías. (mirar)

F Un muchacho en un colegio de Santiago. Completen.

Ricardo es un muchacho chileno. Él ___ (estudiar) en un colegio de Santiago,
                                      ₁

la capital de Chile. Ricardo es un muchacho listo. Él ___ (trabajar) mucho en la
                                                        ₂

escuela. Él ___ (estudiar) inglés. En la clase de inglés los alumnos ___ (hablar)
            ₃   ₄

mucho. A veces ellos ___ (cantar) también.
                      ₅

Yo ___ (estudiar) español en una escuela secundaria en los Estados Unidos.
    ₆

Yo también ___ (trabajar) mucho y ___ (sacar) muy buenas notas en la clase
            ₇   ₈

de español. En la clase nosotros ___ (hablar)
                                  ₉

mucho con el profesor. A veces, nosotros ___
                                          ₁₀

(cantar) y ___ (tocar) la guitarra.
           ₁₁

Después de las clases, los amigos ___ (tomar)
                                   ₁₂

una merienda. A veces nosotros ___ (mirar) la
                                ₁₃

televisión. Cuando no ___ (mirar) la televisión,
                       ₁₄

nosotros ___ (escuchar) discos o ___ (hablar)
         ₁₅   ₁₆

por teléfono.

LEARNING FROM PHOTOS

Ask students to describe the people in the photo on page 6. You may wish to ask questions such as: *¿Es alumno el señor? ¿Qué es el señor? ¿Es alumna la muchacha? ¿Lleva uniforme la muchacha?*

INDEPENDENT PRACTICE

Assign any of the following:
1. Exercises and activities on student pages 2–6
2. Workbook, *Repaso A*

Los verbos *ir, dar* y *estar*

1. Review the forms of the irregular verbs *ir, dar,* and *estar*. Note that they are irregular in the *yo* form. All other forms conform to the pattern of a regular *-ar* verb.

INFINITIVE	IR	DAR	ESTAR
yo	voy	doy	estoy
tú	vas	das	estás
él, ella, Ud.	va	da	está
nosotros(as)	vamos	damos	estamos
vosotros(as)	*vais*	*dais*	*estáis*
ellos, ellas, Uds.	van	dan	están

2. Remember that *estar* is used to express location and how you feel.

> ¿Dónde está Roberto? Está en casa.
> ¿Cómo estás? Estoy bien, gracias.

3. The preposition *a* often follows the verb *ir*. Remember that *a* contracts with *el* to form one word *al*.

> Voy al café. No voy a la tienda.

REPASO   **R–7**

Los verbos **ir, dar y estar**
PRESENTATION *(page 7)*

When going over the explanation, emphasize the fact that the *yo* forms of these three verbs follow the same pattern. Have students repeat *voy, doy,* and *estoy*. Then point out that all other forms are the same as those of a regular *-ar* verb.

LEARNING FROM REALIA

Ask students what the ad on page 7 is for. (crossword puzzle book) You may wish to give the word *crucigrama* for crossword puzzle. Ask them the price of the magazine and where it comes from. (Spain, the price is *150 pesetas*.)

Ejercicio G

It is recommended that you first do Exercise G as an oral activity with books closed. Call on individuals to respond.

PAIRED ACTIVITY

You may also do Exercise G as a paired activity. One student asks the questions and the other responds. After item 4, they can reverse roles.

ANSWERS

Ejercicio G

1. Voy a la escuela…
2. Sí (No), (no) estoy en la escuela ahora.
3. Estoy en la clase de español.
4. Sí (No), (no) voy a la escuela con mis amigos.
5. Vamos a la escuela a pie (en coche, en bus escolar).
6. Sí (No), (no) estoy con mis amigos ahora.
7. Sí (No), ellos (no) están en la clase de español también.
8. Sí (No), el/la profesor(a) de español (no) da muchos exámenes.
9. Después de las clases, vamos a…

F **Entrevista.** Contesten.

1. ¿A qué escuela vas?
2. ¿Estás en la escuela ahora?
3. ¿En qué clase estás?
4. ¿Vas a la escuela con tus amigos?
5. ¿Cómo van Uds. a la escuela?
6. ¿Estás con tus amigos ahora?
7. ¿Están ellos en la clase de español también?
8. ¿Da el/la profesor(a) de español muchos exámenes?
9. ¿Adónde van tú y tus amigos después de las clases?

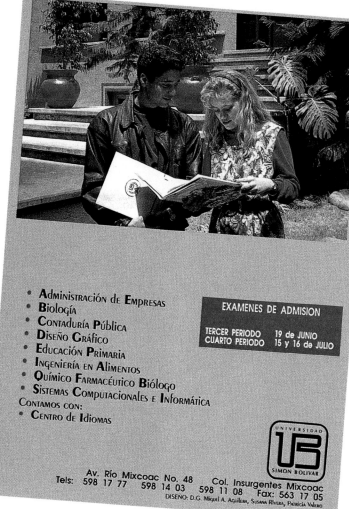

* **A**DMINISTRACIÓN DE **E**MPRESAS
* **B**IOLOGÍA
* **C**ONTADURÍA **P**ÚBLICA
* **D**ISEÑO **G**RÁFICO
* **E**DUCACIÓN **P**RIMARIA
* **I**NGENIERÍA EN **A**LIMENTOS
* **Q**UÍMICO **F**ARMACÉUTICO **B**IÓLOGO
* **S**ISTEMAS **C**OMPUTACIONALES E **I**NFORMÁTICA

CONTAMOS CON:
* **C**ENTRO DE **I**DIOMAS

EXAMENES DE ADMISION

TERCER PERIODO   19 de JUNIO
CUARTO PERIODO   15 y 16 de JULIO

UNIVERSIDAD
US
SIMON BOLIVAR

Av. Río Mixcoac No. 48   Col. Insurgentes Mixcoac
Tels: 598 17 77   598 14 03   598 11 08   Fax: 563 17 05
DISEÑO: D.G. Miguel A. Aguilera, Susana Rivera, Patricia Valero

LEARNING FROM REALIA

The ad on page 8 contains many cognates. You may wish to ask students questions such as: *¿De qué clase de exámenes hablan? ¿Qué universidad es? ¿Dónde está la universidad? ¿Cuándo es el examen para el tercer período? ¿Cuál es el número de FAX de la universidad? ¿Cuál es la dirección de la universidad?*

Ask students to figure out as many of the subjects as they can.

Comunicación

A **Las actividades.** With a classmate prepare a list of activities you do. Separate the activities you have listed into two categories:

EN LA ESCUELA   DESPUÉS DE LAS CLASES

Then write a paragraph telling what you do in school and what you do after school.

B **¿Adónde vas?** With a classmate make up a short conversation using each of the following verbs. Use the model as a guide.

> Estudiante 1: ¿Adónde vas?
> Estudiante 2: ¿Quién, yo? Yo voy a la biblioteca.
> Estudiante 1: ¿Sí? Tomás va a la biblioteca también.

1. ir
2. hablar
3. tocar
4. mirar
5. estar

C **¿Cómo soy…?** Describe yourself to your partner in terms of what you are not. Reverse roles.

> No soy alta; no soy rubia…

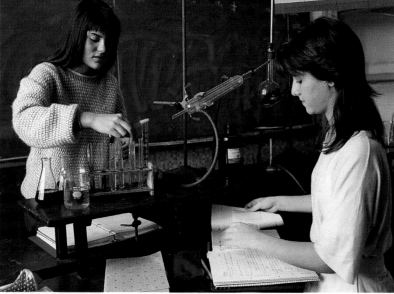

Un colegio en la Argentina

Comunicación

PRESENTATION *(page 9)*

These activities encourage students to use the language on their own. You may let them choose the activities they would like to participate in.

ANSWERS

Actividad A
Answers will vary.

Actividad B
Answers will vary according to the model and cues provided.

Actividad C
Answers will vary.

HISTORY CONNECTION

The school *"Colegio Nacional Nicolás Avellaneda"* is named for the Argentine journalist and politician (1837–1885) who was president of Argentina from 1874–1880. During his presidency, Argentina first exported grain and frozen beef to Europe. He died in a shipwreck while returning from a trip to Europe.

LEARNING FROM PHOTOS

Ask students the following questions about the photo on page 9: *¿Qué estudian las muchachas? ¿Dónde están ellas?* All the equipment is known as: *aparatos de laboratorio.*

INDEPENDENT PRACTICE

Assign any of the following:
1. Exercises and activities on student pages 7–9
2. Workbook, *Repaso A*

OVERVIEW

This chapter reviews greetings, salutations, and farewells. In addition, it recycles vocabulary related to activities that can take place at home, school, or during leisure time. The structures reviewed are the present tense of regular *-er* and *-ir* verbs and *ser,* and the agreement of articles and adjectives.

REVIEW RESOURCES

1. Workbook, *Repaso B*
2. Bell Ringer Review Blackline Masters

Pacing

This review chapter should take four or five days depending on the length of the class, the age of the students, and student aptitude.

REPASO

B

LAS ACTIVIDADES

R–10

LEARNING FROM PHOTOS

The cathedral and the fairway depict the festivities during the *fiestas patronales*. The *fiestas patronales* are traditional in towns and cities in Spain and Latin America. Virtually all towns and cities have a *Santo Patrón* (patron saint) whose day is celebrated with religious ceremonies and entertainment. In larger cities the *fiestas* may last a week or more with bullfights, dances, contests, sporting events, and concerts.

If you have native speakers in your class, ask them the patron saint of their family, town or city, when the *fiestas* take place, and how they are celebrated.

The word for "ferris wheel" is *la noria gigante,* a "merry go round" is a *tíovivo.*

R–11

VOCABULARIO

Los amigos

¡Hola!
¡Hola! ¿Qué tal, Jesús?
Bien, ¿y tú?
Muy bien, gracias.
¡Chao! ¡Hasta luego!
¡Adiós! ¡Hasta luego!

A **Hola.** Say "hi" to a friend in class.

B **¿Cómo te va?** Ask a friend in class how things are going.

C **Adiós.** Say "so long" to a friend in class.

Dos mexicanos

Es Rafael Salas.
Él es de México.
Rafael es mexicano.

Es Carmen Grávalos.
Carmen es mexicana también.
Carmen y Rafael son de
   Guadalajara.
Viven en Guadalajara.
Ellos son alumnos en el colegio Hidalgo, en
   Guadalajara.

En el colegio Rafael y Carmen…
   leen libros y periódicos.
   escriben con lápiz y con bolígrafo.
   comen en la cafetería.
   ven un partido de fútbol.

R–12   REPASO

12

D Rafael y Carmen. Contesten.

1. ¿De dónde es Rafael?
2. ¿De qué nacionalidad es?
3. Y Carmen, ¿de qué nacionalidad es ella?
4. ¿De dónde son Rafael y Carmen?
5. ¿Dónde viven ellos?
6. ¿Dónde son alumnos?

E ¿Qué hacen? Pareen.

1. leer
2. escribir
3. vivir
4. aprender
5. vender
6. comer
7. ver
8. ser
9. subir
10. beber

a. mucho en la escuela
b. al quinto piso
c. una novela
d. un alumno bueno y serio
e. una carta con bolígrafo
f. una limonada
g. en una casa particular
h. una emisión deportiva
i. discos en una tienda en el centro comercial
j. carne, ensalada y papas

F La familia. Completen.

1. La familia ___ en la cocina o en el comedor.
2. La familia ___ la televisión en la sala.
3. Después de la comida mamá ___ una carta a una amiga.
4. Papá ___ el periódico.
5. La familia ___ en una casa privada. La familia no ___ en un apartamento.

G Sustantivos y verbos. Pareen.

1. escribir
2. comer
3. vender
4. beber
5. aprender
6. vivir
7. leer

a. la venta
b. el aprendizaje
c. la escritura
d. la lectura
e. la vivienda
f. la comida
g. la bebida

REPASO   **R–13**

INDEPENDENT PRACTICE

Assign any of the following:
1. Exercises on student page 13
2. Workbook, *Repaso B*

Ejercicios

PRESENTATION (*page 13*)

It is suggested that you go over all the exercises once in class before assigning them as homework.

Ejercicio D

It is recommended that you do Exercise D as an oral activity with books closed.

Ejercicio E

You may wish to give students a few minutes to go over the exercise before calling on individuals to respond aloud.

Expansion of *Ejercicio F*

Upon completion of Exercise F, call on one individual to retell the story about the family in his/her own words.

Ejercicio G

The object of this exercise is to help students recognize new words based on the knowledge of another related word.

ANSWERS

Ejercicio D

1. Él es de México.
2. Él es mexicano.
3. Carmen es mexicana.
4. Rafael y Carmen son de México.
5. Ellos viven en Guadalajara.
6. Son alumnos en el colegio Hidalgo.

Ejercicio E

1. c	6. j
2. e	7. h
3. g	8. d
4. a	9. b
5. i	10. f

Ejercicio F

1. está
2. mira
3. escribe
4. lee
5. vive, vive

Ejercicio G

1. c
2. f
3. a
4. g
5. b
6. e
7. d

13

Structure Teaching Resources

1. Workbook, *Repaso B*
2. Bell Ringer Review Blackline Masters

Los verbos en -er, -ir

Bell Ringer Review

Write the following on the board or use BRR Blackline Master R-4: Answer the following questions in as many ways as you can.
¿Qué comes?
¿Qué aprendes?
¿Qué escribes?
¿Qué ves?

PRESENTATION *(page 14)*

1. Have students repeat the forms of *comer* and *vivir* after you.
2. Write the verbs *leer* and *subir* on the board and have students give you the endings.

Los verbos en *-er, -ir*

1. Review the forms of regular second conjugation, *-er* verbs and third conjugation, *-ir* verbs.

INFINITIVE	COMER	VIVIR
STEM	com-	viv-
yo	como	vivo
tú	comes	vives
él, ella, Ud.	come	vive
nosotros(as)	comemos	vivimos
vosotros(as)	*coméis*	*vivís*
ellos, ellas, Uds.	comen	viven

2. Note that all forms of *-er* and *-ir* verbs are the same except *nosotros* and *vosotros.*

Nosotros comemos.   Nosotros subimos.
Bebemos.   Escribimos.

SE SIENTE...	CON GANAS DE COMER...	¡LO QUE DEBE COMER!
Triste	Alimentos reconfortantes	Sopa, avena, macarrones con queso
Enojada	Alimentos duros crujientes	Palomitas de maíz, apio, manzana
Segura	Comidas picantes	Jugo de tomate con especias, *crudités* con salsas
Avergonzada	Alimentos cremosos	Bananas, yogur descremado
Excitada	Algo dulce	Galletitas "María", caramelos, mazapanes
Tensa	Alimentos salados	Sopa de vegetales, galletitas saltinas
Nerviosa	Alimentos ricos en carbohidratos	Pastas, papas y pan integral
Cansada	Alimentos ricos en proteína	Queso, carne magra y maní

R–14   REPASO

LEARNING FROM REALIA

1. Have students look at the realia on page 14 and tell what its message is. The article describes what people want to eat and what they should eat when they are feeling sad, angry, tired, etc.
2. You may wish to ask students how many "states" or feelings they recognize from the list. You may also ask them to identify as many foods as they can.

H Personalmente. Completen.

1. Yo ___ en ___. (vivir)
2. Yo no ___ en ___. ___ en ___. (vivir)
3. Yo ___ en la calle ___. (vivir)
4. En casa, yo ___ con mi familia. (comer)
5. Nosotros ___ en la cocina. (comer)
6. Después de la comida yo ___ el periódico. (leer)
7. A veces yo ___ una composición para la clase de inglés. (escribir)

I Pregunta. Make up a question for each sentence in Exercise H.

J Vivimos en los Estados Unidos. Contesten.

1. ¿Dónde viven Uds.?
2. ¿Viven Uds. en una casa particular?
3. ¿Viven Uds. en un apartamento?
4. ¿Escriben Uds. mucho en la clase de español?
5. Y en la clase de inglés, ¿escriben Uds. mucho?
6. ¿Comprenden Uds. cuando la profesora habla en español?
7. ¿Reciben Uds. buenas notas en español?
8. ¿Aprenden Uds. mucho en la escuela?
9. ¿Leen Uds. muchos libros?
10. ¿Comen Uds. en la cafetería de la escuela?

El Secreto De Nuestro Éxito En Miami.

No Es Un Secreto.

Mansiones en lotes de ¼ y ½ acre* desde $129,990 a $189,990.

The Mansions
at Lakes of The Meadow
MIAMI - FLORIDA

LEARNING FROM REALIA

Ask students to say all they can about the ad on page 15. You may wish to ask questions such as: *¿Qué venden? ¿Cuáles son los precios? ¿Dónde están las casas? ¿Para quiénes es el anuncio?*

Ejercicios

PRESENTATION *(page 15)*

Ejercicio H

A. Call on each individual to complete two sentences.
B. After going over Exercise H once, call on one individual to read the entire exercise.

Ejercicio I

Students can make up more than one question about each statement.

ANSWERS

Ejercicio H

Answers will vary for items 1–3.
1. vivo
2. vivo, vivo
3. vivo
4. como
5. comemos
6. leo
7. escribo

Ejercicio I

1. ¿Dónde vives?
2. ¿No vives en…? ¿Vives en…?
3. ¿Vives en la calle…?
4. En casa, ¿comes con tu familia?
5. ¿Comen Uds. en la cocina?
6. Después de la comida, ¿lees el periódico?
7. ¿Escribes una composición para la clase de inglés?

Ejercicio J

Answers will vary.
1. Vivimos en…
2. Sí (No), (no) vivimos en una casa particular.
3. Sí (No), (no) vivimos en un apartamento.
4. Sí (No), (no) escribimos mucho en la clase de español.
5. Sí (No), (no) escribimos mucho en la clase de inglés.
6. Sí (No), (no) comprendemos cuando la profesora habla en español.
7. Sí (No), (no) recibimos buenas notas en español.
8. Sí (No), (no) aprendemos mucho en la escuela.
9. Sí (No), (no) leemos muchos libros.
10. Sí (No), (no) comemos en la cafetería de la escuela.

El verbo ser

PRESENTATION (page 16)

Have students open their books to page 16 and repeat the verb forms after you.

PRESENTATION

Ejercicio K

Call on two students with good pronunciation to read the conversation to the class.

Expansion of *Ejercicio K*

Call on a student to retell the story of the conversation in his/her own words.

ANSWERS

Ejercicio K

In-class activity.

El verbo *ser*

Review the forms of the irregular verb *ser*.

SER	
yo	soy
tú	eres
él, ella, Ud.	es
nosotros(as)	somos
vosotros(as)	*sois*
ellos, ellas, Uds.	son

K **La nacionalidad.** Practiquen.

—Roberto, tú eres americano, ¿no?
—Sí, hombre. Soy americano.
—Y tu amiga, ¿es ella americana también?
—¿Quién, Alejandra?
—Sí, ella.
—No, ella es de España.
—Pero Uds. son alumnos en la misma escuela, ¿no?
—Sí, somos alumnos en la escuela Monroe.

LEARNING FROM PHOTOS

1. You may wish to ask the following questions based on the photograph at the top of page 16: *¿Dónde está la muchacha? ¿Es ella alumna? ¿En qué escribe? ¿Con qué escribe? ¿Es una clase pequeña o grande?*
2. Have students look at the photo at the bottom of page 16 and make up sentences using the following words: *alumnos, amigos, hermanos, serios, divertidos.*

L Roberto y Alejandra. Contesten según la conversación.

1. ¿Quién es americano?
2. ¿Quién es de España?
3. ¿Son ellos alumnos en la misma escuela?
4. ¿En qué escuela son ellos alumnos?

M Personalmente. Contesten.

1. ¿Quién eres?
2. ¿De dónde eres?
3. ¿De qué nacionalidad eres?
4. ¿Cómo eres?
5. ¿Qué eres?
6. ¿Dónde eres alumno(a)?

N Dos ecuatorianos. Completen con *ser*.

Marisa Contreras ___ de Guayaquil. Y
                    1
Felipe Gutiérrez ___ de Guayaquil. Los
                   2
dos ___ ecuatorianos y los dos no ___
     3   4
de la capital.

¿De dónde ___ Uds.? ¿ ___ Uds. de
           5   6
la capital de su país?

Nosotros ___ de ___ .
          7

Ecuador

Catedral de Guayaquil

Guayaquil

REPASO   **R–17**

Ejercicios L and M

It is recommended that both these exercises be done orally with books closed.

Expansion of *Ejercicio M*

Upon completion of Exercise M, call on an individual to tell all about himself/herself.

ANSWERS

Ejercicio L

1. Roberto es americano.
2. Alejandra es de España.
3. Sí, son alumnos en la misma escuela.
4. Ellos son alumnos en la escuela Monroe.

Ejercicio M

Answers will vary.

1. Yo soy…
2. Yo soy de…
3. Yo soy…
4. Yo soy…
5. Yo soy…
6. Soy alumno(a) en la escuela…

Ejercicio N

1. es
2. es
3. son
4. son
5. son
6. Son
7. somos

GEOGRAPHY CONNECTION

Have students locate Guayaquil, Ecuador, on the map of South America, page 474. Guayaquil was founded in 1536. Simón Bolívar and José de San Martín met there in 1822 to complete plans for the liberation of South America from Spain. Guayaquil is Ecuador's major port. It has a population of over 1.5 million.

COOPERATIVE LEARNING

Upon completion of Exercise N, have students work in groups of three or four. Each group makes up a story about Marisa and Felipe. Have them come up with as many statements as possible.

INDEPENDENT PRACTICE

Assign any of the following:
1. Exercises and activities on student pages 15–17
2. Workbook, *Repaso B*

Bell Ringer Review

Write the following on the board or use BRR Blackline Master R-5: List as many classroom objects as you can.

Los artículos y los sustantivos

PRESENTATION *(page 18)*

As you go over the explanation, have students repeat the words and example sentences after you. Point to a specific person or object as you use the definite article.

Los artículos y los sustantivos

1. Many Spanish nouns end in *-o* or *-a.* Most nouns that end in *-o* are masculine and most nouns that end in *-a* are feminine. The definite article *el* accompanies a masculine noun and the definite article *la* accompanies a feminine noun.

MASCULINO	FEMENINO
el muchacho	la muchacha
el colegio	la escuela

2. Many Spanish nouns end in *-e.* It is impossible to tell the gender, masculine or feminine, of nouns ending in *-e.*

MASCULINO	FEMENINO
el arte	la calle
el café	la clase
el deporte	la tarde
el padre	la madre

4. To form the plural of nouns ending in the vowels *o, a,* or *e,* you add an *-s.* To nouns ending in a consonant, you add *-es.* Note that *el* changes to *los* and *la* changes to *las.*

MASCULINO	FEMENINO
los muchachos	las muchachas
los deportes	las calles
los profesores	las ciudades

5. In Spanish, you use the indefinite articles *un* or *una* to express "a" or "an." Note that these articles change to *unos* and *unas* in the plural.

SINGULAR	PLURAL
un muchacho	unos muchachos
una muchacha	unas muchachas

R-18   REPASO

18

O **El muchacho y la muchacha.** Completen con *el, la, los* o *las.*

___ muchacho es cubano y ___ muchacha es puertorriqueña. Sus padres son
    1   2

de Ponce en el sur de ___ isla. Ahora ___ dos muchachos viven en ___ ciudad
                        3   4   5

de Miami. Ellos viven en ___ misma calle y van a ___ misma escuela.
                          6   7

P **El plural.** Cambien cada oración a la forma plural.

1. El muchacho es moreno.
2. La muchacha es rubia.
3. El alumno es serio.
4. La escuela es buena.
5. La ciudad es grande.

El departamento de bomberos, Ponce, Puerto Rico

REPASO   **R–19**

Upon completion of Exercise
O, have one student read the
entire exercise as a story.

Ejercicio P

Have students write the plural
sentences. Then have them close
their books, read the plural sentences, and put them back into the
singular.

ANSWERS

Ejercicio O
1. El
2. la
3. la
4. los
5. la
6. la
7. la

Ejercicio P
1. Los muchachos son morenos.
2. Las muchachas son rubias.
3. Los alumnos son serios.
4. Las escuelas son buenas.
5. Las ciudades son grandes.

GEOGRAPHY CONNECTION

Have students locate
Ponce on the map of Puerto
Rico (page 475). The brightly
painted firehouse on page 19
is a very popular tourist
attraction.

LEARNING FROM PHOTOS

The *Parque de bombas* in the photo at the
bottom of page 19 is in the central plaza of
Ponce, Puerto Rico. It was built as an exhibit
hall for an exposition in 1882.

La concordancia de los adjetivos

PRESENTATION *(page 20)*

A. Draw a stick figure of a boy and a girl on the board. Each time you give a masculine form, point to the boy. Each time you give a feminine form, point to the girl.

B. Have students repeat all the example sentences aloud.

La concordancia de los adjetivos

1. Adjectives agree with the nouns they describe. If the noun is feminine, the adjective must be in the feminine form. If the noun is plural, the adjective must be in the plural form. Review the following.

	FEMENINO	MASCULINO
SINGULAR	la amiga rubia una muchacha seria	el amigo rubio un muchacho serio
PLURAL	las amigas rubias unas muchachas serias	los amigos rubios unos amigos serios

2. Adjectives that end in *-e* have two forms. To form the plural you add an *-s*.

   el edificio grande
   los edificios grandes

3. Adjectives that end in a consonant also have two forms. You add *-es* to form the plural.

el curso fácil	**los cursos fáciles**
la lección fácil	**las lecciones fáciles**

LEARNING FROM REALIA

Ask students what they think the ad on page 20 is for. The word for computer in Latin America is usually *computadora*. In Spain the word is *ordenador,* probably from the French *ordinateur.*

Q **Las dos muchachas.** Describan a las muchachas.

R **El amigo.** Describan a un(a) amigo(a).

El presente progresivo *Describing an Action in Progress*

1. The present progressive is used in Spanish to express an action that is presently going on. It is formed by using the present tense of the verb *estar* and the present participle. To form the present participle of most verbs you drop the ending of the infinitive and add *-ando* to the stem of *-ar* verbs and *-iendo* to the stem of *-er* and *-ir* verbs. Study the following forms of the present participle.

INFINITIVE	HABLAR	LLEGAR	COMER	HACER	SALIR
STEM PARTICIPLE	habl- hablando	lleg- llegando	com- comiendo	hac- haciendo	sal- saliendo

2. Note that the verbs *leer* and *traer* have a *y* in the present participle.

   leyendo   **trayendo**

3. Study the following examples of the present progressive.

   ¿Qué está haciendo Elena?
   En este momento está esperando el avión.

REPASO   **R–21**

Ejercicios

PRESENTATION *(page 21)*

Ejercicios Q and R
   After going over these exercises, you may have students describe the boy and the girl in the photos on page 19. They can also describe the group on page 16.

ANSWERS
Ejercicios Q and R
   Answers will vary.

El presente progresivo
PRESENTATION *(page 21)*

A. You may have students call out any verb they can think of. Write the present participle of that verb on the board and have students repeat it.
B. Call on students to read the example sentences on page 21 aloud.

21

Ejercicio S

It is recommended that you do the exercise first orally with books closed. You may wish to do the exercise a second time without providing the cued response.

Ejercicios T and U

Encourage students to be as original as possible in making up their sentences.

ANSWERS

Ejercicio S

1. Los pasajeros están llegando al aeropuerto.
2. Están llegando en taxi.
3. Están viajando a Europa.
4. Están haciendo el viaje en avión.
5. Están facturando el equipaje en el mostrador de la línea aérea.
6. La agente está revisando los boletos y los pasaportes.
7. Los pasajeros están saliendo por la puerta número siete.
8. Están abordando el avión.

Ejercicio T

Answers will vary.

1. (No) Estoy comiendo…
2. (No) Estoy hablando…
3. (No) Estoy estudiando…
4. (No) Estoy bailando…
5. (No) Estoy escribiendo…
6. (No) Estoy aprendiendo…
7. (No) Estoy trabajando…
8. (No) Estoy haciendo un viaje…
9. (No) Estoy leyendo…
10. (No) Estoy saliendo para España.

Ejercicio U

Answers will vary.

22

S **¿Qué están haciendo en el aeropuerto?** Contesten según se indica. (*Answer according to the cues.*)

1. ¿Adónde están llegando los pasajeros? (al aeropuerto)
2. ¿Cómo están llegando? (en taxi)
3. ¿Adónde están viajando? (a Europa)
4. ¿Cómo están haciendo el viaje? (en avión)
5. ¿Dónde están facturando el equipaje? (en el mostrador de la línea aérea)
6. ¿Qué está revisando la agente? (los boletos y los pasaportes)
7. ¿De qué puerta están saliendo los pasajeros para Madrid? (número siete)
8. ¿Qué están abordando? (el avión)

T **Yo (no) estoy…** Formen oraciones. (*Make up a sentence telling whether you are or are not doing each of the following.*)

1. comer
2. hablar
3. estudiar
4. bailar
5. escribir
6. aprender
7. trabajar
8. hacer un viaje
9. leer
10. salir para España

U **¿Qué están haciendo ahora?** Digan lo que están haciendo. (*Tell what the following members of your family or friends are doing now.*)

1. Mi madre
2. Mi padre
3. Mis primos
4. Mis hermanos
5. Yo
6. Mis amigos
7. Mi novio(a) y yo

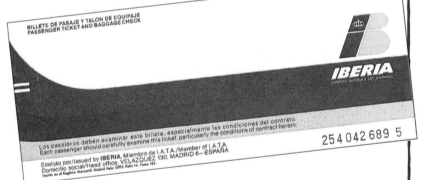

R–22 REPASO

Comunicación

A En la cafetería. You have just met a new student in the school cafeteria. Tell him or her what your nationality is, what languages you speak, what classes you are taking, how many brothers and sisters you have, and what their ages are. Reverse roles.

B Las categorías. With a classmate make up a list of words you know that describe a person. Then divide the words into the following categories.

> descripción física
> personalidad
> características positivas
> características negativas

Continue to work together. Then decide upon a person that fits into all categories and give a complete description of the person.

C Soy… Write a postcard to a pen pal in Puerto Rico. Tell him or her what you look like; where you are from; and where you go to school. Describe your school and after-school activities.

El observatorio de Arecibo, Puerto Rico

Un edificio de apartamentos en el viejo San Juan, Puerto Rico

La catedral de Ponce, Puerto Rico

REPASO **R–23**

OVERVIEW

This chapter reviews vocabulary dealing with plane travel and organized team sports. It also reviews the following structure points: the present tense of stem-changing verbs, the verbs *hacer, poner, traer, salir, tener,* and *venir.*

REVIEW RESOURCES

1. Workbook, *Repaso C*
2. Bell Ringer Review Blackline Masters

Pacing

This review chapter should take three to four days depending on the length of the class, the age of the students, and student aptitude.

REPASO

C

LOS VIAJES Y LOS DEPORTES

R–24

DID YOU KNOW?

Tennis has become very popular in Spanish-speaking countries. The number of international champions from Latin America and Spain increases yearly. You may wish to ask students to identify as many world-class Hispanic tennis players, especially women, as they can.

R–25

25

VOCABULARIO

Un viaje a Lima

—Hola, Jorge. ¿Qué haces, hombre?
—Pues, voy a hacer un viaje a Lima.
—¿A Lima? ¿Cuándo sales?
—Salgo mañana.
—¿Por qué tienes que ir a Lima?
—No tengo que ir. Es que quiero ir.
—¿Qué vas a hacer en Lima?
—Pues, la Argentina juega contra el Perú.
—¡Verdad!

A **Un viaje a Lima.** Contesten según la conversación.

1. ¿Adónde va Jorge?
2. ¿Cuándo sale?
3. ¿Tiene que ir a Lima?
4. ¿Quiere ir?
5. ¿Qué va a hacer en Lima?

R–26 REPASO

Bell Ringer Review

Write the following on the board or use BRR Blackline Master R-7: Write down as many words and expressions as you can think of that have to do with airports or air travel.

Un viaje a Lima

PRESENTATION *(page 26)*

A. Have students share the words they wrote down for the **Bell Ringer Review** above.
B. Now have students repeat each sentence of the conversation after you.
C. Call on pairs of students to read the conversation aloud with as much expression as possible.

Ejercicio B

ANSWERS

Ejercicio A

1. Jorge hace un viaje a Lima.
2. Sale mañana.
3. No, no tiene que ir a Lima.
4. Sí, quiere ir.
5. Jorge va a ver un partido de fútbol.

COOPERATIVE LEARNING

Have students work in pairs and prepare a conversation that takes place at an airport when checking in for a flight. One student is the airline agent and the other is the passenger.

LEARNING FROM REALIA

Have students locate Argentina and Peru on the map of South America on page 474. Ask them to tell, in Spanish, where they are located on the continent. Ask what is shown on the brochure for Argentina. It is a glacier—*un glaciar.* It is the *Glaciar Perito Moreno,* in *lago Argentino,* in the province of Santa Cruz.

Ejercicios

PRESENTATION *(page 27)*

Ejercicio B

1. Have students look at the illustration as they complete the sentences in Exercise B.
2. Go over the exercise once calling on individuals to do the items. Then have one student reread the entire exercise.

Expansion of *Ejercicio C*

You may wish to have students say as much as they can about each sport they identify.

ANSWERS

Ejercicio B

1. **Managua, Nicaragua**
2. **el aeropuerto**
3. **su equipaje (sus maletas)**
4. **boletos, pasaportes**
5. **vuelo**
6. **Managua**
7. **Sale**
8. **pasajeros**

Ejercicio C

1. **el baloncesto**
2. **el fútbol americano**
3. **el fútbol**
4. **el baloncesto**
5. **el fútbol**

B **En el aeropuerto.** Contesten según el dibujo.

1. Los pasajeros hacen un viaje a ___.
2. Los pasajeros están en ___.
3. Ellos llevan (tienen) ___.
4. El agente revisa sus ___ y sus ___.
5. Es el ___ número 110.
6. El vuelo sale para ___.
7. ___ a las 9:20.
8. Los ___ van a abordar el avión.

C **Los deportes.** ¿Que deporte es?

1. hay cinco jugadores en el equipo
2. hay once jugadores en el equipo
3. el portero guarda la portería
4. los jugadores encestan el balón
5. los jugadores juegan en el campo de fútbol

REPASO **R–27**

27

ESTRUCTURA

El presente de los verbos de cambio radical

Bell Ringer Review

Write the following on the board or use BRR Blackline Master R-8: Write down as many words or expressions as you can think of related to each of the following sports: **el fútbol, el básquetbol, el béisbol.**

El presente de los verbos de cambio radical

PRESENTATION *(page 28)*

A. Have students repeat all the verb forms after you.
B. Then have students repeat all the *nosotros* forms.
C. Now have them repeat all the *yo* forms to contrast the stem change.

1. Review the forms of *e > ie* stem-changing verbs. Note that the stem changes in all forms except the *nosotros* and *vosotros*.

INFINITIVE	EMPEZAR	QUERER	PREFERIR
yo	empiezo	quiero	prefiero
tú	empiezas	quieres	prefieres
él, ella, Ud.	empieza	quiere	prefiere
nosotros(as)	empezamos	queremos	preferimos
vosotros(as)	*empezáis*	*queréis*	*preferís*
ellos, ellas, Uds.	empiezan	quieren	prefieren

2. Review the forms of *o > ue* stem-changing verbs. Note that the stem changes in all forms except the *nosotros* and *vosotros*.

INFINITIVE	VOLVER	PODER	DORMIR
yo	vuelvo	puedo	duermo
tú	vuelves	puedes	duermes
él, ella, Ud.	vuelve	puede	duerme
nosotros(as)	volvemos	podemos	dormimos
vosotros(as)	*volvéis*	*podéis*	*dormís*
ellos, ellas, Uds.	vuelven	pueden	duermen

3. Remember that the stem of the verb *jugar* also changes to *ue*.

JUGAR	
yo	juego
tú	juegas
él, ella, Ud.	juega
nosotros(as)	jugamos
vosotros(as)	*jugáis*
ellos, ellas, Uds.	juegan

D **Un juego de fútbol.** Lean.

El juego de fútbol empieza a las dos de la tarde. Hoy juegan los Osos contra los Tigres. Cuando empieza el segundo tiempo, el tanto queda empatado en cero. Los jugadores vuelven al campo. Todos quieren ganar, pero si el tanto no queda empatado, un equipo tiene que perder. ¿Quiénes pierden? Durante el último minuto del partido los Osos meten un gol. El portero de los Tigres no puede parar el balón y los Osos ganan.

Deporte TOTAL El Comercio

Lima, lunes 20 de enero de

Así celebraron los jugadores peruanos el cuarto gol. Nuestra selección deambula, a pesar de sus buenos jugadores.

Sub'23 no convence

Ganó a México 4 a 3
Otra vez bronca y expulsiones

(Pags. 2,3 y 4)   Salto de garrocha frente a la Catedral. (pag 5)

Jaime Yzaga y Julio Granda juntos (pags 8 y 9)
Chemo, el líbero que vino del Sur (pags 10 y 11)
Los 50 años de Cassius Clay (pag 12)
Cómo se prepara Ecuador para la Copa Davis (pag 16)

REPASO   **R–29**

PRESENTATION (*page 29*)
Ejercicio D

   Have students open their books to page 29. Call on individuals to read two or three sentences each.

LEARNING FROM REALIA

   Have students say all they can about the sports page. You may wish to ask: *¿De dónde es el periódico? ¿De qué dos equipos habla? ¿Quién gana, México o Perú? ¿Cuántos goles marca Perú? ¿Y cuántos México?* Ask them how to say "pole vault" (*salto de garrocha*).

Ejercicios

PRESENTATION *(page 30)*

Exercises E–H can be done orally with books closed.

Ejercicio E
You may wish to intersperse the questions while students read Exercise D on page 29.

Expansion of *Ejercicio E*
Call on one student to retell the entire story in his/her own words.

Bell Ringer Review
Write the following on the board or use BRR Blackline Master R-9:
1. Write a list of names for all the members that make up a family.
2. Write a list of words you could use to describe a house or apartment.

ANSWERS

Ejercicio E
1. El juego empieza a las dos de la tarde.
2. Juegan los Osos contra los Tigres.
3. El tanto queda empatado en cero.
4. Los jugadores vuelven al campo.
5. Todos quieren ganar.
6. Si el tanto no queda empatado, tiene que perder un equipo.
7. Los Tigres pierden.
8. El portero de los Tigres no puede parar el balón.
9. No, los espectadores no duermen durante un partido.

Ejercicio F
Answers will vary.
Yo quiero…

Ejercicio G
Answers will vary.
Pablo no quiere…
Pablo prefiere…

Ejercicio H
Answers will vary.
Mis amigos y yo podemos…

Ejercicio I
1. empezamos
2. queremos
3. perdemos, podemos

30

E Los Osos contra los Tigres. Contesten según la lectura.
1. ¿A qué hora empieza el juego de fútbol?
2. ¿Quiénes juegan?
3. ¿Cómo queda el tanto cuando empieza el segundo tiempo?
4. ¿Quiénes vuelven al campo?
5. ¿Qué quieren todos?
6. ¿Tiene que perder un equipo?
7. ¿Quiénes pierden?
8. ¿Qué no puede parar el portero de los Tigres?
9. ¿Duermen los espectadores durante el partido?

F Lo que quiero hacer. Tell five things you want to do.

G Lo que Pablo prefiere hacer. Tell five things Pablo does not want to do. Tell what he prefers to do.

H Lo que podemos hacer. Tell five things you and your friends can do.

I El partido de hoy. Completen.
1. Hoy nosotros ___ a jugar a las dos. (empezar)
2. Nosotros no ___ perder. (querer)
3. Si nosotros ___ el juego de hoy, no ___ jugar mañana. (perder, poder)

J El partido de hoy. Cambien *nosotros* a *yo* en las oraciones del Ejercicio I.

Los verbos con g en la primera persona

1. Review the forms of the irregular verbs *hacer, poner, traer,* and *salir.* Note that they all have a g in the *yo* form.

INFINITIVE	HACER	PONER	TRAER	SALIR
yo	hago	pongo	traigo	salgo
tú	haces	pones	traes	sales
él, ella, Ud.	hace	pone	trae	sale
nosotros(as)	hacemos	ponemos	traemos	salimos
vosotros(as)	hacéis	ponéis	traéis	salis
ellos, ellas, Uds.	hacen	ponen	traen	salen

COOPERATIVE LEARNING ACTIVITY

Have pairs of students prepare short conversations for the following situations:
1. in the taxi (the passenger and the driver):
   The passenger should tell the driver where he/she wants to go, ask how long it will take, and how much it costs. The driver should answer the questions.
2. at the airline counter (the traveller and the airline agent):
   The agent should ask for the tickets, and ask if the traveller has suitcases. The traveller should answer and ask what time the plane leaves and from what gate it leaves.

2. The verbs *tener* and *venir* also have a g in the *yo* form. In addition, the e of the infinitive stem changes to *ie* in all forms except the *nosotros* and *vosotros*.

INFINITIVE	TENER	VENIR
yo	tengo	vengo
tú	tienes	vienes
él, ella, Ud.	tiene	viene
nosotros(as)	tenemos	venimos
vosotros(as)	*tenéis*	*venís*
ellos, ellas, Uds.	tienen	vienen

3. The expression *tener que* followed by an infinitive means "to have to."

   Tenemos que estudiar.
   Tenemos que tomar un examen final.

K **Un viaje imaginario.** Contesten con *sí*.

1. ¿Haces un viaje a España?
2. ¿Haces el viaje en avión?
3. Antes, ¿haces la maleta?
4. ¿Qué pones en la maleta?
5. ¿Cuándo sales?
6. ¿Sales para el aeropuerto en taxi?
7. ¿A qué hora viene el taxi?
8. ¿A qué hora tienes que estar en el aeropuerto?
9. ¿Tienes mucho equipaje?
10. ¿A qué hora sale el vuelo para Madrid?

SECRETARIA GENERAL DE TURISMO
TURESPAÑA

REPASO   **R-31**

INDEPENDENT PRACTICE

Assign any of the following:
1. Exercises and activities on student pages 27–31
2. Workbook, *Repaso C*

Ejercicio J
1. empiezo
2. quiero
3. pierdo, puedo

Los verbos con g en la primera persona

PRESENTATION *(pages 30–31)*
A. Have students repeat all the *yo* forms in the chart on page 30.
B. Then point out to students that all the other forms are the same as those of regular *-er* or *-ir* verbs.
C. Have students repeat all the forms of *tener* and *venir* from the chart on page 31.
D. Have students repeat all the *yo* forms one more time: *hago, pongo, traigo, salgo, tengo,* and *vengo.*

PRESENTATION *(page 31)*
Ejercicio K
A. It is suggested that you do Exercise K orally with books closed. Note that this exercise emphasizes the irregular *yo* form.
B. After going over the exercise once calling on individuals, do the exercise once again. Have one student do items 1–5 and another do items 6–10.

ANSWERS
Ejercicio K
1. Sí, hago un viaje a España.
2. Sí, hago el viaje en avión.
3. Sí, antes hago la maleta.
4. Pongo (mi ropa) en la maleta.
5. Salgo a las…
6. Sí, salgo para el aeropuerto en taxi.
7. El taxi viene a las…
8. Tengo que estar en el aeropuerto a las…
9. Sí, tengo mucho equipaje.
10. El vuelo para Madrid sale a…

PAIRED ACTIVITY
Exercise K can be done as a paired activity. One student asks a question and the other one answers. They then reverse roles.

31

Ejercicio L

Have individual students complete each item.

Ejercicio M

After going over Exercise M, call on individuals to give as much information about their family or their home as they can.

ANSWERS

Ejercicio L

1. hace, pone, sale
2. hacemos, ponemos, salimos
3. haces, pones, haces, sales
4. hacen, ponen, hacen, salen
5. hago, pongo, hago, salgo

Ejercicio M

1. Tengo una familia grande (pequeña).
2. Tengo… hermanos y… hermanas.
3. Tenemos una casa particular (un apartamento).
4. La casa (el apartamento) tiene… cuartos.
5. Sí, tenemos un carro.
6. Sí, tenemos una mascota. Tenemos un perro (un gato).

Note For information concerning the terminology for step-relatives, read *Bienvenidos,* Teacher's Wraparound Edition, Chapter 6, page 55.

L **La maleta.** *Completen con* hacer, poner *o* salir.

1. Juan ___ su maleta. Él ___ una camisa en la maleta. Él ___ para Málaga.
2. Nosotros ___ nuestra maleta. Nosotros ___ blue jeans en la maleta porque ___ para Cancún, en México.
3. ¿Tú ___ tu maleta? ¿Qué ___ en la maleta? ¿Por qué ___ la maleta? ¿Para dónde ___?
4. Mis padres ___ su maleta. Ellos ___ muchas cosas en la maleta. Ellos ___ su maleta porque ___ para Miami.
5. Yo ___ mi maleta. Yo ___ blue jeans y T shirts en mi maleta. Yo ___ mi maleta porque ___ para la Sierra de Guadarrama donde voy de camping.

M **Mi familia y mi casa.** *Preguntas personales.*

1. ¿Tienes una familia grande o pequeña?
2. ¿Cuántos hermanos y cuántas hermanas tienes?
3. ¿Tienen Uds. una casa particular o un apartamento?
4. ¿Cuántos cuartos tiene la casa o el apartamento?
5. ¿Tienen Uds. un carro?
6. ¿Tienen Uds. una mascota? ¿Tienen un perro o un gato?

R–32 REPASO

LEARNING FROM ILLUSTRATIONS

Have students say all they can about the illustration. Have them describe everything the young man is packing. You may wish to ask: *¿Cómo es el señor? ¿Dónde está? ¿Qué hace? ¿Por qué? ¿Qué deporte juega él? ¿De quién es la foto?*

Comunicación

A **¿Adónde vamos?** With a partner decide on a place each of you wants to go to. Tell how you're going to get there and what you're going to do there. Then ask each other questions about your trip. Write a paragraph about your partner's trip. Then compare what each of you have written.

B **Los deportes.** With your partner decide what sport you want to talk about. Make a list of words that describe this sport. Then put the words into sentences and write a paragraph about the sport. Read your paragraph to the class.

Partidos de clasificación - marzo

FECHA	EQUIPO DE CASA	EQUIPO VISITANTE	SEDE	GRUPO
				Europa 2
miércoles 10	San Marino	Turquía		Europa 4
miércoles 24	Chipre	Checoslovaquia	Limasol	1
	Italia	Malta	Palermo	2
	Países Bajos	San Marino		
sábado 27	Austria	Francia	Viena	Europa 6
				Europa 4
miércoles 31	Gales	Bélgica		3
	Dinamarca	España		3
	Irlanda	Irlanda del Norte	Dublín	5
	Hungría	Grecia		1
	Suiza	Portugal	Berna	2
	Turquía	Inglaterra		

C **Mi familia y mi casa.** You and your partner will take turns saying something about your family and your house or apartment. Write down what the other person says. Then compare your families and your house or apartment.

D **Quiero…** Work with a classmate. Each of you will make a list of things you want to do but can't do because you have to do something else. Then compare your lists and see how many things you have in common.

REPASO **R–33**

Scope and Sequence pages 242-267

Topics	Functions	Structure	Culture
Winter sports Clothing Sporting equipment Winter resorts Winter weather	How to describe winter weather How to talk about skiing and skating How to express who you are and what you know How to tell what you know how to do How to discuss what other people say How to describe where people and places are located How to point out people or things	El presente de los verbos *saber, y conocer* El presente del verbo *decir* Los adjetivos demostrativos	Winter sports facilities in Spain and South America Galerías Preciados in Madrid Fjords in Chile and icebergs in Argentina Río Negro in Argentina

CAPÍTULO 9

Situation Cards

The Situation Cards simulate real-life situations that require students to communicate in Spanish, exactly as though they were in a Spanish-speaking country. The Situation Cards operate on the assumption that the person to whom the message is to be conveyed understands no English. Therefore, students must focus on producing the Spanish vocabulary and structures necessary to negotiate the situations successfully. For additional information, see the Introduction to the Situation Cards in the Situation Cards Envelope.

Communication Transparency

The illustration seen in this Communication Transparency consists of a synthesis of the two vocabulary (Palabras 1&2) presentations found in this chapter. It has been created in order to present this chapter's vocabulary in a new context, and also to recycle vocabulary learned in previous chapters. The Communication Transparency consists of original art. Following are some specific uses:

1. as a cue to stimulate conversation and writing activities
2. for listening comprehension activities
3. to review and reteach vocabulary
4. as a review for chapter and unit tests

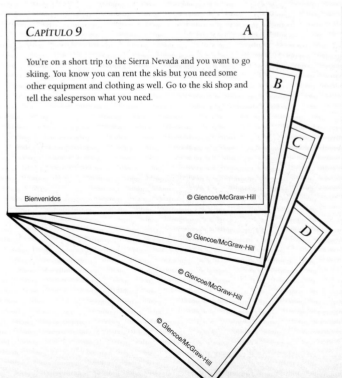

CAPÍTULO 9
Print Resources

	Pages
Lesson Plans	
Workbook	
◆ Palabras 1	89-90
◆ Palabras 2	90-91
◆ Estructura	92-94
◆ Un poco más	95
◆ Mi autobiografía	96
Communication Activities Masters	
◆ Palabras 1	50-51
◆ Palabras 2	52-53
◆ Estructura	54-56
6 Bell Ringer Reviews	23-24
Chapter Situation Cards A B C D	
Chapter Quizzes	
◆ Palabras 1	39
◆ Palabras 2	40
◆ Estructura	41-43
Testing Program	
◆ Listening Comprehension	49
◆ Reading and Writing	50-53
◆ Proficiency	125
◆ Speaking	145

Nosotros y Nuestro Mundo

- ◆ Nuestro Conocimiento Académico *El clima y el tiempo*
- ◆ Nuestro Idioma *La sinalefa*
- ◆ Nuestra Cultura *El clima en Latinoamérica*
- ◆ Nuestra Literatura *"Desde lejos para siempre"* de Nicolás Mihovilovic
- ◆ Nuestra Creatividad
- ◆ Nuestras Diversiones

CAPÍTULO 9
Multimedia Resources

CD-ROM Interactive Textbook Disc 3

Chapter 9 Student Edition
- ◆ Palabras 1
- ◆ Palabras 2
- ◆ Estructura
- ◆ Conversación
- ◆ Lectura y cultura
- ◆ Hispanoparlantes
- ◆ Realidades
- ◆ Culminación
- ◆ Prueba

Audio Cassette Program with Student Tape Manual

Cassette	Pages
◆ 6A Palabras 1	231-232
◆ 6A Palabras 2	232-233
◆ 6A Estructura	233
◆ 6A Conversación	234
◆ 6A Pronunciación	234
◆ 6A Segunda parte	234-236

Compact Disc Program with Student Tape Manual

	Pages
◆ CD 5 Palabras 1	231-232
◆ CD 5 Palabras 2	232-233
◆ CD 5 Estructura	233
◆ CD 5 Conversación	234
◆ CD 5 Pronunciación	234
◆ CD 5 Segunda parte	234-236

Overhead Transparencies Binder

- ◆ Vocabulary   9.1 (A&B); 9.2 (A&B)
- ◆ Pronunciation P-9
- ◆ Communication C-9
- ◆ Maps
- ◆ Fine Art (with Blackline Master Activities)

Video Program

- ◆ Videocassette
- ◆ Video Activities Booklet   26-29
- ◆ Videodisc
- ◆ Video Activities Booklet   26-29

Computer Software (Macintosh, IBM, Apple)

- ◆ Practice Disk
  - Palabras 1 y 2
  - Estructura
- ◆ Test Generator Disk
  - Chapter Test
  - Customized Test

CHAPTER OVERVIEW

In this chapter students will learn to discuss winter sports, the clothing and equipment needed for these sports, and winter resorts in the Spanish-speaking world. They will also learn to talk about winter weather. Students will learn to express whom and what they know, what they know how to do, and the location of people, places, and things by using demonstrative adjectives.

The cultural focus of the chapter is on winter sports facilities in Spain and South America.

CHAPTER OBJECTIVES

By the end of this chapter students will know:

1. vocabulary associated with skiing, ski equipment and clothing, and some ski resort personnel and procedures
2. vocabulary associated with ice skating
3. vocabulary associated with winter weather and weather reports in general
4. the present tense of *saber* and *conocer* and the uses of these verbs
5. the present tense of *decir*
6. demonstrative adjectives

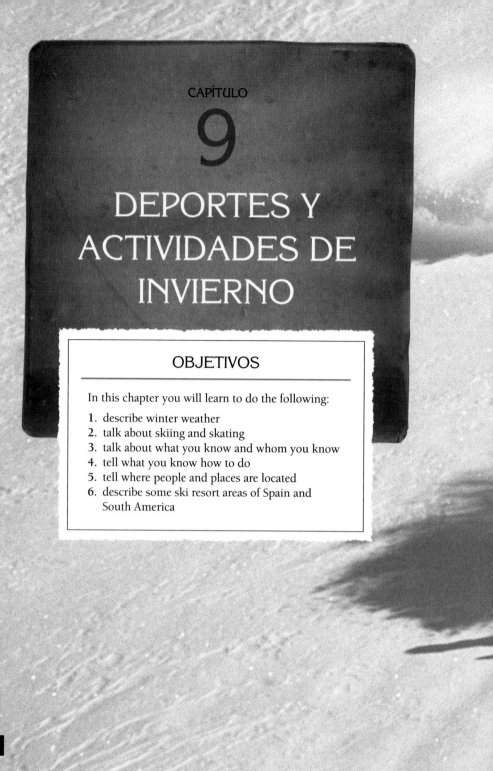

CAPÍTULO

9

DEPORTES Y ACTIVIDADES DE INVIERNO

OBJETIVOS

In this chapter you will learn to do the following:

1. describe winter weather
2. talk about skiing and skating
3. talk about what you know and whom you know
4. tell what you know how to do
5. tell where people and places are located
6. describe some ski resort areas of Spain and South America

242

243

CHAPTER 9 RESOURCES

1. Workbook
2. Student Tape Manual
3. Audio Cassette 6A
4. Vocabulary Transparencies
5. Pronunciation Transparency P-9
6. Bell Ringer Review Blackline Masters
7. Communication Activities Masters
8. Computer Software: Practice and Test Generator
9. Video Cassette, Chapter 9
10. Video Activities Booklet, Chapter 9
11. Situation Cards
12. Chapter Quizzes
13. Testing Program

Pacing

Chapter 9 will require about eight to ten days. However, pacing will vary according to the length of the class, the age of your students, and student aptitude.

Note on Directions to Student Exercises and Activities

Begining with Chapter 9, the English version of the directions to student exercises has been dropped. This has been done to increase the amount of authentic communication in Spanish in the classroom and to provide students with further practice in the target language. You may wish to avoid even mentioning this change and see if students notice it.

LEARNING FROM PHOTOS

After presenting the chapter vocabulary on pages 244–245 and 248–249, you may wish to ask questions about the photo on pages 242–243. *¿Qué deporte practican? ¿Es el esquí de fondo o de descenso? Uno de los esquiadores está haciendo algo diferente. No tiene esquís. ¿Qué tiene? (una plancha) Él está haciendo la plancha sobre la nieve.*

Vocabulary Teaching Resources

1. Vocabulary Transparencies 9.1 (A & B)
2. Audio Cassette 6A
3. Student Tape Manual, pages 231–232
4. Workbook, pages 89–90
5. Communication Activities Masters, pages 50-51, A & B
6. Chapter Quizzes, page 34, *Palabras 1*

Bell Ringer Review

Write the following on the board or use BRR Blackline Master 9-1: Write a list of the sports you have learned in Spanish.

PRESENTATION *(page 244)*

A. Show Vocabulary Transparencies 9.1 (A & B). Point to individual items and have the class repeat the corresponding word or expression after you or the recording on Cassette 6A.
B. As an alternative, you may wish to bring in some props such as sun glasses, ski cap, etc., if you live in an area where winter sports are popular.
C. During the vocabulary presentation ask questions such as *¿Hace frío? ¿Hace frío en el invierno? ¿Cuándo hace frío? ¿Y cuándo nieva? ¿Es una estación de esquí? ¿Qué es? ¿Es un esquiador? ¿Quién es? ¿Esquían los esquiadores en una estación de esquí? ¿Dónde esquían? ¿Quiénes esquían? ¿Cuándo esquían?*

VOCABULARIO

PALABRAS 1

EN LA ESTACIÓN DE ESQUÍ

la nevada

las gafas · el gorro

los guantes de esquí

el anorak

el bastón

el esquí

el frío
el invierno

la temperatura

la bota

¿Qué tiempo hace en el invierno?
Hace frío.
Nieva.
Hay nevadas.
La temperatura baja a cinco grados (centígrados) bajo cero.

el telesilla

la ventanilla

el telesquí

la esquiadora · el esquiador

la boletería

la estación de esquí

244 CAPÍTULO 9

· TOTAL PHYSICAL RESPONSE

(following the Vocabulary presentation)

TPR 1

___, levántate y ven acá, por favor.
Siéntate.
Vamos a hacer gestos.
Ponte las botas.
Ponte los esquís.
Y ahora levántate.

Ponte el anorak.
Ponte las gafas.
Toma el bastón.
Pon el bastón en la mano derecha.
Toma el otro bastón.
Pon este bastón en la mano izquierda.
Y ahora, esquía.
Gracias, ___. Ahora puedes regresar a tu asiento.
Siéntate, por favor.

la cuesta

la pista

el slálom

la nieve

el esquí alpino
el esquí de descenso

el esquí nórdico   el esquí de fondo

Los esquiadores suben la montaña.
Suben en el telesquí.

¿Yo? Yo sé esquiar muy bien.

Anita sabe esquiar bien.
No es principiante. Es experta.
Ella baja la pista.
Baja rápido.

¿Roberto pierde algo?
¿Qué pierde?
Pierde un bastón.
Roberto dice que esquía bien.

Pero conocemos a Roberto.
No sabe esquiar muy bien.
Es un poco fanfarrón.

CAPÍTULO 9   **245**

RECYCLING

In this section, the concept of -*ar* verbs is reinforced with *esquiar* and *bajar*, -*ir* verbs with *subir*, and stem-changing verbs with *perder*.

DRAMATIZATION

You may wish to have students dramatize the following expressions: *subir la montaña, esquiar, bajar la pista, hacer el esquí nórdico, perder algo.*

ABOUT THE LANGUAGE

Gorra is the usual word for cap. However, when talking about a knitted cap, such as a ski cap, the word is *gorro*.

TPR 2

___, levántate y ven acá, por favor.
Ponte en fila.
Espera el telesquí.
Siéntate en el telesquí.
Pon los bastones debajo del brazo izquierdo.
Adiós. Ahora estás en la parte superior de la montaña.
Bájate del telesquí.
Pon un bastón en la mano izquierda y otro en la mano derecha.

Empieza a esquiar.
Baja la pista.
Gracias, ___. Ahora puedes volver a tu asiento.

Ejercicios

Ejercicio A

A. Go over Exercise A with books closed. Call on individuals to respond.

B. You may wish to do the exercise once again with books open.

PAIRED ACTIVITY

Exercise A can be done as a paired activity. One student asks the questions and the other one responds.

Expansion of *Ejercicio A*

Call on a student to describe in his/her own words the winter weather where you live.

Ejercicio B

A. Exercise B can be done with books closed or open.

B. If the answers to Exercise B are all "no" because of the area where you live, you may wish to have students respond as follows: *No, no hay montañas cerca de donde yo vivo pero hay muchas montañas en Colorado (Vermont).*

Ejercicio C

A. It is recommended that you do Exercise C first with books closed.

B. You may go over Exercise C as you present the vocabulary sentences on pages 244–245.

C. You may wish to call on one student to retell the story of the exercise in his/her own words.

ANSWERS

Ejercicio A

Some answers will vary.

1. Los meses de invierno son diciembre, enero y febrero.
2. Sí (No), (no) hace mucho frío donde vivimos nosotros.
3. La temperatura baja hasta los ___ grados.
4. Sí (No), (no) nieva mucho.
5. Sí (No), (no) está nevando hoy.
6. Las nevadas (no) son frecuentes.

Ejercicio B

Answers will vary.

Ejercicios

A **El tiempo en el invierno.** Contesten.

1. ¿Cuáles son los meses de invierno?
2. Donde viven Uds., ¿hace mucho frío en el invierno?
3. ¿Hasta cuántos grados baja la temperatura?
4. ¿Nieva mucho?
5. ¿Está nevando hoy?
6. Las nevadas, ¿son frecuentes o no?

B **¿Esquías o no?** Preguntas personales.

1. ¿Hay montañas cerca de donde tú vives?
2. ¿Nieva en el invierno?
3. ¿Hay estaciones de esquí en las montañas?
4. ¿Hay pistas para principiantes y expertos?
5. ¿Tus amigos saben esquiar?

C **Una excursión de esquí.** Contesten.

1. ¿Qué tienen que llevar los esquiadores?
2. ¿Dónde compran los boletos para el telesquí o el telesilla?
3. ¿Cómo suben la montaña?
4. ¿Quién sabe esquiar bien, Anita o Roberto?
5. ¿Cómo baja ella la pista?
6. ¿Quién no sabe esquiar bien, Anita o Roberto?
7. Pero, ¿qué dice él?
8. ¿Cómo es él?
9. ¿Qué pierde Roberto, un esquí o un bastón?

ADDITIONAL PRACTICE

1. Have students write a list of seven items that they would need on a skiing trip.
2. Have students make up original sentences about skiing.

COOPERATIVE LEARNING

Have students work in groups and make up sentences about someone who is *fanfarrón*. Have them tell what the person does and says to deserve the label *fanfarrón*.

D **A esquiar.** Empareen.

1. esquiar   a. el descenso
2. nevar   b. la subida
3. descender   c. el esquí
4. bajar   d. la pérdida
5. subir   e. la nieve, la nevada
6. perder   f. la bajada

RELACIÓN DE PROVINCIAS, POR ORDEN ALFABÉTICO, EN DONDE EXISTEN ESTACIONES DE NIEVE Y MONTAÑA	
PROVINCIA	NOMBRE DE LA ESTACIÓN
Barcelona	Rasos de Peguera
Burgos	Valle del Sol
	La Lunada
Gerona	La Molina-Supermolina
	Masella
	Nuria
	Vallter, 2.000
Granada	Solynieve
Huesca	Astun
	Candanchú
	Cerler
	El Formigal
	Panticosa
León	Puerto de San Isidro
Lérida	Baqueira-Beret
	Llessui
	Port del Comte
	Super Espot
	Tuca Betren
	Llés
	Sant Joan de L'erm.
Logroño	Valdezcaray
Madrid-Segovia	Puerto de Navacerrada
Madrid	Valcotos
	Valdesquí
Orense	Manzaneda
	Peña Trevinca
Oviedo	Valgrande-Pajares
Santander	Alto Campoo
	Picos de Europa
Segovia	La Pinilla
Teruel	Sierra de Gudar
Tenerife	Las Cañadas del Teide

Ejercicio C

Some answers will vary.

1. **Los esquiadores tienen que llevar esquís (guantes, botas).**
2. **Compran los boletos en la ventanilla.**
3. **Suben en el telesquí.**
4. **Anita sabe esquiar bien.**
5. **Ella baja rápido.**
6. **Roberto no sabe esquiar bien.**
7. **Dice que esquía bien.**
8. **Él es un poco fanfarrón.**
9. **Roberto pierde un bastón.**

PRESENTATION (page 247)

Ejercicio D

Go over Exercise D with books open. You may want to call on individual students to respond orally.

ANSWERS

Ejercicio D

1. c
2. e
3. a
4. f
5. b
6. d

ABOUT THE LANGUAGE

1. **Compound nouns.** If students ask why *telesilla* is *el telesilla*, explain to them that most nouns made up of two parts, i.e., *tele-silla*, are masculine. For example: *el tocacintas, el sacapuntas, el tocadiscos, el paraguas.*
2. In Spain the expression used for *comprar los boletos* is *sacar los billetes.*
3. In many areas of Spain and Latin America, *el ticket* is used rather than *el boleto* or *el billete* when the ticket is very small.

INFORMAL ASSESSMENT
(*Palabras 1*)

Check for understanding by mixing true and false statements about Vocabulary Transparencies 9.1 (A & B). Students either agree by saying *sí, de acuerdo* or do not agree by saying *no, de ninguna manera.*

LEARNING FROM REALIA

Have students look at the names of the ski resorts in Lérida. Ask them if they think the words look like Spanish words. Explain to them that all these words are in *catalán*, the language of *Cataluña*.

INDEPENDENT PRACTICE

Assign any of the following:
1. Workbook, pages 89–90
2. Communication Activities Masters, pages 50-51, *A & B*
3. Exercises on student pages 246–247

VOCABULARIO

PALABRAS 2

EL PATINAJE

el hielo

la pista de patinaje
el patinadero

el patinaje sobre hielo

el patín
los patines

el patinador

el patinaje artístico

el patinaje sobre ruedas

248 CAPÍTULO 9

Vocabulary Teaching Resources

1. Vocabulary Transparencies 9.2 (A & B)
2. Audio Cassette 6A
3. Student Tape Manual, pages 232–233
4. Workbook, pages 90–91
5. Communication Activities Masters, pages 52-53, *C & D*
6. Chapter Quizzes, page 40, *Palabras 2*

Bell Ringer Review

Write the following on the board or use BRR Blackline Master 9-2: Write one sentence for each of the following words:
los jugadores
el equipo
el campo de fútbol
el tablero indicador

PRESENTATION
(pages 248–249)

A. Have students open their books to pages 248–249. Model the vocabulary or play Cassette 6A. Have students repeat in unison.
B. Using Vocabulary Transparencies 9.2 (A & B), say the words and phrases in random order and have volunteers stand at the screen and point to the appropriate illustration.
C. Ask yes/no and either/or questions to elicit the vocabulary. For example: *¿Patinan los muchachos? ¿Patinan o esquían? ¿Tienen patines? ¿Tienen patines o esquís?*
D. You may wish to begin the exercises on page 250 as you present the new vocabulary.

TOTAL PHYSICAL RESPONSE

(following the Vocabulary presentation)
___, levántate y ven acá, por favor.
Siéntate, por favor.
Ponte los patines.
Levántate.
Ve al patinadero.
Patina.
Gracias, ___.
Ahora puedes volver a tu asiento.
Siéntate, por favor.

la cuchilla, la hoja

las ruedas

el monopatín

Y aquella pista es una pista para
el patinaje sobre ruedas.
Es una pista cubierta.

Esta pista es para el patinaje sobre
hielo. Es una pista al aire libre.

Estos patines tienen cuchilla (hoja).

Y aquellos patines tienen ruedas.

PRESENTATION *(page 250)*

Ejercicios A, B, and C

You may want to have students write the answers to all these exercises or just some of them after you have gone over them in class.

RECYCLING

Exercises B and C recycle the skiing vocabulary presented in *Palabras 1* of this chapter.

Note The English is given in Exercise C to show students how different languages use slightly different terminology to convey the same meaning, i.e., indoor rink vs. covered rink.

ANSWERS

Ejercicio A

1. Los jóvenes están patinando en un patinadero al aire libre.
2. Están patinando sobre hielo.
3. Tienen cuchillas.
4. No, no están haciendo el patinaje artístico.

Ejercicio B

1. esquís, bastones
2. botas, guantes, gafas, gorro
3. alpino, descenso
4. slálom
5. nórdico, fondo, subir, bajar
6. ruedas, hielo
7. cubiertos, al aire libre
8. el patinaje artístico

Ejercicio C

1. el esquí de descenso
2. el esquí de fondo
3. el telesquí, telesilla
4. patinar sobre ruedas
5. pista cubierta
6. pista al aire libre
7. el patinaje artístico
8. el monopatín

Ejercicios

A **El patinaje.** Contesten según la foto.

1. Los jóvenes, ¿están patinando en un patinadero cubierto o en un patinadero al aire libre?
2. ¿Están patinando sobre hielo o sobre ruedas?
3. ¿Tienen cuchillas o ruedas sus patines?
4. ¿Están haciendo el patinaje artístico?

B **El esquí y el patinaje.** Completen.

1. Para esquiar es necesario tener dos ___ y dos ___.
2. Los esquiadores llevan ___, ___, ___ y ___.
3. El esquí ___ o de ___ es el esquí que practican los esquiadores que bajan las pistas.
4. El descenso con obstáculos es el ___.
5. En el esquí ___ o de ___, los esquiadores no bajan una pista. Pero tienen que ___ y ___ cuestas.
6. Es posible patinar sobre ___ o ___.
7. Hay patinaderos ___ y ___.
8. Los patinadores que bailan y hacen ballet sobre el hielo practican el ___.

C **La palabra o expresión en español.** ¿Cómo se dice en español?

1. downhill skiing
2. cross country skiing
3. chairlift
4. roller skating
5. indoor rink
6. outdoor rink
7. figure skating
8. skateboard

250 CAPÍTULO 9

ADDITIONAL PRACTICE

Have students write a note to a friend in which they:
1. explain that he/she is going to take a trip to a ski resort
2. say where he/she wants to go and why
3. invite the friend to go along
4. say what the weather is going to be like
5. tell what clothing and equipment the friend will need

INDEPENDENT PRACTICE

Assign any of the following:
1. Workbook, pages 90–91
2. Communication Activities Masters, pages 52-53, *C & D*
3. Exercises on student page 250
4. Computer Software, *Vocabulario*

Comunicación
Palabras 1 y 2

A **En el invierno.** You are travelling in Latin America. A student (your partner) asks you what the winter weather is like where you live and what you do in winter. Tell him or her.

B **Tengo que comprar…** You want to outfit yourself for a ski trip. List everything you need. At the ski shop find out from the salesclerk (your partner) how much each item costs. Let the clerk know what you think of the price. Reverse roles.

> las botas
> Estudiante 1: ¿Cuánto cuestan las botas?
> Estudiante 2: Cuestan trescientos dólares.
> Estudiante 1: Cuestan mucho.

C **Vacaciones de invierno.** You want to go to a ski resort in a Spanish-speaking country. Talk with a travel expert (your partner) about possibilities in the places listed below. Find out about the number of lifts, kinds of slopes, prices, and weather.

1. Portillo, Chile
2. Bariloche, Argentina
3. Solynieve, Spain

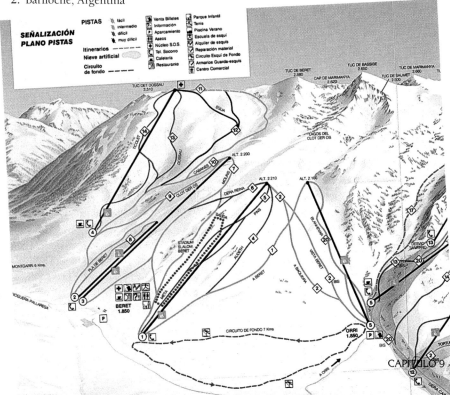

CAPÍTULO 9   **251**

Comunicación
(Palabras 1 and 2)

PRESENTATION *(page 251)*

It is not necessary to do all the activities. You may select those that are most appropriate for your students, or you may permit the students to select the activity or activities they would like to take part in.

ANSWERS

Actividades A, B, and C
Answers will vary.

COOPERATIVE LEARNING

Have students work in pairs. One student is a passenger; the other is an airline reservations clerk. Have them prepare a conversation dealing with a plane reservation to a ski resort. This activity recycles vocabulary from Chapter 8.

LEARNING FROM REALIA

1. Have students look at the legend of the *plano* on page 251 and see how many words they can recognize.
2. Ask the following questions: *¿Es posible hacer el esquí de fondo aquí? ¿Hay circuitos de fondo? ¿Hay nieve artificial? ¿Cuáles son otros deportes que practica la gente aquí?*

251

Structure Teaching Resources

1. Workbook, pages 92–94
2. Student Tape Manual, page 233
3. Audio Cassette 6A
4. Communication Activities Masters, pages 54–56, A-C
5. Chapter Quizzes, pages 41–43, *Estructura*
6. Computer Software

Bell Ringer Review

Write the following on the board or use BRR Blackline Master 9-3: Use the following verbs to form sentences:
hago
pongo
salgo

El presente de los verbos saber y conocer

PRESENTATION (page 252)

A. Have students repeat *sé* and *conozco* as they point to themselves. Explain to them that once again they are going to learn two verbs that are irregular in the *yo* form only.
B. Have students open their books to page 252 and repeat all forms of the verbs in step 1. You may also wish to write the forms on the board.
C. Lead students through steps 2–6 concerning the specific uses of these verbs. Have students read all the example sentences aloud.

INFORMAL ASSESSMENT

Have students make up sentences with *sé* and *conozco*.

ESTRUCTURA

El presente de los verbos
saber y *conocer*

*Expressing Who and What
You Know*

1. Study the following forms of the verbs *saber* and *conocer*, which both mean "to know." As with many irregular verbs you have already learned, *saber* and *conocer* are irregular in the *yo* form only.

INFINITIVE	SABER	CONOCER
yo	sé	conozco
tú	sabes	conoces
él, ella, Ud.	sabe	conoce
nosotros(as)	sabemos	conocemos
vosotros(as)	*sabéis*	*conocéis*
ellos, ellas, Uds.	saben	conocen

2. The verb *saber* means "to know a fact" or "to have information about something."

   Yo sé el número de teléfono.
   Yo sé donde está Madrid.

3. The verb *saber* when followed by an infinitive means "to know how to do something."

   Yo sé esquiar.
   ¿Sabes patinar?

4. When you want to say, "I know," "he knows," etc., the verb *saber* is never used alone. You say:

   Lo sé. Lo sabe.

   In the negative, however, you have a choice.

   No sé. or **No lo sé.**

5. The verb *conocer* means "to know" in the sense of "to be acquainted with."

   Yo conozco a Roberto.
   Conozco el arte mexicano.

6. You need to use the personal *a* with *conocer* when the direct object is a person.

   Conocemos a los hermanos Rodríguez.
   Raúl y Alfredo conocen a Sarita.

252 CAPÍTULO 9

FOR THE NATIVE SPEAKER

Have students write a composition in which they include the following: *¿Cómo es el clima donde Ud. vive? Describa como es el tiempo en las cuatro estaciones del año. Mencione los factores que Ud. cree que afectan el clima, tales como la altitud y la latitud de su ciudad, el efecto de los mares en el clima (si lo hay), los vientos y las lluvias.*

Ejercicios

A **¿Sabes esquiar?** Practiquen la conversación.

—Oye, Teresa, ¿tú sabes esquiar?
—Sí, sé esquiar. Pero no soy experta.
—¿Conoces a Tadeo?
—Sí, conozco a Tadeo, si tú hablas de Tadeo Castaño.
—Sí, hablo de él. No sabes que va a esquiar en las Olimpíadas.
—¡Esquiar en las Olimpíadas! ¡Qué honor para él! ¡Es fantástico!

¿Qué sabe Teresa? Contesten según la conversación.

1. ¿Sabe esquiar Teresa?
2. ¿Sabe esquiar muy bien o bastante bien?
3. ¿Ella conoce a Tadeo?
4. ¿Sabe esquiar?
5. ¿Dónde va a esquiar?

B **¿Qué sabes?** Contesten.

1. ¿Conoces a ___?
2. ¿Sabes su número de teléfono? ¿Cuál es?
3. ¿Sabes su dirección? ¿Cuál es?
4. ¿Sabes su zona postal? ¿Cuál es?
5. ¿Sabes la hora? ¿Qué hora es?
6. ¿Sabes la fecha? ¿Cuál es la fecha de hoy?

C **Lo que yo sé hacer.** Digan todo lo que saben hacer.

CAPÍTULO 9   **253**

Ejercicios

PRESENTATION (page 253)

Ejercicio A

A. Have students repeat each line of the mini-conversation after you once.
B. Call on individuals to read the conversation in pairs. Have them use as much expression as possible.
C. Go over the questions that follow. Have individuals answer with books closed.
D. Then call on one student to retell the information of the conversation in narrative form.

Ejercicio B

It is recommended that you do Exercise B first with books open and then with books closed. This exercise gives students practice hearing *conoces* and *sabes* and answering with the irregular forms *conozco* and *sé.*

Ejercicio C

Some verbs students can use in Exercise C are *cantar, bailar, tocar, esquiar, patinar, hacer, leer, escribir,* and *jugar.*

ANSWERS

Ejercicio A

1. Sí, Teresa sabe esquiar.
2. Sabe esquiar bastante bien.
3. Sí, ella conoce a Tadeo.
4. Sí, él sabe esquiar.
5. Va a esquiar en las Olimpíadas.

Ejercicios B and C

Answers will vary.

ADDITIONAL PRACTICE

Have students point to other students and say they know them. Have them use the name of the student: *Conozco a ___.* Have students expand the activity by giving some information about the person they know.

Yo conozco a ___. Yo sé que él (ella) ___.

LEARNING FROM PHOTOS

Have students look at the photo on page 253 and answer *Sí* or *No: Es una esquiadora. El esquiador hace el esquí nórdico, es decir el esquí de fondo. Lleva gafas. Lleva gorro. Un esquí no está tocando la tierra. El señor tiene una mochila. Lleva un anorak.*

Ejercicio D

Exercise D gives students practice hearing *conoces* and answering with *conozco*. This is important practice because students often want to respond with the same form they heard in the question.

Ejercicio E

A. Have students do Exercise E with books open.

B. You may wish to call on a different student for each item.

C. Then redo the exercise. Have one student take the role of Pepita and the other the role of Sandra.

ANSWERS

Ejercicio D

1. Sí (No), (no) conozco el arte mexicano.

2. Sí (No), (no) conozco la literatura española.

3. Sí (No), (no) conozco la literatura americana.

4. Sí (No), (no) conozco la historia antigua.

5. Sí (No), (no) conozco la historia moderna.

Ejercicio E

P: conoces
S: conozco
P: Sabes
S: sé
P: sabe, sabe, sé
S: conoce
P: conoce, sé, sé, conoce
S: conoce
P: sabes
S: sé, conozco, sé

254

D Algunas cosas que conozco. Contesten con *sí* o *no*.

1. ¿Conoces el arte mexicano?
2. ¿Conoces la literatura española?
3. ¿Conoces la literatura americana?
4. ¿Conoces la historia antigua?
5. ¿Conoces la historia moderna?

E Natalia Isaacs. Completen con *saber* o *conocer*.

PEPITA: Sandra, ¿___ tú a Natalia Isaacs?

SANDRA: Claro que ___ a Natalia. Ella y yo somos muy buenas amigas.

PEPITA: ¿___ tú que ella va a Panamá?

SANDRA: ¿Ella va a Panamá? No, yo no ___ nada de su viaje. ¿Cuándo va a salir?

PEPITA: Pues, ella no ___ exactamente qué día va a salir. Pero ___ que va a salir este mes. Ella va a hacer su reservación mañana. Yo ___ que ella quiere tomar un vuelo sin escala.

SANDRA: ¿Natalia ___ Panamá?

PEPITA: Creo que sí ___ Panamá. Pero yo no ___ definitivamente. Pero yo ___ que ella ___ a mucha gente en Panamá.

SANDRA: ¿Cómo es que ella ___ a mucha gente en Panamá?

PEPITA: Pues, tú ___ que ella tiene parientes en Panamá, ¿no?

SANDRA: Ay, sí, es verdad. Yo ___ que tiene familia en Panamá porque yo ___ a su tía Lola. Y ___ que ella es de Panamá.

La ciudad de Panamá

ADDITIONAL PRACTICE

You may wish to ask the following questions about Exercise E. *¿Conoce Sandra a Natalia? ¿Son ellas buenas amigas? ¿Adónde va Natalia? ¿Sabe Sandra algo de su viaje? ¿Sabe Natalia qué día va a salir? ¿Conoce Natalia Panamá? ¿Conoce ella a mucha gente en Panamá? ¿Tiene ella parientes en Panamá? ¿Conoce Sandra a su tía Lola? ¿Qué sabe Sandra de su tía Lola?*

LEARNING FROM REALIA

Ask students if they recognize the figure on the right side of the magazine cover on page 254. It is from *Las Meninas* by Velázquez (see Fondo Académico page 240). Explain that the other two paintings are renditions of *Las Meninas* done by other artists. (The one in the middle is by Picasso, and the one on the left is by Juan Gris.)

El presente del verbo *decir*

Telling What People Say

The verb *decir*, "to tell," is irregular in the present tense. It has a *g* in the *yo* form and the stem changes from *e* to *i* in all forms except *nosotros* and *vosotros*.

DECIR	
yo	**digo**
tú	**dices**
él, ella, Ud.	**dice**
nosotros(as)	**decimos**
vosotros(as)	***decís***
ellos, ellas, Uds.	**dicen**

A **¿Qué dices de la clase?** Sigan el modelo.

¿Qué dices de la clase de español?
Pues yo digo que es fantástica. Estoy aprendiendo mucho.

1. ¿Qué dices de la clase de matemáticas?
2. ¿Qué dices de la clase de inglés?
3. ¿Qué dices de la clase de ciencias?
4. ¿Qué dices de la clase de educación física?
5. ¿Qué dices de la clase de historia?

B **¿Pablo dice que esquía?**
Contesten según se indica.

1. ¿Qué dice Pablo, esquía bien o no esquía bien? (bien)
2. ¿Dice que es experto? (sí)
3. ¿Y qué dicen Uds.? (no es experto)
4. ¿Por qué dicen eso? (conocemos a Pablo)
5. ¿Están diciendo que es un poco fanfarrón? (sí)
6. ¿Sabe esquiar Pablo? (sí, no muy bien)

ADDITIONAL PRACTICE

Remind students that they have now learned quite a few verbs that are irregular in only the *yo* form of the present tense. Have them repeat the following:

soy
voy
doy
estoy
pongo
salgo
hago
traigo
tengo
vengo
digo
sé
conozco

Have students make up original sentences using these verb forms.

Bell Ringer Review
Write the following on the board or use BRR Blackline Master 9-4: Write the names of all the courses you are presently taking.

El presente del verbo decir

PRESENTATION *(page 255)*

A. With books open to page 255, have students repeat the forms of the verb *decir* after you.
B. Write the forms of the verb on the board. Underline the stem for each form.

Ejercicios

PRESENTATION
(page 255)

Ejercicio A

A. It is recommended that you do Exercise A first with books closed. It gives students ear training in hearing *dices* and responding with *digo*.
B. You may have students answer consistently as in the model or you may have them make up answers based on their own opinions.

Ejercicio B

A. You can do Exercise B with books closed or open.
B. Upon completion of Exercise B, have one student retell all the information in his/her own words.

ANSWERS

Ejercicio A
Answers will vary according to the model.

Ejercicio B
1. Pablo dice que esquía bien.
2. Sí, dice que es experto.
3. Nosotros decimos que no es experto.
4. Nosotros decimos eso porque conocemos a Pablo.
5. Sí, estamos diciéndo que es un poco fanfarrón.
6. Sí, sabe esquiar, pero no muy bien.

Ejercicio C

A. Exercise C can be done with books open.

B. This exercise makes students use all forms of the verb *decir*.

ANSWERS

Ejercicio C

1. digo, dice
2. dicen
3. dicen
4. decimos, dice
5. digo, dicen
6. dice
7. dice

Los adjetivos demostrativos

PRESENTATION (*page 256*)

A. Use a boy, a girl, a book, and a magazine to illustrate the meaning of *este, ese, aquel.* Have the boy stand near you as you say *este muchacho.* Have him stand near another student as you say *ese muchacho.* Have the boy stand in the back of the room away from everyone as you point to him and say *aquel muchacho.* Do the same with a girl, a book, and a magazine.

B. Then have students open their books and read aloud the explanation that appears on page 256.

C. Write the forms of the demonstrative adjectives on the board.

D. Have students read all the example sentences aloud.

PAIRED ACTIVITY

Have students work in pairs. One starts with *digo* and says something. What he/she says can be either correct or wrong. The second student responds with *Lo que dices es verdad,* or *Lo que dices es falso* and corrects the information.

256

C Una discusión. Completen con *decir.*

1. Yo ___ que no y él ___ que sí.
2. ¿Qué ___ Uds.?
3. ¿Uds. ___ que sí?
4. Pues, Uds. y yo ___ que sí y él ___ que no.
5. Pero, hombre, ¿de qué estamos hablando? Estamos hablando de nuestras vacaciones de invierno. Yo ___ que vamos a esquiar y Uds. también ___ que vamos a esquiar.
6. ¿Qué ___ él?
7. Él ___ que vamos a ir a una isla tropical.

Parkas **Ricamato** M.R.
Poleras
Buzos **en Chile**
Estampado
publicitario

Licenza Italia

Fábrica:
SUECIA 2955 ☎ 2740839 [Ñ H10]

Los adjetivos demostrativos   *Pointing Out People or Things*

1. You use the demonstrative adjectives "this," "that," "these," and "those," to point out people or things. The demonstrative adjectives must agree with the noun they modify. Study the demonstrative adjectives in Spanish.

	SINGULAR	PLURAL
MASCULINO	este muchacho ese muchacho aquel muchacho	estos muchachos esos muchachos aquellos muchachos
FEMENINO	esta muchacha esa muchacha aquella muchacha	estas muchachas esas muchachas aquellas muchachas

2. All forms of *este* indicate something near the person speaking. They mean "this," "these" in English.

   Esta revista que tengo yo es muy interesante.

3. All forms of *ese* indicate something close to the person spoken to.

   Roberto, esa revista que tienes es muy interesante.

4. All forms of *aquel* indicate something far away from both the speaker and listener. The forms of both *ese* and *aquel* mean "that," "those" in English.

   Aquel libro que está allá en la mesa es interesante.

5. The adverbs *aquí, allí,* and *allá* indicate relative position: here, there, over there.

256   CAPÍTULO 9

Ejercicios

A ¿**Cuánto es o cuánto cuesta?** Sigan el modelo.

> **las gafas**
> Estudiante 1: ¿Cuánto cuestan las gafas?
> Estudiante 2: ¿De qué gafas habla Ud.? ¿De estas gafas qué están aquí?
> Estudiante 1: No de aquellas gafas que están allá en el mostrador.

1. gafas
2. guantes de esquí
3. esquís
4. patines
5. botas
6. monopatín
7. anorak
8. calculadora
9. bolígrafo
10. mochila

B **El libro que tú tienes.** Completen con *ese/esa* o *aquel/aquellas*.

1. ___ libro que tú estás leyendo es muy interesante. Pero ___ libro que ellos están leyendo allá es muy aburrido, muy pesado.
2. ___ disco que (tú) estás escuchando es fabuloso. Pero ___ disco que ellos están escuchando es horrible.
3. ___ novela que (tú) estás leyendo es una maravilla. Y ___ novela que ellos están leyendo es terrible.
4. ___ botas que estás comprando son fantásticas. Pero ___ botas que ellos están comprando no son muy buenas.
5. ___ esquís que estás mirando son para el esquí alpino y ___ esquís que ellos están mirando son para el esquí nórdico.

NUEVA COLECCION

OPTICAS
Moneda Rotter
CON CLARA VISION DE FUTURO

PUERTO GRAFICO

HUERFANOS 1029 T. 6980465 MONEDA 1152 T. 6960714
MALL PANORAMICO L. 105 T. 6952927 APUMANQUE L. 27 T. 2461591
CENTRO DE LENTES DE CONTACTO ESTADO 359 PISO 6 T. 383665
DIVISION AUDIFONOS. HUERFANOS 1029 PISO 2 T. 6980465

Esquiando en Valle Nevado, Chile

CAPÍTULO 9 **257**

Ejercicios
PRESENTATION (*page 257*)
Ejercicio A: **Paired Activity**
You may wish to have students do Exercise A as a paired activity. As each pair gives their mini-conversation, have the rest of the class listen so they hear the forms of the demonstrative adjectives. Correct any errors or call on another student to correct the error.

Ejercicio B
Go over Exercise B with books open. Call on individual students to read with as much expression as possible.

ANSWERS
Ejercicio A
Answers should follow the model.

Ejercicio B
1. Ese, aquel
2. Ese, aquel
3. Esa, aquella
4. Esas, aquellas
5. Esos, aquellos

ABOUT THE LANGUAGE
You may wish to tell students that the type of skiing that is shown in the photo on page 257 is called *esquí con parapente*.

Conversación 📼

PRESENTATION *(page 258)*

A. Tell students they are going to hear a conversation between Agustín and Carmen. One knows how to ski well and the other does not. Ask them to find out why.

B. Have students listen to the conversation as you play the recording on Cassette 6A, or as you read it to them.

C. With books closed, have students repeat the conversation after you or the recording.

D. Call on pairs of students to read the conversation on page 258 aloud or to dramatize it.

PAIRED ACTIVITY

Have pairs of students make up personal conversations about skiing or skating.

Ejercicio

A. Go over the exercise that follows. This can be done with books closed.

B. With books open have one student answer all the questions.

ANSWERS

1. No, Carmen no esquía mucho.
2. Sí, sabe esquiar un poco.
3. Porque no vive cerca de una estación de esquí.
4. No vive cerca de las montañas.
5. Sí, hay cuestas donde vive.
6. Debe aprender a hacer el esquí de fondo.

Escenas de la vida   *¿Vas a esquiar en las Olimpíadas?*

AGUSTÍN: Carmen, ¿sabes esquiar?
CARMEN: Sí, sé esquiar. Pero no soy experta. Quisiera esquiar más pero no puedo.
AGUSTÍN: No puedes, ¿por qué?

CARMEN: Pues, no vivimos muy cerca de una estación de esquí.
AGUSTÍN: ¿No hay lugares donde hacen nieve artificial?

CARMEN: No, porque no tenemos montañas, sólo cuestas.
AGUSTÍN: Entonces debes aprender a hacer el esquí de fondo. El esquí es un deporte fantástico.

 No es experta. Contesten.

1. ¿Esquía mucho Carmen?
2. ¿Sabe esquiar un poco?
3. ¿Por qué no puede esquiar más?
4. ¿Vive cerca de las montañas?
5. ¿Hay cuestas donde vive?
6. ¿Qué debe aprender Carmen?

258   CAPÍTULO 9

Pronunciación *La consonante g*

The consonant **g** has two sounds, hard and soft. You will study the soft sound in Chapter 10. G in combination with **a**, **o**, **u** (*ga, go, gu*) is pronounced somewhat like the g in the English word "go." To maintain this hard g sound with **e** or **i**, a **u** is placed after the **g**: *gue, gui*.

ga	gue	gui	go	gu
gafa	guerra	guitarra	algo	segundo
gana	guerrilla	Guillermo	pago	guante
paga	Guevara	guía	domingo	seguridad

las gafas

Repeat the following sentences.

La amiga llega y luego toca la guitarra.
Salgo el domingo para Uruguay.
Pongo las gafas y los guantes en la maleta.

Comunicación

A **¿Quién es?** Point out a half dozen members of the class, some near your partner, near you, or away from both of you. Ask your partner who the person is.

B **¿Sabes...?** The following is a list of winter activities. Find out if your partner knows how to do them and if so, how well he or she does them. If your partner doesn't do them ask if he or she wants to learn how.

> **hacer el esquí nórdico**
> **Estudiante 1: ¿Sabes hacer el esquí nórdico?**
> **Estudiante 2: Sí. Lo sé hacer. (No. No lo sé hacer.)**
> **Estudiante 1: ¿Qué tal lo haces? (¿Quieres aprender?)**
> **Estudiante 2: Regular. (No. Es aburrido.)**

1. hacer el esquí nórdico
2. hacer el esquí alpino
3. esquiar el slálom
4. subir la cuesta en telesilla
5. patinar sobre hielo
6. patinar sobre ruedas
7. andar en monopatín

C **¿Qué juegas?** In groups of four, create questions for an opinion poll on winter sports. Interview other groups. Summarize the results of the poll and report to the class.

VALLE NEVADO
CHILE

Pronunciación

PRESENTATION *(page 259)*

Note English speakers tend to want to make the g sound too hard when speaking Spanish. As students repeat *ga, gue, gui, go, gu,* indicate to them that the sound is produced very softly toward the back of the throat.

A. Use Pronunciation Transparency P-9 to model the new sound.
B. You may wish to play the pronunciation section of Audio Cassette 6A.
C. The words and sentences in the *Pronunciación* can also be used as a dictation.

RECYCLING

Using the set of Pronunciation Transparencies, review the key Spanish sounds presented in earlier chapters of the textbook. Point to one of the transparencies and call on volunteers to say the accompanying word or phrase. This is also a good warm-up activity at the beginning of the class hour.

Comunicación

PRESENTATION

Expansion of *Actividad A*
Have students tell as much as they can about the person.

ANSWERS

Actividad A
Answers will resemble the following.
¿Quién es ese muchacho?
¿Quién es aquella estudiante?
¿Quién es esta persona?

Actividad B
Answers should follow the model.

Actividad C
Answers will vary.

LEARNING FROM REALIA

You may wish to ask the following questions about the realia on page 259: *¿Dónde está el Valle Nevado? ¿En qué mes tomaron la fotografía, en enero o en junio? ¿Por qué? ¿Qué opinas? ¿Qué tipo de esquí hacen en Valle Nevado?*

LECTURA Y CULTURA

Bell Ringer Review

Write the following on the board or use BRR Blackline Master 9-6: Write all the geographical terms you have learned in Spanish. For example: montaña, río.

READING STRATEGIES
(page 260)

Note Find out which members of the class are skiers. If your students do not ski because of geographical or socio-economic reasons, you may wish to go over this *Lectura* very quickly.

Pre-reading

Using a wall map, or the maps on pages 473 and 474, point out the geographic locations mentioned in the reading.

Reading

Have students open their books to page 260 and follow along as you read the first paragraph. Then have students read the rest of the *Lectura* silently.

Post-reading

Lead students through the exercises that follow the *Lectura* on page 261.

ESQUIANDO EN UN PAÍS HISPANO

—No esquían en los países hispanos, ¿verdad?

—¿No esquían? ¿Por qué dices eso?

—Porque en los países hispanos siempre hace calor, ¿no? Como no hay invierno, no hace frío.

—¿No hay invierno? ¿Quieres decir que todos los países hispanos son tropicales?

—Pues, si no son tropicales por lo menos siempre hace calor.

—En algunos, sí. Pero no en todos, de ninguna manera. Parece que no conoces bien el mundo hispano. Por ejemplo, el esquí es un deporte muy popular en España.

—¿En España? No puede ser.

—Claro que puede ser. Hay estaciones de esquí a unos kilómetros al norte de Madrid en la Sierra de Guadarrama. Los madrileños pasan el fin de semana esquiando en Navacerrada.

—¿Y allí hacen el esquí alpino?

—Sí, sí, el esquí alpino. Y, ¿no conoces las estupendas estaciones de esquí en Argentina y Chile?

—¡El invierno en la América del Sur! Tengo que estudiar la geografía.

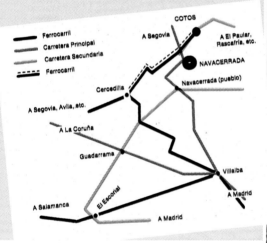

La Sierra Nevada cerca de Granada, España

LEARNING FROM PHOTOS AND REALIA

1. Have students say as much as they can about the photo on page 260.
2. With reference to the map on page 260, ask students the following questions: *¿En qué país está la estación de esquí? ¿Cómo saben que está en España?*
3. Have students explain, *¿Cómo podemos ir (llegar) a Navacerrada?*
4. Have students find, *¿Cuáles son algunas ciudades importantes mencionadas en el plano?*

Estudio de palabras

A ¿Qué es? Busquen una palabra relacionada.

1. las montañas
2. los Alpes
3. el calor
4. los trópicos
5. el invierno
6. la geografía
7. Madrid

a. invernal
b. geográfico
c. montañoso
d. madrileño
e. alpino
f. tropical
g. caluroso

ESCUELA DE SKI PRECIOS EN US$

PRODUCTO	Nº DE LECCIONES/DURACIÓN	PRECIO
Clases colectivas 10 personas máximo	1 lección de 2 horas 5 lecciones de 2 horas c/u 6 lecciones de 2 horas c/u	US$ 16 US$ 64 US$ 72
Clases particulares 1 ó 2 personas	1 lección de 1 hora 5 lecciones de 1 hora c/u	US$ 38 US$ 155
Clases particulares 3 ó 4 personas	1 lección de 1 hora 5 lecciones de 1 hora c/u	US$ 57 por grupo US$ 233 por grupo
Programa y talleres especiales (*) 6 personas máximo	1/2 día Día	US$ 150 por grupo US $300 por grupo
Alas delta		
Parapente		US$ 76
Heliskiing/Helisurf 5 personas máximo	Min. 15 minutos	US$ 57
Safari en nieve 10 personas máximo	1/2 día	desde US$ 61 por persona desde US$ 45 por persona

B La geografía. Completen.

1. Ellos viven en las montañas. Son de una región ___.
2. Y sus primos viven en los trópicos. Viven en una zona ___.
3. La geografía varía. Hay diferencias ___ en las distintas partes del continente.
4. En los trópicos siempre hace calor. Una zona ___ es una región ___.
5. En las zonas polares es casi siempre invierno. La estación ___ dura mucho tiempo.

Comprensión

A ¿Es verdad? Contesten sí o no.

1. Hay estaciones de esquí en todos los países hispanos.
2. Hay estaciones de esquí en algunos países hispanos.
3. Todos los países hispanos son países calurosos.
4. Hay estaciones de esquí cerca de Madrid, la capital de España.

B Datos. Busquen.

1. el nombre de la capital de España
2. las montañas al norte de Madrid
3. el nombre de una estación de esquí cerca de Madrid
4. tres países hispanos donde es popular el esquí

C Inferencia.

This reading selection implies that there is a common misconception among people in the United States about the Spanish-speaking countries. What is that misconception?

Estudio de palabras

ANSWERS

Ejercicio A
1. c
2. e
3. g
4. f
5. a
6. b
7. d

Ejercicio B
1. montañosa
2. tropical
3. geográficas
4. tropical, calurosa
5. invernal

Comprensión

ANSWERS

Comprensión A
1. no
2. sí
3. no
4. sí

Comprensión B
1. Madrid
2. la Sierra de Guadarrama
3. Navacerrada
4. España, Chile y Argentina

Comprensión C
   Que no esquían en los países hispanos. Que todos los países hispanos son tropicales.

EXPANSION
   In addition to the comprehension exercises that appear on page 261, you may wish to ask the following questions: ¿Es el esquí un deporte popular en España? ¿Dónde hay estaciones de esquí? ¿Cuándo van los madrileños a esquiar en Navacerrada? ¿En qué sierra está Navacerrada? ¿En qué otros países de habla hispana hay fantásticas estaciones de esquí?

LEARNING FROM REALIA

   Have students look at the chart on page 261 to find the Spanish equivalents for the following:

1. private class
2. group class
3. special program
4. special workshop
5. snow safari
6. hang glider
7. parachute skiing
8. heliskiing (helicopter lift to snow skiing)

A. Before reading the selection, point out the following areas on the maps (pages 473–474): *Madrid, Sierra de Guadarrama, Sierra Nevada, el Mediterráneo, los Pirineos, la frontera entre Chile y la Argentina, San Carlos de Bariloche, Puerto Montt, Punta Arenas*

B. Have students open their books to pages 262–263 and read silently. You may wish to give them a few true/false statements about what they are reading.

C. Encourage students to look at the photos as they read the material.

DESCUBRIMIENTO CULTURAL

Ya sabemos que no es verdad que siempre hace calor en todos los países hispanos. En Madrid por ejemplo hay un refrán[1] que dice "Nueve meses de invierno y tres meses de infierno". ¿Qué quiere decir este refrán madrileño? Quiere decir que durante nueve meses hace frío en Madrid y durante tres meses es un infierno porque hace muchísimo calor. En Madrid, la temperatura puede subir a los treinta y ocho o cuarenta grados centígrados en el verano. Y en el invierno puede bajar a menos de cero grados centígrados.

Hay estaciones de esquí un poco al norte de Madrid en la Sierra de Guadarrama y también en el norte del país en los Pirineos que forman la frontera con Francia. ¿Saben Uds. que también hay estaciones de esquí en el sur de España? En el invierno mucha gente esquía en la Sierra Nevada mientras la gente del norte de Europa nada en el Mediterráneo a unos 160 kilómetros de las pistas. ¿En qué estado de los Estados Unidos puede la gente esquiar en las montañas, y a unos pocos kilómetros nadar en el mar?

¡El distrito de los lagos! ¿Qué es y dónde está? Pues, es una región fantástica y famosa por su belleza natural. Es una región que tiene muchos lagos y está en los Andes en la frontera entre Chile y la Argentina. En el invierno mucha gente va a esta región a esquiar. Hay estaciones de

La Puerta de Alcalá, Madrid, España

Lago Pehoe, Chile

CRITICAL THINKING ACTIVITY

(Thinking skills: making inferences)

Read the following to the class or write it on the board or on an overhead transparency.

1. **Es la primera vez que Reynaldo esquía. ¿Qué debe hacer?**

2. **Reynaldo no tiene mucha paciencia. La pista designada verde es para principiantes, pero según Reynaldo no es para él. Él quiere bajar la pista roja, la pista para los expertos, para los que saben esquiar muy bien. ¿Cuáles pueden ser las consecuencias de la decisión que toma Reynaldo?**

262

Bariloche, Argentina

Entre Puerto Montt y Punta Arenas en la costa del Pacífico hay ríos, fiordos y glaciares. Muchos turistas dicen que creen que están en Noruega, en Escandinavia.

Y otra cosa interesante—en Punta Arenas hay mucha gente de ascendencia serbo-croata. Si Uds. son de ascendencia alemana o serbocroata, ¿por qué no hacen un viaje al sur de Chile?

[1] refrán   *proverb*   [3] pescar   *to fish*
[2] cazar   *hunt*   [4] madera   *wood*

esquí fabulosas. Pero, ¿cuándo es el invierno en la Argentina y en Chile? El invierno es en los meses de junio, julio y agosto. Cuando es el verano en el hemisferio norte donde están los Estados Unidos, es el invierno en el hemisferio sur.

San Carlos de Bariloche es un pueblo famoso en esta región. Está en la Argentina. En el invierno las pistas de esquí son fabulosas y en las otras estaciones los turistas van a Bariloche para cazar[2], pescar[3] y nadar en los lagos.

Muy cerca de los distritos de los lagos en Chile está Puerto Montt. De Puerto Montt hay vistas preciosas de los picos andinos cubiertos de nieve. Hay también volcanes cubiertos de nieve. Puerto Montt es una pequeña ciudad interesante. Las casas de Puerto Montt son casi todas de madera[4]. Muchos de los habitantes de Puerto Montt son de origen alemán. En el escaparate de una pastelería de esta ciudad en el sur de Chile puede Ud. ver:

Gebürtstagskuchen und Hochzeitskuchen
Tortas para cumpleaños y bodas

Puerto Montt, Chile

CAPÍTULO 9   **263**

(*The Realidades is optional material.*)

PRESENTATION
(pages 264–265)

The main objective of the *Realidades* section is to have students enjoy the photographs and absorb some Hispanic culture. However, if you would like to do more, you may wish to do some of the following types of activities.

A. Before reading the captions, ask students to name as many winter sports as they can. How many of these are part of the Winter Olympics?

B. Have students volunteer to read the captions and answer any questions they find.

C. You may wish to do the following regarding the photos and the realia.

Photo 1: Have students describe the photo in their own words.

Photo 2: Ask the following questions: *¿Cuántas pesetas cuestan los esquís ahora? ¿Cuál es el precio original? Un poco de matemáticas, ¿hay una rebaja (un descuento) de cuántas pesetas? ¿Es una ganga el nuevo precio, el precio rebajado?*

Realia 4: Have students answer the following questions: *¿Qué equipo puedes encontrar en la tienda Martín Pescador? ¿Cuál es la dirección de la tienda? ¿Qué puedes alquilar allí? Además de vender y alquilar equipo, ¿qué más hacen en Martín Pescador? ¿Qué son los nombres alrededor del anuncio?*

REALIDADES

Estos fiordos están en Chile **1**. ¿Qué tal la vista? Espectacular, ¿no?

Este anorak está en una vitrina en Galerías Preciados, una tienda por departamentos en Madrid. **2**

Es un glaciar en la Argentina **3**. ¿Cómo es el clima aquí?

Si vas a Chile y no tienes el equipo necesario para esquiar, puedes ir a Martín Pescador para alquilar lo que necesitas **4**.

Aquí ves un telesilla en la estación de esquí de Río Negro en la Argentina **5**. La nieve es fabulosa, ¿verdad?

264

RAICHLE · DINASTAR · DYNASTY · DACHSTEIN · NORDICA · RAICHLE · SALOMON · NORDICA · RAICHLE · SALOMON LOOK

· ALQUILER de EQUIPOS de SKI ·

martín pescador

SKI ROPA Y ACCESORIOS TALLER ESPECIALIZADO

NAUTICA-PESCA

ARMERIA REPARACIONES CAZA MAYOR Y MENOR

ROLANDO 257
Tel.: (0944) 22275

KASTLE · BLIZZARD · LOOK · TYROLLIA · LOOK · SALOMON · KASTLE · BLIZZARD · LOOK · DINASTAR · DYNASTY · DACHSTEIN

4

5

265

INDEPENDENT PRACTICE

1. Workbook, *Un poco más,* page 95

CULMINACIÓN

PRESENTATION *(page 266)*

RECYCLING

The *Comunicación oral* and *Comunicación escrita* provide various ways for students to recycle and recombine structures and vocabulary associated with clothing, travel, sports activities, weather, making plans, and expressing opinions, preferences, and needs.

Comunicación oral

ANSWERS

Actividad A

Answers will vary but may resemble the following.

¿Vienes mucho a Bariloche a
    esquiar?

¿Sabes esquiar bien?

¿Conoces las estaciones de esquí
    en España? ¿En Noruega?

Actividad B

Answers may resemble the following.

subir en el telesquí

usar patines de ruedas

usar botas y gafas

Comunicación escrita

ANSWERS

Actividades A and B

Answers will vary.

Comunicación oral

A ¿Sabes esquiar? You are on the slopes in Bariloche and meet a young Argentine skier (your partner). Find out as much as you can about your new friend's skiing habits and experience: where he or she goes to ski; how often; how well he or she skis; what equipment he or she has, etc.

B Charada. Get together with a number of classmates. On each of a number of slips of paper write down, in Spanish, an action typical of a particular sport. Randomly distribute the slips. Each player will act out what is on the slip. Everyone tries to guess the sport.

Comunicación escrita

A Una composición. Work with a classmate to create a composition. Follow these five steps:

1. list the words you know that deal with skiing
2. put the words into sentences
3. arrange the sentences in a logical sequence
4. polish the sentences and organize them in a paragraph
5. read your paragraph to the class

B La estación de esquí. You and your group have been contracted to create a magazine ad for Esquimundo, a new ski resort in the Andes. Describe the attractions of the resort in as much detail as possible. After each group has written and polished its ad, it will present it to the class.

266 CAPÍTULO 9

FOR THE YOUNGER STUDENT

Have students paint a mural of a winter scene including people skiing and skating. Have them label it in Spanish. Hang the mural where it can be seen by other people in your school.

Reintegración

A En el aeropuerto. Contesten según se indica.

1. ¿Dónde están ellos? (el aeropuerto)
2. ¿Adónde van? (Santiago)
3. ¿Dónde está Santiago? (Chile)
4. ¿Por qué van a Chile? (a esquiar)
5. ¿Con qué línea o compañía aérea van a viajar? (Lan Chile)
6. ¿Cuánto cuesta el boleto? (mucho)
7. ¿Es un vuelo largo? (sí)
8. ¿Tú haces el viaje también? (no)
9. ¿A qué hora sale su vuelo y a qué hora llega? (a las once de la noche y a las ocho de la mañana)
10. ¿Dónde van a esquiar? (Portillo)

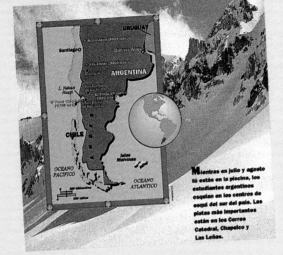

Mientras en julio y agosto tú estás en la piscina, los estudiantes argentinos esquían en los centros de esquí del sur del país. Las pistas más importantes están en los Cerros Catedral, Chapelco y Las Leñas.

B Los deportes. Sigan el modelo.

   Ellos juegan.
   Ellos están jugando.

1. El dribla con el balón.
2. Ella tira la pelota.
3. Yo esquío.
4. Tú haces la plancha de vela.
5. Ellos suben la pista para los expertos.
6. Nosotros hacemos el patinaje artístico.

Vocabulario

SUSTANTIVOS
el invierno
el frío
la nieve
la nevada
la temperatura
el grado

la estación de esquí
el esquí *(skiing; ski)*
el esquí de descenso
el esquí de fondo
el esquí alpino
el esquí nórdico
el slálom
el/la esquiador(a)
la montaña
la cuesta
la pista

el telesquí
el telesilla
la ventanilla
la boletería
el bastón
la bota
las gafas
el gorro
el guante
el anorak
el patinaje
el hielo
el/la patinador(a)
el patinadero
el patín
la cuchilla
la hoja
la rueda

el patinaje sobre hielo
el patinaje artístico
el patinaje sobre ruedas
el monopatín

ADJETIVOS
principiante
experto(a)
fanfarrón(a)
cubierto(a)
rápido(a)

VERBOS
saber
conocer
decir
nevar (ie)
esquiar
patinar

bajar
subir

OTRAS PALABRAS Y
EXPRESIONES
¿Qué tiempo hace?
Hace frío.
Nieva.
bajo cero
al aire libre

PRESENTATION *(page 267)*
Ejercicio A
   Exercise A recycles air travel vocabulary learned in Chapter 8. It also reviews verbs with *g* in the *yo* form.

Ejercicio B
   Exercise B reviews vocabulary related to sports and the progressive tense.

ANSWERS
Ejercicio A
1. Ellos están en el aeropuerto.
2. Van a Santiago.
3. Santiago está en Chile.
4. Van a esquiar.
5. Van a viajar con la línea aérea Lan Chile.
6. El boleto cuesta mucho.
7. Sí, el vuelo es largo.
8. No, no hago el viaje.
9. El vuelo sale a las once de la noche y llega a las ocho de la mañana.
10. Van a Portillo a esquiar.

Ejercicio B
1. Él está driblando con el balón.
2. Ella está tirando la pelota.
3. Yo estoy esquiando.
4. Tú estás haciendo la plancha de vela.
5. Ellos están subiendo la pista para los expertos.
6. Nosotros estamos haciendo el patinaje artístico.

Vocabulario

   There are approximately 10 cognates included in this *Vocabulario* list.

VIDEO
   The video is intended to reinforce the vocabulary, structures, and cultural content in each chapter. It may be used here as a chapter wrap-up activity. See the *Video Activities Booklet* for additional suggestions on its use.

INTRODUCCIÓN (0:32:44)

UNA EXCURSIÓN DE ESQUÍ
(0:33:53)

STUDENT PORTFOLIO

   Written assignments that may be included in students' portfolios are the *Actividades escritas* from page 266 of the student textbook and the *Mi autobiografía* section from the Workbook, page 96.

INDEPENDENT PRACTICE

Assign any of the following:
1. Exercises on student page 267
2. Workbook, *Mi autobiografía,* page 96
3. Chapter 9, Situation Cards

CAPÍTULO 10
Scope and Sequence pages 268-293

Topics	Functions	Structure	Culture
Minor illnesses Symptoms of a cold, flu, or fever Medical exams Body parts Prescriptions	How to describe symptoms of a minor illness How to explain your illness to a doctor How to describe good and bad health habits How to have a prescription filled at a pharmacy How to tell someone where you or others are from How to describe origin and location How to describe characteristics or conditions How to discuss what others do for you	*Ser y estar* Los pronombres *me y te*	Medical services Heath issues in Spanish-speaking countries Hispanic contributions to medicine Visiting a pharmacy in a Spanish-speaking country vs. the U.S. Madrid's Marathon Revista *Saludable*

CAPÍTULO 10

Situation Cards

The Situation Cards simulate real-life situations that require students to communicate in Spanish, exactly as though they were in a Spanish-speaking country. The Situation Cards operate on the assumption that the person to whom the message is to be conveyed understands no English. Therefore, students must focus on producing the Spanish vocabulary and structures necessary to negotiate the situations successfully. For additional information, see the Introduction to the Situation Cards in the Situation Cards Envelope.

Communication Transparency

The illustration seen in this Communication Transparency consists of a synthesis of the two vocabulary (*Palabras 1&2*) presentations found in this chapter. It has been created in order to present this chapter's vocabulary in a new context, and also to recycle vocabulary learned in previous chapters. The Communication Transparency consists of original art. Following are some specific uses:

1. as a cue to stimulate conversation and writing activities
2. for listening comprehension activities
3. to review and reteach vocabulary
4. as a review for chapter and unit tests

CAPÍTULO 10   A

You're spending the summer in Spain and you have a runny nose, stinging eyes, and you're sneezing a lot. You decide to see a doctor. He wants to know if you have any allergies. Tell him about your allergies.

Bienvenidos   © Glencoe/McGraw-Hill

Bienvenidos   Chapter 10   Communication Transparency   C-10

Lesson Plans	**Pages**

Workbook

- Palabras 1 — 97-98
- Palabras 2 — 98-99
- Estructura — 100-102
- Un poco más — 103-105
- Mi autobiografía — 106

Communication Activities Masters

- Palabras 1 — 57-58
- Palabras 2 — 59
- Estructura — 60-62

9 Bell Ringer Reviews — 25-27

Chapter Situation Cards A B C D

Chapter Quizzes

- Palabras 1 — 44
- Palabras 2 — 45
- Estructura — 46-48

Testing Program

- Listening Comprehension — 54
- Reading and Writing — 55-57
- Proficiency — 126
- Speaking — 146

Nosotros y Nuestro Mundo

- Nuestro Conocimiento Académico *Medicinas y médicos*
- Nuestro Idioma *La sinalefa*
- Nuestra Cultura *Biografía de un médico cubano*
- Nuestra Literatura *"Triolet"* de Manuel González Parada
- Nuestras Diversiones

CD-ROM Interactive Textbook Disc 3

Chapter 10 Student Edition
- Palabras 1
- Palabras 2
- Estructura
- Conversación
- Lectura y cultura
- Hispanoparlantes
- Realidades
- Culminación
- Prueba

Audio Cassette Program with Student Tape Manual

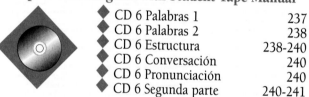

Cassette	**Pages**
6B Palabras 1	237
6B Palabras 2	238
6B Estructura	238-240
6B Conversación	240
6B Pronunciación	240
6B Segunda parte	240-241

Compact Disc Program with Student Tape Manual

- CD 6 Palabras 1 — 237
- CD 6 Palabras 2 — 238
- CD 6 Estructura — 238-240
- CD 6 Conversación — 240
- CD 6 Pronunciación — 240
- CD 6 Segunda parte — 240-241

Overhead Transparencies Binder

- Vocabulary 10.1 (A&B); 10.2 (A&B)
- Pronunciation P-10
- Communication C-10
- Maps
- Fine Art (with Blackline Master Activities)

Video Program

- Videocassette
- Video Activities Booklet — 30-32
- Videodisc
- Video Activities Booklet — 30-32

Computer Software (Macintosh, IBM, Apple)

- Practice Disk
  Palabras 1 y 2
  Estructura
- Test Generator Disk
  Chapter Test
  Customized Test

CHAPTER OVERVIEW

In this chapter students will learn to talk about routine illnesses and describe their symptoms to a doctor. They will use vocabulary associated with medical exams, prescriptions, and minor illnesses such as colds, flu, and headaches. Students will talk about themselves and others using the pronouns *me* and *te*. They will express characteristics and origin using the verb *ser,* and conditions and location using the verb *estar.*

The cultural focus of the chapter is on medical services and health problems in the Spanish-speaking countries.

CHAPTER OBJECTIVES

By the end of this chapter, students will know:

1. vocabulary associated with headaches, colds, fevers, and flu
2. body parts associated with certain minor ailments
3. vocabulary associated with a visit to a doctor's office and a pharmacy
4. the pronouns *me, te,* and *nos,* used as direct and indirect objects
5. the basic uses of *ser* and *estar*

Pacing

Chapter 10 will require about eight to ten days. However, pacing will vary according to the length of the class, the age of your students, and student aptitude.

CAPÍTULO

10

LA SALUD Y EL MÉDICO

OBJETIVOS

In this chapter you will learn to do the following:

1. describe symptoms of a minor illness
2. explain your illness to a doctor
3. describe good and bad health habits
4. have a prescription filled at a pharmacy
5. tell where you and others are from
6. tell where you and others are now
7. describe characteristics and conditions
8. tell what people do for you
9. discuss health issues of concern in both the United States and the Hispanic world

268

CHAPTER PROJECTS

(optional)

1. Obtain a first-aid video from the health department in your school. Use it as a springboard for discussing health and illnesses with the new vocabulary from this chapter.

2. Have students create a poster of a man or woman like that in a doctor's office, labeling in Spanish as many external and internal body parts as they can. This poster can be displayed in the classroom.

269

LEARNING FROM PHOTOS

Note that this pharmacy in Argentina is typical of many in Spanish-speaking countries. It resembles the old apothecary shops that sell only medicines, unlike the modern drugstore. See the apothecary jars in contrast with the up-to-date computer.

Vocabulary Teaching Resources

1. Vocabulary Transparencies 10.1 (A & B)
2. Audio Cassette 6B
3. Student Tape Manual, page 237
4. Workbook, pages 97–98
5. Communication Activities Masters, pages 57-58, A & B
6. Chapter Quizzes, page 44, *Palabras 1*

Bell Ringer Review

Write the following on the board or use BRR Blackline Master 10-1:

Answer the following questions:
1. ¿Cuántos años tienes?
2. ¿Cuántos hermanos tienes?
3. ¿Tienes una familia grande o pequeña?
4. ¿Cuántos son Uds.?
5. ¿Tienen Uds. una mascota?

PRESENTATION

(pages 270–271)

A. Point to yourself as you teach the words *la garganta, la cabeza, el estómago.*
B. You can easily use gestures to teach the following expressions: *enfermo, cansado, nervioso, triste, los escalofríos, toser, estornudar, el dolor de garganta, el dolor de cabeza, el dolor de estómago.*

VOCABULARIO

PALABRAS 1

ESTÁ ENFERMO

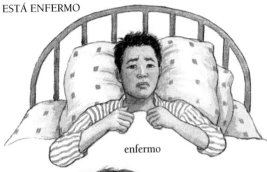

enfermo

cansada

contento

triste

nervioso

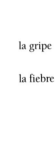

los escalofríos

la gripe

la fiebre

El muchacho tiene la gripe.
Tiene fiebre.

270 CAPÍTULO 10

TOTAL PHYSICAL RESPONSE

(following the Vocabulary presentation)

___, ven acá por favor. Imagínate que estás enfermo(a).
Indícame que estás cansado(a).
Indícame que tienes fiebre.
Indícame que tienes escalofríos.
Indícame que tienes dolor de garganta.
Indícame que tienes dolor de cabeza.
Indícame que tienes dolor de estómago.
Indícame que tienes tos.
Indícame que estás estornudando mucho.
Gracias, ___. Y ahora puedes regresar a tu asiento.

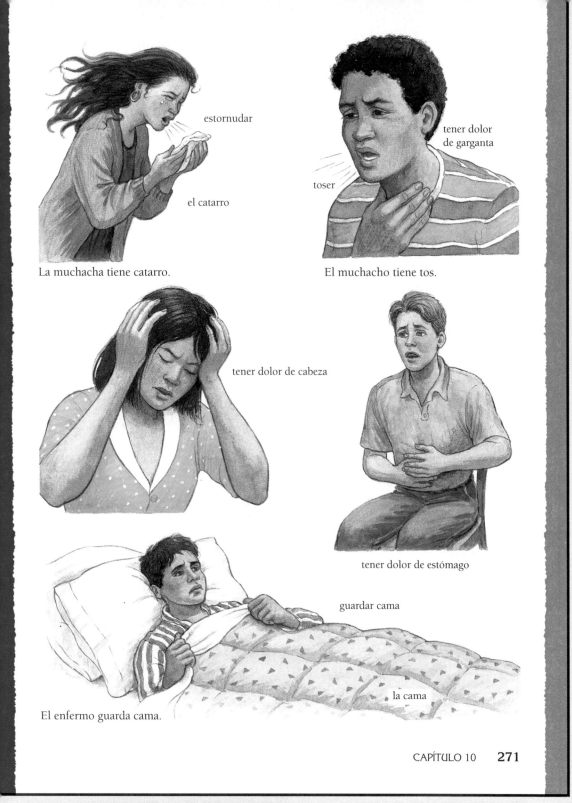

estornudar

el catarro

La muchacha tiene catarro.

tener dolor de garganta

toser

El muchacho tiene tos.

tener dolor de cabeza

tener dolor de estómago

guardar cama

la cama

El enfermo guarda cama.

ABOUT THE LANGUAGE

1. In addition to teaching the word *catarro* for cold, give students *resfriado: Tengo un resfriado* or *Estoy resfriado(a)*.
2. Explain to students that one must be aware of false cognates. The expression *estoy constipado(a)* does not mean to be constipated as one would think. It means "I have a cold." *Estoy estreñido(a)* means "I'm constipated." *Embarazada* does not mean "embarrassed," but "pregnant."

Vocabulary Expansion

Tourists often experience stomach problems when traveling. If you wish, you may give students the following expressions that they may find very useful.

Tengo náuseas.
Tengo diarrea.
Estoy estreñido(a)
    (*constipated*).
Tengo vómitos.
Tengo calambres (*cramps*).

ADDITIONAL PRACTICE

After practicing the *Palabras 1* vocabulary, you may wish to play a game of *Simón dice*. Call the first round yourself and have the students act out the following.

Simón dice: Tienes dolor de cabeza.
Simón dice: Tienes dolor de garganta.
Simón dice: Tienes tos.
Simón dice: Tose.
Simón dice: Estornuda.

Bell Ringer Review

Write the following on the board or use BRR Blackline Master 10-2: Draw a fairly detailed sketch of a person and then label the parts of the body where the following occur:

1. **la tos**
2. **el dolor de cabeza**
3. **el dolor de estómago**
4. **el dolor de garganta**

Ejercicios

PRESENTATION

(pages 272–273)

Ejercicio A

Do Exercise A first with books open. Then call on one student to give all of Roberto's symptoms.

Ejercicio B

Let students say as much as they can about each photo in the exercise.

ANSWERS

Ejercicio A

1. Sí, Roberto está enfermo.
2. Sí, tiene la gripe.
3. Sí, tiene tos.
4. Sí, está estornudando.
5. Sí, tiene fiebre.
6. Sí, tiene escalofríos.
7. Sí, tiene dolor de cabeza.
8. Sí, siempre (a veces, no siempre) está cansado.

Ejercicio B

1. Está contenta.
2. Está triste.
3. Está enfermo.
4. Está tranquila.

Ejercicios

A **El pobre Roberto está enfermo.** Contesten.

1. ¿Está enfermo Roberto?
2. ¿Tiene la gripe?
3. ¿Tiene tos?
4. ¿Está estornudando?
5. ¿Tiene fiebre?
6. ¿Tiene escalofríos?
7. ¿Tiene dolor de cabeza?
8. ¿Está siempre cansado?

B **¿Cómo está?** Contesten según las fotos.

1. ¿Cómo está la señorita? ¿Está triste o contenta?

2. Y el muchacho, ¿cómo está? ¿Está triste o contento?

3. El señor, ¿está bien o está enfermo?

4. Y la joven, ¿está tranquila o está nerviosa?

COOPERATIVE LEARNING

After going over Exercise A, have students work in pairs. Based on the questions in Exercise A, they will make up a conversation between Roberto and his doctor.

C **Y tú, ¿cómo estás?** Preguntas personales.

1. ¿Cómo estás?
2. Cuando estás enfermo, ¿estás de mal humor o de buen humor?
3. Cuando tienes dolor de cabeza, ¿estás contento(a) o triste?
4. Cuando tienes catarro, ¿estás siempre cansado(a) o no?
5. Cuando estás enfermo(a), ¿quieres guardar cama o prefieres ir a una fiesta?
6. Cuando estás enfermo(a), ¿quieres dormir o trabajar?
7. Cuando tienes un examen, ¿estás nervioso(a) o tranquilo(a)?

CAPÍTULO 10 **273**

PRESENTATION *(page 273)*

Ejercicio C

It is suggested that you go over Exercise C first with books closed. For additional reinforcement students can write the answers to the questions as a homework assignment.

ANSWERS

Ejercicio C

Answers will vary.

RECYCLING

As a review of the present progressive, have students answer the following questions about the milk ad. *¿Qué está haciendo la muchacha? ¿Tiene audífonos? ¿Qué está escuchando?*

ABOUT THE LANGUAGE

Ask students if they have heard the word "svelte," which is very similar to the brand name of the milk in the ad, *Sveltes*. In areas of the U.S. where there is a large Jewish population, many people use this Yiddish term for thin.

INFORMAL ASSESSMENT
(Palabras 1)

Check for understanding by miming the symptoms from *Palabras 1*, pages 270–271 and having students tell you what is wrong with you.

CRITICAL THINKING

With reference to the magazine cover on page 273, teach students the meaning of the word *peligro* "danger." Then ask: *¿Qué significa "La mezcla de medicinas, un cóctel peligroso"? Explica.*

INDEPENDENT PRACTICE

Assign any of the following:
1. Workbook, pages 97–98
2. Communication Activities Masters, pages 57-58, A & B
3. Exercises on student pages 272–273

Bell Ringer Review

Write the following on the board or use BRR Blackline Master 10-3: Write some adjectives that describe your family doctor.

PRESENTATION
(pages 274–275)

A. Present the new words using Vocabulary Transparencies 10.2 (A & B). As you point to each item, have students repeat the corresponding word or expression after you two or three times.

B. Have students keep their books closed. Dramatize the following words or expressions from *Palabras 2: abrir la boca, examinar la garganta, me duele la cabeza, me duele la garganta, me duele el pecho, me duele el estómago.*

C. Ask students to open their books to pages 274–275. Have them read along and repeat the new material after you or the recording on Cassette 6B.

VOCABULARIO

PALABRAS 2

LA CLÍNICA Y LA FARMACIA

> La médica me examina la garganta.

el médico

la médica

la consulta del médico
el consultorio del médico

Tomás está en la consulta de la médica.
La médica examina a Tomás.
Tomás abre la boca.

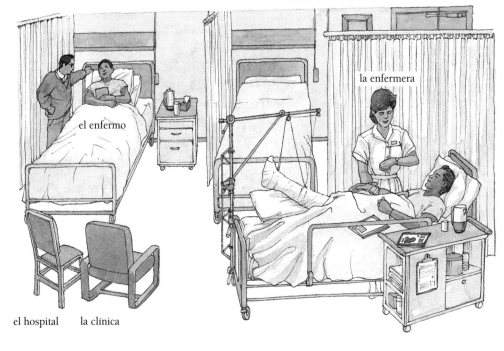

el enfermo

la enfermera

el hospital   la clínica

274   CAPÍTULO 10

Me duele la cabeza.

Me duele la garganta.

Me duele el pecho.

Me duele el estómago.

el farmacéutico

la farmacéutica

la receta

las pastillas
las píldoras
los comprimidos

la farmacia

Tomás va a la farmacia.
La farmacéutica lee la receta.
Ella vende (despacha) los medicamentos.

Nota: Here is a list of cognates related to health and nutrition. You can easily guess the meaning of these words.

la dieta	el síntoma	la fibra
las vitaminas	la alergia	las calorías
la proteína	la dosis	la droga
los ejercicios físicos	la diagnosis	
los ejercicios aeróbicos	los carbohidratos	

CAPÍTULO 10   **275**

RECYCLING

Bring back previously learned vocabulary by asking *¿Dónde te duele?* and point to your stomach, head, arm, foot, finger, and hand.

Vocabulary Expansion

You may wish to give students the following expressions related to a routine visit to the doctor's office.

explicar los síntomas
hacer una diagnosis
tomar la presión (tensión) arterial
tomar el pulso
tomar una radiografía

COGNATES

Have students repeat carefully the cognates at the bottom of page 275. Meaning should cause no problem.

ABOUT THE LANGUAGE

1. Explain to students that many nouns that end in *-ama, -oma* come from Greek, and they take the article *el*. For example: *el síntoma, el programa, el problema, el drama.*
2. Many of the nouns that end in *-osis* take the article *la*. For example: *la diagnosis, la prognosis.*

CROSS-CULTURAL CONNECTION

En los EE.UU. es relativamente reciente que hay muchas señoras médicas. En España y en Latinoamérica no es nada reciente. Siempre ha habido muchas señoras que practican la medicina.

FOR THE NATIVE SPEAKER

1. Ask students about childhood diseases they may have had. If they don't know their names in Spanish, tell them: *sarampión, paperas, tos ferina, varicela* (measles, mumps, whooping cough, chicken pox). Ask them to describe the symptoms of each.

2. Remind students that there are a number of professions in the medical field: *doctores(as), farmacéuticos(as), técnicos(as), enfermeros(as).* Ask them: *¿Cuál es la función de cada profesión? ¿Qué preparación se necesita para ejercer una profesión? ¿Cuál es la importancia de cada profesión en cuanto a la salud del público? ¿Te gustaría ingresar en una de esas profesiones? ¿Por qué sí o por qué no?*

Ejercicios

PRESENTATION (page 276)

Ejercicio A

A. Exercise A can be done with books closed or open.

B. Students should answer with a complete sentence.

Ejercicio B

You may also wish to have students write Exercise B as a homework assignment.

ANSWERS

Ejercicio A

1. Tomás está en la consulta del médico.
2. Tomás está enfermo.
3. El médico examina a Tomás.
4. El enfermero ayuda al médico.
5. El médico examina la garganta.
6. Tomás tiene que tomar una pastilla.
7. El médico receta los antibióticos.
8. Tomás va a la farmacia.
9. El farmacéutico despacha los medicamentos.

Ejercicio B

1. Tomás no está bien. (Está enfermo.)
2. Tomás está en la consulta del médico.
3. Tomás abre la boca.
4. El médico examina la garganta.
5. El médico receta unos antibióticos.
6. El farmacéutico despacha los medicamentos en la farmacia.

Ejercicio C

1. bueno
2. bueno
3. malo
4. bueno
5. malo
6. bueno
7. malo

INFORMAL ASSESSMENT
(Palabras 2)

Have students look at the Vocabulary Transparencies from this chapter and say anything they can about them.

276

Ejercicios

A **En la consulta.** Contesten.

1. ¿Dónde está Tomás? ¿En la consulta del médico o en el hospital?
2. ¿Quién está enfermo? ¿Tomás o el enfermero?
3. ¿Quién examina a Tomás? ¿El médico o el farmacéutico?
4. En el consultorio, ¿quién ayuda al médico? ¿Tomás o el enfermero?
5. ¿Qué examina el médico? ¿El pecho o la garganta?
6. ¿Qué tiene que tomar Tomás? ¿Una inyección o una pastilla?
7. ¿Quién receta los antibióticos? ¿El médico o el farmacéutico?
8. ¿Adónde va Tomás con la receta? ¿A la clínica o a la farmacia?
9. ¿Qué despacha el farmacéutico? ¿Los medicamentos o las recetas?

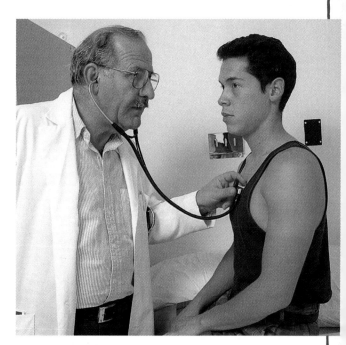

B **Tomás está enfermo.** Corrijan las oraciones falsas.

1. Tomás está muy bien.
2. Tomás está en el hospital.
3. Tomás abre la garganta en la consulta del médico.
4. El médico explica los síntomas a Tomás.
5. El farmacéutico receta unos antibióticos.
6. El médico despacha los medicamentos en la consulta.

C **¿Es bueno o malo para la salud?** Decidan Uds. Escriban en un papel.

	BUENO	MALO
1. Comer carbohidratos		
2. Tomar vitaminas		
3. Tomar drogas		
4. Hacer ejercicios aeróbicos		
5. Fumar cigarrillos		
6. Comer alimentos que contienen fibra		
7. Tomar o beber mucho alcohol		

276 CAPÍTULO 10

ADDITIONAL PRACTICE

Upon completion of Exercise A, have students look at each question and find the word you are defining.

1. *donde el médico examina a sus pacientes que no están muy enfermos*
2. *el que ayuda al médico*
3. *el que receta medicamentos*
4. *el que ayuda al médico*
5. *lo que te da el médico en el brazo*

LEARNING FROM PHOTOS

Ask the following questions about the photo on page 276. *¿Es joven o viejo el paciente? ¿Dónde está? ¿Quién examina al muchacho? ¿Está auscultando al muchacho? ¿Cómo es el muchacho?*

Comunicación
Palabras 1 y 2

A **¿Cómo estás?** You and your partner will take turns asking how each other is feeling. Answer according to the cues and tell why.

> contento(a)
> Estudiante 1: ¿Cómo estás?
> Estudiante 2: Estoy contento(a).
> Estudiante 1: ¿Por qué? (¿Qué pasa?), (¿Qué tienes?)
> Estudiante 2: Sé que voy a sacar una "A" en la clase de español.

1. contento(a)
2. enfermo(a)
3. malo(a)
4. triste
5. cansado(a)
6. nervioso(a)

B **Para tener buena salud…** You and your partner will each write a paragraph about your health habits. You may use any or all of the expressions below. Exchange papers and advise each other how to improve your habits.

> estar de buena salud
> fumar
> hacer ejercicios
> tomar medicamentos
> contar las calorías
> tomar vitaminas
> tener alergias
> comer carbohidratos

C **¿Qué tienes?** You and your partner pretend you each have a common illness. You have to guess the illness by asking each other about your *síntomas*. Use the list below.

1. fiebre
2. escalofríos
3. tos
4. dolor en el pecho
5. dolor de garganta
6. dolor de cabeza
7. estornudar
8. estar cansado(a)

Las Autoridades Sanitarias advierten que:
FUMAR PERJUDICA SERIAMENTE LA SALUD.

Comunicación
(*Palabras 1* and 2)

PRESENTATION (*page 277*)
You may allow students to select the activity or activities they wish to take part in.

PAIRED ACTIVITY
After completing Exercises A and B, have students tell their partner that they think they have the flu or a bad cold. They should tell why they think they are sick by explaining their symptoms. Their partner should respond by giving advice.

ABOUT THE LANGUAGE
In regard to the realia on page 277, tell students that the *autoridades sanitarias* are neither "sanitation workers" nor "sanitary authorities" but rather "health officials."

ANSWERS
Actividad A
Answers should follow the model.
Actividades B and *C*
Answers will vary.

LEARNING FROM REALIA

1. If you taught the word *peligroso* for the realia on page 273, ask students the following questions about the realia on page 277. *El anuncio indica que hay algo muy peligroso. ¿Qué es?*

2. Students will encounter the word *perjudicial* in the *Lectura* of this chapter. You may wish to teach it to students at this point. *Perjudicial: que hace daño, que causa problemas serios.* Then ask *¿Qué perjudica la salud? ¿Es perjudicial fumar?*

ESTRUCTURA

Bell Ringer Review

Write the following on the board or use BRR Blackline Master 10-4: Write as many words as you can that describe a person.

Ser y estar

Note Explain to students that the verb *ser* comes from the Latin verb *esse,* from which the English word *essence* is derived. The verb *ser* is therefore used to describe the essence of something, that which is inherent or characteristic.

The verb *estar,* on the other hand, is derived from Latin *stare,* from which the English word *state* is derived. *Estar* is therefore used to describe a state or a condition.

PRESENTATION *(page 278)*

A. Have students open their books and read the explanation on page 278.
B. Call on someone to read the example sentences aloud.

Ejercicios

PRESENTATION
(pages 278–279)

Ejercicio A
You may wish to have students do Exercise A with books open.

Ser y estar

Describing Characteristics and Conditions

1. In Spanish there are two verbs that mean "to be," *ser* and *estar*. These verbs have separate and distinct uses. *Ser* is used to express inherent traits or characteristics that do not change.

   María es rubia.   **El edificio Colón es muy alto.**

2. *Estar* is used to express temporary conditions or states that can change.

   Tomás está enfermo.   **Está cansado y nervioso.**

Ejercicios

A ¿Cómo es? Formen oraciones según el modelo.

> Alberto   alto/bajo
> *Alberto no es alto. Es bajo.*

1. Teresa   morena/rubia
2. Carlos   aburrido/interesante
3. Lupe   antipática/simpática
4. El curso de español   difícil/fácil
5. La biología   aburrida/interesante

B Rasgos físicos. Digan quién es así.

1. rubio o rubia
2. moreno o morena
3. fuerte
4. bajo o baja
5. alto o alta
6. interesante
7. inteligente
8. simpático o simpática
9. sincero o sincera
10. divertido o divertida

C ¿Cómo eres? Den una descripción personal.

> *Yo soy moreno(a) y…*

278   CAPÍTULO 10

Mejor
tabcin

El primer antigripal efervescente
Para estar bien activo, otra vez

D **¿Cómo está y cómo es?** Describan a cada persona según el dibujo.

1. Joselito

2. Marlena

3. Horacio

4. Inés

5. Roberto

6. Antonia

E **¿Ser o estar?** Formen oraciones con *ser* o *estar*.

1. El médico/muy bueno
2. El muchacho/muy enfermo
3. El médico/inteligente
4. Su consultorio/moderno
5. El paciente/muy enfermo
6. La muchacha/cansada
7. El hospital/grande
8. El edificio/alto
9. Elena/triste
10. Su mamá/nerviosa
11. Joselito/bien
12. Todos/contentos

ADDITIONAL PRACTICE

Have students call out any adjective. Have another student make up a sentence using *ser* or *estar* as appropriate.

INDEPENDENT PRACTICE

Assign any of the following:
1. Workbook, pages 98–99
2. Communication Activities Masters, page 59, *C & D*
3. Exercises on student pages 278–279
4. Computer Software, *Estructura*

Expansion of *Ejercicio A*

Have students change the subject to plural forms. This will review the forms of adjectives as well as the forms of the verb *ser*.

Ejercicio B

Let students give the name of any person they wish.

Ejercicio C

Encourage students to be as thorough as possible based on their knowledge of the language.

ANSWERS

Ejercico A

1. Teresa no es morena. Es rubia.
2. Carlos no es aburrido. Es interesante.
3. Lupe no es antipática. Es simpática.
4. El curso de español no es difícil. Es fácil.
5. La biología no es aburrida. Es interesante.

Ejercicio B

Answers will vary.

Ejercicio C

Answers will vary.

Ejercicio D

Have students look at each illustration as they describe the person.

Expansion of *Ejercicio D*

You may wish to do the exercise a second time and have students add as much information as they can about each illustration.

Ejercicio E

You may wish to have students write their sentences before going over them in class. Then call on students to read the sentences to the class.

ANSWERS

Ejercicio D

1. Joselito está enfermo.
2. Marlena está contenta.
3. Horacio está aburrido.
4. Inés está contenta.
5. Roberto está ocupado.
6. Antonia está cansada.

Ejercicio E

1. es	6. está	11. está
2. está	7. es	12. están
3. es	8. es	
4. es	9. está	
5. está	10. está	

Ser y estar

PRESENTATION *(page 280)*

Note You may wish to emphasize that *estar* is used with both permanent and temporary location. For example: *Madrid está en España. Los alumnos de la señora Rivera están en Madrid ahora.*

Ejercicios

PRESENTATION
(pages 280–282)

Ejercicio A

Give students the model with the appropriate intonation to indicate the naturalness of the exchange.

Ejercicio B

You may have to supply some additional countries to enable students to respond to these questions.

ANSWERS

Ejercicio A
1. Sí, creo que es de Colombia.
2. Sí, creo que es de Guatemala.
3. Sí, creo que es de Puerto Rico.
4. Sí, creo que es de España.
5. Sí, creo que es del Perú.
6. Sí, creo que son de Venezuela.
7. Sí, creo que son de Chile.
8. Sí, creo que son de Costa Rica.

Ejercicio B
Answers will vary but should follow this format:
1. Mis abuelos son de…
2. Mis abuelas son de…
3. Mis padres son de…
4. Yo soy de…

280

Ser y estar   *Telling Origin and Location*

1. The verb *ser* is used to express where someone or something is from.

   La muchacha es de Cuba.
   Las esmeraldas son de Colombia.

2. *Estar* is used to express where someone or something is located.

   Los alumnos están en la escuela.
   Los libros están en el salón de clase.

Ejercicios

A **¿De dónde es?** Contesten según se indica.

   ¿Es cubano el muchacho?
   Sí, creo que es de Cuba.

1. ¿Es colombiana la muchacha?
2. ¿Es guatemalteco el muchacho?
3. ¿Es puertorriqueña la joven?
4. ¿Es española la profesora?
5. ¿Es peruano el médico?
6. ¿Son venezolanos los amigos?
7. ¿Son chilenas las amigas?
8. ¿Son costarricenses los jugadores?

B **¿De dónde es su familia?**
Preguntas personales.

1. ¿De dónde son sus abuelos?
2. ¿De dónde son sus abuelas?
3. ¿De dónde son sus padres?
4. ¿De dónde es Ud.?

Un edificio de apartamentos en Madrid, España

C **¿Dónde está el apartamento?** Formen oraciones según el modelo.

Madrid / España
Madrid está en España.

1. la calle Velázquez/Madrid
2. el piso/la calle Velázquez
3. el piso/un edificio alto
4. el apartamento/cuarto piso
5. el apartamento/a la izquierda del ascensor

D **¿De dónde es y dónde está ahora?** Contesten.

1. Carlos es de Venezuela pero ahora está en México.
   ¿De dónde es Carlos?
   ¿Dónde está ahora?
   ¿De dónde es y dónde está?
2. Ángel es de Colombia pero ahora está en los Estados Unidos.
   ¿De dónde es Ángel?
   ¿Dónde está ahora?
   ¿De dónde es y dónde está?
3. La señora Salas es de Cuba pero ahora está en Puerto Rico.
   ¿De dónde es la señora Salas?
   ¿Dónde está ella ahora?
   ¿De dónde es la señora Salas y dónde está?

E **¿En qué clase estás?** Preguntas personales.

1. ¿Estás en la escuela ahora?
2. ¿Dónde está la escuela?
3. ¿En qué clase estás?
4. ¿En qué piso está la sala de clase?
5. ¿Está la profesora en la clase también?
6. ¿De dónde es ella?
7. ¿Y de dónde eres tú?
8. ¿Cómo estás hoy?
9. Y la profesora, ¿cómo está?
10. ¿Y cómo es?

Ejercicio C
This exercise emphasizes the use of *estar* with permanent location. You may wish to have students write their answers first.

Ejercicio D
The purpose of Exercise D is to contrast the use of *ser* and *estar* and hopefully make it very easy for students to understand the difference between origin and location.

Ejercicio E
It is recommended that you do Exercise E with books closed.

ANSWERS
Ejercicio C
1. La calle Velázquez está en Madrid.
2. El piso está en la calle Velázquez.
3. El piso está en un edificio alto.
4. El apartamento está en el cuarto piso.
5. El apartamento está a la izquierda del ascensor.

Ejercicio D
1. Carlos es de Venezuela. Ahora está en México. Es de Venezuela pero ahora está en México.
2. Ángel es de Colombia. Ahora está en los Estados Unidos. Es de Colombia pero ahora está en los Estados Unidos.
3. La señora Salas es de Cuba. Ahora ella está en Puerto Rico. Es de Cuba pero ahora está en Puerto Rico.

Ejercicio E
Answers will vary.

LEARNING FROM PHOTOS

1. You may wish to explain to students that the type of apartment buildings shown in the photo on page 281 are found in Old Madrid, *el viejo Madrid* or *el barrio viejo*. Many are presently being renovated.
2. You may want to take this opportunity to review some vocabulary taught in Chapter 5 on the topic of houses and apartments.

Ejercicio F

A. Exercise F makes students recombine all the uses of *ser* and *estar*. You may wish to give students a few minutes to scan the exercise before going over it.

B. Have each individual do about three items before calling on the next student. Then, have two individuals do the entire exercise. One does the first half and the other one does the second half.

Expansion of *Ejercicio F*

Call on one student to give a synopsis of the information in his/her own words.

ANSWERS

Ejercicio F

1. es
2. Es
3. es
4. es
5. está
6. está
7. Está
8. Está
9. Está
10. Está
11. está
12. está
13. Está
14. es
15. son
16. son
17. son
18. están
19. están
20. son
21. es
22. Está

F **Un amigo.** *Completen con ser o estar.*

Ángel ___ un amigo muy bueno. ___ muy atlético y ___
      1   2   3
muy inteligente. Además ___ sincero y simpático. Casi
                        4
siempre ___ de buen humor. Pero hoy no. Al contrario, ___
        5   6
de mal humor. ___ muy cansado y tiene dolor de cabeza.
              7
___ enfermo. Tiene la gripe. ___ en casa. ___ en cama.
 8   9   10
La casa de Ángel ___ en la calle 60. La calle 60 está en
                 11
West New York. W.N.Y. no ___ en Nueva York. ___ en New Jersey.
                         12   13
Pero la familia de Ángel no ___ de West New York. Sus padres ___ de
                            14   15
Cuba y sus abuelos ___ de España. Ellos ___ de Galicia, una región
                   16   17
en el noroeste de España en la costa del Atlántico y del mar Cantábrico.
Ángel tiene una familia internacional.

Pero ahora todos ___ en West New York y ___ contentos.
                 18   19
Muchas familias en West New York ___ de ascendencia
                                 20
cubana. El apartamento de la familia de Ángel ___ muy
                                               21
bonito. ___ en el tercer piso y tiene una vista magnífica
        22
de la ciudad de Nueva York.

CUBA aereo 1978 13

CUBA correos 35

XIV JUEGOS

CUBA CORREOS 1982 20

XXI ANIV. CONJUNTO FOLKLORICO NACIONAL

¡VIVELA A TU MANERA!

cuba

Grandeza arquitectónica de La Habana Vieja.
Deportes náuticos en Varadero. Espectáculos de
arte. Museos. Compras. Excursiones. Sabrosa
vida nocturna y la hospitalidad de siempre.

**¡Y mucho tiempo libre
para que vivas como quieras!**

Cuba . A tu manera

282

LEARNING FROM REALIA

1. Ask the following questions about the realia on page 282. *¿Qué ciudad menciona? ¿Cuál es la capital de Cuba? ¿Tiene La Habana un barrio viejo?*

2. You may wish to explain that the ad about Cuba appeared in a Mexican magazine. People from many other countries can travel to Cuba; travel is still very restricted between Cuba and the U.S.

INDEPENDENT PRACTICE

Assign any of the following:

1. Workbook, pages 100–102
2. Communication Activities Masters, pages 60-61, *A & B*
3. Exercises on student pages 280–282

Los pronombres *me, te, nos*

Telling What Someone Does for You

1. *Me* and *te* are object pronouns. They can be used as either a direct object or an indirect object. Note that the object pronoun is placed before the conjugated verb.

> *Me* duele la garganta.
> El médico *me* examina.
> ¿*Te* da una receta?
> Sí, sí. *Me* receta unos antibióticos.

2. The plural form of *me* is *nos*.

> Carlos *nos* llama por teléfono.
> *Nos* invita a la fiesta.
> Él *nos* va a dar una invitación.

Ejercicio

¿Qué te pasa? Contesten.

1. ¿Estás enfermo(a)?
2. ¿Te duele la cabeza?
3. ¿Te duele la garganta?
4. ¿Te duele el estómago?
5. ¿Te examina el médico?
6. ¿Te examina la garganta?
7. ¿Te da la diagnosis?
8. ¿Te receta unas pastillas?
9. ¿Te da una inyección?
10. ¿Te despacha los medicamentos el farmacéutico?

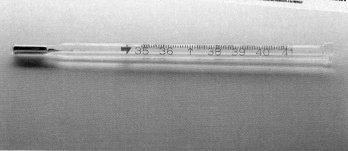

CAPÍTULO 10 **283**

Los pronombres *me, te, nos*

Teaching Tip Only the pronouns *me, te,* and *nos* are presented in this chapter. At this point students do not have to determine direct from indirect object. The pronouns *lo, la, los, las* are presented in Chapter 11, and *le, les* in Chapter 12.

The pronouns *me, te, nos* are presented first because they are less complicated than the third person pronouns. They are both direct and indirect objects. They are the only pronouns that are absolutely necessary for communication. For example, if asked a question with *te,* it is necessary to answer with *me.* When speaking in the third person, one could answer with a noun: *¿Invitaste a Juan? Sí, invité a Juan.*

PRESENTATION (page 283)

A. Have students point to themselves as they say *me* and point to or look at a friend as they say *te.*
B. Have students read the example sentences aloud. You can call on an individual to read them or have the entire class read them in unison.

Ejercicio: **Paired Activity**

This exercise can be done as a paired activity. One student poses the question and another one responds.

ANSWERS
Answers can be negative.

CONVERSACIÓN

Escenas de la vida *En la consulta del médico*

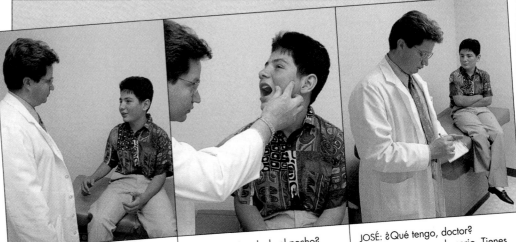

DOCTOR: ¿Qué te pasa, José? Tienes la cara muy roja.
JOSÉ: Ay, doctor López. ¡Qué enfermo estoy!
DOCTOR: No, José. No es tan serio. ¿Cuáles son tus síntomas?
JOSÉ: Pues, doctor, tengo fiebre. Tengo escalofríos. Me duele la garganta. ¡Ay, Dios mío!

DOCTOR: ¿Y te duele el pecho?
JOSÉ: Sí, me duele todo. Y tengo tos.
DOCTOR: Bien, José. ¿Me puedes abrir la boca? Sí, José. Ya veo. La garganta está muy roja.

JOSÉ: ¿Qué tengo, doctor?
DOCTOR: No es nada serio. Tienes la gripe. Te voy a recetar unos antibióticos.

 El pobre José. Contesten.

1. ¿Dónde está José?
2. ¿Con quién habla él?
3. ¿Cómo está José?
4. ¿Qué tiene?
5. ¿Qué abre José?
6. ¿Examina la garganta el médico?
7. ¿Cómo está la garganta?
8. ¿Cuál es la diagnosis del médico?
9. ¿Qué receta el doctor López?

284 CAPÍTULO 10

la boca es la puerta de tu salud

OJOS
CORAZON
PULMONES
RIÑONES
ESTOMAGO
ARTICULACIONES

no te pongas en manos de cualquiera

Ilustre Colegio Oficial de Odontólogos y Estomatólogos

Pronunciación   *Las consonantes* j *y* g

The Spanish j sound does not exist in English. In Spain the j sound is very guttural (coming from the throat). In Latin America the j is much softer.

ja	je	ji	jo	ju
Jaime	Jesús	ají	joven	jugar
hija	ejercicio	Jiménez	viejo	junio
jarabe	equipaje	jirafa	dibujo	julio

G in combination with e or i (*ge, gi*) has the same sound as the j. For this reason you must pay particular attention to the spelling of the words with je, ji, ge, and gi.

ge	gi
general	Gijón
gente	alergia
generoso	gimnasio

Repeat the following sentences.

El hijo del viejo general José trabaja en junio en Gijón.
El jugador hace ejercicios en el gimnasio.
El joven Jaime toma jarabe para la tos.

El general hace ejercicios.

Comunicación

A Me duele. Tell your partner what hurts. Your partner is going to give you practical advice beginning with "Why don't you…?" Reverse roles.

la cabeza
Estudiante 1: Me duele la cabeza.
Estudiante 2: ¿Por qué no tomas aspirinas?

1. la garganta
2. la cabeza
3. el estómago
4. el pecho
5. una mano
6. los pies

B ¿De dónde son? Write down the names of five famous people who are not Americans. See how much your partner knows about them by asking where each person is from and where the place is.

Julio Iglesias
Estudiante 1: ¿De dónde es Julio Iglesias?
Estudiante 2: ¿Es de la Argentina?
Estudiante 1: No.
Estudiante 2: ¿Es de España?
Estudiante 1: Sí, es español. ¿Dónde está España?
Estudiante 2: Está en Europa.

Julio Iglesias, *cantante español*

Ejercicio

ANSWERS

1. José está en el consultorio del médico.
2. Él habla con el médico.
3. José está enfermo.
4. Tiene fiebre, escalofríos y le duele la garganta.
5. José abre la boca.
6. Sí, el médico examina la garganta.
7. La garganta está muy roja.
8. José tiene gripe.
9. El doctor López receta unos antibióticos.

Pronunciación

PRESENTATION (*page 285*)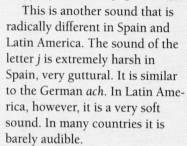

This is another sound that is radically different in Spain and Latin America. The sound of the letter *j* is extremely harsh in Spain, very guttural. It is similar to the German *ach*. In Latin America, however, it is a very soft sound. In many countries it is barely audible.

Since the g and j can present spelling problems, it is recommended that you have students commit to memory the spelling of these words. You may use the words and sentences as a spelling test.

Comunicación

ANSWERS

Actividades A and B

Answers should follow the models.

CRITICAL THINKING ACTIVITY

(*Thinking skills: locating causes*)
Write the following on the board or on an overhead transparency:
1. **Todos hablan del estrés. Hay mucho estrés en la sociedad moderna. ¿Cuáles son algunas causas del estrés?**
2. **Si uno tiene mucho estrés, ¿qué puede hacer para tratar de aliviar el estrés?**

FOR THE NATIVE SPEAKER

Writing The syllables *ge, je, gi, ji* present spelling problems. The spelling of words with these combinations must be memorized. Provide the following list and give a dictation.
ge *gente, margen, germen, recoger, gesto, genio*
je *jefe, jeringa, jeta, garaje*
gi *régimen, registro, gimnasia, gigante, gitano, página*
ji *jíbaro, jinete, jitomate, jirafa*

LECTURA Y CULTURA

Bell Ringer Review

Write the following on the board or use BRR Blackline Master 10-8: Rewrite these sentences, changing the object pronouns in the first two to their plural form, and in the second two sentences to the singular.

1. **Me duele la cabeza.**
2. **Me da una receta.**
3. **Nos invita a la fiesta.**
4. **El médico nos examina.**

READING STRATEGIES
(*page 286*)

Pre-reading

A. Have students scan the passage to look for cognates.
B. Give students a brief synopsis of the *Lectura* in Spanish. Ask a few questions based on it.

Reading

Call on a student to read three or four sentences. Ask several questions to check comprehension before calling on the next student to read. Continue in this way until the selection has been completed.

Post-reading

Assign the reading selection and the exercises that follow as homework. Go over the exercises the next day in class.

ABOUT THE LANGUAGE

The acronym *SIDA*, which stands for AIDS, is usually capitalized. Recently, however, it has been seen in the lower case, *el sida*.

CROSS-CULTURAL COMPARISON

Explain to students that just as here in the U.S., the Spanish-speaking countries all have campaigns to combat drug addiction, alcoholism, and AIDS.

LA SALUD

Hoy día hay mucho interés en la salud y la forma física. En los periódicos y en las revistas de España y de Latinoamérica hay artículos sobre costumbres saludables y costumbres perjudiciales[1] para la salud. Dos recomendaciones que leemos frecuentemente son: mantener una dieta buena con la cantidad adecuada de calorías, vitaminas, carbohidratos, minerales, proteínas y fibra; no tomar drogas ni alcohol.

No hay duda que la dieta es importante. Pero es también importante seguir un programa o régimen de ejercicios físicos. En las grandes ciudades hispánicas hay gimnasios y salones donde la gente practica calistenia y ejercicios aeróbicos. En cada ciudad o pueblo hispano hay parques bonitos. Muchos van al parque a hacer jogging o "footing", a caminar[2] o a correr. Pero la verdad es que la manía que tienen los norteamericanos por ejercicios agotadores[3] no existe en los países hispanos.

Desgraciadamente, hay tres problemas graves en el campo de la salud que tenemos que confrontar. Estos problemas son la adicción a las drogas, el abuso del alcohol y el SIDA. En España hay una campaña de castigos[4] rigurosos contra los conductores de automóviles que manejan (conducen) bajo los efectos o la influencia del alcohol. Y en los grandes supermercados de San Juan, Puerto Rico, uno ve en cada carrito[5] el aviso "El SIDA mata—para más información llamar al 729-8410". Y en todas partes hay programas y campañas para educar a la gente sobre los peligros del uso de las drogas. La drogadicción, el alcoholismo y el SIDA son problemas que tenemos que resolver y vencer[6].

[1] perjudiciales *harmful*
[2] caminar *to walk*
[3] agotadores *exhausting*
[4] castigos *punishment*
[5] carrito *cart*
[6] vencer *overcome, conquer*

LEARNING FROM REALIA

1. Ask the following questions about the realia on page 286. *Este aviso habla de otra cosa muy peligrosa. ¿Cuál es o cuáles son?*
2. Have students repeat aloud: *Sí a la vida. No a las drogas.*

Estudio de palabras

A **Palabras afines.** Busquen doce palabras afines en la lectura.

B **Las palabras derivadas.** Busquen en la lectura las palabra derivadas de las siguientes.

1. abusar
2. recomendar
3. perjudicar
4. la salud
5. el mantenimiento
6. la educación
7. la resolución
8. usar

C **Lo que deben hacer.** Escojan.

1. ___ importante es no tomar drogas ni alcohol.
   a. Una recomendación b. Un régimen c. Una cantidad

2. ___ es un ejercicio físico.
   a. La dieta b. La manía c. La calistenia

3. No es una práctica saludable. La verdad es que puede ser ___ para la salud.
   a. agotadora b. perjudicial c. importante

4. Es bueno para la salud. Es una cosa muy ___.
   a. saludable b. perjudicial c. adecuada

5. El pobre está muy enfermo. Su condición es muy seria, muy ___.
   a. buena b. agotadora c. grave

Comprensión

A **¿Qué es?** Completen.

1. Hoy día dos temas de mucho interés universal son…
2. Una recomendación para mantener buena salud es…
3. Una actividad que es perjudicial (mala) para la salud es…

B **Los problemas.** Contesten.

1. ¿Cuáles son tres problemas graves que existen hoy en el campo de la salud?
2. ¿Existen estos problemas en los Estados Unidos?
3. ¿Existen también en los países hispanos?

C **La idea principal.** Escojan la idea principal de esta lectura.

a. un régimen de ejercicios físicos
b. cómo mantener la salud
c. problemas médicos serios

CLÍNICA
ESPECIALIZADA
SOLUCIÓN DE
ALCOHOLISMO Y
DROGADICCIÓN

671-18-74 (FAX)
671-17-53
594-53-98

AMBIENTE AGRADABLE Y PRIVACIDAD

Estudio de palabras

PRESENTATION *(page 287)*

A. You may wish to have students complete the *Estudio de palabras* exercises before going over them in class.
B. Note that Exercise C involves critical thinking.

ANSWERS

Ejercicio A
1. perjudiciales
2. recomendaciones
3. dieta
4. calorías
5. vitaminas
6. minerales
7. proteínas
8. fibra
9. drogas
10. aeróbicos
11. manía
12. graves

Ejercicio B
1. abuso
2. recomendaciones
3. perjudiciales
4. saludable
5. mantener
6. educar
7. resolver
8. uso

Ejercicio C
1. a   4. a
2. c   5. c
3. b

Comprensión

Note Exercise C involves critical thinking.

ANSWERS

Comprensión A
1. la forma física y la salud
2. una dieta buena
3. fumar (tomar drogas)

Comprensión B
1. Los tres problemas graves que existen hoy en el campo de la salud son la drogadicción, el alcoholismo y el SIDA.
2. Sí, estos problemas existen en los Estados Unidos.
3. Sí, existen también en los países hispanos.

Comprensión C
b

INDEPENDENT PRACTICE

Assign any of the following:
1. Workbook, *Un poco más*, pages 103–104
2. *Estudio de palabras* and *Comprensión* exercises on student page 287

A. You may wish to have students read this material silently.

B. After students read the material, you may wish to have them make a list of differences between a pharmacy in the United States and one in a Spanish-speaking country.

DESCUBRIMIENTO CULTURAL

*E*n los Estados Unidos, si uno quiere o necesita antibióticos, ¿es necesario tener una receta? ¿Quién receta los medicamentos en los Estados Unidos? ¿Quién prepara la receta? ¿Quién despacha los medicamentos en los Estados Unidos?

Pues, en los países hispanos el farmacéutico despacha los medicamentos también. Pero no es necesario tener una receta para comprar antibióticos, por ejemplo. Uno puede explicar sus síntomas al farmacéutico y él o ella puede despachar los medicamentos sin receta. Hay una excepción: las medicinas que contienen sustancias controladas como los narcóticos o el alcohol. El farmacéutico no puede despachar estas medicinas sin receta del médico.

¡Y otra cosa muy importante! El precio de las medicinas en los países hispanos es mucho más bajo que el precio aquí en los EE.UU.

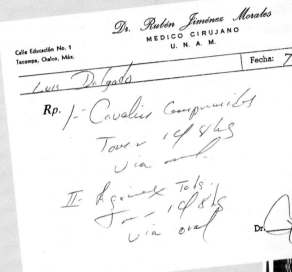

288   CAPÍTULO 10

LEARNING FROM REALIA

1. Ask the following questions about the prescription (realia) on page 288. *¿Cúal es el nombre del médico? ¿Cuál es el nombre del paciente? ¿Dónde está el consultorio del doctor Morales?*

2. Have students choose the correct answer: *¿Es el doctor Jiménez Morales médico cirujano?*

a. *Sí, él examina a sus pacientes.*

b. *Sí, él hace operaciones (intervenciones quirúrgicas). Él opera a sus pacientes.*

c. *Sí, él toma radiografías.*

Santiago Ramón y Cajal

Carlos Juan Finlay y Barres

Las contribuciones del mundo hispano a la medicina son muchas y son importantes. Éstos son algunos ejemplos.

Miguel Servet (1511–1553), médico y humanista español, descubre la circulación pulmonar de la sangre.

El médico cubano, Carlos Juan Finlay y Barres (1833–1915), ayuda a descubrir que un mosquito transmite la fiebre amarilla.

El español, Santiago Ramón y Cajal (1852–1934) recibe el Premio Nobel de Medicina en 1906 por sus investigaciones sobre la estructura del sistema nervioso.

Y AQUÍ EN LOS ESTADOS UNIDOS

La puertorriqueña, Antonia Coello Novello, sirve de Cirujana General de los EE.UU. de 1989–1993.

Antonia Coello Novello

FOR THE NATIVE SPEAKER

Writing Have students select an illness from the list below and write a description of that illness and its symptoms. Then ask them to suggest an appropriate treatment.

catarro/resfriado
gripe
paperas
úlceras estomacales
pulmonía
apendicitis
artritis
cataratas en los ojos

(The Realidades *is optional material.)*

PRESENTATION
(pages 290–291)

The purpose of this section is to have students enjoy the photographs in a relaxed manner in order to gain an appreciation of Hispanic culture. After reading the captions on page 290, you may wish to do the following regarding the photos and realia:

Photo 1: Tell students that *El Corte Inglés* is one of Spain's leading department store chains. It is a sponsor of the Madrid Marathon.

Photo 2:

1. Have students look at the cover of the magazine. You may wish to ask: *¿Cuál es el nombre de la revista? Hay un artículo sobre algo peligroso. ¿Qué es peligroso?* *(autorrecetarse)*

2. Have students find out how the following is said:
   a. del estómago y de los intestinos
   b. decidir por su propia cuenta las medicinas que va a tomar
   c. las radiografías, los rayos equis

Photo 4: Ask the following questions about the photo of the doctor on page 291. *¿Qué profesión tiene el señor? ¿Qué hace él? ¿Dónde está el señor?*

REALIDADES

Es el Maratón Popular de Madrid **1**. Tiene lugar todos los años en el mes de abril. ¿Paticipas de vez en cuando en un maratón? ¿Cuántos kilómetros corres?

Saludable es una revista mexicana **2**. En esta revista hay buenos consejos para la salud.

Es la facultad de medicina de una universidad en un país hispano **3**. ¿Quieres ser médico?

Es un médico hispano **4**. Tiene su consulta en San Francisco. Él tiene muchos pacientes de habla española.

290

CRITICAL THINKING ACTIVITY

(Thinking skills: supporting arguments with reasons)

Write the following on the board or on an overhead transparency: **Prepare Ud. una lista de las características que Ud. considera importantes en un médico. Explique por qué Ud. considera estas características importantes.**

291

INDEPENDENT PRACTICE

1. Workbook, *Un poco más*, page 105

CULMINACIÓN

Comunicación oral

ANSWERS

Actividad A
    Answers will vary.

Actividades B and C
    Answers will vary according to the models.

Comunicación escrita

ANSWERS

Actividades A and B
    Answers will vary.

GEOGRAPHY CONNECTION

Venezuela means "Little Venice." Venice is a city in Italy that has many canals. When the Spanish explorers arrived in Venezuela, they saw many canals that reminded them of *Venecia,* hence the name.

Caracas, a city of four million people, *caraqueños,* has many superhighways. Venezuela is a great producer of petroleum and gasoline. For that reason, automobiles are very popular. In order to alleviate the problem of air pollution, Caracas has an excellent metro system.

Comunicación oral

A **Me parece que…** You and your partner will tell one another a number of practices that each of you thinks are good for your health. If you disagree with your partner, say so, and recommend some changes.

B **¿Qué haces cuando…?** You will ask your partner, and then your partner will ask you what you do in the following circumstances.

> tienes dolor de cabeza
> Estudiante 1: ¿Qué haces si tienes dolor de cabeza?
> Estudiante 2: Tomo aspirina.

1. tienes fiebre
2. estás deprimido(a)
3. estás cansado(a)
4. tienes dolor de cabeza
5. te duelen los pies
6. estás enfermo(a)
7. tienes catarro
8. tienes tos

C **La geografía.** In teams of four students, carry out a "Geography Round Robin." Each team writes five questions testing knowledge of geography. (The writers must know the answers themselves!) Pairs of teams take turns asking each other questions. After each team has faced every other team, tally the results. The team with the most right answers wins.

> ¿Cuál es la capital de Cuba? *Es La Habana.*
> ¿Dónde está Caracas? *Está en Venezuela.*

Comunicación escrita

A **Pero doctor…** You are a doctor who has just examined a slightly overweight "couch potato" who is addicted to junk food and doesn't exercise. Write down your recommendations for this patient to lead a healthier life. Use *tienes que* and *no debes.*

> **Tienes que caminar más.**   **No debes comer chocolates.**

B **No es bueno para la salud.** In groups of three draw up a list of five things—foods, activities, and habits—that may be harmful to your health. Meet with another group to discuss your lists. See how many items you have in common. After your discussion come up with a final list of five items both teams agree on.

292 CAPÍTULO 10

FOR THE YOUNGER STUDENT

1. Have students make colorful get-well cards using some of the expressions they have learned. If someone they know is ill, they can send him/her the cards.
2. Students may work in teams to create a composite "monster." They cut out scrap paper and use markers to make body parts, one per member, including facial features as well as limbs, torsos, hair, etc. They should label the back of each cutout in Spanish. Collect the cutouts and put them in a bag. Call on students one at a time to draw out one body part and pin it to the bulletin board to create a "monster."

Reintegración

LA FAMILIA SALAS PUIG

José Salas Puig vive en Caracas, Venezuela. Su familia tiene un departamento muy bonito en la zona elegante de El Este. José y sus padres son de Venezuela. Son venezolanos. Pero sus abuelos no son de Venezuela. Son de España. Sus abuelos maternos, los Puig, son de Cataluña. Viven en Barcelona. El apellido Puig es un apellido muy catalán.

La madre de José es médica. Tiene su consulta en el centro médico. Trabaja también en el Hospital Británico. El padre de José no es médico. Él es biólogo. Trabaja en un laboratorio donde hacen investigaciones médicas. ¿Y José? ¿Va a ser médico? "De ninguna manera", dice él. "Basta ya de medicina y de ciencias". Él va a ser actor o jugador de fútbol.

La familia Salas Puig. Completen.

1. José Salas Puig ___ en Caracas y yo ___ en ___. (vivir)
2. Ellos ___ en un departamento en El Este y nosotros ___ en un(a) ___ en ___. (vivir)
3. Su familia ___ un departamento y nosotros ___ un(a) ___. (tener)
4. José y sus padres ___ de Venezuela y yo ___ de ___. Mis padres ___ de ___. (ser)
5. El padre de José ___ en un laboratorio. ¿Dónde ___ tus padres? (trabajar)
6. El padre de José ___ investigaciones médicas y yo también ___ investigaciones científicas en la clase de biología. (hacer)

Vocabulario

SUSTANTIVOS	el hospital	la dieta	VERBOS
el catarro	la clínica	la vitamina	ser
la gripe	la cama	la proteína	estar
la fiebre	el síntoma	el carbohidrato	
los escalofríos	la alergia	la caloría	estornudar
la garganta	la diagnosis	la fibra	examinar
la cabeza	el ejercicio		recetar
la boca	la farmacia	ADJETIVOS	despachar
el estómago	el/la farmacéutico(a)	cansado(a)	vender
el pecho	la receta	nervioso(a)	toser
el dolor de garganta	la pastilla	triste	abrir
el dolor de cabeza	la píldora	contento(a)	
el/la enfermo(a)	el comprimido	enfermo(a)	OTRAS PALABRAS Y EXPRESIONES
el/la médico(a)	la droga	bien	
el/la enfermero(a)	el medicamento	físico(a)	guardar cama
la consulta	la medicina	aeróbico(a)	de buen humor
el consultorio	la dosis		de mal humor
			me duele

CAPÍTULO 10   **293**

Reintegración

PRESENTATION *(page 293)*

You may wish to have students read the story about the Puig family aloud. You may then ask questions about it.

RECYCLING

Exercise A reviews many verbs students have already learned.

ANSWERS

Some answers will vary.
1. vive, vivo, ___
2. viven, vivimos, ___ , ___
3. tiene, tenemos, ___
4. son, soy, ___/son ___
5. trabaja, trabajan
6. hace, hago

Vocabulario

There are approximately 19 cognates included in this *Vocabulario* list.

INTRODUCCIÓN   (0:36:54)

LA FARMACIA   (0:37:48)

INTRODUCCIÓN   (0:39:00)

LA CONSULTA   (0:39:52)

Topics	Functions	Structure	Culture
Summer weather Summer leisure activities	How to describe summer weather How to talk about summer sports and activities How to relate actions and events that took place in the past How to refer to persons and things already mentioned	El pretérito de los verbos en *-ar* Los pronombres de complemento directo El pretérito de los verbos *ir* y *ser*	Visiting beaches in Spanish-speaking countries Summer resorts La playa Sol Caribe in Cozumel, Mexico Templo de los Guerreros in Chichén Itzá, Mexico; Viña del Mar, Chile

CAPÍTULO 11

Situation Cards

The Situation Cards simulate real-life situations that require students to communicate in Spanish, exactly as though they were in a Spanish-speaking country. The Situation Cards operate on the assumption that the person to whom the message is to be conveyed understands no English. Therefore, students must focus on producing the Spanish vocabulary and structures necessary to negotiate the situations successfully. For additional information, see the Introduction to the Situation Cards in the Situation Cards Envelope.

Communication Transparency

The illustration seen in this Communication Transparency consists of a synthesis of the two vocabulary (*Palabras 1&2*) presentations found in this chapter. It has been created in order to present this chapter's vocabulary in a new context, and also to recycle vocabulary learned in previous chapters. The Communication Transparency consists of original art. Following are some specific uses:

1. as a cue to stimulate conversation and writing activities
2. for listening comprehension activities
3. to review and reteach vocabulary
4. as a review for chapter and unit tests

CAPÍTULO 11   **A**

You and your Spanish friend Paco are planning to spend a weekend at the beach in Acapulco. Paco is very forgetful. Find out if he has everything he needs for the beach.

Bienvenidos   © Glencoe/McGraw-Hill

© Glencoe/McGraw-Hill

© Glencoe/McGraw-Hill

B

C

D

© Glencoe/McGraw-Hill

Bienvenidos   Chapter 11   Communication Transparency   C-11

Copyright © by Glencoe/McGraw-Hill Publishing Company

CAPÍTULO 11
Print Resources

Lesson Plans	**Pages**

Workbook
- Palabras 1 — 107-109
- Palabras 2 — 110
- Estructura — 111-114
- Un poco más — 115-118
- Mi autobiografía — 119

Communication Activities Masters
- Palabras 1 — 63-64
- Palabras 2 — 65-66
- Estructura — 67-69

5 Bell Ringer Reviews — 28

Chapter Situation Cards A B C D

Chapter Quizzes
- Palabras 1 — 49
- Palabras 2 — 50
- Estructura — 51-53

Testing Program
- Listening Comprehension — 58-59
- Reading and Writing — 60-62
- Proficiency — 127
- Speaking — 147

Nosotros y Nuestro Mundo
- Nuestro Conocimiento Académico *La música*
- Nuestro Idioma *Diptongos*
- Nuestra Cultura *La vida en Latinoamérica*
- Nuestra Literatura *"El grano de oro"* una leyenda
- Nuestra Creatividad
- Nuestras Diversiones

CAPÍTULO 11
Multimedia Resources

CD-ROM Interactive Textbook Disc 3

Chapter 11 Student Edition
- Palabras 1
- Palabras 2
- Estructura
- Conversación
- Lectura y cultura
- Hispanoparlantes
- Realidades
- Culminación
- Prueba

Audio Cassette Program with Student Tape Manual

Cassette	**Pages**
7A Palabras 1	242-243
7A Palabras 2	243-244
7A Estructura	244
7A Conversación	245
7A Pronunciación	245
7A Segunda parte	245-246

Compact Disc Program with Student Tape Manual

- CD 6 Palabras 1 — 242-243
- CD 6 Palabras 2 — 243-244
- CD 6 Estructura — 244
- CD 6 Conversación — 245
- CD 6 Pronunciación — 245
- CD 6 Segunda parte — 245-246

Overhead Transparencies Binder

- Vocabulary 11.1 (A&B); 11.2 (A&B)
- Pronunciation P-11
- Communication C-11
- Maps
- Fine Art (with Blackline Master Activities)

Video Program

- Videocassette
- Video Activities Booklet — 33-35
- Videodisc
- Video Activities Booklet — 33-35

Computer Software (Macintosh, IBM, Apple)

- Practice Disk
  Palabras 1 y 2
  Estructura
- Test Generator Disk
  Chapter Test
  Customized Test

CHAPTER OVERVIEW

In this chapter students will learn to describe summer weather as well as several types of summer sports. Students will also learn to express what they did in the past and to refer back to persons and things already mentioned. In order to do this, they will learn vocabulary associated with warm-weather activities, the preterite of *-ar* verbs, and the object pronouns *lo, la, los, las*. The cultural focus of Chapter 11 is on the extent and beauty of summer resorts in the Spanish-speaking world.

CHAPTER OBJECTIVES

By the end of this chapter students will know:

1. vocabulary associated with leisure time, especially summer seaside activities, and some sports
2. summer weather expressions
3. the preterite of *-ar* verbs
4. the preterite of *ir* and *ser*
5. the direct object pronouns *lo, la, los, las*
6. the names, location, and fame of many resorts in the Spanish-speaking world

Pacing

Chapter 11 will require about eight to ten days. However, pacing will vary according to the length of the class, the age of your students, and student aptitude.

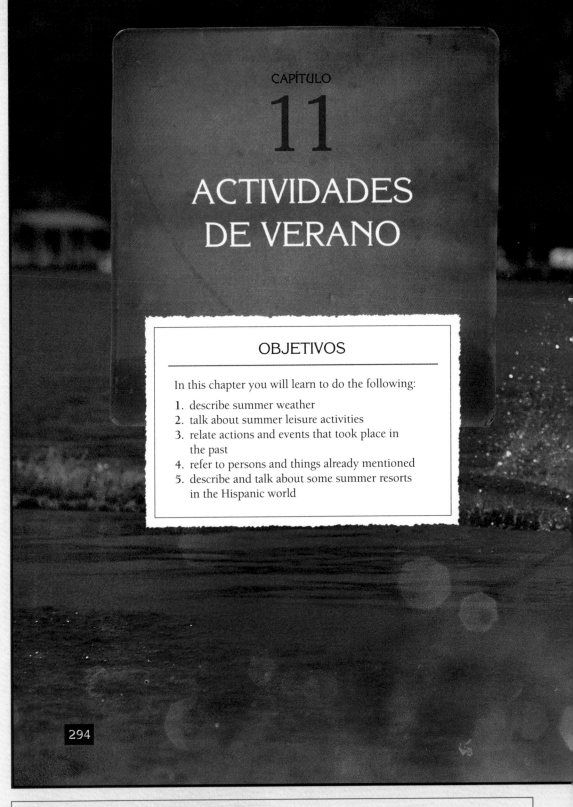

CAPÍTULO

11

ACTIVIDADES DE VERANO

OBJETIVOS

In this chapter you will learn to do the following:

1. describe summer weather
2. talk about summer leisure activities
3. relate actions and events that took place in the past
4. refer to persons and things already mentioned
5. describe and talk about some summer resorts in the Hispanic world

294

CHAPTER PROJECTS

(Optional)

1. Have students share their family's vacation experiences by bringing in photos and vacation memorabilia. You may wish to group students according to where they go on vacation (mountains, beach, camping, city), and have each group tell as much as they can about their vacation there.

2. Have groups plan the ideal four-week vacation trip through a region of their choice in Spain or Latin America.

295

LEARNING FROM PHOTOS

Ask students to tell all they can about the young woman and what she is doing. Some words they may want to know are:
el chaleco salvavidas (life jacket), *el cable de arrastre* (tow line), *el esquí acuático, el mono-squí, la empuñadora.*

Vocabulary Teaching Resources

1. Vocabulary Transparencies 11.1 (A & B)
2. Audio Cassette 7A
3. Student Tape Manual, pages 242–243
4. Workbook, pages 107–109
5. Communication Activities Masters, pages 63-64, *A & B*
6. Chapter Quizzes, page 49, *Palabras 1*

Bell Ringer Review

Write the following on the board or use BRR Blackline Master 11-1: In a brief paragraph, describe typical winter weather in your area.

PRESENTATION
(pages 296–297)

A. Show Vocabulary Transparencies 11.1 (A & B). Point to individual items and have the class repeat the words after you.
B. As an option, you may wish to bring in some props such as sunglasses, suntan lotion, etc.
C. During your presentation ask questions such as the following: *¿Es la playa? ¿Qué es? ¿Es el mar o la arena? ¿Hay arena en la playa? ¿Son olas? ¿Qué son? ¿Dónde hay olas?*

RECYCLING

In this section the concept of *-ar* verbs is reinforced with the new verbs *pasar, usar, bucear, nadar, alquilar,* and *brillar.* In addition, the verbs *tomar* and *esquiar* are recycled.

VOCABULARIO

PALABRAS 1

EL BALNEARIO

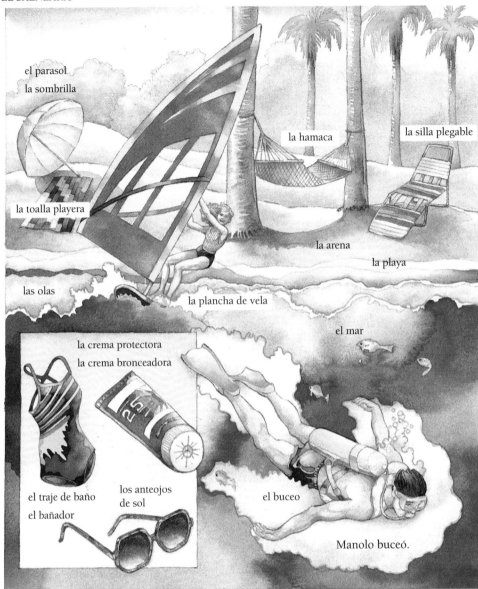

el parasol
la sombrilla
la hamaca
la silla plegable
la toalla playera
la arena
la playa
las olas
la plancha de vela
el mar
la crema protectora
la crema bronceadora
el traje de baño
el bañador
los anteojos de sol
el buceo
Manolo buceó.

TOTAL PHYSICAL RESPONSE

(following the Vocabulary presentation)

TPR 1

___, levántate y ven acá, por favor.
Vas a ir a la playa, pero antes…
Ponte el traje de baño, por favor.
Ponte la crema bronceadora.
Ponte más crema aquí en la cara. *(Point.)*
Ponte los anteojos de sol.

Aquí, toma la sombrilla.
A ver si está dañada. Abre la sombrilla, por favor.
Y toma esta silla plegable.
Ábrela, por favor.
Haz los gestos apropiados.
Nada.
Toma el sol.
Esquía en el agua.
Haz la plancha de vela.
Muy bien, ___. Gracias y siéntate, por favor.

el esquí acuático

Anita nadó.

Paco esquió en el agua.

el fin de semana

SÁBADO DOMINGO

Ayer Gloria fue a la playa.
Ella pasó el fin de semana en la playa.
Ella lo pasó muy bien.
Usó crema protectora.
Tomó el sol.
Tomó (echó) una siesta en la hamaca.

La muchacha alquiló un barquito.

En el verano hace calor.
Hay sol.
El sol brilla en el cielo.

A veces hay nubes.
Cuando hay nubes, está nublado.
A veces hace viento. Llueve.

DRAMATIZATION

You may wish to have students dramatize the following words or expressions: *nadar, esquiar en el agua, tomar el sol, abrir un tubo de crema protectora.*

Vocabulary Expansion

You may give students this additional beach vocabulary:
la tabla hawaiana
correr las olas

INFORMAL ASSESSMENT
(Palabras 1)

Show magazine pictures that depict different types of weather. Have students describe the pictures to the best of their ability.

TPR 2

(Show a picture of a person with a sunburn.)
___, levántate y ven acá, por favor.
Mírate, mi vida. No estás bronceado(a).
    Estás quemado(a).
Ven acá al cuarto de baño.
Quítate los anteojos de sol.
Mírate en el espejo.
Abre el grifo. *(Dramatize. They don't know grifo, "faucet.")*
Lávate la cara con agua fría.

Y ahora, abre el botiquín *(medicine cabinet).*
Saca del botiquín una botella de crema para
    quemaduras.
Ponte la crema en la cara.
Muy bien. Tapa la botella.
Ponla en el botiquín.
Apaga la luz.
Y la próxima vez en la playa, ten más
    cuidado.
Gracias, ___. Ve a tu asiento y siéntate, por
    favor.

Ejercicios

PRESENTATION

(page 298)

Ejercicio A

Exercise A can be done with books open or closed. After going over the exercise once with the entire class, you may wish to repeat it as a group activity. Student 1 reads the question, Student 2 gives the cue, and Student 3 responds. Students can alternate roles with each item.

Expansion of *Ejercicio A*

Upon completion of the exercise, one student can tell all about Gloria in his/her own words.

Note All exercises in the *Vocabulario* section ask students to use only the third person forms of the preterite of *-ar* verbs. Students know these forms from the vocabulary presentation. The preterite will be taught in the *Estructura* section of this chapter. Students will learn to manipulate the preterite forms so that they can tell what they and/or others did.

Ejercicio B

Have students look at the illustrations and respond.

ANSWERS

Ejercicio A
1. Gloria fue a la playa.
2. Fue el viernes.
3. Pasó el fin de semana en la playa.
4. Nadó en el mar.
5. Usó crema protectora.
6. Sí, tomó el sol.
7. Alquiló un barquito.
8. Sí, esquió en el agua.
9. Lo pasó muy bien en la playa.

Ejercicio B
1. Compró unos anteojos de sol.
2. Compró una toalla.
3. Compró crema bronceadora.
4. Compró una silla plegable.

Ejercicios

A **¡A la playa!** Contesten según se indica.

1. ¿Adónde fue Gloria? (a la playa)
2. ¿Cuándo fue? (el viernes)
3. ¿Cuánto tiempo pasó en la playa? (el fin de semana)
4. ¿Dónde nadó? (en el mar)
5. ¿Qué usó? (crema protectora)
6. ¿Tomó el sol? (sí)
7. ¿Qué alquiló? (un barquito)
8. ¿Esquió en el agua? (sí)
9. ¿Cómo lo pasó en la playa? (muy bien)

B **¿Qué compró Lupita?** Contesten según la foto.

Compró…

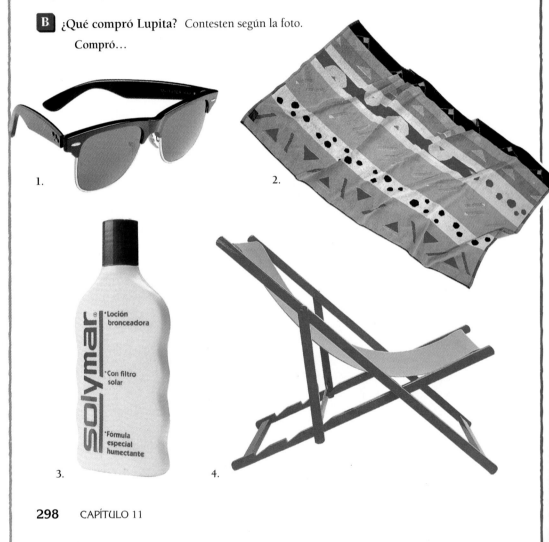

1.

2.

3.

4.

LEARNING FROM REALIA

Have students say all they can about the suntan lotion. You may also wish to ask the following questions: *¿Cuál es el nombre del producto? ¿Por qué tiene ese nombre? ¿Qué tipo de loción es? ¿Tiene filtro solar la loción? ¿Para qué es la "fórmula especial"?*

C ¿Y qué alquiló José? Contesten según la foto.

Alquiló…

1.

2.

3.

4.

D ¿Cuál es la palabra? Completen.

1. Un balneario tiene ___.
2. En la playa hay ___.
3. El Mediterráneo es un ___ y el Caribe es otro ___.
4. En el mar hay ___.
5. En la playa la ___ da protección contra el sol.
6. En el verano hace ___, no hace frío.
7. En el verano hay mucho ___.
8. A veces hay nubes. Cuando hay nubes está ___.
9. A veces también hace ___ y entonces practico la plancha de vela.

PRESENTATION (*page 299*)
Ejercicio C
Have students look at the illustrations and respond.

Ejercicio D
Exercise D is to be done with books open. You may call on one individual to do two items and then move on to someone else.

ANSWERS
Ejercicio C
1. Alquiló un barquito de velas.
2. Alquiló una hamaca.
3. Alquiló un parasol.
4. Alquiló una plancha de vela.

Ejercicio D
1. playa
2. arena
3. mar, mar
4. agua
5. sombrilla
6. calor
7. sol
8. nublado
9. viento

COOPERATIVE LEARNING

Have students work in groups. They will look at Exercise D and make up false statements. For example: *En la playa hay nieve. El Mediterráneo es un océano y el Caribe es otro océano.* The group leader will call on another student to correct the false statement.

INDEPENDENT PRACTICE

Assign any of the following:
1. Workbook, pages 107–109
2. Communication Activities Masters, pages 63-64, *A & B*
3. Exercises on student pages 298–299

Bell Ringer Review

Write the following on the board or use BRR Blackline Master 11-2: Write the names of some things you would need in order to go water skiing.

PRESENTATION
(pages 300–301)

A. Show Vocabulary Transparencies 11.2 (A & B). Point to each item as students repeat the correct word after you two or three times.

B. Give students a word and have them match it with a sport. For example: *la alberca, nadar; el hoyo, jugar (al) golf; la raqueta, jugar al tenis.*

Note To teach the time expressions on the bottom of page 301, write yesterday's date and today's date on the board. Write *hoy* under today's date and *ayer* under yesterday's. Draw an arrow back from *hoy* to *ayer* to indicate past. Write the years for *este año* and *el año pasado.* Then have the class repeat all of the time expressions after you.

LOS DEPORTES

el lago

la piscina
la alberca

la raqueta
la cabeza
el mango
la pelota

el juego de tenis   el tenis

la cancha de tenis

Los amigos jugaron al tenis.   Golpeó la pelota con la raqueta.

TOTAL PHYSICAL RESPONSE

(following the Vocabulary presentation)

TPR 1
___, ven acá, por favor.
Imagínate que vas a jugar al tenis.
Toma la raqueta.
Abre la lata de pelotas.
Cuenta las pelotas.
Dribla o rebota las pelotas.

Rebota una pelota con la raqueta.
Toma una pelota. Sirve.
Gracias, ___. Jugaste muy bien. Y ahora puedes regresar a tu asiento.

TPR 2
___, ven acá.
Aquí tienes tu bolsa de golf. Levanta la bolsa.
Lleva la bolsa al campo de golf.
Toma (saca) un palo de tu bolsa.
Mira el palo.

el green

el campo de golf

el juego de golf
el golf

el palo
el bastón

la bolsa de golf

Golpeó la bola con el bastón.
La bola está en el hoyo.

la bola
la pelota

el hoyo

Nota: To tell about something that happened in the past you may want to use the following expressions:

EL PRESENTE		EL PASADO	
hoy	esta mañana	ayer	el año pasado
esta noche	este año	anoche	la semana pasada
esta tarde	esta semana	ayer por la tarde	anteayer
		ayer por la mañana	

Toma una bola.
Pon la bola en el suelo.
Golpea la bola con el palo.
¡Ah! ¡Qué suerte! La bola entró en el hoyo.
Ve a buscar la bola.
Saca la bola del hoyo.
Gracias, ___. Y ahora siéntate, por favor.

COOPERATIVE LEARNING

Show one of the Vocabulary Transparencies from this chapter. Have students sit in groups. As they look at the Vocabulary Transparencies, they will make up questions informally and in random order. They then call on another group member to respond.

Ejercicios

PRESENTATION (*page 302*)

Ejercicio A

It is suggested that you do Exercise A first with books closed. Change the intonation or pitch of your voice as you give the cue. Call on a student to respond to each item with a complete sentence.

Variation of *Ejercicio A*

Do the exercise a second time. Do not provide the cue and have students come up with the correct word themselves. This is, of course, more challenging and serves as a testing type of activity.

Ejercicios B and C

Exercises B and C must be done with books open.

ANSWERS

Ejercicio A

1. Jugaron al tenis en la cancha de tenis.
2. Jugaron al golf en el campo de golf.
3. Nadaron en la piscina.
4. Golpearon la pelota con la raqueta.
5. Golpearon la pelota con el bastón.
6. En el tenis la pelota pasó por encima de la red.
7. En el golf la bola entró en un hoyo.
8. Los jugadores llevaron los palos en la bolsa de golf.

Ejercicio B

1. la piscina—la natación
2. el palo—el golf
3. la pelota—el golf, el tenis
4. la bola—el golf
5. el hoyo—el golf
6. la raqueta—el tenis
7. la red—el tenis

Ejercicio C

1. una raqueta de tenis
2. unas pelotas de tenis
3. una bolsa de golf
4. unas bolas de golf

302

Ejercicios

A **¿Qué jugaron?** Contesten según se indica.

1. ¿Dónde jugaron al tenis? (en la cancha de tenis)
2. ¿Dónde jugaron al golf? (en el campo de golf)
3. ¿Dónde nadaron? (en la piscina)
4. En el juego de tenis, ¿con qué golpearon la pelota? (la raqueta)
5. En el juego de golf, ¿con qué golpearon la pelota o la bola? (el bastón)
6. ¿En qué juego pasó la pelota por encima de una red? (el tenis)
7. ¿En qué juego entró la bola en un hoyo? (el golf)
8. ¿En qué llevaron los jugadores los palos? (la bolsa de golf)

B **¿Qué deporte es?** Escojan. Escriban en una hoja de papel.

	LA NATACIÓN	EL GOLF	EL TENIS
1. la piscina			
2. el palo			
3. la pelota			
4. la bola			
5. el hoyo			
6. la raqueta			
7. la red			

C **¿Qué compró Eduardo?** Contesten según la foto.

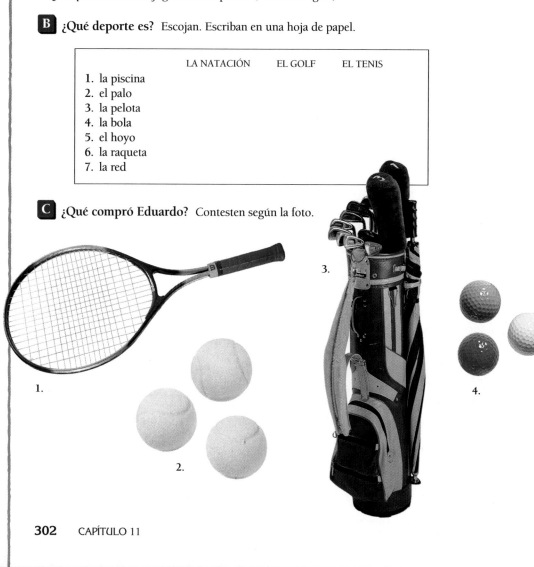

1.

2.

3.

4.

302 CAPÍTULO 11

ADDITIONAL PRACTICE

Have students role-play in pairs. One student plays a foreign student and asks for the following information. The partner provides the answer. Then they switch roles.

1. what the weather is like in the summer in your town
2. if you go to the beach
3. if you swim a lot
4. if you prefer to swim in the ocean or a pool
5. which sports you engage in at the beach

 **D** ¿Cuándo? ¿Hoy o ayer? Contesten según el modelo.

> ¿Hoy?
> *¡Hoy, no! Ayer.*

1. ¿Hoy?
2. ¿Esta semana?
3. ¿Esta noche?
4. ¿Este año?
5. ¿Esta mañana?

Comunicación
Palabras 1 y 2

A ¿Adónde vamos? Together with your partner develop a conversation about plans to go swimming tomorrow. Begin by inviting your partner to go with you. Cover such details as: where to go—pool, lake, or beach; times of departure and return; and things to take along.

B ¿Qué haces? On a separate sheet of paper, fill in the chart for each member in your group, indicating what each person does during each season. When the chart is complete, decide as a group which season is the most active, boring, or interesting. Report to the class.

LAS ESTACIONES			
Primavera	Verano	Otoño	Invierno

C En la playa. Describe three kinds of weather at the beach. Your partner will tell you what he or she likes to do when the day is like that at the beach.

> Estudiante 1: **Hace viento.**
> Estudiante 2: **Cuando hace viento practico la plancha de vela.**

D Dime, por favor. With your partner, develop a list of questions about swimming, then each of you will interview at least two classmates to find out if they go swimming in the summer, when they go, how often, etc. When you finish, compare results.

CAPÍTULO 11 **303**

Structure Teaching Resources

1. Workbook, pages 111–114
2. Student Tape Manual, page 244
3. Audio Cassette 7A
4. Communication Activities Masters, pages 67-69, A–C
5. Chapter Quizzes, pages 51-53, *Estructura*
6. Computer Software, *Estructura*

El pretérito de los verbos en -ar

PRESENTATION (page 304)

A. Have students open their books to page 304. Read grammar step 1 aloud. Then have the class repeat the two example sentences after you.

B. Write the verbs *hablar, tomar,* and *nadar* on the board. Have the class repeat each form after you. After you write the form for one verb on the board, you may wish to have students provide the form for the other verbs. For example, under *hablar,* write *hablé.* Underline the ending. Rather than give the endings for *tomar* and/or *nadar,* ask: If it's *hablé* for *hablar,* what's the form for *tomar? Nadar?* Have students repeat all forms.

C. For step 3, have students look at the examples and note the change in spelling.

D. Have students read the example sentences in step 4.

Note While going over step 3 of the grammar explanation, you may wish to review the following sound/symbol representations:
ca, que, qui, co, cu
ga, gue, gui, go, gu
za, ce, ci, zo, zu

These explain the spelling of *jugó, jugué, buscó, busqué, empezó, empecé.*

304

El pretérito de los verbos en *-ar*   *Describing Past Actions*

1. You use the preterite to express actions that began and ended at a definite time in the past.

   Ayer María pasó el día en la playa.
   Yo, no. Pasé la mañana en la escuela.

2. The preterite of regular *-ar* verbs is formed by dropping the infinitive ending *-ar,* and adding the appropriate endings to the stem. Study the following forms.

INFINITIVE	HABLAR	TOMAR	NADAR	ENDINGS
STEM	habl-	tom-	nad-	
yo	hablé	tomé	nadé	-é
tú	hablaste	tomaste	nadaste	-aste
él, ella, Ud.	habló	tomó	nadó	-ó
nosotros(as)	hablamos	tomamos	nadamos	-amos
vosotros(as)	*hablasteis*	*tomasteis*	*nadasteis*	*-asteis*
ellos, ellas, Uds.	hablaron	tomaron	nadaron	-aron

3. Note that verbs that end in *-gar, -car,* and *-zar* have a spelling change in the *yo* form.

¿Tocaste la guitarra?	Sí, la toqué.
¿Marcaste un tanto?	Sí, marqué un tanto.
¿Llegaste a tiempo?	Sí, llegué a tiempo.
¿Jugaste (al) tenis?	Sí, jugué (al) tenis.
¿Empezaste a jugar?	Sí, empecé a jugar.

4. Study the following examples of the preterite. They all express activities or events that took place at a specific time in the past.

   Ayer María pasó el día en la playa.
   Yo, no. Pasé la mañana en la escuela.
   Pasé la tarde en la piscina donde nadé.
   María nadó y yo nadé. Los dos nadamos.
   Ella nadó en el mar y yo nadé en la piscina.
   Nadamos ayer y anteayer también.

Ejercicios

A Pasó la tarde en la playa. Contesten.

1. Ayer, ¿pasó Rosa la tarde en la playa?
2. ¿Tomó ella mucho sol?
3. ¿Usó crema protectora?
4. ¿Nadó en el mar?
5. ¿Alquiló un barquito?
6. ¿Esquió en el agua?

B ¿Jugaron al tenis? Contesten según se indica.

1. ¿Qué compraron los amigos? (una raqueta)
2. ¿A qué jugaron los jóvenes? (tenis)
3. ¿Jugaron en una cancha cubierta? (no, al aire libre)
4. ¿Golpearon la pelota? (sí)
5. ¿Jugaron individuales (singles) o dobles? (dobles)
6. ¿Quiénes marcaron el primer tanto? (Alicia y José)
7. ¿Quiénes ganaron el partido? (ellos)

Una playa en el Condado, San Juan, Puerto Rico

C ¡A casa! Contesten.

1. Anoche, ¿a qué hora llegaste a casa?
2. ¿Preparaste la comida?
3. ¿Estudiaste?
4. ¿Miraste la televisión?
5. ¿Escuchaste discos?
6. ¿Hablaste por teléfono?
7. ¿Con quién hablaste?

D Pablo, ¿jugaste? Formen preguntas según el modelo.

> ¿Jugó Pablo?
> *No sé. Pablo, ¿jugaste?*

1. ¿Jugó Pablo al baloncesto?
2. ¿Dribló con el balón?
3. ¿Pasó el balón a un amigo?
4. ¿Tiró el balón?
5. ¿Encestó?
6. ¿Marcó un tanto?

EN ABRIL don basket
'FINAL FOUR'
Todo lo que debe saber sobre la fase final del Campeonato de Europa de clubes
VOLKOV
Entrevista con el alero ucraniano, que prepara su regreso a Europa
BASES
Enanos entre gigantes, los bases tienen cada vez más importancia en el éxito de los equipos
CARTWRIGHT
El veterano pivot del Chicago Bulls quiere ganar otra vez el anillo
CAMPEONES
Las mejores fotos de los triunfos del Estudiantes en la Copa del Rey y del Real Madrid en la Copa de Europa
YA EN SU KIOSCO

Ejercicios E and F

Exercises E and F can be done with books closed or open. You may wish to do Exercise F as a paired activity.

Ejercicio G

Exercise G reviews all forms of the preterite of *-ar* verbs. Have students open their books. Call on each student to complete approximately two items. Or allow students to prepare the exercise ahead of time before going over it in class.

Expansion of Ejercicio G

Upon completion of Exercise G, call on one student to retell the entire story in his/her own words.

Ejercicio H

Since Exercise H is a spelling exercise, it need not be done orally. You may wish to use Exercise H as a dictation.

ANSWERS

Ejercicio E

Durante la fiesta mis amigos y yo…

1. … celebramos.
2. … bailamos.
3. … cantamos.
4. … tomamos un refresco.
5. … tomamos fotos.
6. … hablamos.

Ejercicio F

Answers will vary according to the model.

Ejercicio G

1. jugamos
2. pasamos
3. llegué
4. llegaron
5. saqué
6. compraste
7. compré
8. golpeé
9. golpeó
10. voló
11. voló
12. llegó
13. golpeó
14. entró

Ejercicio H

Ayer yo llegué al estadio y empecé a jugar fútbol. Jugué muy bien. No toqué el balón con las manos. Lo lancé con el pie y con la cabeza. Marqué tres tantos.

306

E **Durante la fiesta.** Sigan el modelo.

> celebrar
> *Durante la fiesta mis amigos y yo celebramos.*

1. celebrar
2. bailar
3. cantar
4. tomar un refresco
5. tomar fotos
6. hablar

F **¿Y Uds.? Ayer en la clase de español.** Sigan el modelo.

> **Hablamos mucho en la clase de español.**
> *Y Uds., ¿hablaron también?*

1. Cantamos una canción mexicana.
2. Miramos el mapa.
3. Buscamos la capital de España.
4. Tocamos la guitarra.
5. Tomamos un examen.
6. Escuchamos un disco.

G **Un juego de golf.** Completen.

Ayer, José, sus amigos y yo ____ (jugar) al golf. Nosotros ____ (pasar) la tarde en el campo de golf municipal. Yo ____ (llegar) al campo a las dos y ellos ____ (llegar) a las dos y media. Yo ____ (sacar) mis palos de mi nueva bolsa de golf.

—¿Nueva? ¿Cuándo la ____ (comprar) tú?

—Pues, la ____ (comprar) ayer por la mañana.

Yo ____ (golpear) primero y luego José ____ (golpear). La bola ____ (volar) por el aire y ____ (volar) al green donde ____ (llegar) a tierra. José la ____ (golpear) una vez más y la bola ____ (entrar) en el hoyo.

H **Yo llegué al estadio.** Cambien *nosotros* en *yo*.

Ayer nosotros llegamos al estadio y empezamos a jugar fútbol. Jugamos muy bien. No tocamos el balón con las manos. Lo lanzamos con el pie y con la cabeza. Marcamos tres tantos.

Severiano Ballesteros, golfista español

306 CAPÍTULO 11

LEARNING FROM PHOTOS

Golf is very popular in Spain. Spain boasts a number of world class golf courses. The town of Sotogrande on the Costa del Sol was developed around its world renowned golf course. "Seve" Ballesteros very often plays the course at Sotogrande.

INDEPENDENT PRACTICE

Assign any of the following:
1. Workbook, pages 111–113
2. Communication Activities Masters, page 67, *A*
3. Exercises on student pages 305–306

Los pronombres de complemento directo

Referring to People and Things Already Mentioned

1. Note the following sentences. The words in italics are direct objects. The direct object is the word in the sentence that receives the action of the verb. Note that in Spanish the direct object pronoun comes before the verb.

Elena compró *el boleto*.	Elena *lo* compró.
Compró *los boletos* en la ventanilla.	*Los* compró en la ventanilla.
Elena pone *la crema* en la maleta.	Elena *la* pone en la maleta.
Pone *las toallas* en la maleta.	*Las* pone en la maleta.
Elena conoce *al muchacho*.	Elena *lo* conoce.
Conoce *a los muchachos*.	*Los* conoce.
Roberto conoce *a Elena*.	Roberto *la* conoce.
Conoce *a sus amigas*.	*Las* conoce.

The direct object of each sentence in the first column is a noun. The direct object of each sentence in the second column is a pronoun. Remember that a pronoun is a word that replaces a noun.

2. A direct object pronoun must agree with the noun it replaces. *Lo* replaces a masculine singular noun and *los* replaces a masculine plural noun. *La* replaces a feminine singular noun and *las* a feminine plural noun. The pronouns *lo, la, los,* and *las* replace either a person or a thing.

Elena alquiló *el barquito*.	Elena *lo* alquiló.
Elena ve *a sus amigas*.	Elena *las* ve.

3. Note the placement of the direct object pronoun in a negative sentence. It cannot be separated from the verb by the negative word.

   Elena no *lo* compró.
   Rafael no *la* usó.

Los pronombres de complemento directo

PRESENTATION *(page 307)*

A. Write several of the example sentences from step 1 on the board. Draw a box around the noun object. Circle the pronoun object. Then draw a line from the box to the circle. This visual technique helps many students grasp the concept that one word replaces the other.

B. Have students open their books to page 307. Instead of providing, or having students read the information in step 2, you may wish to have students come up with answers. Does *lo* replace a masculine or a feminine noun? What pronoun replaces a feminine noun?

C. Now lead students through step 3 on page 307.

DEBIDO A UNA ESCASEZ MUNDIAL DE VIENTO TODO LO QUE HACEMOS ES POR UNA RAZON CONCRETA

CAPÍTULO 11 **307**

FOR THE NATIVE SPEAKER

Sometimes students confuse the article with the direct object pronoun. Provide additional practice. For each of the following sentences, have students underline the article(s) once, and the direct object pronoun(s) twice.

1. *Ella nunca los compró.*
2. *Yo la vi haciendo las compras.*
3. *Y ella sí que los miró y los tocó, pero no los compró.*
4. *Ella también miró la cámara, pero no la compró.*
5. *Ella no la compró, pero el hermano la compró.*
6. *Él se interesó en un televisor y lo compró.*

Ejercicios A–D

All these exercises can be done with books closed or open.

Ejercicio A

Have students pretend they are handing the items to someone as they say *Aquí lo tienes.*

ANSWERS

Ejercicio A
1. Aquí lo tienes.
2. Aquí lo tienes.
3. Aquí lo tienes.
4. Aquí la tienes.
5. Aquí la tienes.
6. Aquí los tienes.
7. Aquí los tienes.
8. Aquí los tienes.
9. Aquí las tienes.
10. Aquí las tienes.

Ejercicio B
1. Sí, la compró.
2. Sí, la compró.
3. Sí, los compró.
4. Sí, lo compró.
5. Sí, la compró.
6. Sí, las compró.
7. Sí, la compró.
8. Sí, los compró.

Ejercicio C
1. Sí, la alquiló.
2. Sí, los alquiló.
3. Sí, los alquiló.
4. Sí, lo alquiló.
5. Sí, la alquiló.
6. Sí, la alquiló.

Ejercicio D
Answers will vary.
1. Sí (No), (no) los tengo.
2. Sí (No), (no) los tengo.
3. Sí (No), (no) la tengo.
4. Sí (No), (no) lo pongo.
5. Sí (No), (no) las pongo.
6. Sí (No), (no) las llevo, ([no] las alquilo allí).
7. Sí (No), (no) la alquilo.

Ejercicios

A **Aquí lo tienes.** Sigan el modelo.

> **¿El bañador?**
> *Aquí lo tienes.*

1. ¿El bañador?
2. ¿El traje de baño?
3. ¿El tubo de crema?
4. ¿La toalla?
5. ¿La crema bronceadora?
6. ¿Los anteojos de sol?
7. ¿Los boletos?
8. ¿Los esquís?
9. ¿Las toallas playeras?
10. ¿Las raquetas?

B **Él lo compró.** Sigan el modelo.

> **la toalla**
> *Sí, la compró.*

1. la crema bronceadora
2. la toalla playera
3. los anteojos de sol
4. el traje de baño
5. la bolsa de golf
6. las bolas
7. la raqueta
8. los palos de golf

C **Ella lo alquiló.** Sigan el modelo.

> **¿El barquito?**
> *Sí, lo alquiló.*

1. ¿La plancha de vela?
2. ¿Los esquís?
3. ¿Los palos?
4. ¿El equipo para el buceo?
5. ¿La sombrilla?
6. ¿La hamaca?

D **Sí, los tengo.** Contesten con el pronombre.

1. ¿Tienes los boletos para entrar en la playa?
2. ¿Tienes los anteojos de sol?
3. ¿Tienes la crema bronceadora?
4. ¿Pones el tubo en la bolsa?
5. ¿Pones las toallas en la bolsa también?
6. ¿Llevas las sillas plegables a la playa o las alquilas allí?
7. ¿Alquilas la sombrilla?

En la playa en Tulum, México

COOPERATIVE LEARNING

For additional practice have students work in groups as they redo Exercise B.

E1: ___, ¿compraste la crema bronceadora?
E2: Sí, la compré.
E1: ¿Dónde la compraste?
E2: La compré en ___.
E1: ¿Cuánto te costó?
E2: Me costó ___. (or) Pagué ___.

LEARNING FROM PHOTOS

Tulum, on the coast of Yucatán, is one of the most impressive Mayan ruins. Sixty structures built between the 12th and 15th centuries still stand. Tulum means "City of the New Dawn." When Cortés arrived in 1519, Tulum was the only Mayan city that was still inhabited. Many people who vacation in Cancún rent a car or take an excursion to Tulum.

El pretérito de los verbos *ir* y *ser*   *Describing Past Actions*

1. The verbs *ir* and *ser* are irregular in the preterite tense. Note that they have identical forms.

INFINITIVE	IR	SER
yo	fui	fui
tú	fuiste	fuiste
él, ella, Ud.	fue	fue
nosotros(as)	fuimos	fuimos
vosotros(as)	*fuisteis*	*fuisteis*
ellos, ellas, Uds.	fueron	fueron

2. The context in which each verb is used in the sentence will clarify the meaning. The verb *ser* is not used very often in the preterite.

> El Sr. Martínez fue profesor de español.
> Él fue a España.

> Mi abuelo fue médico.
> Mi abuelo fue al médico.

Ejercicios

A **¿Adónde fuiste ayer?** Preguntas personales.

1. Ayer, ¿fuiste a la escuela?
2. ¿Fuiste a la playa?
3. ¿Fuiste a la piscina?
4. ¿Fuiste al campo de fútbol?
5. ¿Fuiste a la cancha de tenis?
6. ¿Fuiste a las montañas?
7. ¿Fuiste a casa?
8. ¿Fuiste a la tienda?

B **Fui a la escuela.** Contesten.

1. ¿Fuiste a la escuela ayer?
2. ¿Fue tu amigo también?
3. ¿Fueron juntos?
4. ¿Fueron en carro?
5. ¿Fue también la hermana de tu amigo?
6. ¿Fue ella en carro o a pie?

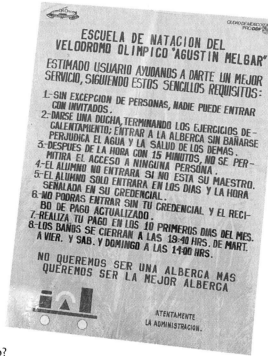

CAPÍTULO 11   **309**

CONVERSACIÓN

PRESENTATION *(page 310)*

A. Tell students they are going to hear a conversation between two young women, Elena and Carmen.

B. Have students close their books. Read the conversation to them or play Cassette 7A.

C. Have the class repeat the conversation once or twice in unison.

D. Call on pairs to read the conversation. Encourage them to be as animated as possible. Change the names of the characters to boy's names.

E. Have pairs act out the conversation for the class allowing them to make any changes that make sense.

Ejercicio

ANSWERS

1. **Carmen fue a la playa.**
2. **No, no invitó a Elena (no la invitó).**
3. **Sí, trató de invitar a Elena.**
4. **Sí, la llamó por teléfono.**
5. **No, Elena no contestó.**
6. **Ella fue a casa de Paco.**
7. **Ellos (Elena y Paco) nadaron en la piscina.**
8. **Carmen nadó en el mar.**

AUDITORY DISCRIMINATION

Give students the following directions in order to practice auditory discrimination: Listen to what I have to say. If it is in the present, raise one hand. If it is in the past, raise both hands. *Hablo, Nadó, Esquío, Miro, Miró, Compro, Pagó.*

Escenas de la vida   *La tarde en la playa*

ELENA: ¿Adónde fuiste ayer?
CARMEN: Pues, fui a la playa.

ELENA: ¿Fuiste a la playa y no me invitaste?
CARMEN: Pues, te llamé por teléfono pero no contestaste.

ELENA: ¡Verdad! Fui a casa de Paco. Nadamos en su piscina.
CARMEN: Pues, Uds. nadaron en la piscina y yo nadé en el mar.

 En la playa.   Contesten.

1. ¿Adónde fue Carmen?
2. ¿Invitó a Elena?
3. ¿Trató de invitar a Elena?
4. ¿La llamó por teléfono?
5. ¿Contestó Elena?
6. ¿Adónde fue ella?
7. ¿Dónde nadaron Elena y Paco?
8. ¿Y dónde nadó Carmen?

310   CAPÍTULO 11

COOPERATIVE LEARNING

Have students work in pairs and make up a conversation using the same type of questions as in the *Conversación* on page 310, but changing the situation to winter and skiing.

INDEPENDENT PRACTICE

Assign any of the following:
1. Workbook, pages 113–114
2. Communication Activities Masters, pages 68–69, B–C
3. Exercises on student pages 309–310

Pronunciación   *La consonante* r

The Spanish trilled **r** sound does not exist in English. When a word begins with an **r** (initial position), the **r** is trilled. Within a word double **r** (rr) is also pronounced as a trilled sound.

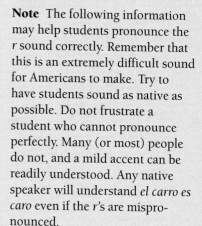

ra	re	ri	ro	ru
raqueta	refresco	Ricardo	Roberto	Rubén
rápido	receta	rico	rojo	ruta

The sound for a single **r** within a word (medial position) does not exist in English either. It is trilled less than the initial **r** or **rr**.

ra	re	ri	ro	ru
parasol	arena	balneario	miro	Aruba
playera	moreno	María	enfermero	Perú

El perrito lleva un parasol rojo.

Repeat the following sentences.

> Rápido corren los carros del ferrocarril.
> La señorita puertorriqueña lleva el parasol rojo al balneario.
> El perrito de Roberto corre en la arena.

Comunicación

A **¿Adónde fuiste?** Ask your partner if he or she went to each of the places on the list last summer. If he or she did, then ask for the specific place. If your partner didn't go there, ask why not. Reverse roles.

> la playa
> Estudiante 1: ¿Fuiste a la playa el verano pasado?
> Estudiante 2: Sí.
> Estudiante 1: ¿A qué playa fuiste?
> Estudiante 2: Fui a Myrtle Beach.

1. la piscina
2. el mar
3. las montañas
4. el campo
5. el lago
6. el campo de golf
7. la playa

En los Pirineos en España

B **En el verano.** Work in groups of four. Each member of your group will list three things that he or she does during the summer. Together, decide what it is that most of the members do, and what is the most interesting thing on the lists. Assign one member of the group to report to the class.

CAPÍTULO 11   **311**

Pronunciación

PRESENTATION *(page 311)*

Note The following information may help students pronounce the *r* sound correctly. Remember that this is an extremely difficult sound for Americans to make. Try to have students sound as native as possible. Do not frustrate a student who cannot pronounce perfectly. Many (or most) people do not, and a mild accent can be readily understood. Any native speaker will understand *el carro es caro* even if the *r*'s are mispronounced.

A. The Spanish *r* sound does not exist in English. A single *r* in medial position is pronounced like a soft *t* in English. The tongue hits the upper part of the mouth in a position similar to when we say "a lot of" (a lotta) very quickly in English.

B. Have students play a game trying to trill the initial *r* or the *rr.* Let them exaggerate as much as they wish and they may get it right.

Comunicación

PRESENTATION

Although we want students to speak freely in these cooperative and communicative activities, they must be based on what students can realistically say based on their knowledge of the language. Since they now know the preterite of *-ar* verbs, they can discuss past events that call for *-ar* verbs. We must be careful not to give activities that would be impossible for students to do, such as discussing a past event that would necessitate the use of *comer*, irregular verbs, or the imperfect. These *Comunicación* activities incorporate all previously learned material, but do not frustrate students by leading them into errors that are beyond their control.

ANSWERS

Actividades A and B
Answers will vary.

LECTURA Y CULTURA

LAS PLAYAS DE LOS PAÍSES HISPANOS

¿Viajar por los países de habla española y no pasar unos días en un balneario? ¡Imposible! Sólo hay que (tiene que) mirar un mapa para ver que en el mundo hispano no faltan[1] playas famosas—famosas aun entre los "jet-setters".

La playa de Luquillo, Puerto Rico

En el verano, cuando hace calor y el sol brilla en el cielo, que en algunos lugares como México, Puerto Rico y Venezuela es todo el año—mucha gente acude o va a los balnearios. Nadan en el mar o sólo toman el sol para volver (regresar) a casa muy tostaditos o bronceados. Los tipos más deportivos esquían en el agua o practican la plancha de vela o la tabla hawaiiana, o como dicen muchos el "surfing". Pero cuidado, si nadas o si esquías en el agua es muy importante usar una crema protectora. Los rayos del sol pueden causar cáncer de la piel.

Los balnearios ofrecen una gran variedad de diversiones[2] como, por ejemplo, casinos, discotecas, canchas de tenis y campos de golf. En fin, hay de todo[3] para todos.

Y tú, el año pasado, ¿nadaste en las aguas cristalinas de Luquillo en Puerto Rico? ¿Practicaste la tabla hawaiiana en la Playa Brava de Punta del Este, Uruguay? ¿Alquilaste un yate en el elegante Club de pescadores en Marbella, España? ¿Bailaste hasta la medianoche en una discoteca de Acapulco? ¿No? Pues, ¿por que no practicas un poquito más[4] el español? Y el año que viene—¡a la playa a disfrutar[5]!

[1] no faltan *aren't lacking*
[2] diversiones *amusements*
[3] todo *everything*
[4] un poquito más *a little more*
[5] disfrutar *to enjoy*

Punta del Este, Uruguay

LEARNING FROM PHOTOS

1. The beach of Luquillo is probably the most scenic in all of Puerto Rico. The water is always calm because the beach is in a cove.

2. Punta del Este is located on a peninsula. Playa Mansa is on the west side where the water is always calm, and Playa Brava is to the east where the water is always turbulent. In Playa Mansa the beachgoers are able to waterski, but in Playa Brava waterskiing is impossible. Punta del Este has a famous golf course where many international tournaments take place.

Estudio de palabras

A Palabras afines. Busquen doce palabras afines en la lectura.

B ¿Qué significa? Busquen la palabra que significa lo mismo.

1. famoso	a. regresar
2. el lugar	b. célebre
3. acude	c. claro
4. tostadito	d. bronceado
5. ofrece	e. el sitio, la localidad
6. cristalino	f. las doce de la noche
7. la medianoche	g. va
8. volver	h. da, provee
9. de habla española	i. donde la gente habla español
10. hay que	j. es necesario

Comprensión

A Los errores. Corrijan las oraciones falsas.

1. Hay pocas playas en el mundo hispano.
2. Hace calor en el invierno.
3. Los balnearios están en la costa.
4. Las diversiones son cosas serias.
5. Él está muy tostado porque toma mucho sol.

B De vacaciones. Completen.

1. Los balnearios tienen ___ bonitas.
2. Los jóvenes bailan en una ___.
3. Juegan al tenis en ___.
4. Juegan al golf en ___.

C Informes. Contesten.

1. ¿Cuáles son los nombres de cuatro playas famosas de los países hispanos?
2. ¿En qué país está cada playa?
3. ¿Cuáles son algunas diversiones que ofrecen los balnearios?

CAPÍTULO 11 **313**

Estudio de palabras

PRESENTATION *(page 313)*

Ejercicio B

After going over Exercise B you may wish to have students use the words in original sentences. This is a rather difficult activity so you may wish to call on talented students.

ANSWERS

Ejercicio A

pasar, mapa, hawaiana, rayos, causar, cáncer, diversiones, casinos, discotecas, cristalinas, yate, imposible

Ejercicio B

1. b
2. e
3. g
4. d
5. h
6. c
7. f
8. a
9. i
10. j

Comprensión

ANSWERS

Comprensión A

1. falsa (Hay muchas playas en el mundo hispano.)
2. falsa (Hace calor en verano.)
3. verdad
4. falsa (Las diversiones son cosas divertidas.)
5. verdad

Comprensión B

1. playas
2. discoteca
3. la cancha de tenis
4. el campo de golf

Comprensión C

1. Luquillo, Playa Brava, Marbella, Acapulco
2. Puerto Rico, Uruguay, España, México
3. casinos, discotecas, canchas de tenis, campo de golf

CRITICAL THINKING ACTIVITY

(Thinking skills: decision making, evaluating consequences)

Write the following on the board or on an overhead transparency:

1. *Maripaz va a la playa. Pero ella sabe que cada vez que va a la playa, no vuelve bronceada. Vuelve quemada. Es un problema para ella. Por consiguiente, ella debe comprar una crema protectora muy fuerte. Ella tiene 1.000 pesos. Quiere comprar un par de anteojos de sol que son fabulosos. Pero si ella compra los anteojos, no va a tener bastante dinero para comprar la crema protectora. ¿Qué debe ella hacer?*

2. *La tentación sale victoriosa. Maripaz compró los anteojos de sol y ella no va a cambiar sus planes. Va a ir a la playa. ¿Cuáles pueden ser las consecuencias de su decisión?*

3. *¿Qué otras alternativas tiene Maripaz?*

PRESENTATION

(pages 314–315)

The information in this section covers a vast part of the globe. You may wish to have students indicate each place on a map.

ABOUT THE LANGUAGE

Paella is actually the name of the pan *(paellera)* in which the meal is prepared, but over time the dish prepared in the pan *(paella)* has taken the name. Students will learn more about *paella* and Spanish cuisine in Level 2 of this series, *A bordo,* Chapter 9.

GEOGRAPHY CONNECTION

Acapulco is one of the oldest and most famous resorts in Mexico. Its full name is *Acapulco de Juárez.* Have students locate it on the map on page 475.

DESCUBRIMIENTO CULTURAL

*E*s verdad que el mundo hispano es famoso por sus playas. La costa occidental de México tiene playas desde Baja California hasta Oaxaca. En el Caribe, en el este, hay playas famosas en Cozumel y Cancún. Y si los turistas no quieren pasar sus vacaciones enteras en la playa, pueden ir a visitar las ruinas mayas en la península de Yucatán.

Puerto Rico, una isla tropical en el Caribe, tiene playas fabulosas. Rincón es el lugar de los campeonatos de tabla hawaiiana o surfing. Rincón está en la costa occidental de Puerto Rico en el canal de la Mona que está entre Puerto Rico y la República Dominicana. Si uno tiene suerte, puede ver desde las playas de esta región las ballenas[1] que saltan[2] del agua.

Punta del Este es un balneario famoso del Uruguay. Punta del Este está en una península muy estrecha[3]. En la península hay pinos y eucaliptos a lo largo de toda la costa. En Punta del Este hay mansiones y condominios de gran lujo. ¿De quiénes son estas residencias fabulosas? La mayoría son de los millonarios argentinos y brasileños que pasan sus vacaciones allí. En el campo de golf de Punta del Este hay frecuentemente campeonatos internacionales.

Cerca de Punta del Este está la isla de Lobos. Es una reserva natural del gobierno uruguayo. En esta isla viven más de 500.000 lobos de mar. La isla está realmente cubierta de lobos de mar. Es una palabra interesante porque en inglés decimos "sea lions", leones, pero en español son lobos o "wolves".

Juan Ashton, surfista puertorriqueño

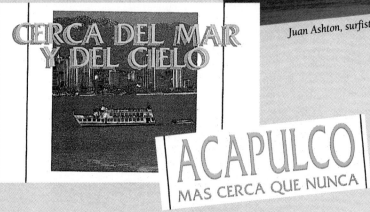

LEARNING FROM PHOTOS

Ask students: *¿En qué playa está Juan Ashton probablemente? (Rincón)*

La playa Montaña de Oro, California

Una paella valenciana

Ya sabemos que muchos habitantes de Puerto Montt son de origen alemán. En la región de Punta del Este y Montevideo, que está muy cerca, hay mucha gente de ascendencia italiana.

Y en España hay playas a lo largo de la costa. En España, si vas a la playa, tienes que comer una paella. ¿Qué es la paella? Es un plato con arroz y muchos mariscos: camarones[4], mejillones[5], almejas[6], langostas[7], etc. La paella es originaria de Valencia, en la costa oriental de España.

Y AQUÍ EN LOS ESTADOS UNIDOS

Todas estas playas están en los EE.UU. ¿Sabes dónde están? Sólo necesitas un mapa de California y de la Florida: Bahía Honda, Trinidad, Pescadero, San Agustín, Cañaveral, Bonita, San Clemente, el Capitán, Ponte Vedra, Laguna, el Presidio de Santa Bárbara, Atascadero, Montaña de Oro.

Ahora sabes dónde están. ¿Sabes qué quieren decir los nombres?

[1] ballenas *whales*
[2] saltan *jump out*
[3] estrecha *narrow*
[4] camarones *shrimp*
[5] mejillones *mussels*
[6] almejas *clams*
[7] langostas *lobster*

R E A L I D A D E S

(The Realidades is optional material.)

PRESENTATION
(pages 316–317)

A. Have students sit back and enjoy the beautiful photographs as they read the information about them in the captions on page 316.

B. You may wish to tell your students that the thatched roof structure seen in **photo 1** is a *bohío*.

Vamos a la playa Sol Caribe en Cozumel, México **1**. Podemos pasar nuestras vacaciones de verano aquí. La playa es maravillosa.

Son condominios en Punta del Este, Uruguay **2**. ¿Por qué no rentas uno?

En Viña del Mar, Chile, también puedes pasar unas vacaciones de verano fabulosas **3**. Pero si quieres ir a la playa para nadar, tienes que ir en diciembre porque Chile está en el hemisferio sur.

Es el templo de los Guerreros en Chichén Itzá **4**. Este centro arqueológico maya está en la península de Yucatán.

316

3

4

317

INDEPENDENT PRACTICE

1. Workbook, *Un poco más,* pages 115–118
2. Student page 313

Comunicación oral
(page 318)

ANSWERS

Actividad A
 Answers will vary.

Actividades B and C
 Answers will vary according to the model.

Comunicación escrita

ANSWERS

Actividades A and B
 Answers will vary.

Comunicación oral

A **De compras.** You are getting ready for a trip to the beach. With your partner make a list of the things you have to buy. Then decide what stores you will go to. At the stores, you and your partner alternate as store clerk and customer in some brief conversations.

B **No, porque. . .** Ask if your partner wants to do the following things this weekend. Your partner is going to play hard to please by saying no and giving a reason.

> jugar al tenis
> Estudiante 1: ¿Quieres jugar al tenis este fin de semana?
> Estudiante 2: No, porque jugué mucho ayer.

1. jugar (al) golf
2. nadar
3. ir a la piscina
4. esquiar en el agua
5. patinar

En la playa en Chile

C **Mi deporte favorito.** Pick your favorite sport and describe it, but incorrectly. Your partner will try to catch the error and then correct your description.

> Estudiante 1: En el fútbol los jugadores tocan el balón con las manos.
> Estudiante 2: De ninguna manera. Los jugadores tocan el balón con los pies o con la cabeza.

Comunicación escrita

A **En el lago.** Write a paragraph about a day you spent at a beach, lake, or pool. Some verbs you may want to use are:

ir	pasar	llamar por teléfono
llegar	nadar	ir a una discoteca
tomar el sol	broncear	bailar
llevar	esquiar en el agua	invitar
alquilar	bucear	escuchar
tomar un refresco	descansar	
tomar una siesta	tomar fotos	

B **Mi diario.** You spent your vacation in Acapulco, Mexico. Write a letter to a friend telling him or her what you did and what you bought.

FOR THE YOUNGER STUDENT

1. Have students draw a map of Spain. On the coastal areas have them write the names of famous beaches. They should highlight these locations by drawing figures of people engaged in various water sports. When finished, students can write a paragraph explaining what is on their map.

2. The same thing can be done for Mexico.
3. Have students draw a beach scene on a piece of paper the size of a postcard. They should include figures to represent themselves. On the back of the paper, have them write to a friend telling about their vacation at the beach.

Reintegración

A **El invierno.** Describan el tiempo en el invierno.

B **Actividades de invierno.** Empleen (usen) cada palabra en una oración.

1. esquiar
2. la pista
3. los esquís
4. el telesquí
5. patinar
6. los patines

C **Tu salud.** Contesten.

1. ¿Cómo estás hoy?
2. ¿Estás cansado(a) o no?
3. ¿Tienes catarro?
4. ¿Tienes tos?
5. Cuando tienes catarro, ¿estornudas mucho?
6. ¿Tienes dolor de garganta?
7. Cuando tienes catarro, ¿te duele el pecho?
8. Si comes algo malo, ¿te duele el estómago?

Vocabulario

SUSTANTIVOS

la playa
el balneario
la arena
el mar
la ola
la sombrilla
el parasol
la hamaca
la silla plegable
la toalla playera
la crema bronceadora
la crema protectora
el traje de baño
el bañador
los anteojos de (para el) sol
el esquí acuático
el barquito
el buceo
la plancha de vela
el fin de semana
la piscina
la alberca
el lago

el verano
el calor
el sol
el cielo

el viento
la nube

el tenis
la cancha de tenis
el juego de tenis
la pelota
la raqueta
el mango
la cabeza
el golf
el campo de golf
el juego de golf
la bolsa de golf
el palo
el bastón
la pelota
la bola
el hoyo
el green

ADJETIVOS

playero(a)
acuático(a)
bronceador(a)
protector(a)
plegable

VERBOS

pasar
bucear
nadar
alquilar
echar
golpear
brillar

OTRAS PALABRAS Y EXPRESIONES

hace calor
hay sol
está nublado
hace viento
llueve
ayer
anteayer
anoche
ayer por la tarde
ayer por la mañana
el año pasado
la semana pasada
hoy
esta noche
esta tarde
esta mañana
este año
esta semana

Reintegración *(page 319)*
RECYCLING

These exercises recycle vocabulary associated with winter activities. You may wish to call on students to contrast winter and summer sports activities.

ANSWERS
Ejercicios A and B
Answers will vary.

Ejercicio C
Some answers will vary.
1. Estoy bien (mal).
2. Sí (No), (no) estoy cansado(a).
3. Sí (No), (no) tengo catarro.
4. Sí (No), (no) tengo tos.
5. Sí (No), cuando tengo catarro (no) estornudo mucho.
6. Sí (No), (no) tengo dolor de garganta.
7. Sí (No), cuando tengo catarro (no) me duele el pecho.
8. Sí (No), si como algo malo (no) me duele el estómago.

Vocabulario

There are approximately nine cognates in this *Vocabulario* list.

VIDEO
The video is intended to reinforce the vocabulary, structures, and cultural content in each chapter. It may be used here as a chapter wrap-up activity. See the *Video Activities Booklet* for additional suggestions on its use.

INTRODUCCIÓN   (0:42:52)

LA PLAYA   (0:44:37)

STUDENT PORTFOLIO

Written assignments that may be included in students' portfolios are the *Actividades escritas* on page 318 and the *Mi autobiografía* section in the Workbook, page 119.

INDEPENDENT PRACTICE

Assign any of the following:
1. Exercises on student page 319
2. Workbook, *Mi autobiografía*, page 119
3. Chapter 11, Situation Cards

Topics	Functions	Structure	Culture
Cultural events Teen dating customs Fondo Académico pages. 352-357	How to discuss movies, plays, and museums How to talk about cultural events How to express cultural preferences How to relate actions or events that took place in the past How to tell for whom something is done How to discuss dating customs in the U.S. vs. those in Spanish-speaking countries	El preterito de los verbos en *-er* e *-ir* Los complementos indirectos *le* y *les*	Teen dating customs and attitudes Cultural preferences Hispanic actors in Hollywood and the Broadway theater Palacio de Bellas Artes El Ballet Folklórico *Nuestro Mundo:* El tiempo Las Matemáticas: El sistema métrico Las Ciencias Naturales: La biología Las Ciencias Sociales: Antropología e Historia

CAPÍTULO 12

Situation Cards

The Situation Cards simulate real-life situations that require students to communicate in Spanish, exactly as though they were in a Spanish-speaking country. The Situation Cards operate on the assumption that the person to whom the message is to be conveyed understands no English. Therefore, students must focus on producing the Spanish vocabulary and structures necessary to negotiate the situations successfully. For additional information, see the Introduction to the Situation Cards in the Situation Cards Envelope.

Communication Transparency

The illustration seen in this Communication Transparency consists of a synthesis of the two vocabulary (*Palabras 1&2*) presentations found in this chapter. It has been created in order to present this chapter's vocabulary in a new context, and also to recycle vocabulary learned in previous chapters. The Communication Transparency consists of original art. Following are some specific uses:

1. as a cue to stimulate conversation and writing activities
2. for listening comprehension activities
3. to review and reteach vocabulary
4. as a review for chapter and unit tests

CAPÍTULO 12   **A**

You're in Spain and you want to see a flamenco performance. Go to the box office and buy a ticket.

Bienvenidos   © Glencoe/McGraw-Hill

B

© Glencoe/McGraw-Hill

C

© Glencoe/McGraw-Hill

D

© Glencoe/McGraw-Hill

Bienvenidos   Chapter 12   Communication Transparency   C-12

Copyright © by Glencoe/McGraw-Hill Publishing Company

CAPÍTULO 12
Print Resources

Nosotros y Nuestro Mundo

- ◆ Nuestro Conocimiento Académico *Las artes plásticas*
- ◆ Nuestro Idioma *El pretérito*
- ◆ Nuestra Cultura *El arte en el mundo hispano*
- ◆ Nuestra Literatura *"El ingenioso hidalgo don Quijote de la Mancha"* de Miguel de Cervantes Saavedra
- ◆ Nuestra Creatividad
- ◆ Nuestras Diversiones

CAPÍTULO 12
Multimedia Resources

CD-ROM Interactive Textbook Disc 3

Chapter 12 Student Edition
- ◆ Palabras 1
- ◆ Palabras 2
- ◆ Estructura
- ◆ Conversación
- ◆ Lectura y cultura
- ◆ Hispanoparlantes
- ◆ Realidades
- ◆ Culminación
- ◆ Prueba

Review: Chapters 9-12
- ◆ Nuestro mundo
- ◆ Repaso: Chapters 9-12
- ◆ Fondo Académico
- ◆ Game: *¿Quién sabe más?*

Audio Cassette Program with Student Tape Manual

Compact Disc Program with Student Tape Manual

Overhead Transparencies Binder

- ◆ Vocabulary 12.1 (A&B); 12.2 (A&B)
- ◆ Pronunciation P-12
- ◆ Grammar G-12
- ◆ Communication C-12
- ◆ Maps
- ◆ Fine Art (with Blackline Master Activities)

Video Program

- ◆ Videocassette
- ◆ Video Activities Booklet 36-37
- ◆ Videodisc
- ◆ Video Activities Booklet 36-37

Computer Software (Macintosh, IBM, Apple)

- ◆ Practice Disk
    Palabras 1 y 2
    Estructura
- ◆ Test Generator Disk
    Chapter Test
    Customized Test

CHAPTER OVERVIEW

In this chapter students will learn how to discuss cultural events and express their cultural preferences. They will also learn to express additional actions in the past. In order to do this they will learn vocabulary associated with films, museums, and the theater. They will learn the preterite of *-er* and *-ir* verbs and the pronouns *le, les*.

The cultural focus of this chapter is on teen dating customs and attitudes, and preferences with regard to cultural events in the Spanish-speaking countries.

CHAPTER OBJECTIVES

By the end of this chapter students will know:

1. vocabulary associated with movies and the theater, including some genres of films and plays
2. vocabulary associated with museums and art, including painting and sculpture
3. the preterite forms of *-er* and *-ir* verbs
4. the preterite forms of *ver* and *dar*
5. the indirect object pronouns *le* and *les*

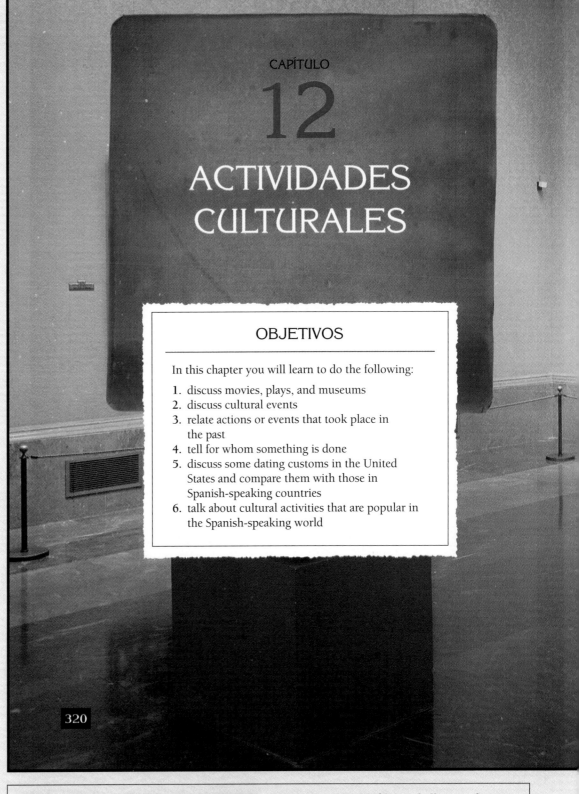

CAPÍTULO

12

ACTIVIDADES CULTURALES

OBJETIVOS

In this chapter you will learn to do the following:

1. discuss movies, plays, and museums
2. discuss cultural events
3. relate actions or events that took place in the past
4. tell for whom something is done
5. discuss some dating customs in the United States and compare them with those in Spanish-speaking countries
6. talk about cultural activities that are popular in the Spanish-speaking world

320

CHAPTER PROJECTS

(optional)

1. Have groups research different Spanish and Latin American painters and/or sculptors. Each group can put on an art show using prints of the artists' most famous works.
2. Visit a local art museum so that students can see different styles of art and, hopefully, some work by Hispanic artists.
3. Show a Spanish film and allow students to discuss it.

321

Pacing

Chapter 12 will require about eight to ten days. However, pacing will vary according to the length of the class, the age of your students, and student aptitude.

LEARNING FROM PHOTOS

The title of this painting is *Las Hilanderas* by Velázquez. Although Velázquez painted kings and other famous people, he also painted more humble figures such as the *hilanderas*.

Have students look at the painting and tell you what *hilanderas* are.

VOCABULARIO

PALABRAS 1

Vocabulary Teaching Resources

1. Vocabulary Transparencies 12.1 (A & B)
2. Audio Cassette 7B
3. Student Tape Manual, pages 247–248
4. Workbook, page 120
5. Communication Activities Masters, pages 70-72, A & B
6. Chapter Quizzes, page 54, *Palabras 1*

PRESENTATION
(pages 322–323)

A. Using Vocabulary Transparencies 12.1 (A & B), play the *Palabras 1* presentation on Cassette 7B. Point to the appropriate illustration as you play the cassette.
B. Have students repeat each word or expression after you two or three times as you point to the corresponding item on the transparency.
C. Now call on individual students to point to the corresponding illustration on the transparency as you say the word or expression.

Vocabulary Expansion

You may wish to give students the following words:
la película policíaca
la película documental
la película de amor
la película de ciencia-ficción
la película de aventuras
la película de vaqueros (del oeste)
una película en versión original
una película doblada
una película con subtítulos

EN EL CINE

la pantalla
el film
la película
la taquilla
la sesión
la entrada
la localidad
el cine
la butaca
la cola   la fila

Independencia

Carlos salió.
Perdió el autobús.

Tomó el metro.
Subió al metro en la estación Independencia.

TOTAL PHYSICAL RESPONSE

(following the Vocabulary presentation)
___, levántate, por favor.
Ven acá. Imagínate que quieres ir al cine.
Ve por el autobús. Allí está la parada.
¡Corre! ¡Anda rápido! Vas a perder el bus.
Ay, ¡qué pena! Perdiste el bus. Pero no hay problema.
Ve a la estación de metro.
Baja al metro.
Espera en el andén.
Aquí viene el metro. Sube.
El metro llega a la estación que quieres. Baja del metro.
Sube la escalera.
Allí está el cine. Ve a la taquilla.
Ponte en fila.
Indica a la taquillera que quieres dos entradas.
Gracias, ___. Y ahora toma tu asiento.

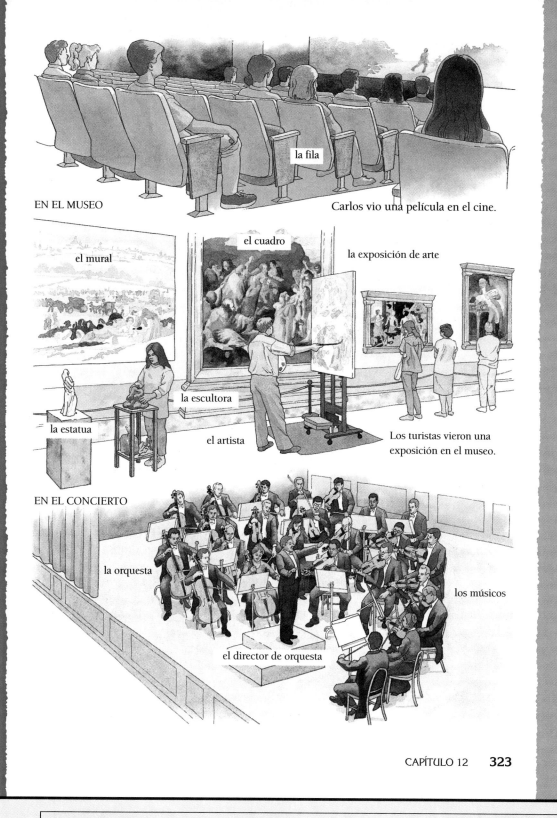

la fila

EN EL MUSEO

Carlos vio una película en el cine.

el mural

el cuadro

la exposición de arte

la escultora

la estatua

el artista

Los turistas vieron una exposición en el museo.

EN EL CONCIERTO

la orquesta

los músicos

el director de orquesta

ABOUT THE LANGUAGE

1. The ticket to a movie or theater is often referred to as *la entrada* rather than *el boleto* or *el billete*. *La taquilla* is the most common word for a movie or theater ticket window, but this does not mean *la ventanilla* is never used. *La localidad* is used for both a ticket or a seat in a theater. The word *la fila* or *la cola* can be used for a line of people.

2. In addition to *la película* and *el film*, you will often hear and see *el filme*.

3. In addition to *el autobús*, the shortened form *el bus* is more and more frequently heard. In the Caribbean area the word for bus is *la guagua*; in Mexico, *el camión*. Other regional terms for bus are *un ómnibus*, *un micro*, *un colectivo* (which in many areas is a public taxi; in Argentina, however, it is a bus), and *una góndola*.

ADDITIONAL PRACTICE

If you give the vocabulary in the Vocabulary Expansion section of this Teacher's Wraparound Edition, read the following movie summaries to students and ask them to identify the type of film.

1. **Los actores y las actrices viven en otro planeta y viajan en el espacio.**
2. **Los policías están buscando a un criminal.**
3. **Es un estudio de los animales en su hábitat natural.**
4. **Dos jóvenes deciden cruzar el océano en una canoa.**

Ejercicios

PRESENTATION (*page 324*)

Ejercicio A

A. Do Exercise A orally with books closed. Call on individuals to respond.

B. Now call on one individual to tell all about Carlos in his/her own words.

Ejercicios B and C

Exercises B and C can be done with books open.

ANSWERS

Ejercicio A

Some answers will vary.

1. Sí, Carlos salió anoche.
2. Fue al cine.
3. Sí, compró una entrada en la taquilla.
4. Asistió a la sesión de la tarde (de la noche).
5. No, Carlos no tomó el autobús.
6. Perdió el autobús.
7. Tomó el metro.
8. Subió al metro en la estación Independencia.

Ejercicio B

1. c
2. b
3. c
4. a
5. b

Ejercicio C

1. butaca
2. entrada
3. taquilla
4. autobús
5. metro
6. las estaciones

Ejercicios

A Al cine. Contesten.

1. ¿Salió anoche Carlos?
2. ¿Adónde fue?
3. ¿Compró una entrada en la taquilla?
4. ¿Asistió a la sesión de la tarde o de la noche?
5. ¿Tomó el autobús Carlos?
6. ¿Por qué no tomó el autobús?
7. ¿Qué tomó?
8. ¿En qué estación subió al metro?

B En la taquilla. Escojan.

1. La gente hace cola ___.
   a. en las butacas   b. en la pantalla   c. en la taquilla
2. Compran ___ en la taquilla del cine.
   a. butacas   b. entradas   c. películas
3. Dan ___ en el cine.
   a. entradas   b. novelas
   c. películas
4. La ___ es una silla o un asiento en el cine o en el teatro.
   a. butaca   b. entrada
   c. taquilla
5. Proyectan la película en ___.
   a. la butaca   b. la pantalla
   c. el metro

C ¿Cuál es la palabra? Den la palabra correcta.

1. un asiento o una silla en el cine o en el teatro
2. un boleto o billete para entrar en el cine o en el teatro
3. la ventanilla o la boletería de un cine o de un teatro
4. un vehículo con ruedas que es un medio de transporte público
5. un medio de transporte subterráneo
6. lugar donde paran los metros

324 CAPÍTULO 12

ADDITIONAL PRACTICE

You may wish to ask students the following questions:

1. ¿Dónde proyectan la película en el cine?
2. ¿Dónde venden (despachan) las entradas?
3. ¿Dónde toman sus asientos los espectadores en el cine?
4. ¿Qué venden o despachan en la taquilla?

LEARNING FROM REALIA

With regard to the realia on page 324, ask students what they think *el Profe* means. Have students draw their own cartoon of *el Profe* and provide a caption.

PALABRAS 2

EN EL TEATRO

la actriz

el actor

el telón

la escena

en el teatro

Los actores dieron una representación de *Bodas de Sangre*.
Los actores y las actrices entraron en escena.

el autor

la obra

El autor García Lorca escribió la obra teatral.

CAPÍTULO 12   **325**

Vocabulary Teaching Resources

1. Vocabulary Transparencies 12.2 (A & B)
2. Audio Cassette 7B
3. Student Tape Manual, pages 248–249
4. Workbook, pages 121–123
5. Communication Activities Masters, pages 73-74, *C & D*
6. Chapter Quizzes, page 55, *Palabras 2*
7. Computer Software, *Vocabulario*

Bell Ringer Review

Write the following on the board or use BRR Blackline Master 12-1: Answer the following questions:
1. ¿Dónde estás a la una de la tarde?
2. ¿Adónde vas después de las clases?
3. ¿Qué haces allí?
4. ¿A qué hora sales de la escuela?
5. ¿A qué hora vuelves a casa?
6. ¿Qué haces después de la cena?

PRESENTATION
(pages 325–326)

A. Show Vocabulary Transparencies 12.2 (A & B). Point to each item and have students repeat the corresponding word or expression after you two or three times.
B. Ask questions of individual students such as the following: ¿Es el actor o la actriz? ¿Es el telón o la escena? ¿Quién es? ¿Qué es?

TOTAL PHYSICAL RESPONSE

(following the Vocabulary presentation)

TPR 1
___, levántate y ven acá, por favor.
Vas a hacer algunos gestos. ¿De acuerdo?
Muy bien, eres escultor. Haz una estatua.
Eres artista. Pinta un cuadro.
Eres actor (actriz). Dile algo al público, a los espectadores.
Eres director de orquesta. Dirige a la orquesta.

C. Then have students open their books and reinforce the new vocabulary by reading the words and sentences on pages 325–326.

Note

1. In *Palabras 1* the preterite forms of the *-er* and *-ir* verbs are in the *-ió* form. In *Palabras 2* the preterite forms presented are *-ió, -ieron*. This enables you to ask questions immediately that students can answer without having to manipulate the verb endings. The other forms will be taught immediately in the *Estructura* section of this chapter.

2. You may wish to point out to students that the drawing of García Lorca on page 325 does in fact resemble the famous writer.

un espectáculo musical

Los espectadores vieron un espectáculo musical.
El público aplaudió.

la cuenta

el mesero

la propina

el menú

la mesa

Después del teatro, María y sus amigos comieron en un restaurante.
El mesero le dio el menú.
Después de la comida, el mesero le dio la cuenta.
Ella le dio (dejó) una propina.

326 CAPÍTULO 12

TOTAL PHYSICAL RESPONSE

TPR 2
___, ven acá, por favor.
Vas a un restaurante.
Entra.
Ve a tu mesa.
Siéntate.
Mira el menú.
Da tu órden al mesero.

Come. Bebe.
Llámale la atención al mesero.
Pídele la cuenta.
Paga. Deja el dinero en la mesa.
Pon un poco más para el mesero. Deja una propina.
Y ahora levántate.
Ve a la puerta. Abre la puerta.
Sal del restaurante.
Gracias, ___. Y ahora puedes volver a tu asiento.

Ejercicios

A **Algunas diversiones.** Contesten.

1. Por la tarde, ¿salió María?
2. ¿Fue al museo?
3. ¿Vio una exposición de arte moderno?
4. Después, ¿fue a un restaurante?
5. ¿Comió en el restaurante?
6. ¿Le dio el menú el mesero?
7. Después de la comida, ¿le dio la cuenta?
8. ¿María le dio una propina al mesero?

B **En el teatro.** Contesten.

1. ¿Quiénes entraron en escena?
2. ¿Qué dieron?
3. ¿Quién escribió la obra?
4. ¿Cuándo aplaudieron los espectadores?

C **¿Dónde?** Escojan y escriban en otro papel.

EL CINE   EL TEATRO   EL MUSEO

1. la representación
2. la película
3. la pantalla
4. la escena
5. la exposición
6. el actor
7. el cuadro
8. la actriz

Museo Arqueológico Nacional

MUSEO DIOCESANO
Nº 033998
ENTRADA
CUENCA

CAPÍTULO 12   **327**

ADDITIONAL PRACTICE

Have students identify the following:
1. *el que escribe libros, novelas, obras teatrales*
2. *el que juega el papel de otra persona en una obra teatral*
3. *el que hace estatuas*
4. *el que toca un instrumento musical*
5. *el que dirige a la orquesta durante un concierto*

INDEPENDENT PRACTICE

Assign any of the following:
1. Workbook, pages 120–123
2. Communication Activities Masters, pages 70–74, *A–D*
3. Exercises on student page 327

Ejercicios

PRESENTATION (*page 327*)

Ejercicios A, B, and C

Exercises A and B can be done with books closed or open. Exercise C should be done with books open.

GEOGRAPHY CONNECTION

With reference to the realia on page 327, Cuenca is a small, lovely city in the province of *Castilla la Nueva.* It is easily accessible from Madrid. It is known for its famous *casas colgadas,* hanging houses that are suspended over an abyss formed by the *Júcar* river.

ANSWERS

Ejercicio A
1. Sí, María salió por la tarde.
2. No, no fue al museo.
3. Sí (No), (no) vio una exposición de arte moderno.
4. Sí, fue a un restaurante después.
5. Sí, comió en el restaurante.
6. Sí, el mesero le dio el menú.
7. Sí, después de la comida le dio la cuenta.
8. Sí, María le dio una propina al mesero.

Ejercicio B
1. Los actores (y las actrices) entraron en escena.
2. Dieron *Bodas de Sangre.*
3. García Lorca escribió la obra.
4. Después de la representación los espectadores aplaudieron.

Ejercicio C
1. la representación—el teatro
2. la película—el cine
3. la pantalla—el cine
4. la escena—el teatro
5. la exposición—el museo
6. el actor—el cine, el teatro
7. el cuadro—el museo
8. la actriz—el cine, el teatro

327

It is not necessary to do all the *Comunicación* activities. You may select those that are most appropriate for your students, or allow students to select the activities they would like to take part in.

ANSWERS

Actividad A

Answers will vary.

Actividad B

Answers will vary.

Actividad C

Answers will vary according to the model and cues.

Comunicación
Palabras 1 y 2

A **¿Vas al cine?** Form groups of four and determine how often each member goes to the movies and what kinds of movies are the most popular. Use the list below. Report to the class on the average amount of movie-going for the group, who goes to the movies most and least frequently, and the most and least popular kinds of movies for the group.

policíaca	de ciencia ficción
cómica	musical
un espectáculo musical	folklórica
una tragedia	documental
una comedia	del oeste
de horror	

B **El concierto.** Call the theater to order tickets for a concert. Your partner is the ticket agent. Make sure you cover all of the following: name of the musical group; time, day, and date of the concert; price of the the tickets; method of payment—cash or credit card.

C **Los museos.** Compare museum visits with your partner. Find out from each other what museums you went to, when you went there, and what you saw. Below are some useful words for your conversation.

arte moderno
Estudiante 1: ¿A qué museo fuiste?
Estudiante 2: Al museo de arte.
Estudiante 1: ¿Y qué viste allí?
Estudiante 2: Vi unos cuadros de Frida Kahlo.

arte moderno	ciencia
arte clásico	historia
tecnología	aviación
antropología	transporte

MUSEO
Frida Kahlo

LONDRES Nº 247
COL. DEL CARMEN
COYOACAN

ADMISION: N$ 5.00

MFK

LEARNING FROM REALIA

Frida Kahlo (1907–1954), the artist, was the wife of the famous Mexican muralist Diego Rivera. In recent years Kahlo's works have received critical acclaim worldwide. Kahlo's home on Calle Londres in Coyoacán is now the Museo de Frida Kahlo. Kahlo was left a partial invalid for life after a bus crash. Despite the constant pain she suffered throughout her life, she was a vibrant, flamboyant, and very creative artist.

El pretérito de los verbos en -er e -ir

Describing Past Actions

1. You have already learned the preterite forms of regular -ar verbs. Study the preterite forms of regular -er and -ir verbs. Note that they also form the preterite by dropping the infinitive ending and adding the appropriate endings to the stem. The preterite endings of regular -er and -ir verbs are the same.

INFINITIVE	COMER	VOLVER	VIVIR	SUBIR	ENDINGS
STEM	com-	volv-	viv-	sub-	
yo	comí	volví	viví	subí	-í
tú	comiste	volviste	viviste	subiste	-iste
él, ella, Ud.	comió	volvió	vivió	subió	-ió
nosotros(as)	comimos	volvimos	vivimos	subimos	-imos
vosotros(as)	comisteis	volvisteis	vivisteis	subisteis	-isteis
ellos, ellas, Uds.	comieron	volvieron	vivieron	subieron	-ieron

2. The preterite forms of the verbs *dar* and *ver* are the same as those of regular -er and -ir verbs.

INFINITIVE	VER	DAR
yo	vi	di
tú	viste	diste
él, ella, Ud.	vio	dio
nosotros(as)	vimos	dimos
vosotros(as)	visteis	disteis
ellos, ellas, Uds.	vieron	dieron

POSADA FLORENTINA
El Tallarín Gordo
PURISIMA 254 TELEFONO 378567

3. Remember that the preterite is used to tell about an event that happened at a specific time in the past.

> Ellos salieron anoche.
> Ayer no comí en casa. Comí en el restaurante.
> ¿Viste una película anoche?

Bell Ringer Review

Write the following on the board or use BRR Blackline Master 12-2: Complete the following in the present tense.
1. José ___ en Santo Domingo. (vivir)
2. Él ___ con su familia a las siete. (comer)
3. Después él ___ sus tareas. (hacer)
4. Luego él ___ una emisión deportiva en la tele. (ver)

El pretérito de los verbos en -er e -ir

PRESENTATION *(page 329)*

A. Write the model verbs on page 329 on the board. Underline the endings and have students repeat each form after you.

B. After you have written a form for *comer,* for example, *yo comí,* you may wish to have students give you the forms for *volver, vivir,* and *subir.*

C. Point out to students that the preterite endings for the -er and -ir verbs are exactly the same.

D. Have students open their books to page 329 and read aloud the example sentences in step 3.

FOR NATIVE SPEAKERS

Just as with -ar verbs, there is a tendency to add an *s* to the *tú* form of the preterite of -er and -ir verbs: *comistes, vivistes, bebistes.* Have students ask the following questions of a classmate:

Pregúntale a un compañero(a)…
1. *qué bebió esta mañana*
2. *a qué hora comió anoche*
3. *qué escribió en la clase de español*

LEARNING FROM REALIA

Have students look at the ad on page 329, concentrating on the large bowl in the middle. Now ask them to guess at the meaning of *tallarín.*

Ejercicios

Ejercicio A

Have students open their books and refer to the illustrations as they respond.

Ejercicios B and C

A. Exercises B and C can be done with books closed or open.

B. You may wish to have students redo Exercise C with any other subject pronoun.

ANSWERS

Ejercicio A

1. Perdió el metro.
2. Subió en Insurgentes.
3. Comió en un café.
4. Le dio una propina.

Ejercicio B

Answers can also be negative.

1. Sí, los amigos salieron anoche.
2. Sí, vieron una función teatral.
3. Sí, los actores dieron una buena representación.
4. Sí, los espectadores aplaudieron.
5. Sí, después ellos comieron en el restaurante.
6. Sí, le dieron una propina al mesero.

Ejercicio C

1. Salí de casa a las ocho.
2. Subí al segundo piso.
3. Asistí a clase.
4. Comprendí la lección.
5. Escribí una carta en español.
6. Vi una película argentina.

Ejercicios

A **¿Para dónde salió ella?** Contesten según el dibujo.

1. ¿Qué perdió?

2. ¿Dónde subió al metro?

3. ¿Dónde comió?

4. ¿Qué le dio al mesero?

B **Los amigos salieron juntos.** Contesten.

1. ¿Salieron los amigos anoche?
2. ¿Vieron una función teatral?
3. ¿Dieron una buena representación los actores?
4. ¿Aplaudieron los espectadores?
5. Después, ¿comieron ellos en el restaurante?
6. ¿Le dieron una propina al mesero?

C **Ayer en la clase de español.** Formen oraciones con *yo.*

1. salir de casa a las ocho
2. subir al segundo piso
3. asistir a clase
4. comprender la lección
5. escribir una carta en español
6. ver una película argentina

COOPERATIVE LEARNING

After going over Exercise C once as a class activity, have students work in groups of four and make up mini-conversations based on the exercise. For example:

E1: ¿Saliste de casa a las ocho?
E2: Sí, salí a las ocho.
E3: ¿Quién no salió a las ocho?
E4: Pues, yo no sé quién no salió a las ocho.

D Yo sé que tú no... Sigan el modelo.

> Yo lo vendí.
> *Pero yo sé que tú no lo vendiste.*

1. Yo lo aprendí.
2. Yo lo comprendí.
3. Yo lo escribí.
4. Yo lo recibí.
5. Yo lo vi.

E ¿Ella salió con él? Completen con el pretérito.

PABLO: José, ¿___ (conocer) tú a Felipe?

JOSÉ: ¿A Felipe? ¿El muchacho nuevo en la clase de español? Sí, lo ___ (conocer). Es un tipo simpático.

PABLO: Sí, lo es. Sabes que él ___ (salir) anoche con Teresa.

JOSÉ: ¿Teresa ___ (salir) con él?

PABLO: Sí, ellos ___ (comer) en el restaurante Sol y luego ___ (ver) una película en el cine Goya.

JOSÉ: ¿Me estás hablando en serio?

PABLO: Pues, hombre. Sí.

JOSÉ: Pero, ¿cómo sabes que ella ___ (salir) con él?

PABLO: Pues, lo sé porque Carmen y yo ___ (salir) con ellos. Nosotros ___ (comer) con ellos en el restaurante pero no ___ (ver) la película porque ___ (volver) a casa.

JOSÉ: ¿Pero es verdad que Uds. ___ (salir) anoche con Teresa y con ese tío Felipe?

PABLO: Sí, José. Pero, ¿qué te pasa, hombre?

JOSÉ: Creo que me estás tomando el pelo.

PABLO: ¡Ja! ¡Ja! No, hombre. No te estoy tomando el pelo. Te estoy hablando en serio.

JOSÉ: Pero, Pablo, ¿no sabes que Teresa es mi novia?

PABLO: ¿Teresa? ¿Es tu novia? ¡Ay, Dios mío! Creo que yo ___ (meter) la pata.

CAPÍTULO 12 **331**

PRESENTATION (*page 331*)

Ejercicio E

A. You may want to allow students to prepare Exercise E ahead of time before going over it in class.

B. Call on different students to read the parts of Pablo and José. Then call on two students to read the entire exercise.

C. Call on another student to give a synopsis of the conversation in his/her own words.

ANSWERS

Ejercicio D

1. Yo lo aprendí. Pero yo sé que tú no lo aprendiste.
2. Yo lo comprendí. Pero yo sé que tú no lo comprendiste.
3. Yo lo escribí. Pero yo sé que tú no lo escribiste.
4. Yo lo recibí. Pero yo sé que tú no lo recibiste.
5. Yo lo vi. Pero yo sé que tú no lo viste.

Ejercicio E

P. conociste
J. conocí
P. salió
J. salió
P. comieron, vieron
J. salió
P. salimos, comimos, vimos, volvimos
J. salieron
P. metí

ABOUT THE LANGUAGE

The expression *meter la pata* is the same as the English "put your foot in your mouth." In Spanish, however, the word used is hoof or paw, rather than a human foot.

LEARNING FROM PHOTOS

This is the *Puerta del Sol* metro station in the center of Madrid. Many lines of the metro converge at *Sol*. Because of this, there are always a lot of people at this station transferring from one line to another.

INDEPENDENT PRACTICE

Assign any of the following:
1. Workbook, pages 124–125
2. Communication Activities Masters, page 75, *A*
3. Exercises on student pages 330–331

PRESENTATION (page 332)

A. You may want to write the following sentences on the board. The arrows will help students understand the concept of direct vs. indirect objects.

a Carmen.

Juan lanzó → el balón ↖

a su amiga.

Ella le dio → el regalo ↖

As students look at these sentences, tell them that Juan doesn't throw Carmen. He throws the ball. To whom does he throw the ball? To Carmen. The ball is the direct object because it receives the action of the verb directly. Carmen is the indirect object because she receives the action of the verb indirectly.

B. Now have students open their books to page 332. Lead them through steps 1–3 and the accompanying example sentences.

C. You may wish to write the example sentences from step 2 on the board and underline the indirect object once and the direct object twice.

D. As you write the sentences from step 2 on the board. Circle *le* and circle *a Juan*. Then draw arrows back and forth to indicate that they are the same person. This visual explanation helps many students.

Note Be sure that students learn that *le* and *les* are both masculine and feminine.

332

Los complementos indirectos *le, les*   *Telling What You Do for Others*

1. You have already learned the direct object pronouns *lo, la, los,* and *las*. Now you will learn the indirect object pronouns *le* and *les*. Observe the difference between a direct object and an indirect object in the following sentences.

Juan lanzó la pelota.   **Juan le lanzó la pelota a Carmen.**

In the above sentences, *la pelota* is the direct object because it is the direct receiver of the action of the verb "threw." Carmen is the indirect object because it indicates "to whom" the ball was thrown.

2. Note the following sentences that have indirect object pronouns.

> **María *le* dio un regalo *a Juan*.**   **Juan *le* dio un regalo *a María*.**
> **María *les* dio un regalo *a sus amigos*.**   **Juan *les* dio un regalo *a sus amigas*.**

The indirect object pronoun *le* is both masculine and feminine. *Les* is used for both the feminine and masculine plural. *Le* and *les* can also be used with a noun phrase.

> **María *le* dio un regalo *a Juan*.**
> **Juan *les* dio un regalo *a sus amigas*.**
> **María y Juan *le* dieron un regalo *a su abuela*.**

3. Since *le* and *les* can refer to more than one person, they are often clarified as follows:

	a él.		a ellos.
Le hablé	a ella.	Les hablé	a ellas.
	a Ud.		a Uds.

Ejercicios

A **Los complementos.** Indiquen el complemento directo y el indirecto.

1. Carlos recibió la carta.
2. Les vendimos la casa a ellos.
3. Conocimos a Elena ayer.
4. Le hablamos a Tomás.
5. ¿Quién tiene el periódico? Tomás lo tiene.
6. El profesor nos explicó la lección.
7. Ella le dio una propina al mesero.
8. Ellos vieron la película en el cine.

B **¿Le hablaste?** Contesten.

1. ¿Le hablaste a Carlos?
2. ¿Le hablaste por teléfono?
3. ¿Le diste las noticias?
4. ¿Y él les dio las noticias a sus padres?
5. ¿Les escribió a sus padres?
6. ¿Les mandó la carta ayer?
7. ¿Les escribió en inglés o en español?

C **El pobre Carlos.** Contesten según los dibujos.

1. ¿Qué le duele?

2. ¿Qué más le duele?

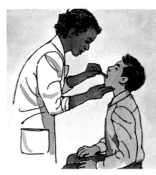

3. ¿Quién le examina la garganta?

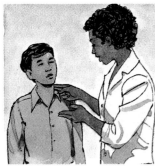

4. ¿Quién le da la diagnosis?

5. ¿Qué le da la médica?

6. ¿Quién le da los medicamentos?

D **En el aeropuerto.** Completen con *le* o *les.*

La señora González llegó al mostrador de la línea aérea en el aeropuerto.

Ella ___ habló al agente. ___ habló en español. No ___ habló en inglés.
    1   2   3

Ella ___ dio su boleto al agente y él lo miró. Ella ___ dio su pasaporte
    4   5

también. El agente ___ dio a la señora su tarjeta de embarque. A bordo del avión
                  6

los asistentes de vuelo ___ hablaron a los pasajeros. ___ dieron la bienvenida
                       7   8

a bordo y ___ explicaron el uso del equipo abordo en el caso de una emergencia.
         9

CAPÍTULO 12   **333**

INDEPENDENT PRACTICE

Assign any of the following:
1. Workbook, page 126
2. Communication Activities Masters, pages 75-76, *B*
3. Exercises on student pages 332–333

Ejercicios

PRESENTATION
(pages 332–333)

Ejercicio A

Exercise A is a diagnostic tool to determine if students understand the concept of direct and indirect objects.

Note It is recommended that you not wait for every student to use these pronouns perfectly. If certain students find the concept difficult, they can still function by answering with nouns. *¿Hablaste a Juan? Sí, hablé a Juan.* Direct and indirect objects will be reintroduced throughout this textbook series.

ANSWERS

Ejercicio A
1. la carta: directo
2. les, a ellos: indirecto; la casa: directo
3. a Elena: directo
4. Le, a Tomás: indirecto
5. el periódico, lo: directo
6. nos: indirecto; la lección: directo
7. una propina: directo; le, al mesero: indirecto
8. la película: directo

ANSWERS

Ejercicio B
1. Sí, le hablé a Carlos.
2. Sí, le hablé por teléfono.
3. Sí, le di las noticias.
4. Sí, él les dio las noticias a sus padres.
5. Sí, les escribió (a sus padres).
6. Sí, les mandó la carta ayer.
7. Les escribió en inglés (en español).

Ejercicio C
1. Le duele la garganta.
2. Le duele la cabeza.
3. La doctora le examina la garganta.
4. La doctora le da la diagnosis.
5. La médica le da una receta.
6. El farmacéutico le da los medicamentos.

Ejercicio D
1. le
2. Le
3. le
4. le
5. le
6. le
7. les
8. Les
9. les

Bell Ringer Review

Write the following on the board or use BRR Blackline Master 12-3: Write some things you do with your friends.

PRESENTATION *(page 334)*

A. To vary procedures, have students listen to the recording on Cassette 7B with books closed.

B. Then ask students to tell you in one or two sentences what the conversation is about. This can be done in either Spanish or English.

C. Have students open their books. Give them two or three minutes to read the conversation silently.

D. Call on one student to read aloud the part of Pablo and another the part of Sarita.

E. Then go over the comprehension questions that follow.

F. Call on one student to retell the information in the conversation in narrative form.

ANSWERS

1. Pablo le dio una llamada telefónica a Sarita.
2. Sarita no contestó.
3. Ella salió.
4. Salió con un grupo de amigos.
5. Fueron a un concierto de rock.
6. Comieron en un restaurante.
7. Sarita no volvió hasta las once y pico.

Escenas de la vida   *Sarita salió anoche*

PABLO: Sarita, ¿saliste anoche?
SARITA: Sí, ¿por qué me preguntas?
PABLO: Pues, te di una llamada y no contestaste.
SARITA: Sí, salí con un grupo de amigos de la escuela.

PABLO: ¿Adónde fueron?
SARITA: Asistimos a un concierto de rock en el Teatro Municipal. Y luego fuimos a comer en un restaurante.

PABLO: ¿A qué hora volviste a casa?
SARITA: Pues, no volví hasta las once y pico.

■ **Una llamada.** Contesten.

1. ¿Quién le dio una llamada telefónica a Sarita?
2. ¿Contestó Sarita?
3. ¿Por qué?
4. ¿Con quiénes salió?
5. ¿Adónde fueron?
6. ¿Dónde comieron?
7. ¿A qué hora volvió Sarita a casa?

Pronunciación   *La* h, *la* y, *la* ll

The **h** in Spanish is silent. It is never pronounced.

> **h**
> hambre   hermano
> hijo   hotel

Y in Spanish can be either a vowel or a consonant. As a vowel it is pronounced exactly the same as the vowel **i**.

> **Juan y María**
> **El piano y la guitarra**

Y is a consonant when it begins a word or a syllable. As a consonant, **y** is pronounced similarly to the English **y** in the word *yoyo*. This sound has several variations throughout the Spanish-speaking world.

> **y**
> ya   playa   playera
> uruguayo ayuda   desayuno

The **ll** is considered a single consonant in Spanish and is a separate letter of the alphabet. In many areas of the Spanish-speaking world it is pronounced the same as the **y**. It too has several variations.

> **ll**
> llama   ella   taquilla
> pantalla lleva   llega
> calle   lluvia

la llave

Repeat the following sentences.

> **La hermana habla hoy con su hermano en el hospital.**
> **Ella llega al hotel en aquella calle.**
> **Ella llega a la taquilla con el billete.**
> **El hombre lleva el desayuno a la playa bajo la lluvia.**

Una llama

CAPÍTULO 12   **335**

Pronunciación

PRESENTATION *(page 335)*

A. In all areas of the Spanish-speaking world the *h* is silent. There is no exception.
B. The *ll* and *y* have several variations. In most areas they are pronounced somewhat like the *yo* in English *yoyo*, or the German *ja*. In Argentina and Uruguay they are pronounced as a *j*, somewhat like the *j* in *Joe*. In Spain you will also hear a *j* sound, similar to the *y* sound Americans make when they pronounce quickly *didya*.
C. Have students repeat all the words carefully after you or the recording on Cassette 7B. The sentences can be used as dictation.

Note You may wish to tell students that it is not unusual for Spanish speakers to misspell words with *y* and *ll*. Since the two letters sound the same, they often mix them up. They will also omit the *h* in words that should have it. Students may enjoy hearing that other people sometimes have spelling problems too.

GEOGRAPHY CONNECTION

The *llama* is found on the high plains of the Andes Mountains. It belongs to the same family as the camel, but, unlike the camel, it has no hump. *Llamas* are never ridden. However, they can carry loads up to 100 pounds. They can work at altitudes that few other animals can tolerate. The *llama* is valued for its meat, milk, and wool. The *alpaca* and the *vicuña* are close relatives. The wool of the *alpaca* is extremely fine. In pre-colonial times, the soft, silky fleece of the *vicuña* was reserved for the royal robes of the Incan kings.

FOR THE NATIVE SPEAKER

Because of the spelling problem with these sounds, you may wish to give the following dictation:
1. *Ellos llegaron al hotel a la hora precisa.*
2. *Él llegó a ser presidente honorario.*
3. *Él llegó a hacerlo hoy a pesar de la lluvia.*
4. *Ella le dió la llave a su yerno.*
5. *Él se cayó en la calle, pero se calló y no lloró.*

Comunicación

Comunicación

A En Madrid. Imagine you are in Madrid speaking with a Spanish friend (your partner) who wants to know the following:

1. if you went out last night
2. if you went out alone or with a group
3. if you have a boyfriend or a girlfriend (Use the word *amigo* or *amiga.*)
4. if you saw a movie last night either at the movies or on television
5. at what time you got home

Now you find out the same things from your partner.

B La última vez. Find out when was the last time your partner did the following things. Reverse roles.

> ver una película
> Estudiante 1: ¿Cuándo viste una película?
> Estudiante 2: Vi una película anoche.

1. ver una película
2. jugar tenis
3. ir a un concierto
4. tomar el metro
5. cenar en un restaurante
6. dar una fiesta

336

Guernica, de Pablo Picasso

C **Artistas famosos.** You and your partner each write down the name, nationality, and at least one well-known work of each of five famous artists or sculptors whose work you have seen in museums, books, TV, etc. Tell your partner the nationality of the artist and the name of a famous work. Your partner has to guess the artist's name. See who gets the most correct answers with the fewest guesses.

Picasso / español / *Guernica*
Estudiante 1: Es español y pintó *Guernica.*
Estudiante 2: ¿Es Salvador Dalí?
Estudiante 1: No.
Estudiante 2: ¿Es Pablo Picasso?

ANSWERS

Actividad C

Answers will vary along these lines:

E1: **Es español y pintó** *Las Meninas.*

E2: **¿Es Pablo Picasso?**

E1: **No.**

E2: **¿Es Velázquez?**

E1: **Sí.**

HISTORY CONNECTION

In 1937 during the Spanish Civil War, German aircraft bombed the ancient Basque city of Guernica, slaughtering hundreds of civilians on market day. The Spaniard Pablo Picasso, appalled by the event, painted *Guernica* as a protest. He was so angered that he completed the work in a very short period of time. You may wish to have students react to the painting and give you their opinion.

CRITICAL THINKING ACTIVITY

(Thinking skills: drawing conclusions)
Write the following on the board or on an overhead transparency:
1. *¿Por qué es importante y útil un sistema de metro en una ciudad grande?*
2. *Mucha gente sale de casa para ir al cine a ver una película. ¿Por qué van al cine cuando pueden alquilar un vídeo y ver una película en casa sin tener que salir?*

LECTURA Y CULTURA

READING STRATEGIES
(*page 338*)

Pre-reading

A. Have students briefly discuss dating customs in the United States.

B. Tell them that they are going to read about dating customs in the Spanish-speaking world. Explain that dating customs are changing, but have students look for some differences between their dating customs and those of their Spanish-speaking counterparts. Also have them look for similarities.

Reading

A. Have students open their books to page 338 and read the selection silently and quickly.

B. Call on an individual to read approximately one-half paragraph. Then stop and ask pertinent comprehension questions.

Post-reading

A. Have students explain the major differences between the terms *boyfriend/girlfriend* and *novio/novia*.

B. After going over the *Lectura* in class, assign it to be read for homework.

C. Also assign the exercises that follow the *Lectura*. Go over them the next day in class.

Estudio de palabras

ANSWERS

1. e
2. g
3. c
4. a
5. f
6. b
7. d

SOLOS O EN GRUPO

Sarita salió anoche. ¿Con quiénes salió? Salió con un grupo de amigos. Fueron al cine donde vieron una película americana. Las películas americanas son muy populares en España y en Latinoamérica. ¿Comprendió Sarita la película? Sí, la comprendió. Ella la vio en versión original que significa que la vio en inglés, no doblada[1] al español. Pero la vio con subtítulos en español.

En España y en los países latinoamericanos en general, una muchacha joven como Sarita no suele[2] salir con sólo un muchacho. Los jóvenes suelen salir más en grupo. Pero es algo que está cambiando. Hoy los jóvenes están saliendo más y más en parejas[3]. Pero, por lo general, los padres de la joven quieren saber con quién está saliendo su hija. Quieren conocer al muchacho. Pero como aquí, lo que quieren los padres y lo que pasa no es siempre lo mismo, ¿verdad?

En español no hay una palabra equivalente a "dating" o "date". Tampoco existe una traducción exacta de "boyfriend" o "girlfriend". Un novio o una novia es la persona con quien un individuo está saliendo exclusivamente. Algún día piensan contraer matrimonio. Un novio o una novia es más que un amigo o una amiga.

[1] doblada   *dubbed*
[2] suele   *tends to, is accustomed*
[3] parejas   *couples*

Estudio de palabras

¿Cuál es la definición? Escojan la definición.

1. soler (suele)
2. exclusivamente
3. la pareja
4. pasar
5. joven
6. la traducción
7. el individuo

a. ocurrir
b. la equivalencia en otra lengua
c. dos personas
d. la persona
e. tener la costumbre, acostumbrar
f. que no tiene muchos años
g. únicamente

338   CAPÍTULO 12

LEARNING FROM PHOTOS

Have students say as much as they can about the photo on page 338.

Comprensión

A Fue al cine. Contesten.

1. ¿Con quién salió Sarita anoche?
2. ¿Adónde fue?
3. ¿Qué vio?
4. ¿Vio una película americana o española?
5. ¿La comprendió?
6. ¿Vio la película en la versión original o doblada?

B ¿Sí o no? Indiquen *sí* o *no.*

1. Aún hoy los jóvenes en España y Latino-américa no pueden salir en parejas.
2. Por lo general, los jóvenes suelen salir con varios compañeros.
3. Los padres de los jóvenes quieren saber con quién están saliendo sus hijos.
4. Un novio es un muchacho con quien sale una joven de vez en cuando.

C ¿Qué es "dating"? Expliquen.

¿Por qué no existe la palabra "dating" en español?

El pasado 15 de agosto en la elegante residencia del Ing. Juan Carlos Suárez y de su esposa la Dra. María Fernanda Ramírez de Suárez, amigos y familiares celebraron la petición de mano de Rebeca, hija única del matrimonio Suárez, por parte del licencia-do Miguel Angel Barrios, hijo del Dr. Antonio Barrios y su distinguida esposa Emilia Acevedo de Barrios. Todos los concurrentes brindaron por la felicidad de la joven pareja que fijó la fecha de la boda para el 17 de julio del año próximo.

CAPÍTULO 12 **339**

Comprensión

ANSWERS

Ejercicio A

1. Sarita salió anoche con un grupo de amigos.
2. Fue al cine.
3. Vio una película.
4. Vio una película americana.
5. Sí, la comprendió.
6. Vio la película en la versión original.

Ejercicio B

1. sí
2. sí
3. sí
4. no

Ejercicio C

Answers will vary.

DID YOU KNOW?

Pepita Jiménez is a novel by the Spanish author Juan Valera (1827–1905). Valera was also a diplomat, and once served in the Spanish Embassy in Washington D.C. You may wish to ask students what they think the story of *Pepita Jiménez* is about from looking at the ad. The plot centers around a young seminarian who falls in love and marries just before he is to be ordained.

LEARNING FROM REALIA

Have students scan the announcement on page 339 and find the following information: Who got engaged? What was the date of the engagement party? When did it take place? How many children do the parents of the fiancée have? When will the wedding take place?

Descubrimiento cultural

(The Descubrimiento *is optional material.)*

PRESENTATION

(pages 340–341)

A. Have students read the information silently.

B. Then let them get together in small informal groups and tell one another in Spanish something they learned from the reading.

HISTORY CONNECTION

Benito Juárez is a great Mexican hero. He led the struggle against the French troops of Maximilian. After his victory, he became president of Mexico from 1858 to 1872. Juárez's birthday, March 21, is a national holiday in Mexico. The city of Juárez, across the border from El Paso, Texas, was named for him.

DESCUBRIMIENTO CULTURAL

A los jóvenes en Latinoamérica les interesan mucho las películas. Como ya sabemos las películas americanas son muy populares. Pero en varios países ruedan muchas películas de habla española. La industria cinematográfica es importante en España, México y la Argentina.

¿Hay un género teatral exclusivamente español? Sí, hay. Es la zarzuela. La zarzuela es una obra dramática de asunto ligero[1], no profundo. Es un tipo de opereta porque en una zarzuela los actores y las actrices cantan y hablan.

En los países hispanos hay algunos museos de fama mundial. Uno es el Prado en Madrid. En el Prado hay exposiciones permanentes de los cuadros de Velázquez, el Greco y Goya—tres pintores españoles famosos.

El Museo de Antropología en la Ciudad de México es otro museo famoso. En la planta baja del museo hay exposiciones de artefactos, templos, etc., de las civilizaciones indígenas precolombinas—artefactos de los mayas, los toltecas y los aztecas. En el primer piso hay exposiciones de las culturas indígenas que existen en México en la actualidad.

Es imposible hablar de la cultura mexicana y no hablar de los famosos murales de Diego Rivera, José Clemente Orozco y David Alfaro Siqueiros. Los murales de Rivera son de carácter revolucionario. Él pintó para educar al pueblo. Sus murales tienen como tema la vida, la historia y los problemas sociales mexicanos.

Ya sabemos que los españoles viajaron por las Américas en busca de oro y plata. En Bogotá, Colombia y en Lima, Perú, hay museos de oro. La cantidad de objetos de oro en estos dos museos es increíble.

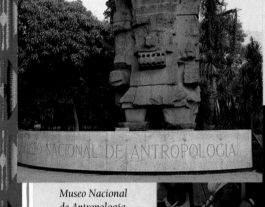

Museo Nacional de Antropología, México, D.F.

El presidente Benito Juárez, mural de José Clemente Orozco

CRITICAL THINKING ACTIVITY

(Thinking skills: drawing conclusions and problem solving)

Write the following on the board or on an overhead transparency: *¿Dónde prefiere vivir la mayoría de la gente que tiene mucho interés en las actividades culturales? ¿Por qué?*

INDEPENDENT PRACTICE

Assign the following: Workbook, *Un poco más,* pages 127–129

El ballet folklórico de México es famoso. Los domingos hay una presentación en el Palacio de Bellas Artes en la capital.

Varias ciudades hispanas tienen metro, un sistema de transporte subterráneo. Madrid tiene un sistema de metros. Es bastante viejo. Caracas, la Ciudad de México y Santiago de Chile tienen sistemas de metro fantásticos. Las estaciones están muy limpias[2] y los trenes no hacen ruido[3]. Son muy modernos.

Una estación de metro en México, D.F.

Y AQUÍ EN LOS ESTADOS UNIDOS

Hace mucho tiempo que los artistas hispanos tienen gran importancia en Broadway y Hollywood. Nuestras abuelas recuerdan a César Romero, hijo de cubanos y descendiente del héroe José Martí; a Desi Arnaz, otro cubano de múltiples talentos; y al puertorriqueño José Ferrer, gran intérprete de Cyrano.

Los puertorriqueños Raúl Julia y Rita Moreno siguen recibiendo aplausos y premios por su gran talento. Rita Moreno es ganadora del Óscar, del Tony, del Emmy y del Grammy. Rubén Blades, panameño, con un título de Harvard, es músico, actor y político. Andy García y María Conchita Alonso, hijos de cubanos, son grandes estrellas. También son estrellas Edward James Olmos, y Vicki Carr, de ascendencia mexicana.

El teatro puede inspirar y enseñar. El director y productor mexicoamericano, Luis Valdez es fundador del Teatro Campesino, que lleva obras de teatro a los barrios latinos de California y el suroeste. Miriam Colón Valle, actriz, directora y productora, es la fundadora y presidenta del Puerto Rican Travelling Theater. Ella y su grupo llevan obras de teatro a las calles del barrio latino de Nueva York.

[1] ligero   *light*
[2] limpias   *clean*
[3] ruido   *noise*

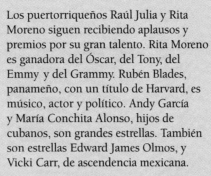
Luis Valdez

Andy García

Rita Moreno

CAPÍTULO 12   **341**

LEARNING FROM PHOTOS

You have learned that some other Spanish-speaking cities have a subway system. Which ones? (*México, Caracas, Santiago de Chile, Madrid*)

REALIDADES

(*The* Realidades *is optional material.*)

PRESENTATION

Have students look at the photos for enjoyment. After they read the captions on page 342 you may want to share the following additional cultural information with them:

Photo 1: Tenochtitlán was founded in 1345 on a marshy island in Lake Texcoco. It is estimated that its population was between 200,000 and 300,000. In 1521, after a three-month siege, the Spaniard Hernán Cortés and his army conquered Tenochtitlán and captured the Aztec leader Cuauhtémoc. Mexico City was subsequently built by the Spaniards on the ruins of Tenochtitlán.

The model of Tenochtitlán shown on pages 342–343 is located in the *Museo Nacional de Antropología* in Mexico City. It is undoubtedly one of the best archeological museums in the world. It houses a tremendous collection of treasures from all the pre-Hispanic cultures of Meso-America. The upper floor contains wonderful displays of the current indigenous peoples of Mexico.

Photo 2: The *Palacio de Bellas Artes* was originally intended to only be an opera house. Now it is also a national museum. The building is known for its architecture and its paintings by famous Mexican artists such as Rufino Tamayo and the muralists Rivera, Orozco, and Siqueiros.

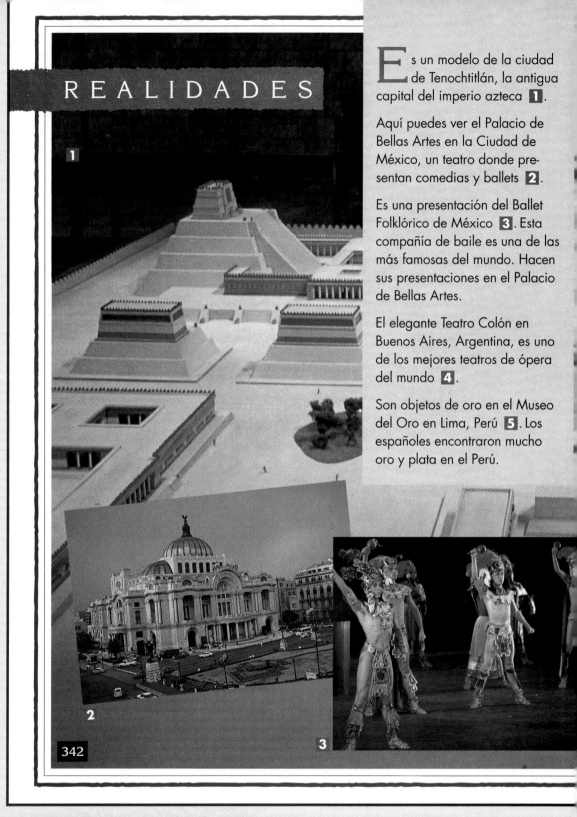

2

342

3

E s un modelo de la ciudad de Tenochtitlán, la antigua capital del imperio azteca **1**.

Aquí puedes ver el Palacio de Bellas Artes en la Ciudad de México, un teatro donde presentan comedias y ballets **2**.

Es una presentación del Ballet Folklórico de México **3**. Esta compañía de baile es una de las más famosas del mundo. Hacen sus presentaciones en el Palacio de Bellas Artes.

El elegante Teatro Colón en Buenos Aires, Argentina, es uno de los mejores teatros de ópera del mundo **4**.

Son objetos de oro en el Museo del Oro en Lima, Perú **5**. Los españoles encontraron mucho oro y plata en el Perú.

DID YOU KNOW?

In the *Palacio de Bellas Artes*, Diego Rivera reconstructed his mural *Man in Control of His Universe*. This mural had originally been commissioned for the Radio City Music Hall in New York City. However, it was taken down because of its political message. It contains a face of Lenin.

Photo 5: The *Museo del Oro* contains more than 6,500 pieces of gold, including bowls, cups, plates, and ceremonial objects. Other great works of indigenous art, mostly larger ones, were unfortunately melted down by the Spaniards during the colonial period.

343

LEARNING FROM PHOTOS

The photo of the Teátro Colón shows the typical wide avenues of Buenos Aires. The center of the city is the *Plaza de Mayo* with the *Casa Rosada,* the home of the president. The *Avenida de Mayo* stretches from the *Plaza de Mayo* to the National Congress, 1.6 kilometers away. The *Avenida 9 de Julio* commemorates Argentina's independence from Spain on July 9, 1816.

Comunicación oral
(page 344)

ANSWERS

Actividad A
 Answers will vary.

Actividad B
 Answers will vary.

Actividad C
 Answers will vary according to the model.

Comunicación escrita

ANSWERS

Actividades A–D
 Answers will vary.

CULMINACIÓN

Comunicación oral

A **Los novios.** Work in groups of four. In your group find out: how many have a *novio(a)*; if they do, do they go out with anyone else; do their parents know or want to meet their *novio(a)*.

B **¿Quién es más culto?** You and your partner each prepare a list of favorite activities. Compare your lists and rate the activities as cultural or non-cultural. Decide who is the more "cultured" type.

C **¿Qué hiciste?** Using the cues provided, tell your partner when you usually do the following things, but that yesterday you did something different. Reverse roles.

> comer a las ___
> *Suelo comer a las doce, pero ayer comí a las dos.*

1. comer a las ___
2. beber ___
3. salir para la escuela a las ___
4. llegar a casa a las ___
5. ver ___ a las ocho
6. hablar por teléfono con ___

Comunicación escrita

A **Anoche conocí a…** Make an entry in your diary about a special person you met (*conocer*) last night at a concert. Tell what time you arrived at the concert and exactly where and when you saw the person. Tell the person's age and what school he or she attends. Write down that you gave the person your phone number, and that the person gave you his or hers.

B **Una carta.** Your friend Lupita Delgado lives in Santiago de Chile. She has written to you asking what "dating" means. Write to her explaining the meaning of "dating," and of "boyfriend" and "girlfriend" in the United States.

C **El fin de semana pasado.** Make a list of five things that you did last weekend. Share your list with your partner. Did you do any of the same things? If so, write them down.

D **Tiene que ser…** Write a short paragraph describing an ideal boyfriend or girlfriend. Exchange papers with your partner and correct any errors. Discuss the corrections with each other, rewrite the paragraphs, and read them to the class.

344 CAPÍTULO 12

FOR THE YOUNGER STUDENT

1. Have students illustrate a poster that advertises a movie in Spanish (real or imaginary), giving the names of the stars, the type of film, and the time and location of the film.

2. Have students make a poster in Spanish for the school play. Include the following information: title of the play, date, time, location, actors, price of the tickets, and a statement encouraging people to attend.

Reintegración

A **El año pasado.** Contesten.

1. ¿Esquiaste el invierno pasado?
2. ¿Nadaste el verano pasado?
3. ¿Esquiaste en el agua?
4. ¿Patinaste?
5. ¿Adónde fuiste?
6. ¿Con quién fuiste?
7. ¿Lo pasaron Uds. bien?
8. ¿Jugaste al tenis?

B **¿Qué deporte es?** Identifiquen.

1. El jugador tiró o lanzó el balón con el pie.
2. La pelota pasó por encima de la red.
3. Él tiró el balón y encestó.
4. Marcó un gol.
5. La pelota entró en el hoyo.
6. Es necesario tener una raqueta.
7. Es necesario jugar con palos.
8. Ella bateó un jonrón.

Vocabulario

SUSTANTIVOS

el cine
la película
el film(e)
la pantalla
el teatro
la escena
el telón
el actor
la actriz
el/la autor(a)
la obra
la representación
el espectáculo
la taquilla
la sesión
la cola
la fila
la entrada
la localidad
la butaca

el museo
el arte
la exposición
el/la artista
el/la escultor(a)
el cuadro
el mural

la estatua
el concierto
el/la músico
la orquesta
el/la director(a)

el restaurante
el/la mesero(a)
la mesa
el menú
la cuenta
la propina

el transporte
el metro
la estación

ADJETIVOS

público(a)
artístico(a)
musical
teatral
subterráneo(a)

VERBOS

parar
dejar
asistir
aplaudir

OTRAS PALABRAS Y EXPRESIONES

perder el autobús
entrar en escena
dar (presentar) una película

CAPÍTULO 12   **345**

Reintegración

PRESENTATION (*page 345*)
   Exercises A and B reinforce the preterite of *-ar* verbs.

ANSWERS

Ejercicio A
   Answers can also be negative.
1. Sí, esquié el invierno pasado.
2. Sí, nadé el verano pasado.
3. Sí, esquié en el agua.
4. Sí, patiné.
5. Fui a (Acapulco).
6. Fui con…
7. Sí, lo pasamos bien.
8. Sí, jugué al tenis.

Ejercicio B
1. fútbol
2. tenis
3. baloncesto
4. fútbol
5. golf
6. tenis
7. golf
8. béisbol

Vocabulario
   There are approximately 24 cognates in this *Vocabulario* list.

VIDEO
   The video is intended to reinforce the vocabulary, structures, and cultural content in each chapter. It may be used here as a chapter wrap-up activity. See the *Video Activities Booklet* for additional suggestions on its use.

ACTIVIDADES CULTURALES
(0:48:19)

STUDENT PORTFOLIO

   Written assignments that may be included in students' portfolios are the *Actividades escritas* on page 344 and the *Mi autobiografía* section in the Workbook, page 130.

INDEPENDENT PRACTICE

   Assign any of the following:
1. Exercises on student page 345
2. Workbook, *Mi autobiografía*, page 130
3. Chapter 12, Situation Cards

(optional material)

OVERVIEW

All the readings presented in the *Nuestro Mundo* section are authentic, uncut texts from publications of the Hispanic world. Students should be encouraged to read the text for overall meaning, but not intensively, word for word. Students should find satisfaction in their ability to derive meaning from "real" texts. Each reading is related to a theme or themes covered in the previous four chapters.

PRESENTATION *(page 346)*

Have students study the weather map and tell all they can about it. You may wish to ask them questions such as: *¿Qué país es el más grande en el mapa? ¿Dónde hace sol? ¿Dónde llueve?* etc.

Ejercicios

PRESENTATION

Ejercicio A

Have students respond orally as they look at the weather map.

ANSWERS

Ejercicio A

1. para las 12 horas
2. chubasco
3. Sevilla, Málaga, Melilla
4. Madrid, Valladolid, Valencia, Palma

GEOGRAPHY CONNECTION

The typical conditions of a geographical zone have to do with the climate (*el clima*). These conditions are stable. They don't vary much through the years. For example: Summers are hot and winters are cold. It rains during certain months of the year. *El tiempo* (the weather) refers to the atmospheric conditions at a given time. It can vary from day to day.

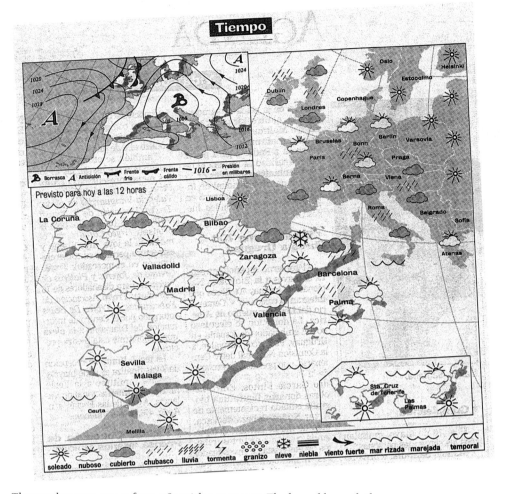

The weather map comes from a Spanish newspaper. The legend beneath the map shows the symbols for the different phenomena. Study the map and try to answer the questions.

A **El tiempo.** Contesten.

1. For what time of day is the weather being predicted?
2. What is the weather like in Barcelona?
3. Name three areas where it will be sunny today.
4. Where will it be partially cloudy?

LEARNING FROM REALIA

The box at the upper-left corner of the weather map on page 346 shows barometric pressure in milibars. You may wish to call students' attention to the box and ask: *¿Qué tiempo hace cuando la presión es alta? Y, ¿qué tiempo hace cuando la presión es baja?* (rising barometric pressure usually indicates fair weather) *¿Dónde en Europa probablemente hace mal tiempo?*

B ¿Qué quiere decir? Digan en español.

1. rain showers
2. storm
3. hail
4. snow
5. partly cloudy
6. sunny
7. rain
8. choppy seas
9. Stockholm
10. Athens
11. Warsaw
12. London

C El cuadro. Contesten.

1. In the lower right-hand corner of the chart there is a box. What is represented in the box?
2. In similar U.S. weather maps, what are represented in boxes like that?

DICIEMBRE – ENERO Nº 17, Santiago

TRAVELING

El sol brilla en el hemisferio sur. Es época de vacaciones. Playas, lagos, campos y ciudades se ven diferentes. Todo lo entretenido está al aire libre. En Santiago, el teatro y la música invaden los parques, y siempre existe la posibilidad de arrancarse, aunque sea por el día, a las playas del litoral central o a los hermosos lagos de los alrededores. Le invitamos a celebrar con nosotros, bajo el sol del verano, un buen año que termina y deseamos de corazón que el próximo año sea el mejor de su vida.

This is an excerpt from a guide for tourists published in Santiago, Chile.

D ¿Dónde dice? Busquen dónde en el artículo dice lo siguiente:

1. where the sun shines
2. what time of the year it is
3. what it is that "invades" the parks of Santiago
4. where you can get away to "if only for a day"
5. what is ending, what is beginning, and what will be celebrated
6. what "seems different"

E ¿Qué quiere decir? Contesten.

The article says that four things look "different" at this time of the year. What are they?

F ¡Piensen! Contesten.

There seems to be something incongruous about the weather and the activities described, and the months of the year. Why? Explain.

PRESENTATION (*page 347*)

A. You may wish to assign the questions as written homework, or have students do them orally in class.
B. Students should look at the weather map as they do this exercise.

Ejercicio D
Have students find the place in the text where the information is located and read it aloud.

Ejercicio E
Have students respond orally. They only have to find the place in the text and read it in Spanish.

ANSWERS

Ejercicio B
1. chubasco
2. tormenta
3. granizo
4. nieve
5. nuboso
6. soleado
7. lluvia
8. mar rizada
9. Estocolmo
10. Atenas
11. Varsovia
12. Londres

Ejercicio C
1. Santa Cruz de Tenerife y Las Palmas (las Islas Canarias)
2. Alaska and Hawaii

Ejercicio D
1. en el hemisferio sur (line 1)
2. es época de vacaciones (line 1)
3. el teatro y la música (line 3)
4. a las playas del litoral central o a los hermosos lagos de los alrededores (lines 4-5)
5. un buen año, el próximo año, un buen año que termina (lines 6-7)
6. playas, lagos, campos y ciudades (line 2)

Ejercicio E
beaches, lakes, countryside, and cities

Ejercicio F
The passage talks about New Year's, going to the beach, and summer vacation in December and January. The article is from Chile where the seasons are opposite from those in North America.

OVERVIEW

This section reviews the key grammatical structures and vocabulary from Chapters 9–12. The topics were first presented on the following pages: present tense of *saber* and *conocer,* page 252; *ser* and *estar,* page 278; direct object pronouns, pages 283, 307; preterite of regular verbs, 304, 329; preterite of *ir* and *ser,* page 309.

Lectura

PRESENTATION *(page 348)*

A. Read the *Lectura* to the class as they listen with books closed.

B. Now have students open their books to page 348 and read the *Lectura* silently.

C. Call on individual students to read several sentences aloud. Ask comprehension questions after each student has read.

Ejercicio

PRESENTATION

Students may do this exercise either orally or as a reading task.

ANSWERS

1. b   4. a
2. c   5. a
3. b   6. c

Estructura

Saber y conocer

PRESENTATION

(pages 348–349)

A. Read the rules for the use of *saber* and *conocer* to the class.

B. Ask for examples of known facts and of people or abstract topics with which one is acquainted.

C. Review the paradigms for *saber* and *conocer* on page 349.

D. Emphasize the irregular *yo* forms, *sé* and *conozco.* Point out that the other forms are regular.

CAPÍTULOS 9–12

Lectura *Fuimos al teatro*

Ayer mis hermanos y yo tomamos el metro y fuimos al teatro. Vimos una comedia excelente. El autor de la comedia es de Francia. La dieron en el Teatro Guerrero. Ese teatro es viejo pero elegante. Está en la Avenida Central. Yo sé que los actores principales son famosos, pero no los conozco. El público les dio una gran ovación al final. Cuando salimos del teatro empezó a nevar y decidimos tomar un taxi para regresar a casa.

En el teatro. Escojan.

1. La familia fue al teatro ___.
   a. a pie   b. en metro   c. en taxi

2. Ellos vieron ___.
   a. una película   b. un drama   c. una comedia

3. El autor es ___.
   a. español   b. francés   c. norteamericano

4. Guerrero es el nombre del ___.
   a. teatro   b. autor   c. actor

5. El teatro tiene muchos ___.
   a. años   b. actores   c. pisos

6. La joven no conoce ___.
   a. el teatro   b. al autor   c. a los actores

Estructura

Saber y conocer

1. Both *saber* and *conocer* mean "to know." *Saber* is used for expressing knowledge of simple facts.

   Yo sé la palabra.

2. *Conocer* means "to know" in the sense of "to be acquainted with." It is also used to express knowledge of abstract or complex issues or topics.

   Conozco al senador. Conocemos la ciudad.
   Ella conoce la historia de México.

Teatro María Guerrero

CENTRO DRAMÁTICO NACIONAL

COMBATE
*de negro
y de perros*

de BERNARD-MARIE KOLTÈS

Traducción: SERGI BELBEL
Dirección: MIGUEL NARROS

Escenografía y vestuario:
CHRISTOPH SCHUBIGER   KATRIN FURLER

Por orden de intervención:
ALAIN LUKUSA   SANCHO GRACIA
PILAR BAYONA   ANTONIO VALERO

LEARNING FROM REALIA

Have students tell you all they can about the theater program cover. You may wish to ask them: *¿En qué teatro dan la obra? ¿Qué obra es? ¿Quién es el autor de la obra? ¿Quién es el traductor? ¿Quién es el director?*

Review the present tense forms of *saber* and *conocer*.

INFINITIVE	SABER	CONOCER
yo	sé	conozco
tú	sabes	conoces
él, ella, Ud.	sabe	conoce
nosotros(as)	sabemos	conocemos
vosotros(as)	sabéis	conocéis
ellos, ellas, Uds.	saben	conocen

A **¿Qué sabes?** Completen con *saber* o *conocer*.

Yo no ___ dónde vive Luis Tovar. Tú ___ a Luis,
₁   ₂
¿verdad? Pero, ¿tú ___ dónde él vive? Quiero hablar
₃
con Luis, porque él ___ esquiar muy bien, y quiero
₄
aprender. También quiero ___ a su hermana Sonia.
₅
Sonia ___ a mi hermana, pero no me ___. Ella no
₆   ₇
___ que yo soy amigo de Luis.
₈

Ser y estar

1. *Ser* is used to denote origin.

    Paco es de México. Los libros son de Chile. Soy de Puerto Rico.

2. *Estar* is used to denote location.

    Ellos están en la playa. El periódico está en la mesa.

3. *Ser* is used to describe characteristics of a person or thing that are relatively permanent.

    La ciudad es grande. Somos altos. Ella es inteligente.

4. *Estar* is used to describe conditions that are temporary or liable to change.

    Estoy cansada. El día está oscuro. La comida está fría.

B **¿Dónde está?** Completen con la forma apropiada de *ser* o *estar*.

1. La Sra. Fernández ___ muy inteligente.
2. Ella ___ de Honduras.
3. Ella ___ en Texas ahora.
4. Ella ___ profesora de español.
5. Hoy ella no ___ bien. Tiene fiebre.
6. Por eso ___ en casa.
7. Su casa ___ en la ciudad y ___ muy bonita.

CAPÍTULOS 9–12 REPASO   **349**

349

Los pronombres de complemento directo y indirecto

1. The object pronouns *me, te,* and *nos* can function as either direct or indirect object pronouns. Note that the object pronouns in Spanish precede the conjugated verb.

    Juan *me* vio.   **Juan *me* dio el libro.**

2. *Lo, los, la,* and *las* function as direct object pronouns only. They can replace persons or things.

    Pablo compró *el boleto.*   Pablo *lo* compró.
    Pablo compró *los boletos.*   Pablo *los* compró.
    Elena compró *la raqueta.*   Elena *la* compró.
    Elena compró *las raquetas.*   Elena *las* compró.
    Yo vi *a los muchachos.*   Yo *los* vi.

3. *Le* and *les* function as indirect object pronouns only.

    Yo *le* escribí una carta (a él, a ella, a Ud.).
    Yo *les* escribí una carta (a ellos, a ellas, a Uds.).

C **¿Qué llevas?** Cambien los sustantivos.

1. Llevo *los esquís* a la cancha.
2. También llevo *las botas.*
3. Compro *el boleto* en la taquilla.
4. Veo *a mi hermana* en el telesquí.
5. Doy el boleto *a mi hermana.*
6. Ella da sus esquís *a los muchachos.*

El pretérito de los verbos regulares

Review the preterite tense forms of regular verbs. The preterite is used to express an action completed in the past.

estudiar	yo estudié, tú estudiaste, él/ella/Ud. estudió, nosotros(as) estudiamos, *vosotros(as) estudiasteis,* ellos/ellas/Uds. estudiaron
comer	yo comí, tú comiste, él/ella/Ud. comió, nosotros(as) comimos, *vosotros(as) comisteis,* ellos/ellas/Uds. comieron
escribir	yo escribí, tú escribiste, él/ella/Ud. escribió, nosotros(as) escribimos, *vosotros(as) escribisteis,* ellos/ellas/Uds. escribieron

D Esta mañana. Completen.

Esta mañana yo ___ (tomar) el desayuno a las siete. Después mi hermana y
yo ___ (salir) de casa. Ella ___ (subir) al bus para ir a la escuela, pero yo ___
(decidir) ir a pie. Nosotros no ___ (llegar) a la misma hora. En la escuela
algunos estudiantes ___ (estudiar) y ___ (aprender) un poco de historia.
Yo ___ (leer) un libro. Mi hermana ___ (escribir) unas lecciones. A las tres
yo ___ (meter) mis libros y cuadernos en la mochila, y nosotros ___ (volver)
a casa.

(Los números debajo de los espacios: 1 tomar, 2 salir, 3 subir, 4 decidir, 5 llegar, 6 estudiar, 7 aprender, 8 leer, 9 escribir, 10 meter, 11 volver)

El pretérito de *ir* y *ser*

The preterite tense forms of *ir* and *ser* are identical. Review them.

ir	yo fui, tú fuiste, él/ella/Ud. fue, nosotros fuimos, *vosotros fuisteis*, ellos/ellas/Uds. fueron
ser	yo fui, tú fuiste, él/ella/Ud. fue, nosotros fuimos, *vosotros fuisteis*, ellos/ellas/Uds. fueron

E Fuimos al cine. Completen.

1. El sábado pasado nosotros ___ al cine.
2. Las películas no ___ muy buenas.
3. Yo ___ a la taquilla por mi dinero.
4. El taquillero no ___ muy simpático.
5. Entonces Adela ___ a hablar con el dueño del cine.
6. Y tú, ¿adónde ___ el sábado pasado?

Comunicación

Los deportes. Tell a student from Latin America what sports you participated in last summer and last winter, how well you played them, and which was your favorite and why. Reverse roles.

Las matemáticas: El sistema métrico

OVERVIEW

The three readings in this section deal with the metric system, nutrition, and the Inca civilization. You may wish to allow students to choose one selection that appeals to their particular interests, or have the whole class read all three selections.

Antes de leer

PRESENTATION (page 352)

A. Assign the *Antes de leer* exercises as homework prior to the reading.

B. Go over the assignment in class. Ask students to write the metric system units for length on the board. Give them the following units in Spanish and ask individual students to put the English equivalent next to each one on the board:
1. *el metro*
2. *el centímetro*
3. *el milímetro*
4. *el kilómetro*

C. Have students go over step 2 orally.

D. Ask students for the metric units for weights and liquids. Have them write them on the board. For example: miligram, gram, kilogram; centiliter, liter. Give them the following units in Spanish and ask individual students to put the English equivalent next to each one on the board:
1. *el mililitro*
2. *el litro*
3. *el gramo*
4. *el kilogramo*

LAS MATEMÁTICAS: EL SISTEMA MÉTRICO

Antes de leer

The metric system is used in most of the world for measuring length, mass, and volume; meters, liters, and grams. The English system of measures, traditionally used in Great Britain and the U.S., consists of feet, miles, pounds, and ounces.

1. Review the English names for the major units of measure for length in the metric system.
2. Review the metric equivalents of inches, yards, miles, pounds, and ounces.

Lectura

En la mayoría de los países del mundo se usa el sistema métrico decimal. El sistema métrico decimal emplea las siguientes unidades básicas. Para medir la longitud, el metro; para el peso, el kilogramo; y para los líquidos, el litro.

Longitud: El metro se puede usar para medir la longitud, la anchura[1] y la altura. El metro original se determina en 1796 dividiendo en diez millones de partes iguales la longitud para el cuadrante de

meridiano que va desde Dunkerque en Francia hasta Barcelona en España, pasando por París. En París, en el Museo de Artes y Oficios, conservan la barra de platino[2] que mide[3] el metro original. El metro moderno (1983) es igual a la distancia que viaja la luz en un vacío[4] en 1/299.792.459 de un segundo.

El sistema tradicional inglés se basa en la pulgada[2] y el pie. La tradición dice que el "pie" original es el pie de un rey de Inglaterra. Es obvio que todos no tenemos los pies iguales.

Las medidas tradicionales para peso en los EE.UU. son la onza, la libra y la tonelada. Las medidas para líquidos son la onza, la pinta, el cuarto y el galón. Uds. saben que hay 16 onzas en una libra, y 2.000 libras en una tonelada. En el sistema métrico decimal las medidas de peso se basan en el kilogramo (kg). Un kilogramo es igual a 2.2 libras. Es decir, una libra es un poco menos que medio kilogramo. Las medidas para líquidos se basan en el litro (L). Una botella de vino contiene 750 mililitros o 75 centilitros. Una lata de refresco contiene 354 mililitros. Un litro contiene un poco más que un cuarto; un litro es equivalente a 1,0567 cuarto. Un cuentagotas[5] contiene aproximadamente un mililitro.

LEARNING FROM PHOTOS

Major highways in Spain are *Carreteras Nacionales, Autopistas,* or *Autovías.* The *Carreteras Nacionales* carry the designation *N* plus a Roman numeral. There is also a marker at every kilometer showing the distance from that point to Madrid. Ask students how much information they can get from the photo on page 352.

FONDO ACADÉMICO

Para medir cantidades o distancias inferiores o superiores al kilogramo, litro o metro se usan unidades que se forman con los siguientes prefijos:

kilo × 1000	kilogramo = 1000 gramos
hecta × 100	hectámetro = 100 metros
deca × 10	decalitro = 10 litros
deci: 10	decilitro = 1/10 litro
centi:100	centímetro = 1/100 metro
mili: 1000	miligramo = 1/1000 gramo

Podemos convertir las unidades de un sistema a otro.

SISTEMA MÉTRICO DECIMAL		SISTEMA INGLÉS
1 m	=	39,37 pulgadas (1,094 yardas)
1 km	=	0,621 millas
1 litro	=	1,0567 cuartos

¹ anchura *width*
² platino *platinum*
³ mide *measures*
⁴ vacío *vacuum*
⁵ pulgada *inch*
⁶ cuentagotas *eyedropper*

Después de leer

A **El sistema métrico.** Contesten.

1. ¿Qué podemos medir con el sistema métrico decimal?
2. ¿Qué es lo que dividen para determinar el metro original?
3. ¿En cuántas partes la dividen?
4. ¿Cuáles son las unidades básicas del sistema métrico decimal?
5. ¿En qué se basa el sistema inglés para medir la longitud?
6. ¿Quién es más grande, una persona que pesa 200 libras o 100 kilos?
7. ¿Cuántas onzas son 354 mililitros?
8. ¿Cuál contiene menos líquido, un cuarto o un litro?
9. ¿Más o menos cuántos litros hay en un galón?

B **Las medidas.** ¿Dónde dice lo siguiente?

1. how the original meter was determined
2. what the most common metric units are
3. the length of the modern meter
4. on what the English system is based
5. the contents of an eyedropper

C **Seguimiento.** Den la respuesta en unidades métricas.

1. ¿Cuál es la distancia entre la escuela y tu casa?
2. ¿Cuál es tu altura?
3. ¿Cuál es el largo de un campo de fútbol americano?
4. ¿Cuánto mide un jugador profesional de baloncesto?
5. ¿Cuánto pesa un jugador profesional de fútbol americano?

FONDO ACADÉMICO **353**

Lectura
PRESENTATION
(pages 352–353)

A. Have students read the passage silently.
B. Select individual students to read paragraphs aloud.
C. Ask the questions in *Después de leer* Exercise A and have students answer orally.

Después de leer
PRESENTATION *(page 353)*

A. Have students write short answers to Exercise A for homework.
B. Do Exercise B in class.
C. Exercise C can be done either orally in class or as homework to be reviewed in class.

ANSWERS
Ejercicio A
1. la longitud, el peso y los líquidos
2. la longitud para el cuadrante de meridiano que va desde Dunkerque hasta Barcelona
3. diez millones
4. el kilogramo, el litro y el metro
5. la pulgada y el pie
6. una persona que pesa 100 kilos
7. 12
8. un cuarto
9. 4

Ejecicio B
1. page 352, paragraph 1
2. page 352, paragraph 1
3. page 352, paragraph 2
4. page 352, paragraph 3
5. page 352, paragraph 4

Ejercicio C
Answers will vary.

CRITICAL THINKING ACTIVITY

(Thinking skills: supporting opinions; solving problems)

1. Ask students to comment on the following: *¿Cuál es más práctico, el sistema métrico o el sistema inglés? ¿Por qué?*
2. Present the following problem to figure out:

Tú tienes un carro americano en la Argentina. Sabes que da 25 millas por galón de gasolina. Quieres viajar de Buenos Aires a las cataratas de Iguazú, una distancia de unos 1.100 kilómetros. Más o menos, ¿cuántos litros de gasolina tienes que comprar?

Las ciencias naturales: La biología

Antes de leer

PRESENTATION *(page 354)*

A. Call on students to explain and give examples of a food chain.

B. Have students put three headings on the board:
   1. *productores*
   2. *consumidores primarios*
   3. *consumidores secundarios*

   Hand individual students pictures or drawings of the following and ask them to place them under the appropriate heading:
   a. a cat or dog
   b. a head of lettuce
   c. a rabbit or mouse
   d. an eagle or hawk
   e. a deer, moose, or elk
   f. vegetable
   g. a human

C. Have students skim the passage and identify the following cognates that are not obvious: consumers, predators.

Lectura

PRESENTATION *(page 354)*

A. Have students read the passage silently.

B. Select students to ask comprehension questions about the passage.

C. Ask students to define in Spanish:
   a. *herbívoro*
   b. *carnívoro*
   c. *omnívoro*

LAS CIENCIAS NATURALES: LA BIOLOGÍA

Antes de leer

All living things, both plants and animals, need nutrients of one sort or another to maintain life. You probably already know something about the "food chain." Review the steps in the food chain prior to reading the following selection.

Lectura

Un gaucho argentino

Los humanos comemos para vivir. Nada puede vivir sin alguna forma de alimentación[1]. Las plantas producen su propia alimentación con la ayuda de la energía del sol. La cadena[2] alimentaria comienza con una planta verde. Las plantas verdes son los únicos *productores*, y forman la materia orgánica. Los humanos, los animales y todos los otros seres vivos son consumidores. Los consumidores se dividen en dos grupos: los consumidores primarios y los consumidores secundarios. Los consumidores primarios comen las plantas verdes. No comen carne. Los animales herbívoros se alimentan exclusivamente de plantas. Los consumidores secundarios comen los animales herbívoros. Son animales carnívoros o depredadores. Algunos consumidores secundarios comen plantas y animales. Ellos son omnívoros. Los humanos, ¿somos herbívoros u omnívoros? Y tú, ¿eres consumidor primario o secundario? ¿Qué son los vegetarianos?

[1] alimentación *food*
[2] cadena *chain*

LEARNING FROM PHOTOS

Ask students the following questions about the photos on pages 354–355:

1. *En la foto de un gaucho, ¿son los animales productores, consumidores primarios o consumidores secundarios?*

2. *En la foto de los leones, ¿qué son estos animales?*

3. *¿En qué foto o fotos hay herbívoros? ¿Carnívoros? ¿Productores?*

DID YOU KNOW?

Argentina is one of the major world producers and consumers of beef. It is also one of the four major exporters of grain.

FONDO ACADÉMICO

Las pampas argentinas

Puente Romano, Córdoba, España

Después de leer

A ¿Consumidores o productores?
Escojan.

1. Los únicos productores son ___.
   a. los humanos   b. las plantas

2. Los elefantes son consumidores ___.
   a. primarios   b. secundarios

3. Los depredadores son consumidores ___.
   a. primarios   b. secundarios

4. Los animales herbívoros son
   consumidores ___.
   a. primarios   b. secundarios

5. Los depredadores están al ___ de la
   cadena alimentaria.
   a. comienzo   b. final

B La clasificación. Clasifiquen los
siguientes organismos.

PRODUCTORES
CONSUMIDORES PRIMARIOS
CONSUMIDORES SECUNDARIOS

perros	flores	gatos
plantas	humanos	papas
bacterias	amebas	elefantes
tigres	burros	

C Seguimiento. Preparen tres
cadenas alimentarias lógicas.

grano > ratón > gato

Después de leer

PRESENTATION *(page 355)*

A. Have students do Exercise A
   orally in class.
B. Assign Exercises B and C as
   homework.

ANSWERS
Ejercicio A
1. b
2. a
3. b
4. a
5. b

Ejercicio B
   Productores: plantas, flores,
papas
   Consumidores primarios: amebas, bacterias, burros, elefantes
   Consumidores secundarios:
tigres, humanos, gatos, perros

Ejercicio C
   Answers will vary.

CRITICAL THINKING ACTIVITY

*(Thinking skills: making inferences, drawing
conclusions)*
   Ask students to discuss the following
question: *¿Qué son los humanos? ¿Consumidores primarios o secundarios? ¿Herbívoros,
carnívoros u omnívoros?* The discussion
should focus on differences in diet among
people.

355

Las ciencias sociales: Antropología e historia
Antes de leer

PRESENTATION *(page 356)*

A. Assign the *Antes de leer* task for homework.

B. Review the homework in class prior to doing the reading. Call on students to answer the following questions:
   1. *¿Qué países cubre el imperio inca?* (See map on page 357.)
   2. *¿Qué nombre tiene el rey de los incas?*
   3. *¿Qué productos cultivan los incas?*
   4. *¿Cuál es la capital del imperio inca?*
   5. *¿Cuál es la lengua de los incas?*

C. Tell students that they are going to read about the Incas and their civilization. Find out if they know of other pre-Columbian civilizations in the Americas. They should be able to identify the Mayas and the Aztecs. Give them the names in Spanish (*los mayas, los aztecas*) and ask a student to put them on the board. Ask them to locate the lands of the Mayas and Aztecs on the map on page 475. (The Aztecs were in central México, the Mayas were in the Yucatan and Central America.)

LAS CIENCIAS SOCIALES: LA ANTROPOLOGÍA Y LA HISTO

Antes de leer

Hiram Bingham found the "lost Inca city" of Machu Picchu in 1911. Locate the area inhabited by the Incas and briefly review their history.

Lectura

Los primeros incas viven alrededor del lago Titicaca mucho antes de llegar los españoles. De allí van al norte, al Valle del Cuzco. Allí fundan la ciudad del Cuzco que más tarde es el centro de su imperio. El jefe de los incas se llama el Inca—el jefe o señor. La leyenda dice que el imperio comienza con Manco Capac y su hermana Mama Ocllo durante el siglo XIII. Durante su época más importante, los incas ocupan el Ecuador, Perú, Bolivia y el norte de Chile y la Argentina, un territorio de más de un millón de km^2 con más de 12 millones de personas. La economía se basa en la agricultura. Cultivan maíz[1], papas y otras plantas, y crían[2] llamas, alpacas y vicuñas. La leyenda dice que el Inca desciende del Sol. Su imperio se

Una calle en Cuzco, Perú

Vista panorámica de Cuzco

Alpacas

LEARNING FROM PHOTOS

The *vicuña*, *llama*, and *alpaca* are all related to the camel. They are much valued for their wool.

DID YOU KNOW?

One of the grains cultivated by the Incas is now considered a "miracle grain." It is *quinoa*. Five hundred years ago the Incas thought it had magical powers. It is now an important source of income and food for Ecuadorean peasants. CARE helped reintroduce the crop to the region some years ago.

divide en cuatro *suyos*. Los suyos se dividen en *provincias*, las provincias en *distritos* y cada distrito en varios *ayllúes*. Cada ayllú se forma de un grupo de familias que son parientes. Los incas construyen templos, puentes[3], carreteras y acueductos. La ciudad de Machu Picchu es un magnífico ejemplo de construcción incaica. La lengua de los incas es el *quechua*.

[1] maíz *corn*
[2] crían *raise*
[3] puentes *bridges*

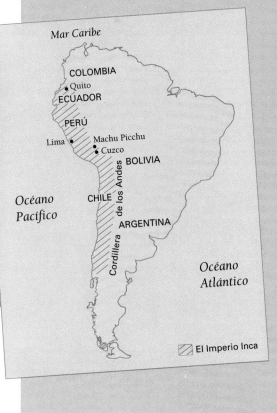

La ciudad de Machu Picchu, Perú

Después de leer

A **Los incas.** Contesten.

1. ¿Cuál es el territorio del imperio inca?
2. ¿Dónde viven los incas al principio?
3. ¿Qué animales crían, y qué plantas cultivan?
4. ¿Por qué son importantes Manco Capac y Mama Ocllo?
5. ¿Cuántos habitantes tiene el imperio inca?

B **Un gran imperio.** ¿Dónde dice lo siguiente?

1. what the Incas built
2. from whom or what their leader descended
3. where they went when they left their original home

C **Seguimiento.** Describan, en español, la organización política del imperio inca.

Lectura

PRESENTATION
(pages 356–357)

A. Have students skim the reading passage and locate the cognates for empire, occupy, legend, descend, and district.
B. Have students read the passage silently.
C. Assign a group of four to five students to develop questions about the passage. After the reading, students in the "question" group take turns asking their questions of the other class members.

Después de leer

PRESENTATION *(page 357)*

A. Assign Exercise A as homework. You may wish to accept short written answers. Review homework in class.
B. Do Exercise B orally in class. Students should find the line where the reference is located and read it.
C. In Exercise C students may describe the organization orally, or you may wish to have them draw an "organization chart."

ANSWERS

Ejercicio A
1. Ecuador, Perú, Bolivia y el norte de Chile y la Argentina
2. alrededor del lago Titicaca
3. Crían llamas, alpacas y vicuñas; cultivan maíz, papas y otras plantas.
4. La leyenda dice que el imperio comienza con ellos.
5. más de 12 millones

Ejercicio B
1. page 357, lines 5–7
2. page 356, lines 23–25
3. page 356, lines 3–4

Ejercicio C
Answers will vary.

CAPÍTULO 13
Scope and Sequence pages 358-383

Topics	Functions	Structure	Culture
Clothing Colors Shopping for clothes Likes, dislikes, and preferences	How to identify and describe articles of clothing How to talk about what you and others wear for different occasions How to shop for clothing How to discuss likes and dislikes How to express interest, boredom, and surprise How to make negative statements	Verbos como *interesar* y *aburrir* El verbo *gustar* Las palabras negativas y afirmativas	Teen styles of clothing Clothing stores in Spanish-speaking countries Outdoor markets European vs. U.S. sizing Hispanic designers Calle Serrano in Madrid Market in Chichicastenango, Guatemala

CAPÍTULO 13

Situation Cards

The Situation Cards simulate real-life situations that require students to communicate in Spanish, exactly as though they were in a Spanish-speaking country. The Situation Cards operate on the assumption that the person to whom the message is to be conveyed understands no English. Therefore, students must focus on producing the Spanish vocabulary and structures necessary to negotiate the situations successfully. For additional information, see the Introduction to the Situation Cards in the Situation Cards Envelope.

Communication Transparency

The illustration seen in this Communication Transparency consists of a synthesis of the two vocabulary (*Palabras 1&2*) presentations found in this chapter. It has been created in order to present this chapter's vocabulary in a new context, and also to recycle vocabulary learned in previous chapters. The Communication Transparency consists of original art. Following are some specific uses:

1. as a cue to stimulate conversation and writing activities
2. for listening comprehension activities
3. to review and reteach vocabulary
4. as a review for chapter and unit tests

CAPÍTULO 13   A

You're in Madrid and you decide to go shopping for clothes at the Galerías Preciados. Tell the salesperson what you want to buy.

B

C

D

Bienvenidos   © Glencoe/McGraw-Hill

© Glencoe/McGraw-Hill

© Glencoe/McGraw-Hill

© Glencoe/McGraw-Hill

Bienvenidos   Chapter 13   Communication Transparency   C-13

Copyright © by Glencoe/McGraw-Hill Publishing Company

CAPÍTULO 13
Print Resources

	Pages
Lesson Plans	

Workbook
- Palabras 1 — 136
- Palabras 2 — 137-138
- Estructura — 139-142
- Un poco más — 143-144
- Mi autobiografía — 145

Communication Activities Masters
- Palabras 1 — 77-79
- Palabras 2 — 80-81
- Estructura — 82-85

6 Bell Ringer Reviews — 30-31

Chapter Situation Cards A B C D

Chapter Quizzes
- Palabras 1 — 58
- Palabras 2 — 59
- Estructura — 60-62

Testing Program
- Listening Comprehension — 73
- Reading and Writing — 74-77
- Proficiency — 129
- Speaking — 150

Nosotros y Nuestro Mundo
- Nuestro Conocimiento Académico *El mercadeo*
- Nuestro Idioma *Metáforas y símiles*
- Nuestra Cultura *Biografía de un diseñador famoso*
- Nuestra Literatura *"La camisa de Margarita"* de Ricardo Palma
- Nuestra Creatividad
- Nuestras Diversiones

CAPÍTULO 13
Multimedia Resources

CD-ROM Interactive Textbook Disc 4

Chapter 13 Student Edition
- Palabras 1
- Palabras 2
- Estructura
- Conversación
- Lectura y cultura
- Hispanoparlantes
- Realidades
- Culminación
- Prueba

Audio Cassette Program with Student Tape Manual

Cassette	**Pages**
8A Palabras 1	254-255
8A Palabras 2	255-256
8A Estructura	256
8A Conversación	256
8A Pronunciación	256
8A Segunda parte	257-258

Compact Disc Program with Student Tape Manual

CD 8 Palabras 1	254-255
CD 8 Palabras 2	255-256
CD 8 Estructura	256
CD 8 Conversación	256
CD 8 Pronunciación	256
CD 8 Segunda parte	257-258

Overhead Transparencies Binder

- Vocabulary 13.1 (A&B); 13.2 (A&B)
- Pronunciation P-13
- Communication C-13
- Maps
- Fine Art (with Blackline Master Activities)

Video Program

Videocassette	
Video Activities Booklet	38-40
Videodisc	
Video Activities Booklet	38-40

Computer Software (Macintosh, IBM, Apple)

- Practice Disk
  - Palabras 1 y 2
  - Estructura
- Test Generator Disk
  - Chapter Test
  - Customized Test

CHAPTER OVERVIEW

In this chapter students will learn to identify and describe articles of clothing, to talk about what they and others wear for different occasions, and to communicate in various situations that arise when shopping for clothes. They will express likes and dislikes as well as interest, surprise, etc. They will also learn how to make negative statements.

The cultural focus of Chapter 13 is on teen styles and clothing stores in Spanish-speaking countries, including boutiques, department stores, and outdoor markets.

CHAPTER OBJECTIVES

By the end of this chapter students will know:

1. vocabulary used to describe clothing, including size and color
2. some basic vocabulary and structures necessary for locating items and speaking with salespeople in various types of clothing stores
3. the use of verbs like *interesar, sorprender, aburrir*
4. the verbs *gustar* and *encantar*
5. negative expressions

Pacing

Chapter 13 will require about eight to ten days. However, pacing will vary according to the length of the class, the age of your students, and student aptitude.

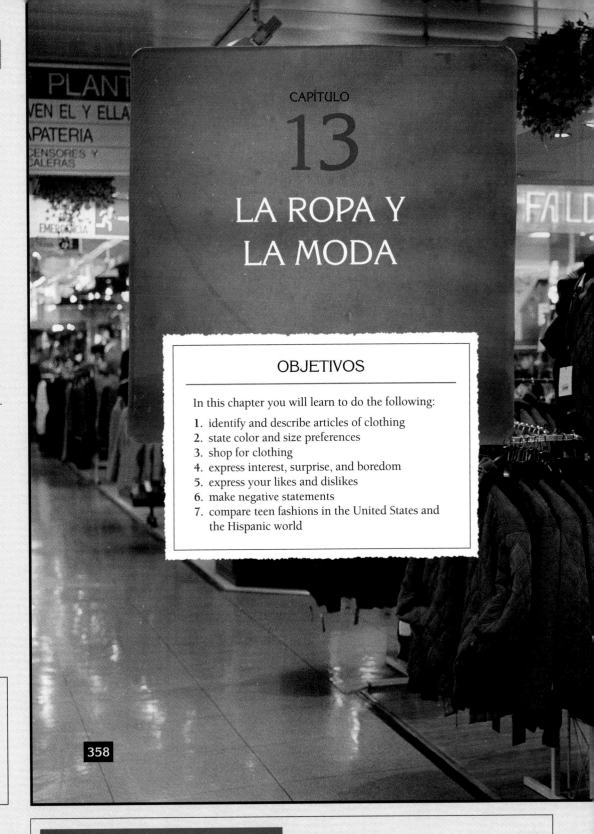

CAPÍTULO

13

LA ROPA Y LA MODA

OBJETIVOS

In this chapter you will learn to do the following:

1. identify and describe articles of clothing
2. state color and size preferences
3. shop for clothing
4. express interest, surprise, and boredom
5. express your likes and dislikes
6. make negative statements
7. compare teen fashions in the United States and the Hispanic world

358

CHAPTER PROJECTS

(optional)

1. Have students prepare some magazine ads for clothing.
2. Have pairs of students prepare a skit that takes place at a clothing store. One is the client, the other, the store clerk.

359

LEARNING FROM PHOTOS

After presenting the vocabulary on pages 360–361, do the following:

1. Look at the photograph on pages 358–359 and identify as many items as you can (*la bufanda* is the scarf).
2. What does *moda urbana* mean? *¿Es para el campo o para la ciudad?*
3. *Moda en fin de semana. ¿Qué opinas? ¿Es un estilo formal o informal?*
4. What do they sell in the department with neon lights?
5. The sign giving directions is incomplete. Can you, however, make out any words?

Vocabulary Teaching Resources

1. Vocabulary Transparencies 13.1 (A & B)
2. Audio Cassette 8A
3. Student Tape Manual, pages 254–255
4. Workbook, page 136
5. Communication Activities Masters, pages 77-79, A & B
6. Chapter Quizzes, page 58, *Palabras 1*

Bell Ringer Review

Write the following on the board or use BRR Blackline Master 13-1: Write a list of all the sports equipment you know. Keep your list.

PRESENTATION
(pages 360–361)

A. Identify articles of clothing students are actually wearing. Have the class repeat each item after you once or twice. Ask *¿Qué es?* and have a student respond.
B. Show Vocabulary Transparencies 13.1 (A & B). Have students repeat each item after you or the recording on Cassette 8A.
C. Ask questions about page 361, referring to the vocabulary transparency. For example: *¿Quién va de compras? ¿Con quién habla? ¿Dónde? ¿Le gustan los zapatos? ¿Le sientan bien o no? ¿Cuánto cuestan? ¿Es mucho o no? ¿Son baratos o caros los zapatos?*
D. Play a game using the new vocabulary by having students tell what someone in the class is wearing. The student giving the description calls on classmates to guess who is being described.

360

VOCABULARIO

PALABRAS 1

DE COMPRAS

el escaparate
el traje
la camisa
la gabardina
la chaqueta
el blusón
el T shirt
la camiseta
la talla
el tamaño
el abrigo
el saco
el precio
la corbata
el blue jean
los calcetines
los pantalones
la tienda de ropa para caballeros (señores)

la vitrina
el sombrero
el cinturón
la blusa
el suéter
el jersey
las medias
el vestido
la falda
la tienda de ropa para damas (señoras)

360 CAPÍTULO 13

360

Juan va de compras.
Habla con el dependiente en la tienda de ropa.

¿Te gustan estos zapatos?
¿Te sientan bien?
¿Cómo te sientan?

Sí, me gustan y me sientan bien.

Los zapatos no cuestan mucho.
No son caros.
Son baratos.
¿Cuánto cuestan?
Cuestan 1.000 pesos.
Juan paga en la caja.
Paga con una tarjeta de crédito.

el número

Pero a José no le interesa nada.
Nunca le gusta nada.

CAPÍTULO 13   **361**

Decides comprar los zapatos. Ve a la caja.
Saca tu tarjeta de crédito de tu bolsillo o de
    tu cartera.
Paga.
Gracias, ___. Ahora puedes sentarte.

DID YOU KNOW?

Clothing sizes in Europe and the United States are different. Many garments today carry labels with both European and American sizes. Ask students what size shoe the young man in the illustration is trying on (46). Ask them to figure out what the equivalent U.S. size would be. Ask them what size shoe they would ask for in a Spanish shoe store (chart is on page 379).

ABOUT THE LANGUAGE

1. *El saco* is used for both a man's and a woman's jacket. In Spain *la chaqueta* or *la americana* are common terms. In Mexico the word *chamarra* is used. Other kinds of outer jackets are *la cazadora, el blusón, el chaquetón.* One will also hear *gabán* used for jacket.
2. In many areas of Latin America, *medias* is used for women's stockings and men's socks.
3. *El terno* is a three-piece suit, usually including *el pantalón, el chaleco,* and *el saco.*
4. Another word for belt, in addition to *cinturón,* is *la correa.*
5. The word *zapatería* can mean a shoe store (shoe department) or a shoe factory. Another term is *tienda de (departamento de) calzado.*
6. Other words for sweater are *la chompa* and *el pulóver.* Blue jeans are called *blue jeans* or *blujins, vaqueros,* and *pantalones de mezclilla.*

RECYCLING

Recycle earlier material by having students describe each person as well as what the person is wearing.

Vocabulary Expansion

In addition to the articles of clothing given here, you may wish to give the names of some undergarments: **la ropa interior** (underwear); **la camiseta** (undershirt); **los calzoncillos** (underpants); **las bragas** (panties); **los pantis** (pantyhose); **el sostén** (bra); **la combinación/el refajo/las enaguas** (slip); Some accessories are **el pañuelo** (handkerchief); **la cartera** (wallet); **la bolsa** (purse); **el reloj** (watch); **el anillo** (ring); **el pendiente** (pendant); **el brazalete** (bracelet).

Note Many other articles of clothing will be presented in later chapters as they are needed.

Ejercicios

Ejercicio A

It is recommended that you do Exercise A first with books open as a class activity. You may do the exercise a second time as a group activity. Students can work in groups of three. One reads the question, another gives the cue, and the third responds. They can change roles with each item.

Expansion of *Ejercicio A*

Upon completion of Exercise A, have one student retell all the information in his/her own words.

Ejercicio B

Recycling After presenting *Palabras 2* of this chapter, you may have students look at the illustrations of Exercise B again and give a brief description of each item of clothing.

ANSWERS

Ejercicio A

1. El dependiente trabaja en la tienda.
2. Los zapatos están en el escaparate.
3. El cliente compra un par de zapatos.
4. Su número es 43.
5. El precio de los zapatos es 600 pesos.
6. Cuestan 600 pesos.
7. No, no son demasiado caros.
8. Son bastante baratos.
9. El señor quiere una camisa.
10. Su talla es 38.
11. No, no quiere nada más.
12. El cliente paga en la caja.

Ejercicio B

1. sombreros
2. corbatas
3. camisas
4. trajes
5. chaquetas
6. calcetines

Ejercicios

A **Está comprando zapatos.** Contesten según se indica.

1. ¿Quién trabaja en la tienda? (el dependiente)
2. ¿Dónde están los zapatos? (en el escaparate)
3. ¿Qué compra el cliente? (un par de zapatos)
4. ¿Cuál es su número? (43)
5. ¿Cuál es el precio de los zapatos? (600 pesos)
6. ¿Cuánto cuestan? (600 pesos)
7. ¿Son demasiado caros? (no)
8. ¿Cómo son? (bastante baratos)
9. ¿Qué más quiere el señor? (una camisa)
10. ¿Cuál es su talla? (38)
11. ¿Quiere algo más? (No, nada)
12. ¿Dónde paga el cliente? (en la caja)

B **En la tienda de ropa para caballeros.** Contesten según la foto.

¿Qué venden en la tienda de ropa para señores?

1.

2.

3.

4.

5.

6.

ADDITIONAL PRACTICE

After completing Exercises B and C on pages 362–363, reinforce with the following: Have students tell about *la ropa que llevan* and ask them *¿Cómo te sienta(n)?*

C **En la tienda de ropa para señoras.** Contesten según la foto.

¿Qué venden en la tienda de ropa para señoras?

1.
2.
3.
4.
5.
6.

D **¿Qué estilo es?** Escojan. Escriban en otro papel.

```
                    FORMAL          DEPORTIVO
    1. los tenis
    2. la corbata
    3. el jersey
    4. el saco, la chaqueta
    5. el vestido
    6. las sandalias
    7. el T shirt
    8. el blue jean
```

E **Sí, me sienta(n) bien.** Contesten.

1. Los zapatos que llevas, ¿te sientan bien?
2. La camisa o la blusa que llevas, ¿cómo te sienta?
3. El blue jean que compraste ayer, ¿te sienta bien?
4. El blusón que compraste, ¿te sienta bien o no?
5. Los tenis que compraste, ¿cómo te sientan?

CAPÍTULO 13   **363**

PRESENTATION *(page 363)*

Ejercicio C

Recycling After presenting *Palabras* 2 of this chapter, you may have students look at the illustrations in Exercise C again and give a brief description of each item of clothing.

Ejercicio D

If there is any disagreement in categorizing these articles of clothing, have students defend their opinions.

Ejercicio E

Note Exercise E serves as an introduction to the grammar points that will be presented in this chapter.

ANSWERS

Ejercicio C
1. faldas
2. suéteres
3. vestidos
4. sandalias
5. blusas
6. cinturones

Ejercicio D
1. los tenis—deportivo
2. la corbata—formal
3. el jersey—deportivo
4. el saco, la chaqueta—formal
5. el vestido—formal
6. las sandalias—deportivo
7. el T shirt—deportivo
8. el blue jean—deportivo

Ejercicio E
1. Sí, me sientan bien.
2. Me sienta bien.
3. Sí, me sienta bien.
4. Sí, me sienta bien.
5. Me sientan bien.

INDEPENDENT PRACTICE

Assign any of the following:
1. Workbook, page 136
2. Communication Activities Masters, pages 77-79, *A & B*
3. Exercises on student pages 362–363

PALABRAS 2

Vocabulary Teaching Resources

1. Vocabulary Transparencies 13.2 (A & B)
2. Audio Cassette 8A
3. Student Tape Manual, pages 255–256
4. Workbook, pages 137–138
5. Communication Activities Masters, pages 80-81, *C & D*
6. Chapter Quizzes, page 59, *Palabras 2*
7. Computer Software, *Vocabulario*

Bell Ringer Review

Write the following on the board or use BRR Blackline Master 13-2: Take the list of sports equipment you wrote for Palabras 1 and identify the sport each item is used for.

LA ROPA Y LOS COLORES

la manga corta

la manga larga

el tacón alto

el tacón bajo

estrecho

pequeño

ancho

grande

el botón

el zíper

la cremallera

una blusa a rayas

un saco a cuadros

364   CAPÍTULO 13

(following the Vocabulary presentation)

Note You may vary the articles of clothing and their colors according to what the students are wearing.

Atención, todos. Si Uds. llevan un artículo de ropa que yo menciono, levántense.

Veo un pantalón blanco.

Veo una camiseta negra.
Veo una camisa azul.
Veo un T shirt rojo.
Veo una falda verde.
Veo un short beige.
Veo un pantalón crema.
Veo un jean negro.
Veo un jean azul.
Gracias, todos. Y ahora siéntense.

Estos zapatos no me sientan bien.
Son demasiado estrechos.
Me aprietan.

Los colores

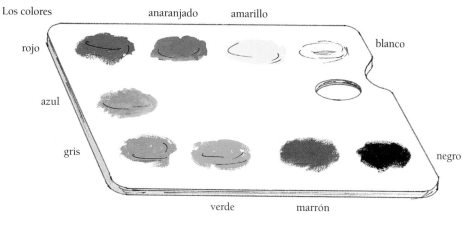

Nota: There are many nouns in Spanish that are used to describe a color. They are the names of fruits, gems, etc. Some of these words are: *crema, vino, café, oliva, marrón,* and *turquesa.* These words do not agree with the noun they accompany because they are not adjectives. They don't change form. For example, *zapatos color café,* or simply, *zapatos café.*

COOPERATIVE LEARNING

Have students work in groups. Each group makes a list of several people that everyone in the group knows. The people can be celebrities or classmates who are not in the room. Then, each student chooses one of the people and describes what that person is probably wearing today. The other students try to guess who it is, choosing from the list.

FOR THE NATIVE SPEAKER

A number of colors are given different names in different regions. For example, red, brown, and blue have a variety of names. Show students these and other colors and ask them what they call them. There are also different names for articles of clothing. Ask them what names they use for such articles as *suéter, saco, falda, tenis,* etc.

Ejercicios

Ejercicio A

It is recommended that you do Exercise A with books open as a class activity.

Ejercicio B

Have students work in pairs. One reads the question and the other responds. They can change roles with each question.

Ejercicio C

Before going over Exercise C, have students review the names of the colors on page 365. This exercise can be done as a paired activity.

ANSWERS

Ejercicio A

1. mangas cortas
2. mangas largas
3. tacón bajo
4. larga
5. a cuadros
6. cremallera

Ejercicio B

Some answers will vary.

1. Sí (No), (no) quiere comprar la camisa.
2. Sí (No), (no) le gusta (la camisa).
3. Sí (No), (no) le queda bien.
4. Es (azul, blanca, etc.).
5. Tiene mangas largas (cortas).
6. Sí (No), (no) hace juego con la corbata.

Ejercicio C

Answers will vary.

Ejercicios

A ¿Cómo es? Contesten según el dibujo.

1. ¿Esta camisa tiene mangas largas o mangas cortas?

2. ¿Esta blusa tiene mangas largas o cortas?

3. ¿Estos zapatos tienen tacón alto o bajo?

4. ¿Esta falda es larga o corta?

5. ¿Este saco es a rayas o a cuadros?

6. ¿Este blusón tiene botones o cremallera?

B Juan quiere esta camisa. Contesten.

1. ¿Juan quiere comprar la camisa?
2. ¿Le gusta?
3. ¿Le queda bien?
4. ¿De qué color es?
5. ¿Tiene mangas largas o cortas?
6. ¿Hace juego con la corbata?

C Mi color favorito. ¿Cuál es su color favorito para cada prenda?

1. una camisa
2. un traje
3. un vestido
4. zapatos
5. un abrigo
6. una gabardina

LEARNING FROM ILLUSTRATIONS

Ask students to compare the shirt (1) with blouse (2) in detail. They should talk about *mangas, botones, colores,* and *bolsillos* (pockets).

GRATIS

ADELANTATE
A LA MODA
OTOÑO-INVIERNO
CON VENCA

Comunicación
Palabras 1 y 2

A **Mis prendas favoritas.** You and your partner have to buy clothes for four people you know. Take turns describing what you will buy for each person.

B **¿Qué me pongo?** With a partner prepare a list of articles of clothing. For each article indicate the season during which you would wear it and whether it is formal or informal.

C **¿Qué ropa llevo?** You and your partner are going to San Juan, Puerto Rico for a few days. You plan to go out one evening to a fancy restaurant and salsa club. You will also go to the beach and do a little sight-seeing. List all the clothes you're going to take. Compare your list with your partner's list and tell each other if you think each item is necessary and appropriate.

D **Sí, señor(a).** You are working this summer in a local clothing store. A South American millionaire (your partner) comes in to get a completely new wardrobe. Find out what the customer wants and sell as much as you can.

Bell Ringer Review

Write the following on the board or use BRR Blackline Master 13-3: Complete the following sentences.

1. ___ es un curso interesante.
2. ___ es un curso aburrido.
3. ___ es un curso fabuloso.
4. ___ es un curso divertido.
5. ___ es un curso fácil.
6. ___ es un curso difícil.

Comunicación

PRESENTATION *(page 367)*
(Palabras 1 and 2)

Actividad A
Have students work in pairs. Encourage them to use *le sienta bien* and *le gusta.*

Actividad B
Have students consider the four seasons so that the list is as complete as possible.

Actividad C
Have students work in pairs.

Actividad D
Tell students that they can use some of the questions of Exercise A on page 362. These questions can help students do this exercise in conversational form.

ANSWERS
Actividades A–D
Answers will vary.

ESTRUCTURA

Structure Teaching Resources

1. Workbook, pages 139–142
2. Student Tape Manual, pages 256
3. Audio Cassette 8A
4. Communication Activities Masters, pages 82-85, A-C
5. Chapter Quizzes, pages 60-62, *Estructura*
6. Computer Software, *Estructura*

Verbos como interesar *y* aburrir

Note The verbs in this section, *interesar, aburrir, sorprender,* and *molestar,* function exactly the same in Spanish as they do in English. This makes them an excellent introduction to the verb *gustar,* which is so often confusing for students. Once they see *interesar* and realize that *gustar* functions the same way, it is much easier for them to grasp the concept.

PRESENTATION
(pages 368–369)

Read the explanation on page 368 to students. Have students repeat each of the example sentences.

Ejercicios

ANSWERS

Ejercicio A

1. El álgebra me interesa. No me aburre.
2. La geometría me interesa. No me aburre.
3. La historia me interesa. No me aburre.
4. El español me interesa. No me aburre.
5. La geografía me interesa. No me aburre.

Verbos como *interesar* y *aburrir*

How to Express Interest and Boredom

Interesar "to interest," *aburrir* "to bore," *sorprender* "to surprise," *enojar, enfadar* "to annoy," and *molestar* "to bother" function the same in Spanish as in English. They are always used with an indirect object.

> **Aquel libro me interesa.** *That book interests me.*
> **Aquellos libros me interesan.** *Those books interest me.*
> **A Juan le aburre la historia.** *History bores John.*
> **A Juan le aburren las ciencias.** *The sciences bore John.*
> **Me sorprendió la noticia.** *The news surprised me.*
> **Me sorprendieron sus reacciones.** *Their reactions surprised me.*
> **Nuestra reacción les molestó.** *Our reaction bothered them.*

Ejercicios

A ¿Te interesa o te aburre? Sigan el modelo.

> **la biología**
> *La biología me interesa. No me aburre.*

1. el álgebra
2. la geometría
3. la historia
4. el español
5. la geografía

B ¿Te interesan o te aburren? Sigan el modelo.

> **Las películas policíacas**
> *Las películas policíacas me aburren. No me interesan.*

1. las ciencias
2. las matemáticas
3. las lenguas
4. las ciencias sociales
5. las ciencias naturales

368 CAPÍTULO 13

LEARNING FROM REALIA

You may wish to ask the following questions about the realia on page 368. *¿Para quiénes es el anuncio? ¿Es este anuncio de una revista de los Estados Unidos o de un país latinoamericano? ¿Qué días dan la super película? ¿A qué hora dan la película? ¿A qué se refiere la palabra "centro"?*

C ¿Te enoja o no? ¿Quién te enoja?

1. ¿El profesor?
2. ¿Mamá?
3. ¿Tu hermano?
4. ¿Papá?
5. ¿Tu hermana?
6. ¿Tus hermanos?
7. ¿Tus amigos?

D En la tienda de ropa. Contesten.

1. ¿A Roberto le interesa la camisa?
2. ¿Le sienta bien la camisa?
3. ¿Le sorprende el precio?
4. ¿A Roberto le interesan los zapatos también?
5. ¿Le sientan bien?
6. ¿Le aprietan?

El verbo *gustar*   *Expressing Likes and Dislikes*

1. The verb *gustar* is used in Spanish to convey the meaning "to like." Its literal meaning is "to be pleasing to." It takes an indirect object the same as verbs like *interesar, sorprender*, etc. Note the following sentences.

> ¿Te gusta esta camisa?
> Sí, me gusta mucho.
> Y me gustan estas corbatas también.
> ¿A Juan le gusta el estilo formal o informal?
> Le gusta el "look" informal.
> Le gustan mucho los blue jeans.
> A mis amigos les gusta el blue jean con un suéter.

2. The verb *gustar* is used with an infinitive to tell what you like to do.

> Me gusta esquiar.
> ¿Te gusta comer?
> A los alumnos no les gusta estudiar.
>
> *Me gusta más* means "I prefer."
>
> Me gusta más esa camisa que la otra.

3. *Encantar* "to love" (inanimate things), is used the same as *gustar.*

> ¿Te gusta esta camisa? Ah, sí. Me encanta.

CAPÍTULO 13   **369**

INDEPENDENT PRACTICE

Assign any of the following:
1. Workbook, page 139
2. Communication Activities Masters, page 82, *A*
3. Computer Software, *Estructura*
4. Exercises on student pages 368–369

*Ejercicio B*
1. Las ciencias me aburren. No me interesan.
2. Las matemáticas me aburren. No me interesan.
3. Las lenguas me aburren. No me interesan.
4. Las ciencias sociales me aburren. No me interesan.
5. Las ciencias naturales me aburren. No me interesan.

Ejercicio C
Answers will vary.
1. El profesor (no) me enoja.
2. Mamá (no) me enoja.
3. Mi hermano (no) me enoja.
4. Papá (no) me enoja.
5. Mi hermana (no) me enoja.
6. Mis hermanos (no) me enojan.
7. Mis amigos (no) me enojan.

Ejercicio D
Answers will vary.
1. Sí (No), (no) le interesa la camisa.
2. Sí (No), (no) le sienta bien la camisa.
3. Sí (No), (no) le sorprende el precio.
4. Sí (No), (no) le interesan los zapatos también (tampoco).
5. Sí (No), (no) le sientan bien.
6. Sí (No), (no) le aprietan.

El verbo gustar

Note *Gustar* conveys the meaning "to like" although that is not its literal meaning. Tell students that *gustar* functions the same as verbs like *interesar* or *sorprender,* which they have already learned. It is strongly recommended that you not do any English translation. It tends to confuse the students and make the point more difficult.

PRESENTATION *(page 369)*
A. Have students read the example sentences in steps 1–3 aloud.
B. You may wish to read the sentences once substituting *interesar* with *gustar* to show students that the two verbs function exactly the same.

Ejercicios

PRESENTATION

(page 370)

Ejercicios A–C

All of these exercises can be done with books closed or open.

ANSWERS

Ejercicio A

Answers can be negative. When they are, *Me aburre* replaces *Me interesa.*

1. Me gusta mucho la música. Me interesa.
2. Me gusta mucho el arte. Me interesa.
3. Me gusta mucho el ballet. Me interesa.
4. Me gusta mucho la ópera. Me interesa.
5. Me gusta mucho el cine. Me interesa.

Ejercicio B

Answers can be negative, too.

1. Rodolfo, ¿te gustan las ciencias?
   Sí, me gustan las ciencias.
2. Rodolfo, ¿te gustan las lenguas extranjeras?
   Sí, me gustan las lenguas extranjeras.
3. Rodolfo, ¿te gustan las matemáticas?
   Sí, me gustan las matemáticas.
4. Rodolfo, ¿te gustan las bellas artes?
   Sí, me gustan las bellas artes.
5. Rodolfo, ¿te gustan los deportes?
   Sí, me gustan los deportes.

Ejercicio C

1. Sí, le gustan mucho.
2. Sí, le gusta mucho.
3. Sí, le gusta mucho.
4. Sí, le gusta mucho.
5. Sí, le gustan mucho.

370

Ejercicios

A **¿Te gusta o no te gusta?** Sigan el modelo.

> la historia
> *Me gusta mucho la historia. (No me gusta la historia.)*
> *Me interesa. (Me aburre.)*

1. la música
2. el arte
3. el ballet
4. la ópera
5. el cine

B **¿Te gustan o no?** Preparen una mini-conversación según el modelo.

> las ciencias
> Estudiante 1: Rodolfo, ¿te gustan las ciencias?
> Estudiante 2: Sí, me gustan las ciencias. (No, no me gustan.)

1. las ciencias
2. las lenguas extranjeras
3. las matemáticas
4. las bellas artes
5. los deportes

C **Sí, le gusta.** Contesten según el modelo.

> ¿Juan va a comprar estos zapatos?
> *Sí, le gustan mucho.*

1. ¿María va a comprar estas sandalias?
2. ¿Juan va a comprar este bañador?
3. ¿María va a comprar este blue jean?
4. ¿Juan va a comprar esta gabardina?
5. ¿María va a comprar estos tenis?

COOPERATIVE LEARNING

Have students work in teams of four. The first team member gives the name of a student on one of the school sports teams. The second makes a statement about the team this person plays on. The third tells whether he/she likes or dislikes that particular sport and whether he/she attends the games. The fourth team member writes down everything that is said.

D A tus amigos, ¿qué les gusta hacer? Contesten según el dibujo.

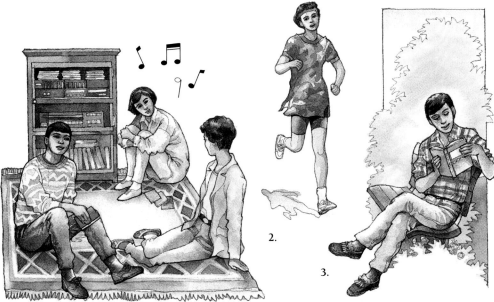

1.

2.

3.

4.

5.

E Me gusta comer. Digan todo lo que les gusta hacer.

F Me gusta la música rock. Digan lo que les gusta.

Ejercicio D
 Have students refer to the illustrations on page 371 as they respond.

Ejercicios E and F
 Encourage students to say as much as they can.

ANSWERS
Ejercicio D
1. Les gusta escuchar música.
2. Le gusta correr.
3. Le gusta leer.
4. Le gusta comer.
5. Les gusta patinar.

Ejercicios E and F
 Answers will vary.

COOPERATIVE LEARNING

Have students work in groups. One states what he/she likes. From that one statement, have students make up a free conversation.
E1: Me gusta la biología.
E2: ¿Te gusta? ¿De veras?
E3: Sí, yo sé que a ___ le gusta.
E2: ___, ¿por qué te gusta la biología?
E1: Pues, me gusta porque quiero ser médico(a).

INDEPENDENT PRACTICE

1. Workbook, pages 140–141
2. Communication Activities Masters, page 83, *B*
3. Computer Software: *Estructura*
4. Exercises on student pages 370–371

Bell Ringer Review

Write the following on the board or use BRR Blackline Master 13-4: Write some things you like to do in your leisure time.
Me gusta ___.

Las palabras negativas y afirmativas

PRESENTATION *(page 372)*

A. Present negative expressions by holding up an object such as a book or pencil, or looking at something as you say *Tengo algo. Veo algo.* Then put the object away or look away and say *No tengo nada. No veo nada.*

B. Have a student stand by you as you say *Veo a alguien.* Then have the person go away as you say *Ahora no veo a nadie.*

C. Lead students through steps 1–3 on page 372.

Note Point out to students that the words *nada, nadie,* and *nunca* can stand alone as short answers. For example: *¿Qué tienes? Nada. ¿Quién habla? Nadie. ¿Cuándo vas? Nunca.*

Las palabras negativas y afirmativas
Expressing Affirmative and Negative Ideas

1. The words *nada, nunca,* and *nadie* are negative words. Note how they are used.

AFIRMATIVAS	NEGATIVAS
Él tiene algo en la mano.	Él no tiene nada en la mano.
Ella siempre esquía.	Ella nunca esquía.
Ella ve a alguien.	Ella no ve a nadie.
Él también estudia alemán.	Él tampoco estudia alemán.

Alguien and *nadie* always refer to people. Therefore, you usually use the personal *a* when they are the direct object of the verb.

2. Unlike English, in Spanish you can use more than one negative word in the same sentence.

Nunca hablo francés con nadie.
No compro nada nunca.
Yo no quiero nada tampoco.

3. *También* is used to confirm an affirmative statement.

Siempre estudio después de las clases. Y yo también.

Tampoco is used to confirm or agree with a negative statement.

No estudié para el examen de química. Ni yo tampoco
or Yo tampoco.

Ejercicios

A **¿Nada, nunca o nadie?** Contesten con *no*.

1. ¿Hay algo en la mochila?
2. ¿Tienes algo en la mano?
3. ¿Ves a alguien en la sala?
4. ¿Hay alguien en la cocina?
5. ¿Siempre cantas con tus amigos?
6. ¿Siempre lees algo?
7. ¿Siempre le escribes a tu abuelita?

B **¿Y tú?** Indiquen si están de acuerdo.

> Yo no compro en esa tienda.
> *Yo tampoco.*

1. Yo siempre prefiero ir en avión.
2. Yo juego mucho al fútbol.
3. Yo no canto mucho.
4. Yo no conozco a Juan.
5. Yo estudio mucho.
6. Yo nunca toco la guitarra.

PRESENTATION *(page 373)*

Exercises A and B can be done with books closed or open.

ANSWERS

Ejercicio A

1. No hay nada en la mochila.
2. No tengo nada en la mano.
3. No veo a nadie en la sala.
4. No hay nadie en la sala.
5. Nunca canto con mis amigos.
6. Nunca leo nada.
7. Nunca le escribo a mi abuelita.

Ejercicio B

1. Yo también.
2. Yo también.
3. (Ni) Yo tampoco.
4. (Ni) Yo tampoco.
5. Yo también.
6. (Ni) Yo tampoco.

ADDITIONAL PRACTICE

After completing the exercises on page 373, write the following verbs on the board:

> veo
> quiero
> tengo
> compro
> digo
> escribo
> aprendo

Have students use either *algo* or *alguien* with each verb. Then have them put their sentences in the negative with *nada* or *nadie*.

PRESENTATION *(page 374)*

A. Have students open their books to page 374. Without reading the conversation, have them look at the photos and guess what the conversation is about.

B. Now have students listen to the conversation on Cassette 8A. Then have them repeat the conversation after you.

C. Call on two individuals to read the conversation in its entirety with as much expression as possible.

D. Do the comprehension exercise that follows the conversation.

ANSWERS

1. El cliente está hablando con el dependiente.
2. Está en la tienda de ropa para señores.
3. Quiere una camisa.
4. Su talla es cuarenta y dos.
5. Quiere el color blanco.
6. Quiere mangas largas.
7. Le gusta mucho la camisa a rayas.
8. La camisa es (cuesta) ocho mil pesos.
9. Sí, le sorprende el precio.
10. No es muy cara.

CONVERSACIÓN

Escenas de la vida *En la tienda de ropa para señores*

DEPENDIENTE: Sí, señor.
CLIENTE: Quisiera una camisa, por favor.
DEPENDIENTE: Su talla, por favor.
CLIENTE: Cuarenta y dos.

DEPENDIENTE: ¿Qué color le gusta?
CLIENTE: Blanco.
DEPENDIENTE: De acuerdo. ¿Le gustan más las mangas largas o cortas?
CLIENTE: Largas, por favor.
DEPENDIENTE: ¿Qué tal le gusta esta camisa a rayas?

CLIENTE: Mucho. ¿Cuánto es?
DEPENDIENTE: Ocho mil pesos.
CLIENTE: Ocho mil. Me sorprende. No es muy cara.

 **Quisiera…** Contesten.

1. ¿Con quién está hablando el cliente?
2. ¿Dónde está?
3. ¿Qué quiere?
4. ¿Cuál es su talla?
5. ¿Qué color quiere?
6. ¿Quiere mangas largas o cortas?
7. ¿Qué tal le gusta la camisa a rayas?
8. ¿Cuánto es la camisa?
9. ¿Le sorprende el precio al cliente?
10. ¿Por qué le sorprende?

374 CAPÍTULO 13

COOPERATIVE LEARNING

Have students work in pairs and prepare a skit based on buying an item of clothing either for themselves or as a gift for someone else.

FOR THE NATIVE SPEAKER

Some Spanish-speaking countries use U.S. sizes; others use metric or European sizes. If there are students from different Hispanic countries, ask them to tell what sizes they use in those countries: *¿Qué número (tamaño) usan para los zapatos (blusas /camisas/ pantalones /medias /sacos /abrigos)?*

Pronunciación   *Las consonantes* ñ *y* ch

The **ñ** is a separate letter of the Spanish alphabet. The mark over it is called a *tilde*. Note that it is pronounced similarly to the **ny** in the English word *canyon*. Repeat the following.

ñ

señora	señor	pequeño	montaña
año	otoño	España	cumpleaños

Ch is also considered a separate letter of the Spanish alphabet. It is pronounced much like the **ch** in the English word *church*. Repeat the following.

ch

chaqueta	estrecho	ancho
chocolate	muchacho	chileno

Repeat the following sentences.

> El señor español sube las montañas cada año en el otoño.
> El muchacho chileno lleva una chaqueta ancha color chocolate.

una chaqueta
color chocolate

Comunicación

A **En la tienda.** You are in the clothing department of Galerías Preciados, a large Madrid department store. A classmate will play the salesperson.

1. Describe the things you want.
2. Tell the clerk your size.
3. Try on each item and tell the clerk how it fits.
4. Find out the price and if you can pay with a credit card.

B **No me sienta bien.** You are the salesperson and your partner is the customer, inside the dressing room. Ask your partner if he or she likes each item and how it fits. Your partner likes them all, but none fits quite right.

> pantalones
> Estudiante 1: ¿Le gustan los pantalones?
> Estudiante 2: Sí, me gustan.
> Estudiante 1: ¿Cómo le quedan?
> Estudiante 2: Son un poco grandes.

zapatos	camiseta	chaqueta	tenis
blue jean	camisa	sandalias	pantalones

C **¿Y qué compraste?** A Mexican exchange student (your partner) won a $1000 gift certificate at the local mall. Find out the following.

1. what he or she bought
2. how much each item cost
3. where he or she shopped
4. where he or she ate

PRESENTATION (*page 375*)

Most students have no particular problem with these sounds. Have them pronounce each word carefully after you or the recording on Cassette 8A. You may also wish to use the sentences as a dictation.

Comunicación

PRESENTATION

Allow students to select the activity or activities they wish to take part in. They can work in pairs.

ANSWERS

Actividades A, B, and C
Answers will vary.

FOR THE NATIVE SPEAKER

Negative Words *Nada* and *nadie* are frequently mispronounced in many parts of the Spanish-speaking world. *Nada* become *ná*, and *nadie* becomes *naide*.

ADDITIONAL PRACTICE

After completing Activities A, B, and C on page 375, have students write a short composition describing the things they want to buy. Have them give the price of each item, its size, and where they go shopping.

LECTURA Y CULTURA

READING STRATEGIES

(page 376)

Pre-reading

If possible, share with students some clothing ads from popular Spanish magazines such as *Marie Claire, Hombre,* and *Vanidades.*

Reading

Have students read the selection once silently.

Teaching Tip

A. Adherence to a pre-set time limit will encourage students to read all the material and not get bogged down every time they think they don't know a word. Encourage students to read for ideas, rather than word for word.

B. Call on an individual to read a few sentences aloud. Ask comprehension questions. Call on other students to respond.

Post-reading

Call on volunteers to summarize in their own words what they have learned from the reading selection.

Estudio de palabras

ANSWERS

Ejercicio A

1. generalizar	6. formales
2. favorito	7. versátil
3. informal	8. crema
4. dinámico	9. sofisticado
5. ocasiones	10. diferencia

LA MODA

¿Cómo es la moda en España y en Latinoamérica? ¿Qué estilo está en onda[1]? Pues, es difícil saber. ¿Por qué? Porque la moda cambia rápidamente como aquí en los Estados Unidos. Lo que hoy está de moda, mañana está pasado de moda.

Pero podemos generalizar un poco y decir que ahora el estilo favorito de los jóvenes es informal y dinámico. Para los muchachos un blue jean con una camisa amplia. Y para ocasiones más formales—el estilo clásico—el versátil saco azul marino con una camisa azul y pantalones color crema.

Y para las jóvenes hay más variedad y flexibilidad aunque los estilos cambian de un día para otro. En un grupo de tres o cuatro chicas una puede llevar un traje pantalón con un cinturón sofisticado; otra lleva una falda con una blusa con cuello sin espalda, abotonada como un saco; y otra lleva blue jean con un blusón.

¿Cuál es el estilo que te gusta más ahora? ¿Te gusta el estilo deportivo o clásico? ¿Qué opinas? ¿Hay mucha diferencia entre la moda de los jóvenes en los Estados Unidos y los jóvenes en España o Latinoamérica?

[1] onda *in*

Estudio de palabras

A **Palabras afines.** Busquen diez palabras afines en la lectura.

B **¿Cuál es la palabra?** Busquen una expresión equivalente.

1. está en onda	a. un evento
2. en este momento	b. un tipo de chaqueta
3. versátil	c. muy popular
4. favorito	d. ahora, actualmente
5. una ocasión	e. predilecto
6. el saco	f. que sirve para muchas ocasiones

Comprensión

A ¿Verdad o no? Contesten con *sí* o *no.*

1. Es fácil describir la moda entre los jóvenes españoles y latinoamericanos.
2. La moda no cambia mucho en los países latinos.
3. En este momento el estilo que está de moda es más bien formal y clásico.
4. Hay muy poca diferencia entre lo que llevan los jóvenes aquí y lo que llevan en los países de habla española.

B Un conjunto. Describan un conjunto bonito, atractivo para ir a los siguientes lugares: el colegio, el cine, una fiesta.

★ LO QUE ESTÁ IN

ARETES
Largos
En forma de botones
Dorados mate
Formas geométricas
En forma de gotas

BRAZALETES
Grandes
De metal

COLLARES
Gargantillas
Collares pegados al cuello
Antiguos
Perlas falsas o reales

DETALLES
Tonos metálicos
Con diseños de animales selváticos
Cintas
Antigüedades

RELOJES
De brazalete
Deportivos
Con personajes de caricaturas

PRENDEDORES
Formas abstractas
Broches

LO QUE ESTÁ OUT

Los accesorios pequeños
Aretes minúsculos
Varios collares

VOGUE MÉXICO

Empacando para un crucero
Tijuana, la frontera inquieta

CAPÍTULO 13 **377**

Ejercicio B
1. c
2. d
3. f
4. e
5. a
6. b

Comprensión

PRESENTATION *(page 377)*

Comprensión A
Have students correct any false statements in this exercise.

Comprensión B
This exercise can provide an overall review of this chapter.

ANSWERS

Comprensión A
1. no
2. no
3. no
4. sí

Comprensión B
Answers will vary.

CRITICAL THINKING ACTIVITY

(Thinking skills: drawing conclusions, giving opinions)

Write the following on the board or on a transparency or read the information to the students:

1. *En su opinión, ¿es necesario gastar o pagar mucho dinero por la ropa o no? Defienda sus opiniones.*

2. *Es obligatorio llevar uniforme a la escuela. Discuta las ventajas y las desventajas.*

PRESENTATION *(page 378)*

Depending upon the interest of the class, you may skip this material completely or merely have students read the material once silently. If you choose to treat this section in depth, use any of the *Lectura* suggestions given in earlier chapters.

HISTORY CONNECTION

A very large percentage of the Guatemalan population are descendants of the famous Mayans. As in other areas of South and Central America, the Indians were greatly suppressed by their Spanish conquerors. However, the native people of Guatemala remained defiantly apart from the culture of their conquerors. The highland Mayans of Guatemala retained their own cultural identity. This cultural identity continues to be very strong.

DESCUBRIMIENTO CULTURAL

*E*n Latinoamérica o en España, como aquí, hay muchos tipos de tiendas diferentes adonde va la gente a comprar ropa. Hay grandes almacenes o tiendas de departamentos. En las ciudades hay también pequeñas tiendas elegantes, donde los precios son bastante altos. En estas tiendas venden la ropa de los grandes modistas (diseñadores) como Cartier, Balenciaga, etc.

Hay también tiendas que tienen precios bajos porque siempre tienen ofertas especiales, rebajas (precios reducidos) y gangas[1]. Tienen muchos saldos o liquidaciones[2].

En algunos países hay mercado al aire libre. En estos mercados venden muchos productos indígenas. Tienen suéteres de lana, sarapes, ponchos, etc. que son fantásticos y muy razonables.

Hoy en día hay también muchos centros comerciales. Los centros comerciales se encuentran por lo general en las afueras de una ciudad. Un centro comercial tiene una aglomeración de tiendas diferentes. También los grandes hoteles tienen centros comerciales.

Un mercado al aire libre en Guatemala

Un centro comercial en Buenos Aires, Argentina

378 CAPÍTULO 13

LEARNING FROM PHOTOS

1. You may wish to ask the following questions about the mall in the photo on page 378: *¿Dónde está el centro comercial? ¿Es bonito? ¿Cuántos pisos tiene? ¿Es elegante? ¿Tiene muchas tiendas?*
2. After asking questions, have students describe the photo in their own words.

Los tamaños de aquí y de Europa no son los mismos. Aquí tiene Ud. las diferencias.

TALLAS EN ESTADOS UNIDOS Y EN EUROPA

BLUSAS Y SUÉTERES

Estados Unidos	32	34	36	38	40	42	44
Europa	40	42	44	46	48	50	52

VESTIDOS Y TRAJES DE SEÑORA

Estados Unidos	10	12	14	16	18	20
Europa	38	40	42	44	46	48

TRAJES Y ABRIGOS DE CABALLERO

Estados Unidos	36	38	40	42	44	46
Europa	46	48	50	52	54	56

CAMISAS

Estados Unidos	14	14½	15	15½	15¾	16	16½	17
Europa	36	37	38	39	40	41	42	43

CALCETINES

Estados Unidos	9½	10	10½	11	11½
Europa	38-39	39-40	40-41	41-42	42-43

ZAPATOS DE SEÑORA

Estados Unidos	4	5	6	7	8	9	10	11
España	32	34	36	38	40	42	44	46

MEDIAS

Estados Unidos	8	8½	9	9½	10	10½
Europa	0	1	2	3	4	5

Y AQUÍ EN LOS ESTADOS UNIDOS

Carolina Herrera, venezolana, y Oscar de la Renta, dominicano, son modistos famosos que viven y diseñan en los Estados Unidos. Herrera diseñó el vestido de boda de Caroline Kennedy, hija del presidente John F. Kennedy.

Paloma Picasso, hija del famoso pintor español Pablo Picasso, nació en Francia pero se considera una diseñadora hispana. Ella diseña joyas[3] para la famosa casa Tiffany. También diseña perfumes y cosméticos.

[1] gangas *bargains*
[2] liquidaciones *sales*
[3] joyas *jewelry*

Paloma Picasso

LEARNING FROM REALIA

Have students look for their own sizes on the chart on page 379.

LEARNING FROM PHOTOS

Paloma and Claude, Picasso's two children, were born in France. Pablo Picasso lived in France from his student days at the turn of the century until his death in 1973.

PRESENTATION
(pages 380–381)

The main objective of this section is to have students enjoy the photographs and Hispanic culture. You may, however, also wish to do the following activities.

A. Have students read page 380 aloud. Ask them about similarities or differences between the markets in the photographs.

B. Ask them about the clothes that the people are wearing and guess the season. After reading the captions on page 380, you may wish to share the following information regarding the photos and realia:

Photo 1: *La calle Serrano* in Madrid is in a wealthy section of the city. The U.S. Embassy is in the same area. The street was named for Francisco Serrano Domínguez, a politician and general (1810–1885).

Photo 3: *El Rastro* is one of the most famous flea markets in the world. Although there are some permanent, and sometimes expensive, antique shops in the area, it is in the street where all the "action" takes place. People set out their used clothing, tools, old books, and magazines. Everything imaginable is to be found in the stalls of el *Rastro* every Sunday.

Realia 4: Spanish teens love to use shortened forms of words. This is very "in." Have students look for the word *prepa* on the magazine cover. Ask them to guess what *prepa* stands for *(La preparatoria).*

Realia 5: *Liquidación* means "sale."

REALIDADES

La calle Serrano en Madrid **1**. ¿Es una calle muy bonita, verdad?

Es un mercado al aire libre en Chichicastenango, Guatemala **2**. Los colores de la ropa son muy brillantes.

Es el famoso mercado del Rastro en Madrid **3**. Este mercado tiene lugar todos los domingos.

Es la portada de la revista "Eres", una revista para jóvenes muy popular en México **4**.

Es una liquidación, una venta en una tienda en Buenos Aires **5**. ¿Qué vas a comprar?

380

INDEPENDENT PRACTICE

1. Workbook, *Un poco más,* pages 143–144

RECYCLING

The *Comunicación oral* and *Comunicación escrita* activities allow students to use vocabulary and grammar from this chapter in open-ended, real-life settings. They also give students the opportunity to re-use the vocabulary and structures taught in previous chapters.

Comunicación oral

PRESENTATION *(page 382)*

Activities A, B, and C may serve as a means to evaluate speaking skills. You may wish to assign a grade based on the student's ability to communicate in Spanish.

Teaching Tip For students who are uncomfortable speaking in public, you may try working with a "cassette mail" system. Students record the assigned task in a private setting and give you the cassette. You can then record your evaluative comments and return the cassette to them. Use the evaluation criteria given on page 62 of this Teacher's Wraparound Edition.

ANSWERS

Actividades A–C

Answers will vary.

Comunicación escrita

ANSWERS

Actividades A–C

Answers will vary.

Comunicación oral

A **Una blusa por favor.** You sell clothing in a boutique. A Latin American tourist (your partner) comes in and wants to buy a blouse. The tourist wants to see a variety of styles before making a decision. Help by asking questions and offering advice.

B **El Oscar.** You and your partner are covering the Oscars for a Colombian radio station. Take turns describing in detail what each of the following stars is wearing.

1. Michael Jackson
2. Tom Selleck
3. Cher
4. Andy García
5. Denzel Washington
6. Jodie Foster

C **Le voy a comprar…** With your partner make a list of family members and the gifts you would buy for each one. Explain why you chose each gift.

Comunicación escrita

A **¿Qué está "in"?** With your partner make a list of clothing styles you think are "in" and "out" for high school students. Write down a description of each style and report to the class.

B **Lo que está en onda.** You are covering a fashion show in New York for a Spanish fashion magazine. Write an article of at least two paragraphs decribing the show. Include what's "in," what's "out," and what the new "look" is for next season according to the top designers.

C **Por catálogo.** Last week you ordered several items of clothing from a mail order house in Mexico. When you received the items and tried them on you discovered that some were too short, too long, the wrong color, too tight, too big, etc. Write a letter to the mail order house that includes: a brief description of the events leading to the problem; a statement of the problem; what you think the company should do about it.

> Muy señores míos:
> La semana pasada compré una blusa y un blusón. El color de la blusa no me gusta y el blusón me queda muy grande. Quiero cambiar (exchange) la blusa por otro color y el blusón por una talla más pequeña.
>
> Atentamente,
> Mariela García

FOR THE YOUNGER STUDENT

1. Set up a clothing store in the room, using items of clothing or pictures from a magazine. Have pairs of students make up skits between a salesperson and a client buying a gift for someone.
2. Have students make collages using magazine photos, advertisements, fabric, etc. Then have them describe their collages.

Reintegración

 Al cine. Contesten con *sí.*

1. ¿Fuiste al cine anoche?
2. ¿A qué cine fuiste?
3. ¿Qué película viste?
4. ¿Cuántas entradas compraste en la taquilla?
5. ¿Te gustó la película?
6. ¿Fuiste al cine con tus amigos?
7. Después, ¿fueron Uds. a tomar una merienda?
8. ¿Qué tomaste?
9. ¿Comiste?
10. ¿Qué comiste?
11. ¿Quién pagó, tú o tu amigo(a)?
12. ¿A qué hora volviste a casa?

Vocabulario

SUSTANTIVOS
la tienda de ropa
　para caballeros
　(señores)
　para damas (señoras)
el escaparate
la vitrina
el mostrador
el/la dependiente
el/la cliente
la caja
la tarjeta de crédito
la camisa
la corbata
el traje
los pantalones
la chaqueta
el saco
las medias
los calcetines
el blue jean
el T shirt
la camiseta
el suéter
el jersey
la blusa
la falda
el vestido
el sombrero
el cinturón
el abrigo
la gabardina
el blusón

los zapatos
las sandalias
los tenis
el precio
el color
el número
el tamaño
la talla
la manga
el tacón
el botón
la cremallera
el zíper

ADJETIVOS
corto(a)
largo(a)
ancho(a)
estrecho(a)
caro(a)
barato(a)
blanco(a)
rojo(a)
verde
negro(a)
amarillo(a)
gris
anaranjado(a)
azul

VERBOS
interesar
aburrir
enojar

Oscar de la Renta, diseñador dominicano que vive en los Estados Unidos

enfadar
sorprender
molestar
gustar
encantar

OTRAS PALABRAS Y
EXPRESIONES
demasiado
bastante
a rayas
a cuadros
de color
　crema
　vino
　café
　oliva
　marrón

hacer juego con
me sienta bien
me queda bien
me aprieta

¿cuánto cuesta?
nada
nadie
nunca
ni yo tampoco
algo
alguien
siempre
también

CAPÍTULO 13　**383**

Topics	Functions	Structure	Culture
Train travel Buying a ticket Procedures at a railway station	How to use words and expressions related to train travel How to purchase a train ticket and request information about arrivals and departures How to talk about events or activities that took place at definite time in the past How to identify various types of trains and services	El pretérito de los verbos *hacer, querer y venir* El pretérito de otros verbos irregulares	Train Travel in Spain, Central America, and South America Railroads in the U.S. Visiting Cuzco, Peru Train schedules

CAPÍTULO 14

Situation Cards

The Situation Cards simulate real-life situations that require students to communicate in Spanish, exactly as though they were in a Spanish-speaking country. The Situation Cards operate on the assumption that the person to whom the message is to be conveyed understands no English. Therefore, students must focus on producing the Spanish vocabulary and structures necessary to negotiate the situations successfully. For additional information, see the Introduction to the Situation Cards in the Situation Cards Envelope.

Communication Transparency

The illustration seen in this Communication Transparency consists of a synthesis of the two vocabulary (*Palabras 1&2*) presentations found in this chapter. It has been created in order to present this chapter's vocabulary in a new context, and also to recycle vocabulary learned in previous chapters. The Communication Transparency consists of original art. Following are some specific uses:

1. as a cue to stimulate conversation and writing activities
2. for listening comprehension activities
3. to review and reteach vocabulary
4. as a review for chapter and unit tests

CAPÍTULO 14   A

You're at the ticket window for the luxury train El Talgo. Buy a ticket for Paris. Give the ticket agent all the necessary information.

B

C

D

Bienvenidos   © Glencoe/McGraw-Hill

© Glencoe/McGraw-Hill

© Glencoe/McGraw-Hill

© Glencoe/McGraw-Hill

Bienvenidos   Chapter 14   Communication Transparency   C-14

Andén

Copyright © by Glencoe/McGraw-Hill Publishing Company

	Pages
Lesson Plans	

Workbook

Communication Activities Masters

6 Bell Ringer Reviews — 32-33

Chapter Situation Cards A B C D

Chapter Quizzes

Testing Program

Nosotros y Nuestro Mundo

- Nuestro Conocimiento Académico *El gobierno y la política*
- Nuestro Idioma *Regionalismos*
- Nuestra Cultura *Poblaciones indígenas de Latinoamérica*
- Nuestra Literatura *"¡Quien sabe!"* de José Santos Chocano
- Nuestra Creatividad
- Nuestras Diversiones

CD-ROM Interactive Textbook Disc 4

Chapter 14 Student Edition
- Palabras 1
- Palabras 2
- Estructura
- Conversación
- Lectura y cultura
- Hispanoparlantes
- Realidades
- Culminación
- Prueba

Audio Cassette Program with Student Tape Manual

Compact Disc Program with Student Tape Manual

Overhead Transparencies Binder

- Vocabulary 14.1 (A&B); 14.2 (A&B)
- Pronunciation P-14
- Communication C-14
- Maps
- Fine Art (with Blackline Master Activities)

Video Program

Computer Software (Macintosh, IBM, Apple)

- Practice Disk
  - Palabras 1 y 2
  - Estructura
- Test Generator Disk
  - Chapter Test
  - Customized Test

CHAPTER OVERVIEW

In this chapter students will learn to communicate when traveling by train in a Spanish-speaking country. They will also learn the preterite forms of irregular verbs. The cultural focus is on train travel in Spain, and some interesting train trips in Central and South America.

CHAPTER OBJECTIVES

By the end of this chapter students will know:

1. vocabulary associated with facilities, personnel, and procedures at a railroad station and on board a train
2. the preterite of *hacer, querer,* and *venir*
3. the preterite of *estar, andar,* and *tener*
4. the preterite of *poder, poner,* and *saber*

CHAPTER 14 RESOURCES

1. Workbook
2. Student Tape Manual
3. Audio Cassette 8B
4. Vocabulary Transparencies
5. Pronunciation Transparency P-14
6. Bell Ringer Review Blackline Masters
7. Communication Activities Masters
8. Computer Software: Practice and Test Generator
9. Video Cassette, Chapter 14
10. Video Activities Booklet, Chapter 14
11. Situation Cards
12. Chapter Quizzes
13. Testing Program

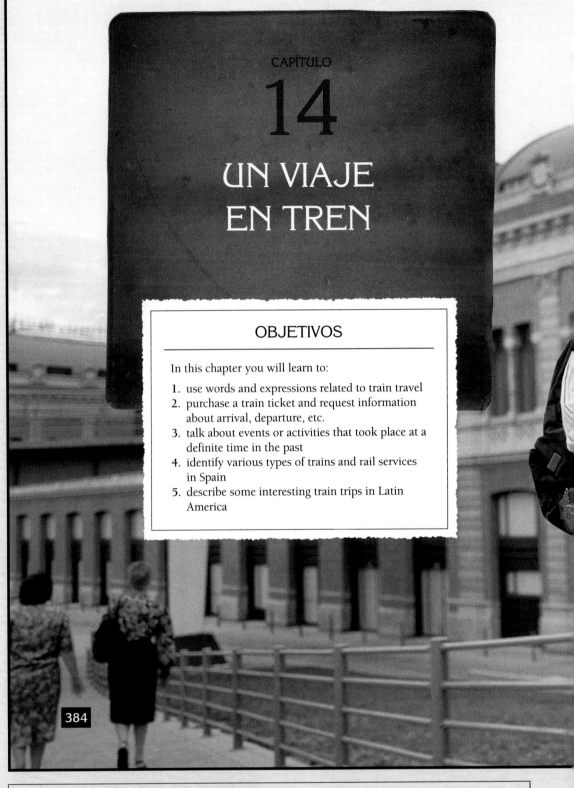

CAPÍTULO

14

UN VIAJE EN TREN

OBJETIVOS

In this chapter you will learn to:

1. use words and expressions related to train travel
2. purchase a train ticket and request information about arrival, departure, etc.
3. talk about events or activities that took place at a definite time in the past
4. identify various types of trains and rail services in Spain
5. describe some interesting train trips in Latin America

384

CHAPTER PROJECTS

(optional)

1. Have groups plan a rail trip through Spain using a guide such as the one from Eurail (available at many travel agencies). Give them a time limit and have them include at least one overnight stay. They should plan arrival and departure times and the length of each stop on the itinerary. Groups can describe their trip to the class.

2. Have the groups select one city from their itinerary and find out some information about it. They can do a brief report for a presentation to the class.

385

Pacing
    Chapter 14 will require about eight to ten days. However, pacing will vary according to the length of the class, the age of your students, and student aptitude.

LEARNING FROM PHOTOS

The young man and woman are in front of the Atocha train station in Madrid. They are looking at a booklet describing the AVE (*Alta Velocidad Española*), the high-speed train that links Madrid with Sevilla. The Atocha station, renovated in the 1990s, is one of the oldest railroad stations in Spain. Trains leave Atocha for Andalucía and the Levante (Valencia, Murcia, Alicante).

Note A magazine article on *El AVE* appears in Level 3 of this textbook series, *De viaje*.

VOCABULARIO

Vocabulary Teaching Resources

1. Vocabulary Transparencies 14.1 (A & B)
2. Audio Cassette 8B
3. Student Tape Manual, pages 259–260
4. Workbook, pages 146–147
5. Communication Activities Masters, page 86, *A & B*
6. Chapter Quizzes, page 63, *Palabras 1*

Bell Ringer Review

Write the following on the board or use BRR Blackline Master 14-1: Complete the following sentences.

1. Los pasajeros hacen ___ en el mostrador de la línea aérea.
2. Los pasajeros ___ su equipaje.
3. El equipaje ___ tiene que caber debajo del asiento o en el compartimiento.
4. Los pasajeros en un aeropuerto tienen que pasar por ___.
5. Los pasajeros tienen que mostrar su ___.

PALABRAS 1

EN LA ESTACIÓN DE FERROCARRIL

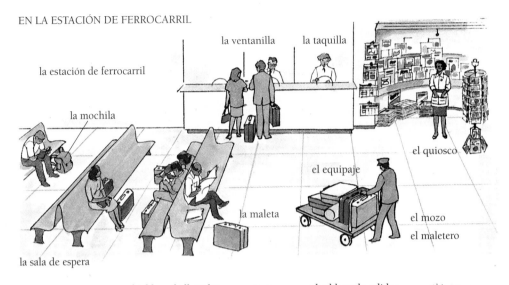

la ventanilla la taquilla

la estación de ferrocarril

la mochila

el quiosco

el equipaje

la maleta

el mozo

el maletero

la sala de espera

el tablero de llegadas   el tablero de salidas

Madrid
Pais Vasco

el boleto   el billete

RENFE

el billete sencillo

el billete de ida y vuelta

el horario

386   CAPÍTULO 14

TOTAL PHYSICAL RESPONSE

(following the Vocabulary presentation)

Getting Ready

A piece of paper with the word *maleta* written on it can represent a suitcase.

TPR 1

___, levántate y ven acá, por favor.
Vas a hacer algunos gestos. Aquí tienes una maleta.
Toma la maleta. Mira la maleta.
Abre la maleta. Pon la ropa en la maleta.
Cierra la maleta.
Ve al teléfono. Llama un taxi.
Toma la maleta y ve a la calle.
Espera el taxi.
El taxi llega. Pon la maleta en la maletera del taxi. Abre la puerta del taxi.
Sube al taxi. Siéntate.
Gracias, ___. Y ahora puedes volver a tu asiento.

el tren
el vagón
el andén
la vía

La señora hizo un viaje.
Hizo el viaje en tren.
Tomó el tren (fue en tren) porque no quiso ir en carro.

El mozo vino con el equipaje.
Otro mozo puso el equipaje en el tren.

El tren salió del andén número tres.
Los pasajeros estuvieron en el andén.

PRESENTATION
(*pages 386–387*)

A. Have students close their books. Using Vocabulary Transparencies 14.1 (A & B), point to each item and model the word. Have students repeat each item several times after you.

B. Have students listen once to Cassette 8B for additional reinforcement.

C. Point to items on the transparency at random and call on an individual to identify the item you are pointing to.

D. When presenting the contextualized sentences, you may wish to ask some questions. For example: *¿Qué hizo la señora? ¿Cómo hizo el viaje? ¿Por qué tomó el tren? ¿Con qué vino el mozo? ¿Dónde puso el otro mozo el equipaje? ¿De qué andén salió el tren?*

INFORMAL ASSESSMENT
(*Palabras 1*)

A. After presenting all the vocabulary from *Palabras 1*, show the Vocabulary Transparencies again and let students identify items at random.

B. Then have students make up questions about what they see on the transparencies. You may answer the questions or have them call on other students to answer.

TOTAL PHYSICAL RESPONSE

TPR 2

Getting Ready

Have your desk be *la ventanilla*. One student can be *el agente* and another student can be *el pasajero*. Numbers on the board can represent *los andenes*. A piece of paper with the word *boleto* or *billete* can be the ticket.
___, **levántate y ven acá.**

Ésta es la estación de ferrocarril. Estamos en la sala de espera. Dame la maleta. Ve a la ventanilla. Compra un boleto.
Págale al agente.
Toma tu boleto. Mira el boleto.
Pon el boleto en tu bolsillo.
Ven acá. Toma la maleta.
Busca el andén número dos.
Ve al andén. Espera el tren.
Aquí viene el tren. Sube al tren.
Gracias, ___. Regresa a tu asiento.

PRESENTATION
(page 388)

Ejercicio A

A. It is recommended that you do this exercise first with books closed.

B. You may wish to do it a second time with books closed providing no cues.

Expansion of *Ejercicio A*

Call on one student to retell the story in his/her own words.

GEOGRAPHY CONNECTION

1. The *tarifas* (fares) on the information board in the Buenos Aires railroad station on page 388 are from Retiro to Tigre. You may wish to explain to students that *el Tigre* is a lovely delta area not far from Buenos Aires. Many people have modest weekend homes along the canals. The homes are lovely but rustic, and there's no electricity. People go there to get away from the hustle of the city.

2. On the map of Spain on page 473 have students locate Burgos. Burgos was the home of *El Cid*, Spain's national hero.

ANSWERS

Ejercicio A

1. **La señora vino a la estación en taxi.**
2. **Puso sus maletas en la maletera del taxi.**
3. **Fue a la ventanilla.**
4. **Compró un boleto.**
5. **Compró un boleto de ida y vuelta.**
6. **Compró un billete de segunda clase.**
7. **Puso su billete en su bolsa.**
8. **Consultó el horario.**
9. **Fue al andén.**
10. **El tren salió del andén número tres.**
11. **Hizo el viaje en tren porque no quiso ir en coche.**

La estación de ferrocarril El Retiro, Buenos Aires, Argentina

Ejercicios

A **En la estación de ferrocarril.** Contesten según se indica.

1. ¿Cómo vino la señora a la estación? (en taxi)
2. ¿Dónde puso sus maletas? (en la maletera del taxi)
3. En la estación, ¿adónde fue? (a la ventanilla)
4. ¿Qué compró? (un boleto)
5. ¿Qué tipo de boleto compró? (de ida y vuelta)
6. ¿En qué clase? (segunda)
7. ¿Dónde puso su billete? (en su bolsa)
8. ¿Qué consultó? (el horario)
9. ¿Adónde fue? (al andén)
10. ¿De qué anden salió el tren? (del número tres)
11. ¿Por qué hizo la señora el viaje en el tren? (no quiso ir en coche)

388 CAPÍTULO 14

LEARNING FROM REALIA

The ticket on page 388 is from Madrid to Burgos. Trains leave *Chamartín* for Asturias, Santander, Vascongadas, Barcelona, and France. The third Madrid train station is the *Estación del Norte*. Trains leave from here for northwestern Spain (*la Coruña*). You may wish to ask students the following: *¿Qué día hace el viaje el pasajero? ¿Cuánto cuesta el billete? ¿Cuál es la distancia del viaje? (364 kilómetros) ¿Qué día y a qué hora compraron el billete? ¿En qué clase viaja el pasajero?*

B **Antes de abordar el tren.** Escojan.

1. ¿Dónde espera la gente el tren?
   a. en la ventanilla   **b.** en la sala de espera   **c.** en el quiosco

2. ¿Dónde venden o despachan los billetes?
   a. en la ventanilla   **b.** en el equipaje   **c.** en el quiosco

3. ¿Qué venden en el quiosco?
   a. boletos   **b.** maletas   **c.** periódicos y revistas

4. ¿Qué consulta el pasajero para verificar la hora de salida del tren?
   a. la llegada   **b.** la vía   **c.** el horario

5. ¿Quién ayuda a los pasajeros con el equipaje?
   a. el mozo   **b.** el tablero   **c.** el andén

6. ¿De dónde sale el tren?
   a. de la ventanilla   **b.** del andén
   c. del tablero

C **El billete del tren.** Contesten.

1. ¿De qué estación sale el tren?
2. ¿Adónde va el tren?
3. ¿Cuál es la fecha del billete?
4. ¿A qué hora sale el tren?
5. ¿A qué hora llega el tren?
6. ¿Está el asiento en la sección de fumar o de no fumar?
7. ¿Qué clase de billete es?
8. ¿Con qué pagó el/la pasajero(a)?

CAPÍTULO 14   **389**

PRESENTATION (*page 389*)
Ejercicio B
   Exercise B is to be done with books open.

Ejercicio C
   Have students refer to the ticket as they respond to the questions.

ANSWERS
Ejercicio B
1. b
2. a
3. c
4. c
5. a
6. b

Ejercicio C
1. El tren sale de la estación de Cuenca.
2. El tren va a Atocha en Madrid.
3. La fecha del billete es el 20 de marzo.
4. El tren sale a las 6:31 P.M.
5. El tren llega a las 9:00 P.M.
6. Está en la sección de no fumar.
7. Es un billete de segunda clase.
8. El/la pasajero(a) pagó con pesetas.

COOPERATIVE LEARNING

   Have students work in pairs. Have them look at the ticket on page 389 and question one another about the information on it.

INDEPENDENT PRACTICE

   Assign any of the following:
1. Workbook, pages 146–147
2. Communication Activities Masters, page 86, *A & B*
3. Exercises on student pages 388–389

Bell Ringer Review

Write the following on the board or use BRR Blackline Master 14-2: Complete the following. **La compañía de aviación anuncia la ___ de su ___ 102 con ___ a Madrid por la ___ número tres. Embarque inmediato.**

PRESENTATION

(page 390)

A. Model the new words using Vocabulary Transparencies 14.2 (A & B). Have students repeat the new words chorally after you or the recording on Cassette 8B.

B. After the vocabulary has been presented orally, students can open their books to pages 390–391 and read the new words and statements.

C. You may wish to play a guessing game with opposites. Have students give you the opposite of the following words.
   subir
   libre
   a tiempo
   un boleto de ida y vuelta
   la llegada

VOCABULARIO

PALABRAS 2

EN EL TREN

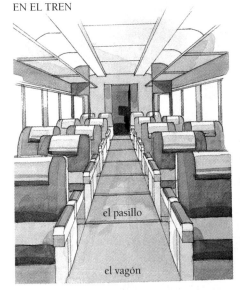

el pasillo

el vagón

el compartimiento

el revisor

la litera

el coche-cama

el coche-comedor

390 CAPÍTULO 14

TOTAL PHYSICAL RESPONSE

(following the Vocabulary presentation)

Getting Ready

Set up an area in front of the classroom as *el tren* and place three chairs together. Tell students that those chairs are the seats in the train. Then call on one student to act as *pasajero(a)*.

___, levántate y ven acá, por favor.
Sube al tren. Busca tu asiento.
Pon tu maleta en el asiento. Abre la maleta.
Saca un libro de la maleta.
Cierra la maleta.
Pon la maleta en el compartimiento.
Siéntate. Toma tu asiento.
Abre tu libro. Lee el libro.
Gracias, ___. Y ahora puedes volver a tu asiento.

el asiento

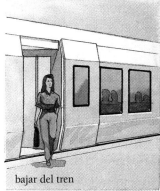

ocupado   libre

reservado

ABOUT THE LANGUAGE

Note that we have used the expression *bajar del tren*, which is grammatically correct. In many areas of Latin America one will hear *bajarse del tren*. Among contemporary novelists one will sometimes encounter examples of *bajar* and *bajarse* in the same work.

bajar del tren   subir al tren   transbordar

Los pasajeros subieron al tren.
El tren salió a tiempo.
No salió tarde.
No salió con retraso (con una demora).

Los pasajeros van a transbordar en la próxima
estación, la próxima parada.

FOR THE NATIVE SPEAKER

This is an opportunity for a linguistics lesson. The topic is the *ferrocarril*. The *ferrocarril* is really a *hierro-carril*, the *f* from old Spanish having become an *h* in modern Spanish. Ask students if they can think of words with an *f* in English that have an *h* in Spanish. For example: falcon-*halcón*; fig-*higo*. In Spanish *fuego* comes from *hogar*, *horno* was *forno*, *hermano* was *fermano*, and *hierro* was *fierro*. Have students look for examples of words with an *h* in modern Spanish that used to be written with an *f*. You may wish to tell them that *fierro* is still used in the countryside for *iron* and *branding iron*.

Ejercicios

PRESENTATION *(page 392)*

Ejercicio A

This exercise can be done with books closed or open. You may call on one student to do one or two items. If the student makes an error, call on another student to correct it.

Ejercicio B

Have students answer the questions about the drawing. Then allow them to say anything they can about the drawing in their own words.

Ejercicio C

Have students locate Granada, Málaga, and Benidorm on a map.

ANSWERS

Ejercicio A

1. Sí, subieron a bordo los pasajeros.
2. No, el tren no salió tarde.
3. No salió con una demora.
4. Sí, el revisor vino.
5. Sí, él revisó los boletos.

Ejercicio B

1. Sí, este tren tiene compartimientos.
2. Tiene un pasillo central.
3. Hay dos asientos a cada lado del pasillo.
4. Hay asientos libres.
5. No, el tren no está completo.
6. No, no hay pasajeros de pie en el pasillo.

Ejercicio C

1. paradas
2. paradas
3. transbordar
4. transbordar, estación, parada
5. revisor

Ejercicios

A **En el tren.** Contesten.

1. Cuando llegó el tren a la estación, ¿subieron los pasajeros a bordo?
2. ¿El tren salió tarde?
3. ¿Con cuántos minutos de demora salió?
4. ¿Vino el revisor?
5. ¿Revisó él los boletos?

B **El tren.** Contesten según el dibujo.

1. ¿Tiene este tren compartimientos?
2. ¿Tiene el coche o vagón un pasillo central o lateral?
3. ¿Cuántos asientos hay a cada lado del pasillo?
4. ¿Hay asientos libres o están todos ocupados?
5. ¿Está completo el tren?
6. ¿Hay pasajeros de pie en el pasillo?

C **Un viaje en tren.** Completen.

1. Entre Granada y Málaga el tren local hace muchas ___.
2. El expreso o el rápido no hace muchas ___.
3. No hay un tren directo a Benidorm. Es necesario cambiar de tren. Los pasajeros tienen que ___.
4. Los pasajeros que van a Benidorm tienen que ___ en la próxima ___ o ___.
5. ¿Cómo lo sabes? El ___ nos informó que este tren no es directo.

392 CAPÍTULO 14

COOPERATIVE LEARNING

Have pairs of students make up as many sentences as they can about travel. They can read their sentences to each other and decide if they deal with train or air travel. They should categorize their sentences under the headings *Viajes en avión* and *Viajes en tren*. Finally, have them reorganize their sentences to tell two stories, one about train travel and another about air travel.

Comunicación
Palabras 1 y 2

A El Talgo. You are an exchange student in Spain. You have just returned to Madrid from a trip to Paris. You travelled from Madrid to Paris on the luxury train El Talgo. The train left Madrid at 6:15 p.m. The trip took fifteen hours but the train arrived in Paris one hour late. The train had a dining car and a sleeping car with sleeping berths. It made only two stops: in Burgos and at the French border in the town of Hendaye. You have been asked to tell the class about your trip. Include in your talk:

1. the price of the ticket
2. what time you boarded the train
3. when the train left the station
4. the number of stops and where
5. when and how well you slept
6. what time you arrived in Paris
7. what you think of El Talgo
8. if you recommend it or not, and why

B ¿A qué hora…? With your group study a map of Spain. One member of the group will be the RENFE (Red Nacional de Ferrocarriles Españoles) ticket agent in Madrid. Each member will choose two cities from the map. Take turns asking the ticket agent: the price of a round-trip second class ticket; if there is a dining car; the time the train leaves Madrid; the time it arrives at the city; if the train is always on time.

C Quiero ir a… You are planning a train trip from Santiago to Puerto Montt in Chile. Get as much information as you can from the travel agent (your partner). Make sure you cover such things as:

la estación de donde sale	el coche-cama	la litera
la estación adonde llega	la hora que sale	la hora que llega
el número de paradas	la tarifa de ida y vuelta	el coche-comedor

D En tren o en avión. With a classmate, compare train and air travel. For each fact that you state about train travel, your partner will state the corresponding fact about air travel.

Estudiante 1: El tren sale de la estación.
Estudiante 2: El avión sale del aeropuerto.

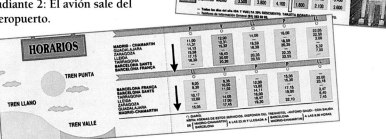

CAPÍTULO 14   **393**

LEARNING FROM REALIA

1. Have students look at the prices on the realia on page 393. Ask students: Which train do you think is the fastest and most comfortable? Why?
2. Ask students? *¿Cuál es el descuento si uno compra un billete de ida y vuelta? (20 por ciento) ¿Cuál es una ciudad importante entre Madrid y Barcelona? ¿Hace parada el tren en esta ciudad?*

INDEPENDENT PRACTICE

Assign any of the following:
1. Workbook, pages 147–148
2. Communication Activities Masters, pages 87-88, *C & D*
3. Exercises on student page 392
4. Computer Software, *Vocabulario*

Comunicación
(Palabras 1 and 2)

PRESENTATION *(page 393)*

Select whichever activities you want to do, or allow students to select the activity they would like to take part in. Different groups can do different activities.

ANSWERS
Actividad A
Answers may include the following.
1. El billete costó…
2. Subí al tren a las…
3. El tren salió a las…
4. El tren paró… veces.
5. Dormí… toda la noche.
6. Llegué a París a las…
7. Me gusta mucho El Talgo.
8. Le recomiendo El Talgo porque…

Actividad B
Answers will vary.

Actividad C
Answers may include the following.
¿De qué estación sale el tren?
¿A qué hora sale?
¿Cuántas paradas hace?
¿Hay coche-cama?
¿Hay coche-comedor?
¿A qué estación llega?
¿A qué hora llega?
¿Cuánto cuesta el billete?
¿Hay literas?

Actividad D
Answers will vary according to the model.

ESTRUCTURA

Structure Teaching Resources

1. Workbook, pages 149–150
2. Student Tape Manual, page 261
3. Audio Cassette 8B
4. Communication Activities Masters, page 89, A & B
5. Chapter Quizzes, pages 65–66, *Estructura*
6. Computer Software,

Bell Ringer Review

Write the following on the board or use BRR Blackline Master 14-3: Write a sentence using each of the following expressions in the present tense.

hacer un viaje
poner la ropa en la maleta
salir para la estación de ferrocarril
venir en tren

El pretérito de los verbos hacer, querer y venir

PRESENTATION *(page 394)*

A. Read the grammar points on page 394 to the class.
B. Have the class repeat the verb forms aloud.
C. Call on an individual to read the example sentences.
D. Point out to students that all these irregular verbs have the ending *-e* in the *yo* form.

Note Many of the verbs students will be learning in this chapter are not used very frequently in the preterite. For this reason, it is recommended that you do not spend a great deal of time on this topic. The most important verbs are *venir, hacer,* and *poner.*

El pretérito de los verbos *hacer, querer y venir*   *Relating Past Actions*

1. The verbs *hacer, querer,* and *venir* are irregular in the preterite. Note that they all have an *-i* in the stem and the endings for the *yo* and *él, ella,* and *Ud.* forms are different from the endings of the regular verbs.

INFINITIVE	HACER	QUERER	VENIR
yo	hice	quise	vine
tú	hiciste	quisiste	viniste
él, ella, Ud.	hizo	quiso	vino
nosotros(as)	hicimos	quisimos	vinimos
vosotros(as)	hicisteis	quisisteis	vinisteis
ellos, ellas, Uds.	hicieron	quisieron	vinieron

2. The verb *querer* has a special meaning in the preterite.

Quise ayudar.   *I tried to help.*
No quise ir en carro.   *I refused to go by car.*

LEARNING FROM PHOTOS

Bicycle racing has become popular in the U.S. in recent years. In Europe and South America it has long been a major sport. The premier event is the *Tour de France.* Spanish cyclists have won the *Tour* a number of times. In the 1990s Miguel Indurain won three consecutive times. In Spain, the great race is the *Vuelta a España.*

Ejercicios

A **¿Cómo viniste?** Contesten.

1. ¿Viniste a la estación en taxi?
2. ¿Viniste en un taxi público o privado?
3. ¿Hiciste el viaje en tren?
4. ¿Hiciste el viaje en el expreso o en el rápido?
5. ¿Lo hiciste en tren porque no quisiste ir en coche?

B **¿Por qué no quisieron?** Completen las conversaciones.

1. —Ellos no ___ (hacer) el viaje
   —¿No lo ___ (querer) hacer?
   —No, de ninguna manera.
   —Pues, ¿qué pasó entonces? ¿Lo ___ (hacer) o no lo ___ (hacer)?
   —No, no lo___ (hacer).
2. —¿Por qué no ___ (venir) Uds. esta mañana?
   — Nosotros no ___ (venir) porque no ___ (hacer) las reservaciones.
3. —Carlos no ___ (querer) hacer la cama.
   —Entonces, ¿quién la ___ (hacer)?
   —Pues, la ___ (hacer) yo.
   —¡Qué absurdo! ¿Tú la ___ (hacer) porque él no la ___ (querer) hacer?

CONDUZCASE CON PRUDENCIA

ZONA DE SERVICIO
Comida, café, copa y vídeo. Estos son los ingredientes de un viaje apetecible. Mézcielos a su gusto. En tren. En su próximo viaje estamos para servirle. Sin parar.

ESTACIONAMIENTO RESERVADO
Al salir de viaje aparque bien su coche. En tren. En Auto-expreso alcanzará los 160 Km/h, sin tocar el acelerador. Llegará a su destino, sin cambiar la marcha.

TRANSPORTE ESCOLAR
Si tienes menos de 11 años, juega a los trenes en la guardería. Si tienes más, disfruta de las ventajas que tiene el tren mientras tus hijos juegan.

VISTA PANORAMICA
Con vistas al campo o con vistas a la playa. Usted elige. Sólo tiene que asomarse a la ventanilla y disfrutar. Sólo tiene que viajar en tren.

VELOCIDAD RECOMENDADA 160 Km/h.
Viaje sin límites. En tren. A 160 Km/h , cuando menos lo espere, llegará a su destino. Haga cálculos.

VIA LIBRE
Reservada para usted. En el tren dispone de una vía exclusiva, sin atascos. La única vía donde usted tiene preferencia siempre.

OBRAS
Obras públicas para disfrutar en privado. Cómodamente. No pare hasta llegar al final. Hasta su destino.

AFLOJENSE LOS CINTURONES
Así viajará más cómodo. Sin aprietos. Sin agobios. Sin molestias de ninguna clase. Así viajará en el tren.

HOTEL
Tenemos plazas para todos. Para que viaje con toda comodidad, en coche-cama o literas. No se pierda el tren.

RENFE MEJORA TU TREN DE VIDA

CAPÍTULO 14   **395**

Ejercicios

PRESENTATION *(page 395)*

Ejercicios A and B

A. You may wish to assign Exercises A and B as homework. Then go over them orally in class.
B. Exercise B can be done as a paired activity.

Expansion of *Ejercicio B*

You may wish to have several students quickly present the mini-conversations to the class.

ANSWERS

Ejercicio A

Answers will vary.
1. Sí (No), (no) vine en taxi.
2. Vine en un taxi público (privado).
3. Sí (No), (no) hice el viaje en tren.
4. Hice el viaje en el expreso (en el rápido).
5. Sí, lo hice en tren porque no quise ir en coche.

Ejercicio B
1. hicieron
   quisieron
   hicieron
   hicieron
   hicieron
2. vinieron
   vinimos
   hicimos
3. quiso
   hizo
   hice
   hiciste
   quiso

Bell Ringer Review

Write the following on the board or use BRR Blackline Master 14-4:
1. Write three things you have to do.
2. Write three things you can do.
3. Write three things you want to do.
4. Write three things you know how to do.

El pretérito de otros verbos irregulares

PRESENTATION *(page 396)*

A. Read the grammar explanation on page 396 to the class.

B. Have the class repeat the verb forms aloud.

C. Call on an individual to read the example sentences.

ABOUT THE LANGUAGE

You may wish to point out to students that the expression *andar a pie* means "to walk." This can also be expressed with the verb *caminar*. To take a walk, however, is *dar un paseo*.

PAIRED ACTIVITY

Have students work in pairs and make up as many sentences as they can using the verbs given on pages 394 and 396. They then write their sentences as questions and read them to each other.

El pretérito de otros verbos irregulares

Describing Past Actions

1. The verbs *estar, andar,* and *tener* are irregular in the preterite. They all have a -*u* in the stem.

INFINITIVE	ESTAR	ANDAR	TENER
yo	estuve	anduve	tuve
tú	estuviste	anduviste	tuviste
él, ella, Ud.	estuvo	anduvo	tuvo
nosotros(as)	estuvimos	anduvimos	tuvimos
vosotros(as)	*estuvisteis*	*anduvisteis*	*tuvisteis*
ellos, ellas, Uds.	estuvieron	anduvieron	tuvieron

2. The verb *andar* means "to go" but not to a specific place. The verb *ir* is used with a specific place. Note the following.

> **Fueron a Toledo.** *They went to Toledo.*
>
> **Anduvieron por las plazas pintorescas de Toledo.**
> *They wandered through (walked around) the picturesque squares of Toledo.*

3. The verbs *poder, poner,* and *saber* are also irregular in the preterite. Like the verbs *estar, andar,* and *tener,* they all have a -*u* in the stem.

INFINITIVE	PODER	PONER	SABER
yo	pude	puse	supe
tú	pudiste	pusiste	supiste
él, ella, Ud.	pudo	puso	supo
nosotros(as)	pudimos	pusimos	supimos
vosotros(as)	*pudisteis*	*pusisteis*	*supisteis*
ellos, ellas, Uds.	pudieron	pusieron	supieron

4. Like *querer,* the verbs *poder* and *saber* have special meanings in the preterite.

> **Pude parar.** *(After trying hard) I managed to stop.*
> **No pude parar.** *(I tried but) I couldn't stop.*
> **Yo lo supe ayer.** *I found it out (learned it) yesterday.*

FOR THE NATIVE SPEAKER

Some irregular preterite forms present a pronunciation problem. There is a tendency to substitute *o* for *u* in *poder*. For example: *Yo no podí*. It is also common to hear *pusí* for *puse* because of forms like *salí, volví,* etc. This also occurs with *estuví* for *estuve, anduví* for *anduve,* and *tuví* for *tuve*. If this is a problem with the group, practice the correct forms. Provide practice by having them respond to questions such as? *¿Dónde estuviste anoche? ¿Dónde pusiste la mochila? ¿Tuviste tiempo para hacer la tarea ayer?*

Ejercicios

A **¿Estuviste en la estación?** Contesten según se indica.

1. ¿Estuviste ayer en la estación de ferrocarril? (sí)
2. ¿Tuviste que tomar el tren a Toledo? (sí)
3. ¿Pudiste comprar un billete reducido? (no)
4. ¿Tuviste que mostrar tu tarjeta de identidad estudiantil? (sí)
5. ¿Dónde la pusiste? (no sé)
6. ¿La perdiste? (sí, creo)
7. ¿Cuándo supiste que la perdiste? (cuando llegué a en la estación)

B **Estuve en el mercado.** Completen.

El otro día yo ___ (estar) en el mercado de
              1
Chichicastenango, en Guatemala. Ramón ___
                                         2
(estar) allí también. Nosotros ___ (andar) por el
                                3
mercado pero no ___ (poder) comprar nada.
                  4
No es que no ___ (querer) comprar nada, es
             5
que no ___ (poder) porque ___ (ir) al
        6   7
mercado sin un quetzal.

Ejercicios

PRESENTATION *(page 397)*

Ejercicios A and B

A. It is suggested that you go over Exercise A orally with books closed.

B. Exercise B can also be done as a paired activity.

C. Have students read the story in Exercise B aloud.

Expansion of *Ejercicio B*

A. Have a student retell all the information in his/her own words.

B. Call on students to make up a question about each statement.

ANSWERS

Ejercicio A

1. Sí, ayer estuve en la estación de ferrocarril.
2. Sí, tuve que tomar el tren a Toledo.
3. No, no pude comprar un billete reducido.
4. Sí, tuve que mostrar mi tarjeta de identidad estudiantil.
5. No sé dónde la puse.
6. Sí, creo que la perdí.
7. Supe que la perdí cuando llegué a la estación.

Ejercicio B

1. estuve
2. estuvo
3. anduvimos
4. pudimos
5. quisimos
6. pudimos
7. fuimos

INDEPENDENT PRACTICE

Assign any of the following:

1. Workbook, pages 149–150
2. Communication Activities Masters, page 89, A & B
3. Exercises on student pages 395 and 397

LEARNING FROM REALIA

1. The form at the bottom of page 397 is for a type of tax collected by the town. Ask students? *¿Para qué pueblo o ciudad es? ¿En qué país está? ¿En qué departamento del país está? ¿Cuál es la moneda del país?*
2. Have students find the word for "receipt."

Conversación

PRESENTATION *(page 398)*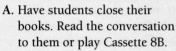

A. Have students close their books. Read the conversation to them or play Cassette 8B.

B. Have the class repeat each line after you once.

C. Call on two students to read the conversation with as much expression as possible.

D. After completing the exercise, have students retell the story in their own words.

ANSWERS

1. **La señorita está en la ventanilla.**
2. **Ella va a Madrid.**
3. **Quiere un billete sencillo.**
4. **Lo quiere para hoy.**
5. **Quiere viajar en segunda clase.**
6. **Sí, la señorita es estudiante.**
7. **Sí, hay una tarifa reducida para estudiantes.**
8. **La señorita tiene su tarjeta de identidad estudiantil.**
9. **Con el descuento estudiantil el billete cuesta (es) tres mil pesetas.**
10. **El tren sale a las 10:10 P.M.**
11. **El tren sale del andén número 8.**

Escenas de la vida *En la ventanilla*

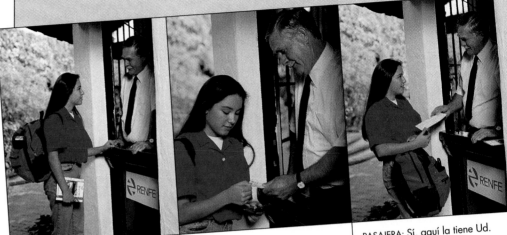

PASAJERA: Un billete para Madrid, por favor.
AGENTE: ¿Sencillo o de ida y vuelta?
PASAJERA: Sencillo, por favor.
AGENTE: ¿Para cuándo, señorita?
PASAJERA: Para hoy.

AGENTE: ¿En qué clase, primera o segunda?
PASAJERA: En segunda. ¿Tiene Ud. una tarifa reducida para estudiantes?
AGENTE: Sí. ¿Tiene Ud. su tarjeta de identidad estudiantil?

PASAJERA: Sí, aquí la tiene Ud.
AGENTE: Con el descuento son tres mil pesetas.
PASAJERA: ¿A qué hora sale el próximo tren?
AGENTE: Sale a las veinte y diez del andén número ocho.
PASAJERA: Gracias.

 De viaje. Contesten.

1. ¿Dónde está la señorita?
2. ¿Adónde va?
3. ¿Qué tipo de billete quiere?
4. ¿Para cuándo lo quiere?
5. ¿En qué clase quiere viajar?
6. ¿Es estudiante la señorita?
7. ¿Hay una tarifa reducida para estudiantes?
8. ¿Qué tiene la señorita?
9. ¿Cuánto es el billete con el descuento estudiantil?
10. ¿A qué hora sale el tren?
11. ¿De qué andén sale?

398 CAPÍTULO 14

Pronunciación *La consonante* x

An **x** between two vowels is pronounced much like the English **x** but a bit softer.

exacto	conexión	éxito
examen	flexible	próximo

When **x** is followed by a consonant, it is often pronounced like an **s**.

extranjero	explicar	exclamar
Extremadura	extraordinario	excusar

Repeat the following sentence.

El extranjero tomó el examen en Extremadura.

un examen
extraordinario

Comunicación

A ¿Por qué no quieres…? Recently your best friend (your partner) has been turning down all your invitations to do things together. Ask him or her why. Your partner should give some interesting excuses.

> ir a patinar
> Estudiante 1: ¿Por qué no quisiste ir a patinar?
> Estudiante 2: No quise porque la gente que patina no me gusta.

1. ir a patinar
2. jugar al tenis
3. ir al cine
4. venir a la fiesta de ___
5. ir a la piscina
6. asistir al concierto de música clásica

B ¿Qué hiciste? Ask your partner what he or she did last Saturday, last Sunday, and last night. Reverse roles.

C ¿Dónde estuviste? Find out if your partner was at the following places or events. He or she will answer "yes" or "no" and give a reason. Reverse roles.

> el centro comercial
> Estudiante 1: ¿Estuviste en el centro comercial?
> Estudiante 2: No, porque tuve que estudiar.

1. el concierto de Bach
2. la fiesta de cumpleaños de ___
3. el partido de baloncesto
4. la reunión del club de español
5. la biblioteca

D En Buenos Aires. You are at the train station in Buenos Aires, Argentina. You want to buy a ticket for Mar del Plata. Your partner is the ticket agent.

1. Tell the ticket agent what you want.
2. Get the price.
3. Find out at what time the next train leaves.
4. Ask for the track number.

CAPÍTULO 14   **399**

Pronunciación

PRESENTATION (*page 399*)

A. Whenever *x* is followed by a consonant, it is pronounced as *s*. There are no variations to this.

B. There is, however, a variation in the pronunciation of *x* between two vowels. In some areas it is *s* (*esacto*), and in some areas it is *gs* (*eg-sacto*).

Comunicación

RECYCLING

These activities recycle a considerable amount of vocabulary learned in previous chapters on topics including sports and leisure time activities.

PRESENTATION (*page 399*)

You may allow students to select the activities they wish to take part in.

ANSWERS

Actividad A
Answers will vary but should resemble the model.

Actividad B
Answers to the following questions will vary.
¿Qué hiciste el sábado pasado?
¿Qué hiciste el domingo pasado?
¿Qué hiciste anoche?

Actividad C
Answers will vary but should resemble the model.

Actividad D
Answers will vary but should resemble the following.
Quiero un boleto para Mar del Plata.
¿Cuánto cuesta?
¿Cuándo sale el próximo tren?
¿De qué andén sale?

DID YOU KNOW?

The Argentine railroads were built and originally run by the British. The Argentine Pampa has the densest network of railroads in South America. (Have students locate the Pampa region on a map.) Argentina's railroads were nationalized in 1948 by then dictator Juan Perón. In the 1990s the railroads were again privatized.

CRITICAL THINKING ACTIVITY

Argentina has the most developed rail system in South America. The topography of the country is an important reason. You may wish to ask students: *Miren el mapa de la Argentina. Argentina tiene más ferrocarriles que los otros países de la América del Sur. ¿Por qué?*

READING STRATEGIES
(page 400)

Pre-reading

Have students quickly scan the reading on page 400 to find as many cognates as they can.

Reading

A. To vary the presentation of the *Lectura* selection, have students close their books and listen as you read to them. Ask them to tell you what they have understood.

B. Read the *Lectura* again as students follow along in their books.

C. Call on individuals to read about three sentences. After every three sentences ask a few comprehension questions.

Post-reading

Upon completion of the reading selection, go over the exercises that accompany it.

ABOUT THE LANGUAGE

Note that the expression *sacar el billete* is used in Spain. In Latin America one would say *comprar el boleto.*

UNA EXCURSIÓN EN TREN

*U*n grupo de alumnos de la señora Rivera hicieron un viaje a España durante las vacaciones de primavera. La señora Rivera los acompañó. Pasaron unos ocho días en Madrid e hicieron excursiones a las cercanías[1] de la capital.

Un día fueron a Toledo. Hicieron el viaje de Madrid a Toledo en tren. Salieron del hotel y tomaron el autobús a la estación de Atocha. Los trenes para Toledo salen de esta estación. La señora Rivera fue a la ventanilla, donde compró o como dicen los madrileños, "sacó", un billete para cada alumno. Luego, verificó[2] la hora de salida del próximo tren en el tablero "Cercanías". Hay también trenes de largo recorrido que van a ciudades lejanas. Pero Toledo está en las cercanías de Madrid, a sólo 100 kilómetros de la capital.

El entierro del conde de Orgaz, de El Greco

Después de una hora en el tren, los alumnos llegaron a Toledo. Todos los alumnos pusieron su billete de vuelta en su mochila y salieron a conocer esta ciudad histórica. Anduvieron por las callejuelas y plazas pintorescas. Visitaron la catedral, una de las sinagogas y la pequeña iglesia de Santo Tomé. ¿Por qué fueron a esta iglesia pequeña? Para ver el famoso cuadro *El entierro del Conde de Orgaz* de El Greco. El famoso pintor, El Greco, nació en Creta, Grecia, pero pasó la mayor parte de su vida en Toledo. Los alumnos estuvieron muy impresionados por la belleza[3] extraordinaria de esta obra maestra que el artista pintó en 1585, en honor del Conde de Orgaz.

[1] cercanías *outskirts*   [3] belleza *beauty*
[2] verificó *checked*

La iglesia de Santo Tomé

La sinagoga Santa María la Blanca, Toledo, España

Estudio de palabras

A **Palabras afines.** Busquen diez palabras afines en la lectura.

B **¿Cuál es la otra palabra?** Pareen.

1. hicieron un viaje
2. siete días
3. excursión
4. el lugar
5. la vuelta
6. de largo recorrido
7. fabuloso
8. la callejuela
9. la sinagoga
10. el pintor

a. el sitio
b. calle estrecha
c. fantástico
d. viajaron
e. una semana
f. el regreso
g. viaje
h. el templo judío
i. de larga distancia
j. el artista

Una calle en Toledo, España

Comprensión

A **En Toledo.** Contesten.

1. ¿Dónde pasaron las vacaciones de primavera los alumnos de la señora Rivera?
2. ¿Cuántos días estuvieron en Madrid?
3. ¿Adónde hicieron excursiones?
4. ¿Cómo fueron a Toledo?
5. ¿De qué estación salió el tren?
6. ¿Qué compró (sacó) la señora Rivera?
7. ¿Dónde pusieron los alumnos su billete de vuelta?
8. ¿Por dónde anduvieron los alumnos?
9. ¿Qué lugares turísticos visitaron?
10. ¿Qué vieron en la iglesia de Santo Tomé?

B **Datos.** Identifiquen.

1. el nombre de un pintor español
2. la ciudad donde pasó la mayor parte de su vida el pintor
3. el año en que el pintor pintó el cuadro
4. el nombre de uno de sus cuadros más famosos
5. el nombre de la iglesia donde está este cuadro

C **El Greco.** Decidan.

1. Si el pintor pintó este cuadro en 1585, ¿en qué siglo vivió?
2. El pintor tiene el apodo de El Greco. Su verdadero nombre es Doménikos Theotokópoulos. La lectura dice que este pintor pasó la mayor parte de su vida en Toledo. ¿Qué opina Ud.? ¿Por qué tiene el apodo El Greco?

LEARNING FROM ART

1. *Este cuadro de El Greco está en la Iglesia de Santo Tomé en Toledo. Es El entierro del Conde de Orgaz. Es uno de los cuadros más famosos del pintor. En el cuadro aparece el hijo del pintor. Dicen que El Greco mismo es la sexta persona a la derecha. Noten que las figuras que pinta El Greco parecen elongadas. Algunos críticos dicen que esto expresa un sentido místico y espiritual. Otros creen que esto se debe a un defecto visual del pintor.*

2. *Toledo fue un centro de cultura hebrea en España antes del siglo XV. España tuvo una población judía de cientos de miles de personas.*

Estudio de palabras
ANSWERS

Ejercicio A
1. acompañó
2. excursiones
3. tren
4. hotel
5. verificó
6. catedral
7. famoso
8. Grecia
9. extraordinaria
10. artista

Ejercicio B
1. d   6. i
2. e   7. c
3. g   8. b
4. a   9. h
5. f   10. j

Comprensión
ANSWERS

Comprensión A
1. Los alumnos de la señora Rivera pasaron las vacaciones de primavera en Madrid.
2. Estuvieron en Madrid ocho días.
3. Hicieron excursiones a las cercanías de la capital.
4. Fueron a Toledo en tren.
5. El tren salió de la estación de Atocha.
6. La señora Rivera sacó los billetes.
7. Los alumnos pusieron su billete de vuelta en la mochila.
8. Los alumnos anduvieron por las callejuelas y plazas pintorescas.
9. Hicieron una visita a la catedral y a la pequeña iglesia de Santo Tomé.
10. Vieron el cuadro *El entierro del Conde de Orgaz* en la iglesia de Santo Tomé.

Comprensión B
1. El Greco
2. Toledo
3. 1585
4. *El entierro del Conde de Orgaz*
5. La iglesia de Santo Tomé

Comprensión C
1. Él vivió en el siglo dieciséis.
2. Él tiene el apodo El Greco porque él es griego (nació en Grecia).

Descubrimiento cultural

(The Descubrimiento is optional material.)

Note Some of the areas in South and Central America mentioned here are fascinating. You may want to expose all students to this information even if they just read it silently.

PRESENTATION

(pages 402–403)

A. You may have students read the selection, or you may read it aloud for the entire class while they follow the reading in their own books.

B. After the reading have a discussion about it and any other information related to it.

GEOGRAPHY CONNECTION

Have students look at the map of Panamá on page 475 as they read about the location of Colón and la Ciudad de Panamá.

DESCUBRIMIENTO CULTURAL

¿Te gusta viajar en tren? A muchos les gusta hacer una excursión en tren de vez en cuando. Mientras viajan, pueden observar el paisaje.

Y si te interesa el paisaje, hay tres viajecitos que tienes que hacer en Latinoamérica. El primero es el viaje de Cuzco a Machu Picchu en el Perú. Cada día, a las siete de la mañana un tren de vía estrecha[1] sale de la estación de San Pedro en Cuzco y llega a las diez y media a Machu Picchu. Cuzco está a 3.469 metros sobre el nivel del mar[2]. El tren tiene que bajar a 2.300 metros para llegar a Machu Picchu —¡tiene que bajar 1.100 metros! En Machu Picchu están las ruinas fabulosas de los incas. Es una ciudad entera, totalmente aislada[3], en un pico andino al borde de un cañón. Un dato histórico increíble es que los españoles nunca descubrieron a Machu Picchu durante su conquista del Perú. Los historiadores creen que Machu Picchu fue el último refugio de los nobles incas que se escaparon de los españoles. Si los españoles no encontraron a Machu Picchu, ¿quien lo encontró? Hiram Bingham, el explorador y senador de los Estados Unidos, lo encontró en 1911. ¿Cómo llegó Bingham a Machu Picchu? ¡A pie! Hoy, hay solamente dos maneras de ir a Machu Picchu. ¿Cuáles son? A pie, como llegó Bingham, o en el tren que sale de Cuzco a las siete de la mañana.

Otro viaje interesante es el de San José, Costa Rica, a Puntarenas. San José, la capital, está a una altura de 1.135 metros y Puntarenas está al nivel del mar, en una región tropical de la costa del Pacífico. El pequeño tren con bancos de madera tiene que bajar las montañas como una víbora[4]. Para los naturalistas es fascinante ver que en sólo dos horas cambia la vegetación entre la zona fresca montañosa y la zona tórrida tropical.

[1] estrecha *narrow gauge*   [3] aislada *isolated*
[2] nivel del mar *sea level*   [4] víbora *snake*

Machu Picchu

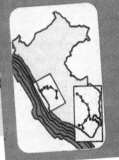

EMPRESA NACIONAL DE FERROCARRILES DEL PERU

FERROCARRIL DEL CENTRO 1

FERROCARRIL DEL SUR 2

CRITICAL THINKING ACTIVITY

(Thinking skills: evaluating information)

Write the following on the board or on an overhead transparency: Have students help Mr. Ugarte with his decision.

El señor Ugarte es venezolano. Él hace un viaje a los Estados Unidos. Quiere ir de Nueva York a Wáshington, D.C., la capital. Él puede ir de Nueva York a Wáshington en avión o en tren. El viaje en tren tarda unas tres horas y media, *en avión una hora. Por lo general, la estación de ferrocarril está en el centro mismo de la ciudad y los aeropuertos están fuera de la ciudad, y a veces bastante lejos del centro. Pero no es el caso en Wáshington. El aeropuerto nacional está muy cerca del centro de la ciudad. Pero los aeropuertos de Nueva York están bastante lejos de la ciudad y hay mucho tráfico. ¿Qué debe hacer el señor Ugarte? ¿Por qué?*

El canal de Panamá

El tercer viaje es el de la ciudad de Panamá a Colón. El tren cruza el istmo de Panamá. Durante algunas partes del recorrido, los pasajeros pueden ver el canal. ¡Una cosa muy interesante! El tren sale de Panamá, en la costa del Océano Pacífico, y termina en Colón, en la costa del Caribe. El Pacífico está al oeste y el Caribe está al este, ¿no? Sí, es verdad. Pero, a causa de la forma del istmo, este tren viaja hacia el noroeste para llegar al noreste. Colón, en el Caribe, está al noroeste de Panamá que está en el Pacífico. Si Uds. no lo creen, tienen que mirar el mapa.

Y AQUÍ EN LOS ESTADOS UNIDOS

Entre 1880 y 1900 se construyeron líneas de ferrocarril por todo el suroeste de los EE.UU., Texas, Nuevo México, Arizona, California, el norte y después, todo México. Las vías cruzaron la frontera en Nogales, El Paso y Laredo.

Las compañías trajeron a miles de mexicanos para trabajar en la construcción y el mantenimiento de las vías. Muchos de ellos se quedaron en el suroeste.

Al principio los mexicanos que vinieron a trabajar vinieron del norte de México. Pero cuando las líneas se extendieron más al sur de Zacatecas, vinieron a los EE.UU. mexicanos de toda la república. Así, la primera gran migración de mexicanos a los EE.UU. fue uno de los resultados de la construcción de los ferrocarriles.

Trabajadores mexicanos

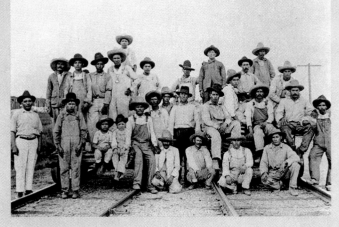

LEARNING FROM REALIA

Miren el folleto de la Empresa Nacional de Ferrocarriles del Perú en la página 402. ¿Cuál es el punto ferroviario más alto del mundo?

FOR THE NATIVE SPEAKER

Have students write a short composition in which they indicate whether they prefer to travel by train or by plane. They should give their opinion and then support it with at least three reasons, for example: *precio, comodidad, seguridad.*

REALIDADES

(*The* Realidades *is optional material.*)

PRESENTATION
(*pages 404–405*)

A. The purpose of this section is to have students enjoy the photographs. If they want to say something about the photographs in Spanish, let them. If they have any questions, let them ask.

B. After reading the captions on page 404 you may wish to share the following information with the class regarding the photos and captions.

Photo 1: The massive stone constructions in Cuzco were created without the use of mortar. Each piece had to be carefully placed and fit without machinery or animal power.

Art 2: Have students look at the painting and describe what they see in it. Although the work dates from the 16th century, a number of structures in it still dominate the landscape of Toledo today, most notably the Cathedral and the Alcázar. Ask students if they can identify them in the painting. El Greco's *Vista de Toledo* now hangs in the Metropolitan Museum of Art in New York City.

Realia 3: The Talgo was the fastest and most luxurious of all the Spanish trains. However, the new *AVE* (1992) is a high-speed train that can go faster than the French TGV or the Japanese bullet train.

Note A magazine article about *El AVE* appears in Level 3 of this textbook series, *De viaje*.

GEOGRAPHY CONNECTION
Have students look at a map of Spain and trace the route of the train from Málaga to Madrid.

Es una muralla de la fabulosa ciudad de Cuzco en los Andes del Perú **1**. Si quieres visitar las famosas ruinas incaicas de Machu Picchu, puedes tomar el tren de Cuzco.

Es el cuadro de El Greco, *Vista de Toledo* **2**.

Es el horario de El Talgo **3**. El Talgo es un tren de lujo con coches elegantes, aire acondicionado, comidas riquísimas y buen servicio.

Este joven espera el tren en la estación de Málaga en el sur de España **4**. ¿Viajas mucho en tren? ¿Adónde vas?

404

INDEPENDENT PRACTICE

Assign the following:
1. Workbook, *Un poco más*, pages 151–153

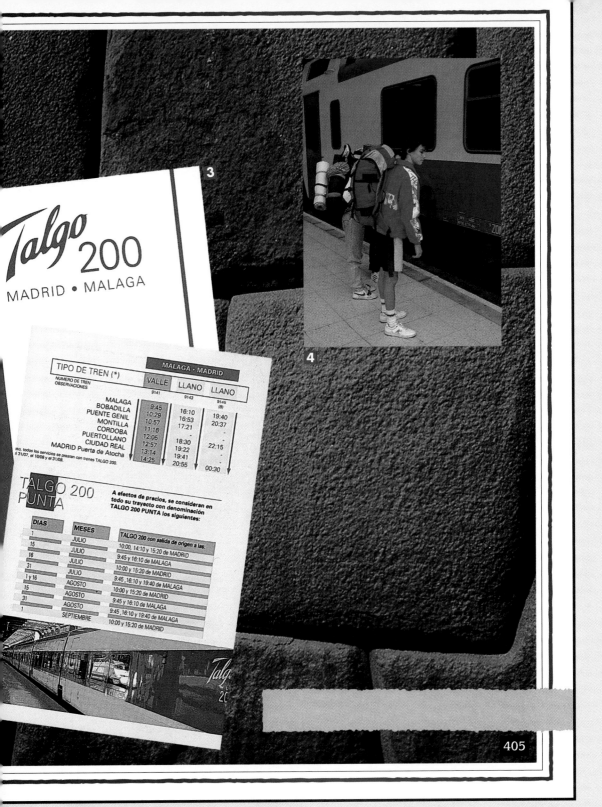

3

4

Talgo **200**

MADRID • MALAGA

TIPO DE TREN (*)	MALAGA · MADRID		
NUMERO DE TREN OBSERVACIONES	VALLE	LLANO	LLANO
	9141	9143	9145 (B)
MALAGA	9:45	16:10	19:40
BOBADILLA	10:29	16:53	20:37
PUENTE GENIL	10:57	17:21	
MONTILLA	11:16	-	-
CORDOBA	12:05	18:30	22:15
PUERTOLLANO	12:57	19:22	-
CIUDAD REAL	13:14	19:41	-
MADRID Puerta de Atocha	14:25	20:55	00:30

80, todos los servicios se prestan con trenes TALGO 200.
al 31/07, el 16/08 y el 31/08.

TALGO 200 PUNTA

A efectos de precios, se consideran en todo su trayecto con denominación TALGO 200 PUNTA los siguientes:

DIAS	MESES	TALGO 200 con salida de origen a las:
1	JULIO	10:00, 14:10 y 15:20 de MADRID
15	JULIO	9:45 y 16:10 de MALAGA
16	JULIO	10:00 y 15:20 de MADRID
31	JULIO	9:45, 16:10 y 19:40 de MALAGA
1 y 16	AGOSTO	10:00 y 15:20 de MADRID
15	AGOSTO	9:45 y 16:10 de MALAGA
31	AGOSTO	9:45, 16:10 y 19:40 de MALAGA
1	SEPTIEMBRE	10:00 y 15:20 de MADRID

Talgo 2C

405

LEARNING FROM PHOTOS

Have students say all they can about photo 4. You might ask questions such as: *¿Están en una estación de ferrocarril? ¿En qué parte de la estación están? ¿En qué llevan sus cosas los jóvenes?*

405

RECYCLING

The *Comunicación oral* and *Comunicación escrita* activities recycle vocabulary and structures from this and previous chapters. Success in these activities should be based more on the students' ability to convey messages rather than strict grammatical accuracy.

HISTORY CONNECTION

The Roman aqueduct of Segovia is one of the best preserved Roman remains in the entire world. It is built of huge boulders. Absolutely no cement was used. The aqueduct brought water to Segovia from Riofrío, some 16 kilometers from the town. Because the aqueduct was built without cement, it is said that if one central boulder were removed, the entire aqueduct would collapse.

Comunicación oral

ANSWERS

Actividad A

Answers may resemble the following.

E1: Buenos días. ¿Puedo ver su pasaporte?

E2: Aquí lo tiene Ud. ¿Vamos a llegar a París a tiempo?

E1: No, vamos a llegar con una hora de demora. Estuvimos mucho tiempo en Burgos.

Actividades B and C

Answers will vary.

Comunicación escrita

ANSWERS

Actividades A, B, and C

Answers will vary.

Comunicación oral

A Su pasaporte. You are the *revisor* on the train from Madrid to Paris and your partner is the *viajero(a)*. You knock on the compartment door, greet your partner, and ask if you can see his or her ticket and passport. Your partner shows them to you and asks if the train is going to arrive in Paris on time. You say that it is going to arrive one hour late because it stopped in Burgos too long.

B De paseo. You have been away on a study tour for ten days and have just returned to school after missing two days of classes. Find out from the exchange student from Venezuela (your partner) what has been going on and what you've missed. Reverse roles. Some things you might want to know are:

1. what he or she did during vacation
2. how the school's teams did
3. any parties you missed (*perder*)
4. what went on in different classes
5. any tests you may have missed

C El tren, el bus o el avión. Work in groups of four. With your group compile a list of advantages and disadvantages (*ventajas y desventajas*) for each of three methods of transportation. Make sure you include such things as: speed, price, location of terminals or stations, and anything else you consider important. Polish your list and have one person present it to the class.

Comunicación escrita

A En Segovia. Mrs. Rivera's class visited Ávila and Segovia, two famous historic cities near Madrid. Get information about these cities in an encyclopedia or other source, and describe what Mrs. Rivera's students saw and did there.

B Machu Picchu. You have just taken the train from Cuzco to Machu Picchu. Write an entry in your diary about the trip. Include your impressions of the scenery, the weather conditions, etc.

Acueducto romano en Segovia, España

C Las listas. You plan to take an overnight train trip and need to get organized. Write a list of everything you need to do. Include such things as going to the travel agent, buying train tickets, making reservations for a berth, packing your suitcase, buying items you will need, etc. Make as complete a list as possible. Compare your list with a classmate's. Did you forget anything?

406 CAPÍTULO 14

FOR THE YOUNGER STUDENT

Have students create a play about a train trip and present it to the class. The characters in the play are:

un viajero o pasajero

una viajera o pasajera

el agente de RENFE (Red Nacional de Ferrocarriles Españoles)

el mozo

el revisor

STUDENT PORTFOLIO

Written assignments that may be included in students' portfolios are the *Actividades escritas* on page 406 and the *Mi autobiografía* section in the Workbook, page 154.

Reintegración

A **Preparaciones para un viaje.** Contesten.

1. ¿Hiciste la maleta?
2. ¿Qué pusiste en la maleta?
3. Antes de hacer el viaje, ¿compraste ropa nueva?
4. ¿Dónde la compraste?
5. ¿Qué compraste?
6. ¿Te costó mucho?
7. ¿Le diste el dinero a la empleada en la tienda?
8. El viaje que hiciste, ¿lo hiciste en tren?
9. ¿A qué hora salió el tren de la estación de ferrocarril?

B **Los cursos que me interesan.** Contesten.

1. ¿Cuáles son los cursos que te interesan?
2. ¿Cuáles son los cursos que no te interesan, que te aburren?
3. ¿Cuáles son los deportes que te interesan?
4. ¿Cuáles son los deportes que no te interesan, que te aburren?
5. ¿Cuáles son los cursos que te gustan más?

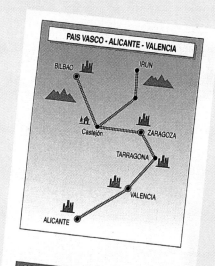

Vocabulario

SUSTANTIVOS
la estación de ferrocarril
la ventanilla
la taquilla
el billete de ida
  y vuelta
el billete sencillo
el horario
la sala de espera
el quiosco
el tablero de llegadas
el tablero de salidas
el mozo
el maletero
la maleta
la mochila
el equipaje
el andén
la vía
el tren

el vagón
el coche
el pasillo
el compartimiento
el asiento
el coche-cama
la litera
el coche-comedor
el revisor

la estación
la parada
el retraso
la demora

ADJETIVOS
libre
ocupado(a)
reservado(a)
sencillo(a)
próximo(a)

VERBOS
esperar
bajar(se) del tren
transbordar
subir al tren

OTRAS PALABRAS Y EXPRESIONES
tarde
a tiempo
con retraso
con una demora

PRESENTATION *(page 407)*

Exercise A reviews the preterite. Exercise B reviews verbs like *interesar, gustar.*

ANSWERS

Ejercicio A
Answers will vary.
1. Sí (No), (no) hice la maleta.
2. Puse… en la maleta.
3. Sí (No), (no) compré ropa nueva.
4. La compré en un centro comercial.
5. Compré…
6. Sí (No), (no) me costó mucho.
7. Sí (No), (no) le di el dinero a la empleada en la tienda.
8. Sí (No), (no) hice el viaje en tren.
9. El tren salió a las…

Ejercicio B
Answers will vary.
1. Me interesan…
2. Me aburren (la geografía, las matemáticas).
3. Me interesan (el béisbol, el fútbol).
4. Me aburren (el tenis, el golf).
5. Los cursos que me gustan más son (el español, la educación cívica).

Vocabulario

There are approximately three cognates included in this *Vocabulario* list.

VIDEO

The video is intended to reinforce the vocabulary, structures, and cultural content in each chapter. It may be used here as a chapter wrap-up activity. See the *Video Activities Booklet* for additional suggestions on its use.

INTRODUCCIÓN   *(0:56:45)*

UN VIAJE EN TREN   *(0:58:15)*

LEARNING FROM REALIA

Have students scan the realia and note with the aid of the symbols how many expressions they can understand.

INDEPENDENT PRACTICE

Assign any of the following:
1. Exercises on student page 407
2. Workbook, *Mi autobiografía,* page 154
3. Chapter 14, Situation Cards

Topics	Functions	Structure	Culture
Restaurants Food items and eating utensils	How to order food or beverages at a restaurant How to identify different foods How to identify eating utensils and dishes How to explain how you like certain foods prepared How to talk about present and past events/activities How to describe some of the many cuisines in Spanish-speaking countries	El presente de los verbos con el cambio *e > i* El pretérito de los vebos con el cambio *e > i y o > u*	Regional differences in Hispanic cuisine Eating customs and traditions Hispanic cuisine in the U.S. Casa Botín in Madrid An outdoor café in Mexico City A typical dish from Spain: *cochinillo asado*

CAPÍTULO 15

Situation Cards

The Situation Cards simulate real-life situations that require students to communicate in Spanish, exactly as though they were in a Spanish-speaking country. The Situation Cards operate on the assumption that the person to whom the message is to be conveyed understands no English. Therefore, students must focus on producing the Spanish vocabulary and structures necessary to negotiate the situations successfully. For additional information, see the Introduction to the Situation Cards in the Situation Cards Envelope.

Communication Transparency

The illustration seen in this Communication Transparency consists of a synthesis of the two vocabulary (*Palabras 1&2*) presentations found in this chapter. It has been created in order to present this chapter's vocabulary in a new context, and also to recycle vocabulary learned in previous chapters. The Communication Transparency consists of original art. Following are some specific uses:

1. as a cue to stimulate conversation and writing activities
2. for listening comprehension activities
3. to review and reteach vocabulary
4. as a review for chapter and unit tests

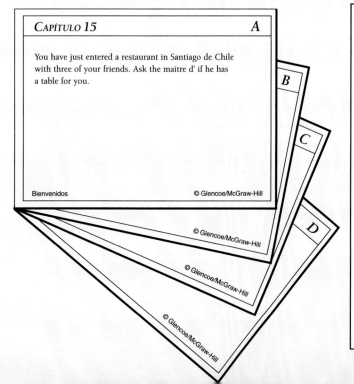

CAPÍTULO 15
Print Resources

	Pages

Lesson Plans

Workbook
- Palabras 1   155
- Palabras 2   156
- Estructura   157-158
- Un poco más   159-161
- Mi autobiografía   162

Communication Activities Masters
- Palabras 1   90-91
- Palabras 2   92-93
- Estructura   94-95

6 Bell Ringer Reviews   34-35

Chapter Situation Cards A B C D

Chapter Quizzes
- Palabras 1   67
- Palabras 2   68
- Estructura   69-70

Testing Program
- Listening Comprehension   82
- Reading and Writing   83-86
- Proficiency   131
- Speaking   152

Nosotros y Nuestro Mundo
- Nuestro Conocimiento Académico *La salud*
- Nuestro Idioma *Vulgarismos*
- Nuestra Cultura *Alimentos*
- Nuestra Literatura *"El cuervo y el zorro"* de Félix de Samaniego
- Nuestra Creatividad
- Nuestras Diversiones

CAPÍTULO 15
Multimedia Resources

CD-ROM Interactive Textbook Disc 4

Chapter 15 Student Edition
- Palabras 1
- Palabras 2
- Estructura
- Conversación
- Lectura y cultura
- Hispanoparlantes
- Realidades
- Culminación
- Prueba

Audio Cassette Program with Student Tape Manual

Cassette	**Pages**
9A Palabras 1	264-265
9A Palabras 2	265-266
9A Estructura	266-267
9A Conversación	267
9A Pronunciación	268
9A Segunda parte	268-272

Compact Disc Program with Student Tape Manual

CD 9 Palabras 1	264-265
CD 9 Palabras 2	265-266
CD 9 Estructura	266-267
CD 9 Conversación	267
CD 9 Pronunciación	268
CD 9 Segunda parte	268-272

Overhead Transparencies Binder

- Vocabulary 15.1 (A&B); 15.2 (A&B)
- Pronunciation P-15
- Communication C-15
- Maps
- Fine Art (with Blackline Master Activities)

Video Program

Videocassette	
Video Activities Booklet	44-46
Videodisc	
Video Activities Booklet	44-46

Computer Software (Macintosh, IBM, Apple)

- Practice Disk
  Palabras 1 y 2
  Estructura
- Test Generator Disk
  Chapter Test
  Customized Test

CHAPTER OVERVIEW

In this chapter students will learn how to order food in a restaurant. They will learn to identify additional food items and eating utensils. Students will also learn the present and preterite of stem-changing verbs.

The cultural focus of this chapter is on the regional differences in Hispanic cuisine and some differences in eating customs.

CHAPTER OBJECTIVES

By the end of this chapter students will learn to do the following:

1. order food or beverages at a restaurant
2. identify foods
3. identify eating utensils
4. describe and identify regional dishes from various areas of the Spanish-speaking world
5. use stem-changing verbs such as *pedir, servir, preferir,* and *dormir* in the present and preterite

CHAPTER 15 RESOURCES

1. Workbook
2. Student Tape Manual
3. Audio Cassette 9A
4. Vocabulary Transparencies
5. Pronunciation Transparency P-15
6. Bell Ringer Review Blackline Masters
7. Communication Activities Masters
8. Computer Software: Practice and Test Generator
9. Video Cassette, Chapter 15
10. Video Activities Booklet, Chapter 15
11. Situation Cards
12. Chapter Quizzes
13. Testing Program

CAPÍTULO
15
EN EL RESTAURANTE

OBJETIVOS

In this chapter you will learn to do the following:

1. order food or beverage at a restaurant
2. identify some food
3. identify eating utensils and dishes
4. explain how you like certain foods prepared
5. talk about present and past events and activities
6. describe some of the many cuisines of the Hispanic world
7. compare some U.S. and Hispanic dining habits

408

CHAPTER PROJECTS

(optional)

1. Plan a class outing to an inexpensive restaurant that serves food from a Spanish-speaking country.
2. Prepare a dish from one of the Spanish-speaking countries, or have students prepare some Hispanic foods and bring them to class.
3. Have the Spanish Club prepare a banquet or snack. You may even invite the parents for a "Spanish" dinner.

409

Pacing

Chapter 15 will take eight to ten class sessions. Pacing will depend on the length of the class, the age of the students, and student aptitude.

LEARNING FROM PHOTOS

This cafe is in the Plaza Mayor in the heart of Old Madrid. The plaza was constructed by Felipe II, whose statue stands in it. The statue was removed and stored during the construction of a huge parking lot beneath the plaza.

Bell Ringer Review

Write the following on the board or use BRR Blackline Master 15-1: Write a list of the foods you have learned.

PRESENTATION
(*pages 410–411*)

A. Show Vocabulary Transparencies 15.1 (A & B). Point to individual items and have students repeat each word after you two or three times.

B. Intersperse the presentation with simple questions that enable students to use the new words.

ABOUT THE LANGUAGE

1. The word *mesero* is used for waiter throughout Latin America. In Spain, however, the word used is *camarero*.
2. The word *el menú* is universally understood. Other words frequently used for menu are: *la minuta* and *la carta.*

Note We have taught the words *la pimienta* and *la sal* but not *el pimentero* and *el salero* since these are rarely used. One would say *la sal, por favor.*

VOCABULARIO

PALABRAS 1

EL RESTAURANTE

el menú

el mesero

el cocinero

la mesa

la tarjeta de crédito

la cuenta

la propina

Tengo hambre. Quiero comer.
Tengo sed. Voy a beber algo.

410 CAPÍTULO 15

TOTAL PHYSICAL RESPONSE

(*following the Vocabulary presentation*)

TPR 1
___, ven acá, por favor.
Vas a poner la mesa.
Cubre la mesa con un mantel.
Dobla las servilletas.
Pon un plato en la mesa.
Luego pon la cucharita y el cuchillo a la derecha.

Pon el tenedor a la izquierda. Gracias, ___.

TPR 2
___, ven acá, por favor.
Vas a hacer unos gestos.
Toma el menú. Abre el menú.
Lee el menú. Cierra el menú.
Corta la carne con el cuchillo. Come.
Bebe. Deja una propina para el mesero.
Gracias, ___. Regresa a tu asiento.

la pimienta la sal el vaso la taza el platillo

la servilleta el plato la cuchara la cucharita

el tenedor el cuchillo

el mantel

pedir

freír

La señorita pide el menú.

El cocinero fríe (está friendo) las papas.

servir

El mesero le sirve la comida.

COOPERATIVE LEARNING

   Have students work in pairs. One student gives the name of a food or beverage. The other asks: *¿Tienes sed?* or *¿Tienes hambre?*
E1: *Un sándwich.* **E2:** *Ah, ¿tienes hambre?*

DID YOU KNOW?

   In Spain and most of Latin America pepper shakers hardly ever appear on a table except in international restaurants and hotels.

Ejercicios

A En el restaurante. Contesten.

1. ¿Cuántas personas hay en la mesa?
2. ¿Pide María el menú?
3. ¿Le trae el menú el mesero?
4. ¿María pide?
5. ¿El mesero le sirve?
6. ¿El mesero le sirve bien?
7. Después de la comida, ¿le pide la cuenta al mesero?
8. ¿Le trae la cuenta el mesero?
9. ¿Paga con su tarjeta de crédito María?
10. ¿María le da (deja) una propina al mesero?
11. ¿Tiene hambre María?
12. Después de la comida, ¿tiene hambre María?

B El mesero pone la mesa. Completen.

1. Para comer los clientes necesitan ___, ___, ___ y ___ .
2. Dos condimentos son la ___ y la ___ .
3. El mesero cubre la mesa con ___ .
4. En la mesa el mesero pone una ___ para cada cliente.
5. El niño pide un ___ de leche y sus padres piden una ___ de café.
6. Ellos tienen ___ y piden una botella de agua mineral.

EN MEXICO
COMO EN EL EXTRANJERO
¡Qué bueno es pagar con Banamex!

TARJETAS
Banamex
TODO CON EL PODER DE SU FIRMA

C ¿Qué necesitas? Contesten según el modelo.

> ¿Para tomar leche?
> *Para tomar leche, necesito*
> *un vaso.*

1. ¿Para tomar agua?
2. ¿Para tomar café?
3. ¿Para comer la ensalada?
4. ¿Para comer el postre?
5. ¿Para cortar la carne?

D Palabras relacionadas. Busquen una palabra relacionada..

1. la mesa	a. la cuenta
2. la cocina	b. el servicio
3. costar	c. la bebida
4. servir	d. el cocinero
5. freír	e. la comida
6. comer	f. el mesero
7. beber	g. frito

Ejercicios C and D

It is recommended that you go over the exercises once in class before assigning them for homework. Exercise C can be done with books open or closed. Exercise D should be done with books open.

ANSWERS
Ejercicio C
1. **Para tomar agua, necesito un vaso.**
2. **Para tomar café, necesito una taza.**
3. **Para comer la ensalada, necesito un tenedor.**
4. **Para comer el postre, necesito una cucharita (un tenedor).**
5. **Para cortar la carne, necesito un cuchillo.**

Ejercicio D
1. **f**
2. **d**
3. **a**
4. **b**
5. **g**
6. **e**
7. **c**

LEARNING FROM REALIA AND PHOTOS

1. You may wish to ask students about the ad on page 413. Ask students what *refinada, limpia,* and *yodatada* mean. *Yodatada* will be a challenge. Ask them what is added to salt in the U.S. (iodine in iodized salt).
2. Ask students to describe the table setting, telling everything they can about it.

INDEPENDENT PRACTICE

Assign any of the following:
1. Workbook, page 155
2. Communication Activities Masters, pages 90–91, *A & B*
3. Exercises on student pages 412–413

Bell Ringer Review

Write the following on the board or use BRR Blackline Master 15-2: Complete using the past tense.

1. Anoche yo no ___ en casa. (comer)
2. Mis amigos y yo ___ en un restaurante. (comer)
3. Yo ___ al restaurante en el metro pero mis amigos ___ el autobús. (ir, tomar)
4. El mesero nos ___ un servicio muy bueno. (dar)

PRESENTATION
(pages 414–415)

You may wish to use some suggestions from previous chapters for the presentation of the new vocabulary on pages 414–415.

VOCABULARIO

PALABRAS 2

LAS COMIDAS

la carne

el pollo

el pescado

los mariscos

las frutas

las legumbres
los vegetales
las verduras

la tortilla

TOTAL PHYSICAL RESPONSE

(following the Vocabulary presentation)
___ levántate y ven acá, por favor.
Estamos en el restaurante Mendoza.
Siéntate, ___.
Toma el menú.
Ábrelo.
Lee el menú.
Llama al mesero.
___, ven acá. Tú vas a ser el mesero.
___, pídele al mesero lo que quieres comer.
___, escribe lo que pide.
Ve a la cocina.
Vuelve con la comida.
Sirve la comida.
Pon los platos en la mesa.
___, come.

el pan

el jamón

el huevo

el aceite

el queso

la papa

los frijoles
las habichuelas

la lechuga

el arroz

¿Cómo le gusta el biftec?

casi crudo

a término medio

bien hecho (cocido)

María pidió un biftec.
El mesero le sirvió el biftec.
Él le sirvió el biftec como lo pidió.
La comida está deliciosa, muy rica.
No está mala.

Nota: En los Estados Unidos hay muchos restaurantes mexicanos. ¿Sabes lo que son los tacos, las enchiladas, las tostadas, las flautas, las fajitas, el guacamole?

ABOUT THE LANGUAGE

1. Explain to students the difference between *La comida está buena* and *La comida es buena*. (*La comida está buena significa que está deliciosa, que está muy rica, que tiene buen sabor. La comida es buena significa que es buena para la salud. Contiene vitaminas, etc.*)
2. *La papa* is used for potato throughout Latin America. *La patata* is used in Spain.
3. Beans of different kinds are a staple in the diet of the Caribbean, Mexico, and Central America. Words used for beans include *frijoles*, *fréjoles*, *habichuelas*, *judías*, and *porotos*. Green beans or string beans are *judías verdes*, *chauchas*, *vainitas*, *ejotes*, and *porotos verdes*.
4. In parts of Mexico *los huevos* is to be avoided because of a vulgar connotation. *Los blanquillos* is used instead. *Los huevos* has a vulgar connotation in many other areas too, but its use for "eggs" is not avoided.

Vocabulary Expansion

You may wish to give students the following additional food-related vocabulary.
los entremeses (appetizers)
la sopa (soup)
el plato principal (main dish)
el postre (dessert)
los dulces (sweets, candy)
vegetariano (vegetarian)

RECYCLING

To review the verb *gustar*, ask several students, ¿*Cómo te gusta la carne?* Students respond using *Me gusta ___*. Ask another student: *___, ¿cómo te gusta la carne?*
Do the same with *hamburguesas* to elicit the plural, *gustan*.

TOTAL PHYSICAL RESPONSE

Ah, tenemos un problema. Pediste la carne bien hecha y el mesero te sirvió la carne casi cruda. Llama al mesero.
___, ve a la mesa.
___, dale el plato.
Pide la cuenta.
Mira la cuenta.
Saca el dinero de tu bolsillo o de tu cartera.
Paga.

Levántate.
Sal del restaurante.
Gracias, ___. Ahora puedes volver a tu asiento.
Y tú también, ___. Gracias.

PRESENTATION (*page 416*)

Ejercicio A

It is recommended that Exercise A be done with books closed.

Expansion of *Ejercicio A*

Call on one student to retell in his/her own words María's restaurant experience.

Ejercicios B and C

Exercises B and C review the verb *gustar*, which was presented in Chapter 14.

ANSWERS

Ejercicio A

Some answers will vary.

1. Sí, María fue al restaurante anoche.
2. Le sirvió el mesero.
3. Sí, pidió un biftec.
4. Lo pidió (bien hecho).
5. Sí, también pidió una ensalada.
6. Sí, el mesero le sirvió una ensalada de lechuga y tomate.
7. Le sirvió una comida deliciosa.

Ejercicio B

Some answers will vary.

1. Sí (No), (no) me gusta la ensalada.
2. Sí (No), (no) me gusta la ensalada con aceite y vinagre.
3. Sí (No), (no) me gusta el biftec.
4. Me gusta el biftec (bien hecho, casi crudo, a término medio).
5. Sí, me gusta el sándwich de jamón y queso. Me gusta más tostado.
6. Sí (No), (no) me gusta la tortilla de queso.
7. Sí (No), (no) me gusta el jamón con huevos.

Ejercicio C

1. Sí (No), (no) me gustan las frutas.
2. Sí (No), (no) me gusta la lechuga.
3. Sí (No), (no) me gustan los huevos.
4. Sí (No), (no) me gusta el pan.
5. Sí (No), (no) me gusta el pescado.
6. Sí (No), (no) me gustan las papas (patatas).

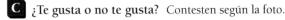

Ejercicios

A **Cenó en el restaurante.** Contesten.

1. ¿Fue María al restaurante anoche?
2. ¿Quién le sirvió?
3. ¿Pidió María un biftec?
4. ¿Cómo lo pidió?
5. ¿Pidió también una ensalada?
6. ¿Le sirvió el mesero una ensalada de lechuga y tomate?
7. ¿Le sirvió una comida deliciosa o una comida mala?

B **Sí, me gusta.** Preguntas personales.

1. ¿Te gusta la ensalada?
2. ¿Te gusta la ensalada con aceite y vinagre?
3. ¿Te gusta el biftec?
4. ¿Te gusta el biftec casi crudo, a término medio o bien hecho?
5. ¿Te gusta el sándwich de jamón y queso? ¿Te gusta más tostado?
6. ¿Te gusta la tortilla de queso?
7. ¿Te gusta el jamón con huevos?

C **¿Te gusta o no te gusta?** Contesten según la foto.

1.   2.   3.

4.   5.   6.

LEARNING FROM PHOTOS

1. Bananas have various names in the Spanish-speaking world. They are known as *bananas, bananos, guineos, plátanos,* and *cambures.* There are also many varieties of bananas, some for eating raw, others for boiling or frying. On the plate on page 416 are *plátanos, uvas, naranjas, limón,* and *chirimoya.*

2. This type of lettuce (romaine) is the usual lettuce in Spain. Iceberg lettuce is virtually unknown.

3. The yolk of the egg is called *la yema,* and the white, *la clara.*

4. You may also mention that in Spanish a fish in the sea is *un pez* and when it is caught and on the table it is *un pescado.*

Comunicación
Palabras 1 y 2

A **¿Qué comen?** The home economics class at the school in Honduras where you are an exchange student wants to know all about eating habits in the United States. Tell the class:

1. where people eat each meal
2. at what time Americans eat each meal
3. some things people eat
4. what people drink with their meals

B **¿Qué quieres?** You and your partner go out to a restaurant for breakfast, lunch, and dinner. You never know what to order. Your partner will give you a few suggestions. You turn down each suggestion and then you order something totally different. Reverse roles.

> el desayuno
> Estudiante 1: No sé qué pedir para el desayuno.
> Estudiante 2: ¿Por qué no pides huevos fritos?
> Estudiante 1: No me gustan los huevos.
> Estudiante 2: ¿Por qué no pides cereal?
> Estudiante 1: No, quiero otra cosa.
> Estudiante 2: ¿Por qué no pides jamón?
> Estudiante 1: No, voy a pedir pan y café.

C **En el restaurante.** You go to a restaurant in Caracas. Your partner is the server. Do the following:

1. Ask for the menu.
2. Find out what the specialties of the house are.
3. Give the server your order.
4. Ask what there is to drink and order something.
5. Ask for the bill.

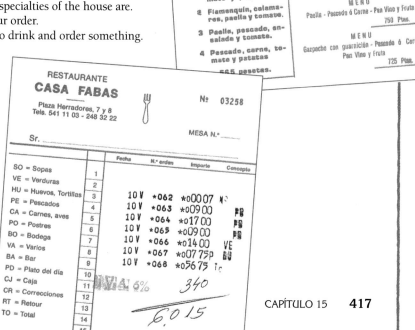

Mesón Restaurante "EL TABLON"
PATIO ANDALUZ (REFRIGERADO)
Cardenal González, 75 - Teléfono 47 60 61 - CORDOBA

COMBINADOS

1 Chuleta, huevo, tomate y patatas.
2 Flamenquín, calamares, paella y tomate.
3 Paella, pescado, ensalada y tomate.
4 Pescado, carne, tomate y patatas
565 pesetas.

MENU
Sopa - Pescado ó Carne - Pan Vino y Fruta
725 Ptas.

MENU
Paella - Pescado ó Carne - Pan Vino y Fruta
750 Ptas.

MENU
Gazpacho con guarnición - Pescado ó Carne
Pan Vino y Fruta
725 Ptas.

RESTAURANTE
CASA FABAS
Plaza Herradores, 7 y 8
Tels. 541 11 03 - 248 32 22

Nº 03258
MESA N.º ____
Sr. ____

SO = Sopas
VE = Verduras
HU = Huevos, Tortillas
PE = Pescados
CA = Carnes, aves
PO = Postres
BO = Bodega
VA = Varios
BA = Bar
PD = Plato del día
CJ = Caja
CR = Correcciones
RT = Retour
TO = Total

CAPÍTULO 15   **417**

PRESENTATION *(page 417)*

You may wish to let students select the activity or activities they wish to do.

ANSWERS

Actividad A
Answers will vary.

Actividad B
Answers will vary but should follow the model.
el almuerzo
E1: No sé qué pedir para el almuerzo.
E2: ¿Por qué no pides una tortilla?
E1: No me gustan las tortillas.
E2: ¿Por qué no pides unas flautas?
E1: No, quiero otra cosa.
E2: ¿Por qué no pides unas enchiladas?
E1: No, voy a pedir una ensalada.

Actividad C
Answers will vary.

INFORMAL ASSESSMENT

Have students call out at random any item of food they know. Write the foods on the board and have students use them in sentences. Or, have students categorize them: *legumbres, frutas, carne, pescado, marisco, postre (dulces).*

LEARNING FROM REALIA

Have students look at the menu from *El Tablón,* and the bill from *Casa Fabas* on page 417. Ask them questions about both. For example, what the least expensive item on the menu is (*combinados* at 565 pesetas); what the addresses of these restaurants are; what the category of *Casa Fabas* is (1 fork); and what the percentage of *IVA* is (*impuesto sobre valor adquirido,* value added tax).

INDEPENDENT PRACTICE

Assign any of the following:
1. Workbook, page 156
2. Communication Activities Masters, pages 92–93, *C & D*
3. Exercises and activities on student pages 416–417

ESTRUCTURA

Structure Teaching Resources

1. Workbook, pages 157–158
2. Student Tape Manual, pages 266–267
3. Audio Cassette 9A
4. Communication Activities Masters, pages 94-95, *A & B*
5. Computer Software, *Estructura*
6. Chapter Quizzes, pages 69-70, *Estructura*

Bell Ringer Review

Write the following on the board or use BRR Blackline Master 15-3: Answer the following questions.

1. ¿Te gusta la carne?
2. ¿Te gustan los mariscos?
3. ¿Cuáles son algunas legumbres que te gustan?
4. ¿Te gusta el postre?
5. ¿Qué te gusta beber?

El presente de los verbos con el cambio *e > i*

PRESENTATION *(page 418)*

A. Have students open their books to page 418. Write the verb forms on the board. Underline the stem and have students repeat each form after you.

Note Oral practice with these verbs is important because, if students pronounce them correctly, they will be inclined to spell them correctly.

B. When going over the verb *seguir*, review with students the following sound-symbol sequence: *ga, gue, gui, go, gu.*

El presente de los verbos con el cambio *e > i*   *Describing People's Activities*

1. The verbs *pedir, servir, repetir, freír,* and *seguir,* "to follow," are stem-changing verbs. The *e* of the infinitive stem, *pedir, servir,* changes from *e* to *i* in all forms of the present tense except the *nosotros* and *vosotros* forms. Note the following.

INFINITIVE	PEDIR	SERVIR	FREÍR
yo	pido	sirvo	frío
tú	pides	sirves	fríes
él, ella, Ud.	pide	sirve	fríe
nosotros(as)	pedimos	servimos	freímos
vosotros(as)	*pedís*	*servís*	*freís*
ellos, ellas, Uds.	piden	sirven	fríen

2. Note the spelling of the verb *seguir.*

SEGUIR	
yo	sigo
tú	sigues
él, ella, Ud.	sigue
nosotros(as)	seguimos
vosotros(as)	*seguís*
ellos, ellas, Uds.	siguen

RESTAURANTE
Los Remos
(antes Parque Moroso)
PRIMERA CASA EN PESCADOS Y MARISCOS
AMBIENTE SELECTO ✱ VIVEROS PROPIOS

Ctra. Coruña, km. 12,700 ✱ Telfs. 207 72 30 - 207 73 36
ABIERTO DOMINGOS MEDIODÍA

P PARKING PROPIO

LEARNING FROM REALIA

Have students look at the drawing on the card and figure out the meaning of *Los Remos.* Have students answer the following questions: *¿Qué sirven en Los Remos? ¿Dónde está el restaurante? ¿Cuántos números de teléfono tiene? ¿A qué hora abren el restaurante los domingos? ¿Es posible estacionar el carro allí?*

Ejercicios

A **Lo que yo pido.** Digan si piden lo siguiente o no.

1.

2.

3.

4.

5.

6.

B **Lo que pedimos en el restaurante.** Sigan el modelo.

> A Juan le gusta el pescado. ¿Qué pide él?
> *Él pide pescado.*

1. A Teresa le gustan los mariscos. ¿Qué pide ella?
2. A Carlos le gusta el biftec. ¿Qué pide él?
3. A mis amigos les gustan las legumbres. ¿Qué piden ellos?
4. A mis padres les gusta mucho la ensalada. ¿Qué piden ellos?
5. Nos gusta el postre. ¿Qué pedimos?
6. Nos gustan las tortillas. ¿Qué pedimos?

C **Vamos al restaurante.** Completen.

Cuando mi amiga y yo ___ (ir) al restaurante, nosotros ___ (pedir) casi
        1   2
siempre un biftec. Yo lo ___ (pedir) casi crudo y ella lo ___ (pedir) bien
                          3   4
hecho. A mi amiga le ___ (gustar) mucho las papas fritas. Ella ___ (decir) que
                      5   6
le ___ (gustar) más cuando el cocinero las ___ (freír) en aceite de oliva.
    7   8

D **Cuando voy a un restaurante.** Preguntas personales.

1. Cuando vas a un restaurante, ¿qué pides?
2. ¿Cómo pides la carne?
3. ¿Y cómo pides las papas? Si no pides papas, ¿pides arroz?
4. ¿Qué más pides con la carne y las papas o el arroz?
5. ¿Quién te sirve en el restaurante?
6. Si te sirve bien, ¿qué le dejas?

CAPÍTULO 15   **419**

INDEPENDENT PRACTICE

Assign any of the following:
1. Workbook, page 157
2. Communication Activities Masters, page 94, *A*
3. Exercises on student page 419

Ejercicios

PRESENTATION *(page 419)*

Ejercicio A

  Have students look at the illustrations as they answer.

Ejercicio B

A. Exercise B reviews *gustar* as students use the new verb *pedir.*

B. It is recommended that Exercise B be done orally with books closed.

Ejercicio C

  After completing Exercise C, have one student retell all the information in his/her own words.

Ejercicio D

  After completing Exercise D, permit students to tell anything else they do when they go to a restaurant.

ANSWERS

Ejercicio A

  Answers will vary.

Ejercicio B

  Answers will vary but should resemble the following.
1. Ella pide mariscos.
2. Él pide biftec.
3. Ellos piden legumbres.
4. Ellos piden ensalada.
5. Pedimos postre.
6. Pedimos tortillas.

Ejercicio C

1. vamos
2. pedimos
3. pido
4. pide
5. gustan
6. dice
7. gustan
8. fríe

Ejercicio D

  Answers will vary but may resemble the following.
1. Pido un sándwich de queso y una ensalada de frutas.
2. La pido (Pido la carne) bien hecha (casi cruda).
3. Pido papas fritas. Sí, si no pido papas, pido arroz.
4. Pido ensalada.
5. Un mesero (o una mesera) me sirve.
6. Le dejo una propina si me sirve bien.

Bell Ringer Review

Write the following on the board or use BRR Blackline Master 15-4: Unscramble the following sentences.

1. tacos/los/sirve/restaurante/ el mesero/en el
2. pimienta/pide/Juan/sal/la/ y/la
3. y/el/Sofía/fríen/pescado/ papas/las/y Jaime

El pretérito de los verbos con el cambio e>i, o>u

PRESENTATION *(page 420)*

Have students repeat the verb forms on page 420 paying particular attention to the stem and the correct pronunciation.

El pretérito de los verbos con el cambio *e > i, o > u*

Describing People's Activities in the Past

1. The verbs *pedir, repetir, freír, servir,* and *seguir* have a stem change in the preterite also. The *e* of the infinitive stem changes to *i* in the *él* and *ellos* forms.

INFINITIVE	PEDIR	REPETIR	SEGUIR
yo	pedí	repetí	seguí
tú	pediste	repetiste	seguiste
él, ella, Ud.	pidió	repitió	siguió
nosotros(as)	pedimos	repetimos	seguimos
vosotros(as)	*pedisteis*	*repetisteis*	*seguisteis*
ellos, ellas, Uds.	pidieron	repitieron	siguieron

2. The verbs *preferir* and *dormir* "to sleep" also have a stem change in the preterite. The *e* in *preferir* changes to *i* and the *o* in *dormir* changes to *u* in the *él* and *ellos* forms.

INFINITIVE	PREFERIR	DORMIR
yo	preferí	dormí
tú	preferiste	dormiste
él, ella, Ud.	prefirió	durmió
nosotros(as)	preferimos	dormimos
vosotros(as)	*preferisteis*	*dormisteis*
ellos, ellas, Uds.	prefirieron	durmieron

Other verbs conjugated like *preferir* and *dormir* are *sugerir* "to suggest" and *morir* "to die."

FOR THE NATIVE SPEAKER

Some students may have a pronunciation problem with certain forms of irregular verbs in the preterite. In a few areas there is a tendency to pronounce the *e* in some positions as an *i*, for example, *repití* for *repetí*. If this is a problem, provide practice in using the correct form.

Ejercicios

A **¿No te sirvieron bien?** Contesten.

1. ¿Qué pediste en el restaurante? (un biftec)
2. ¿Cómo lo pediste? (casi crudo)
3. ¿Cuántas veces repetiste "casi crudo"? (dos veces)
4. ¿Y cómo sirvió el mesero el biftec? (bien hecho)
5. ¿Qué hiciste? (pedí otro biftec)
6. ¿Qué pidió tu amigo? (puré de papas)
7. ¿Y qué pasó? (el cocinero frió las papas)
8. ¿Qué sirvió el mesero? (papas fritas)
9. ¿Pidieron Uds. una ensalada? (sí)
10. ¿Qué pidieron para la ensalada? (aceite y vinagre)
11. ¿Y con qué sirvió las ensaladas el mesero? (con mayonesa)
12. ¿Le dieron Uds. una propina al mesero? (no)

B **Yo preparé la comida.** Completen con el pretérito.

1. Anoche mi hermano y yo ___ la comida para la familia. (preparar)
2. Yo ___ el pescado. (freír)
3. Mi hermano ___ las papas. (freír)
4. Mamá ___ la mesa. (poner)
5. Y papá ___ la comida. (servir)
6. Todos nosotros ___ muy bien. (comer)
7. A todos nos ___ mucho el pescado. (gustar)
8. Mi hermano y mi papá ___ el pescado. (repetir)
9. Luego yo ___ el postre, un sorbete. (servir)
10. Después de la comida mi hermano echó (tomó) una siesta. Él ___ media hora. (dormir)
11. Yo no ___. No me gusta dormir inmediatamente después de comer. (dormir)

CAPÍTULO 15   **421**

Ejercicios
PRESENTATION (*page 421*)
Ejercicios A and *B*
Upon completion of Exercises A and B, students can retell the situations in their own words.

ANSWERS
Ejercicio A
1. Pedí un biftec en el restaurante.
2. Lo pedí casi crudo.
3. Repetí "casi crudo" dos veces.
4. El mesero sirvió el biftec bien hecho.
5. Pedí otro biftec.
6. Mi amigo pidió puré de papas.
7. El cocinero frió las papas.
8. El mesero sirvió papas fritas.
9. Sí, pedimos una ensalada.
10. Pedimos aceite y vinagre para la ensalada.
11. El mesero sirvió las ensaladas con mayonesa.
12. No, no le dimos una propina al mesero.

Ejercicio B
1. preparamos
2. freí
3. frió
4. puso
5. sirvió
6. comimos
7. gustó
8. repitieron
9. serví
10. durmió
11. dormí

COOPERATIVE LEARNING

Have students work in groups of three to make up mini-conversations.

E1: Fui a un restaurante y pedí ___.
E2: ¿Qué más pediste?
E1: Pedí ___.
E3: ¿Qué tal te gustó(aron)?
E1: ___.
E3: Y tu amigo(a), ¿qué pidió?
E1: Pidió ___.

INDEPENDENT PRACTICE

Assign any of the following:
1. Workbook, page 158
2. Communication Activities Masters, page 95, *B*
3. Exercises on student page 421

CONVERSACIÓN

Bell Ringer Review

Write the following on the board or use BRR Blackline Master 15-5: Write three things you would possibly say to or ask a waiter at a café.

PRESENTATION (page 422)

A. Have students close their books. Tell them that they will hear a conversation between Raquel and a waiter. Then read the conversation to them or play Cassette 9A.

B. After introducing the conversation, you may wish to set up a café in the classroom and have groups of students perform the conversation for the class.

C. Have students retell the conversation in their own words.

Ejercicio

ANSWERS

1. el menú
2. el biftec
3. el biftec
4. a término medio
5. la cuenta
6. la cuenta
7. está incluído

Escenas de la vida *En el restaurante*

RAQUEL: El menú, por favor.
MESERO: ¡Cómo no! ¡En seguida!
RAQUEL: Gracias.

MESERO: Esta noche le recomiendo el biftec. Está muy bueno.
RAQUEL: De acuerdo, el biftec, por favor.
MESERO: ¿Y cómo le sirvo el biftec? ¿Cómo le gusta?
RAQUEL: A término medio, por favor.

(Después de la comida)
RAQUEL: La cuenta, por favor.
MESERO: En seguida, señorita.
RAQUEL: ¿Está incluído el servicio?
MESERO: Sí, está incluído.

■ **El mesero.** Completen.

1. El mesero me trae ___ .
2. Él me recomienda ___.
3. Yo pido ___.
4. El mesero me sirve el biftec ___.
5. Después de comer, yo le pido ___.
6. Él me trae ___.
7. Él dice que el servicio ___.

422 CAPÍTULO 15

LEARNING FROM PHOTOS

Have students describe the photo at the bottom of page 422 as completely as possible.

Pronunciación   *La acentuación*

1. The rules of stress or accentuation in Spanish are simple. Words ending in a vowel, **n**, or **s** are accented on the next-to-last syllable.

   señor**i**ta   C**a**rmen   pre**pa**ras

2. Words ending in a consonant (except **n** or **s**) are accented on the last syllable.

   se**ñor**   ca**lor**   Ma**drid**   universi**dad**

3. Words that do not follow the above rules must have a written accent mark over the stressed syllable.

   árbol   **Ló**pez   capi**tán**

4. A word of one syllable (monosyllabic) does not take an accent unless the same word can have two different meanings. The written accent mark distinguishes between words that are spelled alike but have different meanings.

tú	*you*	sí	*yes*	él	*he*
tu	*your*	si	*if*	el	*the*

el árbol del capitán López

Comunicación

A **En el restaurante.** You are having dinner in a small restaurant near the Ramblas in Barcelona, Spain. Your partner will be the server.

1. Ask for the menu.
2. One of the specialties of the restaurant is charcoal-broiled chicken, *pollo al carbón*. Order the chicken.
3. Decide what you want with the chicken and order it.
4. Order a dessert.
5. Ask for the check.
6. Find out if the service is included.

B **Una reservación.** You have just heard a commercial on the radio about a great Mexican restaurant, *El Charro*. You call the restaurant to make reservations for Saturday night. Your partner is the restaurant manager.

1. Request a table for two for Saturday night.
2. Tell what time you want it for.
3. Give your name (*A nombre de…*).
4. Ask if you can pay with a credit card.
5. Thank the manager and say goodbye.

C **¿Qué preparamos?** Work in groups of three. You need to create three special menus for RENFE: a vegetarian menu (*vegetariano*), a low-fat menu (*bajo en grasas*), and an exotic "gourmet" menu. Discuss your recommendation, prepare the menus, and present them to the class.

CAPÍTULO 15   **423**

LECTURA Y CULTURA

Bell Ringer Review

Write the following on the board or use BRR Blackline Master 15-6: Rewrite these sentences in the singular form.
1. Ellos siguieron el camino.
2. Dormimos hasta muy tarde el viernes.
3. Las chicas prefirieron estudiar.
4. Los alumnos repitieron las preguntas.

READING STRATEGIES
(*page 424*)

Reading

A. You may wish to divide this reading selection into parts, each part dealing with a different area and cuisine. Assign each part to a group. Each group is responsible for telling other class members about the cooking in their area. Everyone should read paragraph 1.

Group 1: paragraph 2 (México)
Group 2: paragraph 3 (España)
Group 3: paragraph 4 (la Argentina)
Group 4: paragraph 5 (el Caribe)

B. After students have made their reports, have the class read the *Lectura* once silently.

Post-reading

Assign the exercises that follow as a homework assignment. Go over them in class the following day.

LA COMIDA EN UN RESTAURANTE HISPANO

¿Qué es la cocina hispana? La cocina "hispana" no existe porque hay una gran variedad de cocinas. La cocina varía de un país a otro. La cocina española no es la comida mexicana y ésta no es la comida argentina. Vamos a ver algunos ejemplos.

La comida mexicana es muy popular en los Estados Unidos. Hay muchos restaurantes mexicanos en este país. Algunos sirven comida típicamente mexicana y otros sirven variaciones que vienen del sudoeste de los EE.UU. donde vive mucha gente de ascendencia mexicana. La base de muchos platos mexicanos es la tortilla que es un tipo de panqueque de maíz. Con las tortillas los mexicanos preparan tostadas, tacos, enchiladas, etc. Rellenan[1] las tortillas con pollo, carne de res, queso, y frijoles.

En España comen tortillas también, pero no son de maíz. Los españoles preparan las tortillas con huevos. La tortilla a la española es una tortilla con patatas y cebollas[2]. La cocina española es muy buena y variada. Los cocineros preparan muchos platos con el aceite de oliva.

En la Argentina reina el biftec, o como dicen los argentinos, "el bife". En las pampas argentinas hay mucho ganado[3] y en los restaurantes argentinos sirven mucho bife. Cuando pides bife, le tienes que decir al mesero cómo lo quieres, casi crudo, a término medio o bien hecho.

En el Caribe, en Puerto Rico, la República Dominicana y Cuba, la gente come mucho pescado y muchos mariscos. Una carne favorita es el puerco o lechón. Sirven el pescado o la carne con arroz, frijoles (habichuelas) y tostones. Para hacer tostones el cocinero corta plátanos en rebanadas[4] y las fríe.

[1] rellenan *they fill*
[2] cebollas *onions*
[3] ganado *cattle*
[4] rebanadas *slices*

Lechón asado

Tapas

Un restaurante en México

LEARNING FROM PHOTOS

1. Have students look at the photos on page 424 and find the following items: *aceitunas, tortilla a la española, arroz, habichuelas, aceite y vinagre, papas, calamares, salchichas.*

2. Because of the late dinner hour in Spain (10 or 11 P.M.), people will often go to a café or restaurant for *tapas* at 6 or 7 P.M. in order to *matar el hambre,* until dinner time. The word *tapa* is said to come from a little plate that was placed atop a glass of wine. A tidbit would be on the plate. As *tapas* have become more elaborate, the custom of the free *tapa* has all but disappeared.

Estudio de palabras

A **Palabras afines.** Busquen diez palabras afines en la lectura.

B **Más palabras.** Busquen una palabra relacionada.

1. comer	a. la variedad, la variación
2. cocinar	b. la base, básico
3. variar	c. la comida, el comedor
4. servir	d. la preparación
5. basar	e. la cocina, el cocinero
6. preparar	f. el servicio, el servidor, el sirviente

Comprensión

A **¿Sí o no?** Contesten.

1. La cocina es la misma en casi todos los países de Latinoamérica.
2. Hay mucha diferencia entre la cocina de un país y otro.
3. A veces hay una diferencia entre un plato mexicano en México y el mismo plato mexicano del sudoeste de los EE.UU.
4. Hay una gran diferencia entre una tortilla mexicana y una tortilla española.
5. Las pampas están en España.

B **¿Qué cocina es?** Identifiquen la cocina.

1. el aceite de oliva
2. tortillas de maíz
3. carne de res
4. enchiladas
5. arroz y frijoles
6. el lechón

C **¿Qué les parece?** ¿Qué opina Ud.? De las cocinas mencionadas, ¿cuáles son sus favoritas? ¿Pueden Uds. decir por qué?

RESTAURANTE "EL ARRABAL"
C/REAL ARRABAL, 9 · TOLEDO

PRIMER GRUPO: Entremeses y Sopas

1. - Entremeses Variados	400. - Ptas.
2. - Ensalada Mixta	300. - "
3. - Sopas de Pasta	300. - "
4. - Sopa de Verduras	300. - "
5. - Jugo de Frutas	150. - "
6. - Gazpacho Andaluz	250. - "
7. - Consomé	250. - "

SEGUNDO GRUPO: Verduras y Huevos

8. - Guisantes Salteados	400. - Ptas.
9. - Alcachofas Salteadas	450. - "
10. - Judías Verdes Salteadas	400. - "
11. - Espárragos con Mayonesa	800. - "
12. - Fabada Asturiana	400. - "
13. - Paella Valenciana (Personas)	1.500. - "
14. - Tortilla Francesa	300. - "
15. - Huevos Fritos con Jamón	450. - "
16. - Espagueti	400. - "

TERCER GRUPO: Carnes y Pescados

17. - Filete de Ternera	500. - Ptas.
18. - Entrecott a la Plancha	1.200. - "
19. - Chuletas de Cordero	700. - "
20. - Chuletas de Cerdo	400. - "
21. - Carne de Ternera en Salsa	700. - "
22. - Pollo Asado	400. - "
23. - Lenguado a la Romana	900. - "
24. - Merluza a la Romana	600. - "
25. - Trucha a la Navarra	600. - "
26. - Perdiz Estofada (1/2)	800. - "
27. - Cordero Estofado	900. - "

CUARTO GRUPO: Postres

28. - Piña	300. - Ptas.
29. - Pijama	500. - "
30. - Flan	150. - "
31. - Melocotón en Almíbar	250. - "
32. - Helado	200. - "
33. - Fruta del Tiempo	200. - "
34. - Queso	300. - "
35. - Tarta Helada	400. - "

MENU DE LA CASA

SE COMPONE DE DOS PLATOS, POSTRE, PAN Y VINO.

Precio
900. Ptas

ESPECIALIDAD DEL DÍA

ZARZUELA DE MARISCOS

IVA NO INCLUIDO

Estudio de palabras
ANSWERS
Ejercicio A
1. varía
2. popular
3. restaurantes
4. ascendencia
5. base
6. preparan
7. sirven
8. bife
9. crudo
10. favorita

Ejercicio B
1. c
2. e
3. a
4. f
5. b
6. d

Comprensión
ANSWERS
Comprensión A
1. no
2. sí
3. sí
4. sí
5. no

Comprensión B
1. española
2. mexicana
3. argentina
4. mexicana
5. mexicana, caribe (antillana)
6. caribe

Comprensión C
Answers will vary.

LEARNING FROM REALIA

Have students order what they want from the menu.

INDEPENDENT PRACTICE

Assign any of the following:
1. Workbook, *Un poco más*, pages 159–160
2. Exercises on student page 425

PRESENTATION
(pages 426–427)

A. Have students read the information in the *Descubrimiento
cultural* section silently.
B. If there are any Hispanic restaurants in your area, you may
wish to tell students about
them.

DESCUBRIMIENTO CULTURAL

*C*uando la gente va a un restaurante en un país hispano suele pedir más de un plato. Empiezan con un entremés como un cóctel de camarones o una sopa. En España, sirven las legumbres o verduras en un plato aparte. Nunca beben café con la comida. Toman el café después de la comida.

Tampoco es muy común beber agua con la comida. Pero si alguien quiere agua, pide con frecuencia una botella de agua mineral. Si tú vas a un restau- rante y pides una botella de agua mineral, el mesero te va a preguntar si quieres el agua con gas o sin gas. ¿Cómo le vas a contestar? ¿Cuál prefieres?

Y AQUÍ EN LOS ESTADOS UNIDOS

Podemos probar platos de todas las cocinas hispanas sin tener que salir de los Estados Unidos. Hace muchos años[1] que restaurantes españoles y mexicanos en todas las grandes ciudades norteameri- canas sirven comidas típicas y tradicio- nales. La comida mexicana también es popular hoy como una opción entre las variedades de comida rápida.

CRITICAL THINKING ACTIVITY

(Thinking skills: making inferences)
    Write the following on the board or on an overhead transparency: *La señora Segreda decide que esta noche no va a preparar la cena. ¿Cuáles son las opciones que tiene la familia de la señora Segreda?*

Los restaurantes hispanos en los EE.UU. son elegantes y humildes, grandes y pequeños. Los más interesantes, quizás[2], son aquéllos que se establecieron para servir a sus clientes en los barrios hispanos. La Calle 8, en Miami, por ejemplo, tiene extraordinarios restaurantes cubanos. En Nueva York, en Queens, hay restaurantes colombianos, peruanos, argentinos y puertorriqueños que sirven a sus clientes los platos que les hacen recordar a su patria. En Newark, New Jersey, en la Calle Ferry, hay restaurantes españoles fundados por emigrantes gallegos[3] hace cincuenta años. Y en San Francisco, California, hay hoteles con restaurantes que se establecieron para los pastores vascos[4]. Los pastores pasaban meses en la sierra con sus ovejas[5]. En San Francisco podían recibir su pago[6], dormir en una cama limpia, comer una buena comida vasca y hablar en vascuence.

Y en todo el suroeste de los EE.UU. hay lugares en donde se puede comer una comida hispana, nativa de los EE.UU., preparada por norteamericanos de ascendencia mexicana, comida hispana y al mismo tiempo tan americana como cualquiera.

[1] hace muchos años   *it's been many years*
[2] quizás   *perhaps*
[3] gallegos   *from Galicia, Spain*
[4] pastores vascos   *Basque shepherds*
[5] ovejas   *sheep*
[6] el pago   *pay*

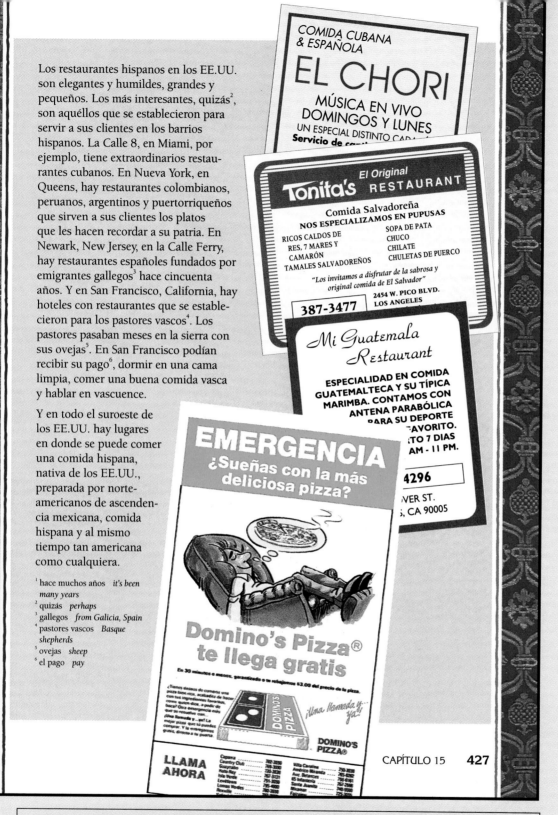

CAPÍTULO 15   **427**

FOR THE NATIVE SPEAKER

1. **Conversation** Among North Americans it is common to invite acquaintances to one's home for a meal, even though they are not close friends. Most Hispanics prefer to invite acquaintances to a restaurant to eat. Have students comment. You may wish to get them started by asking: *¿Creen Uds. que esto es verdad? ¿Cuál de las costumbres es más apropiada y por qué?*

2. **Writing** Divide the group according to ethnic background, if possible: Cuban-Americans, Puerto Ricans, Mexican-Americans, etc. Ask each group to prepare a menu for a restaurant specializing in cuisine from their region. They must offer a variety of dishes.

PRESENTATION
(*pages 428–429*)

The objective of this section is student enjoyment. However, if you would like to do something more, do the following activities.

A. Ask students if they have ever been to a Mexican, Spanish, Cuban or any other Hispanic restaurant. Ask them to describe the ambiance.

B. Using your own resources, show students photos, cookbooks, or sample menus.

C. If possible, plan a field trip to an ethnic restaurant.

D. After reading the captions on page 428, you may wish to share the following information and ask questions regarding the photos and realia:

Photo 2: The restaurant shown here is Casa Botín, near the Plaza Mayor in Old Madrid. It first opened in 1725, and it was one of Ernest Hemingway's favorite restaurants.

Photo 3: Have students compare the two *tortillas* and describe the differences.

Photo 4: Have students describe the setting of this restaurant.

Photo 5: The *cochinillo* of Madrid is a *lechón* in the Caribbean.

REALIDADES

Es un restaurante en Buenos Aires, Argentina **1**. ¿Qué puedes pedir en este restaurante?

El famoso restaurante Casa Botín está en Madrid **2**. Es un restaurante muy antiguo y famoso. La especialidad es el cochinillo asado.

Una tortilla española y una tortilla mexicana son diferentes **3**. Las dos son deliciosas, ¿verdad?

Es un restaurante al aire libre en la Ciudad de México **4**. ¿Quieres comer aquí? ¿Qué vas a pedir?

El cochinillo asado es un plato típico de España **5**. ¿Quieres comer cochinillo? ¡Buen provecho!

428

Assign the following:
1. Workbook, *Un poco más,* page 161

4

5

429

LEARNING FROM PHOTOS

The floors of these restaurants in Mexico, Argentina, and Spain all have tile floors (*suelo de losa/baldosa/loseta/azulejos*). Ask the students what the advantages of tile floors are and why they are so popular in many Spanish-speaking countries (they are easy to clean and they stay cool).

Comunicación oral

ANSWERS

Actividad A

Answers will vary but may include the following.

1. ¿Qué clase de restaurante te gusta?
2. ¿Dónde está el restaurante?
3. ¿Qué sirven?
4. ¿Qué te gusta pedir?
5. ¿Es económico o caro?
6. ¿Es bueno el servicio?
7. ¿Es grande o pequeño?
8. ¿Con quién te gusta ir?

Actividades B and C

Answers will vary.

Comunicación escrita

ANSWERS

Actividades A, B, and C

Answers will vary.

Comunicación oral

A **Mi restaurante favorito.** Work with a classmate. Find out the following about each other's favorite restaurant.

1. the kind of restaurant
2. where it is
3. what foods they specialize in
4. what each of you likes to order
5. if it is expensive or inexpensive
6. what the service is like
7. if the restaurant is big or small
8. with whom you like to go

B **¡Qué comida!** You have just spent a year traveling in Spain, Mexico, Argentina, and Puerto Rico. The president of a local cooking club (your partner) asks you to come to its meeting to discuss the food and restaurants of the countries you have visited and to answer a list of questions about your culinary experience in each country. Explain what is eaten in each of the countries you visited, what are the ingredients in some typical dishes, and what you ate and drank while traveling. Also answer your partner's questions.

C **La cocina japonesa.** There are ethnic restaurants almost everywhere in the United States. A visitor from Guatemala (your partner) asks you if there are different ethnic restaurants nearby. For each one, tell whether or not you like that kind of cooking (*la cocina*), whether you go to the restaurant or not, and if you do, what you order there.

chino	cubano	francés
mexicano	italiano	argentino
japonés	español	

Comunicación escrita

A **El menú.** You and your partner have been hired by an airline to plan the menus for the passengers in first class. Write a dinner menu for the flight from New York to Buenos Aires. Then present your menu to the class. The class will vote on the best menu.

B **Y ahora, un anuncio.** You and your group have been hired by *El Charro* to do a new radio commercial. Write an ad that will encourage people to go to the restaurant. Name some of the dishes and tell how delicious they are. Indicate whether the restaurant is expensive or not. Include the address and phone number, the days it opens, and the hours of operation. Polish the ad and assign one person to "broadcast" the ad to the class.

FOR THE YOUNGER STUDENT

1. Have students make lists in their notebooks of the things they would and would not order in a restaurant. Encourage them to add to these lists as they learn more foods. Tell students to learn the words for the items they order.

2. Tell students they are going to open a restaurant of their own. Have them give it a name and prepare a special menu for the restaurant.

C Puede pedir… You and your partner own a travel agency in Montevideo. Since your clients have many questions about American food and eating customs in the U.S., prepare some guidelines about American food and customs for them. Then make suggestions about what they can order for breakfast, lunch, and dinner and describe typical dishes.

Reintegración

A En el pasado. Cambien al pretérito.

1. Voy a la escuela.
2. Llego a las ocho.
3. Le digo "buenos días" al profesor.
4. Aprendo algo nuevo.
5. Tomo un examen.
6. Saco una nota buena en el examen.
7. Escribo una composición.
8. Salgo de la escuela.
9. Voy al campo de fútbol.
10. Juego (al) fútbol.
11. Vuelvo a casa.
12. Como.

B Yo no, Juan. Cambien *yo* en *Juan* en las oraciones del Ejercicio A.

Vocabulario

SUSTANTIVOS
el restaurante
la mesa
el/la mesero(a)
el menú
la cuenta
la tarjeta de crédito
la propina

el tenedor
el cuchillo
la cuchara
la cucharita
el plato
el vaso
la taza
el platillo
el mantel

la servilleta
la comida
la carne
el biftec
el pollo
el jamón
los mariscos
el pescado
las legumbres
las verduras
los vegetales
las habichuelas
los frijoles
las frutas
la papa
la lechuga
el huevo

la tortilla
el queso
el pan
el arroz
la sal
la pimienta
el aceite

ADJETIVOS
delicioso(a)
rico(a)
malo(a)
crudo(a)

VERBOS
pedir (i,i)
servir (i,i)
freír (i,i)

repetir (i,i)
seguir (i,i)
preferir (ie,i)
dormir (ue,u)
morir (ue,u)

OTRAS PALABRAS Y
EXPRESIONES

casi crudo
a término medio
bien cocido (hecho)
tener hambre
tener sed

Reintegración
RECYCLING

These exercises reinforce all types of verbs in the present and the preterite.

ANSWERS
Ejercicio A
1. Fui a la escuela.
2. Llegué a las ocho.
3. Le dije "buenos días" al profesor.
4. Aprendí algo nuevo.
5. Tomé un examen.
6. Saqué una nota buena en el examen.
7. Escribí una composición.
8. Salí de la escuela.
9. Fui al campo de fútbol.
10. Jugué (al) fútbol.
11. Volví a casa.
12. Comí.

Ejercicio B
1. Juan fue a la escuela.
2. Juan llegó a las ocho.
3. Juan le dijo "buenos días" al profesor.
4. Juan aprendió algo nuevo.
5. Juan tomó un examen.
6. Juan sacó una nota buena.
7. Juan escribió una composición.
8. Juan salió de la escuela.
9. Juan fue al campo de fútbol.
10. Juan jugó fútbol.
11. Juan volvió a casa.
12. Juan comió.

Vocabulario

There are approximately eight cognates included in this *Vocabulario* list.

VIDEO
The video is intended to reinforce the vocabulary, structures, and cultural content in each chapter. It may be used here as a chapter wrap-up activity. See the *Video Activities Booklet* for additional suggestions on its use.

INTRODUCCIÓN (1:00:11)

EL RESTAURANTE (1:02:06)

STUDENT PORTFOLIO

Written assignments that may be included in students' portfolios are the *Actividades escritas* on page 430 and the *Mi autobiografía* section in the Workbook, page 162.

INDEPENDENT PRACTICE

Assign any of the following:
1. Exercises on student page 431
2. Workbook, *Mi autobiografía*, page 162
3. Chapter 15, Situation Cards

Topics	Functions	Structure	Culture
Daily routines Grooming habits Camping	How to describe personal grooming habits How to talk about your daily routine How to describe a camping trip How to tell about things you do for yourself How to discuss what others do for themselves	Los verbos reflexivos Los verbos reflexivos de cambio radical	Outdoor living Popularity of camping Drugstores Pamplona, Spain Herbologists in the U.S. A youth hostel in Spain Arte iberofenicio: "La Dama de Elche" *Nuestro Mundo:* trucos culinarios
Fondo Académico pages: 464-469			Las Ciencias Naturales: La medicina La sociología La Literatura

CAPÍTULO 16

Situation Cards

The Situation Cards simulate real-life situations that require students to communicate in Spanish, exactly as though they were in a Spanish-speaking country. The Situation Cards operate on the assumption that the person to whom the message is to be conveyed understands no English. Therefore, students must focus on producing the Spanish vocabulary and structures necessary to negotiate the situations successfully. For additional information, see the Introduction to the Situation Cards in the Situation Cards Envelope.

Communication Transparency

The illustration seen in this Communication Transparency consists of a synthesis of the two vocabulary (*Palabras 1&2*) presentations found in this chapter. It has been created in order to present this chapter's vocabulary in a new context, and also to recycle vocabulary learned in previous chapters. The Communication Transparency consists of original art. Following are some specific uses:

1. as a cue to stimulate conversation and writing activities
2. for listening comprehension activities
3. to review and reteach vocabulary
4. as a review for chapter and unit tests

CAPÍTULO 16   **A**

You are going on a camping trip in the Pyrenees. A Spanish friend is going camping for the first time. Tell him/her what he/she will need.

B

C

D

Bienvenidos   © Glencoe/McGraw-Hill

© Glencoe/McGraw-Hill

© Glencoe/McGraw-Hill

© Glencoe/McGraw-Hill

Bienvenidos   Chapter 16   Communication Transparency   C-16

Copyright © by Glencoe/McGraw-Hill Publishing Company

CAPÍTULO 16
Print Resources

	Pages
Lesson Plans	

Workbook
- Palabras 1 — 163-164
- Palabras 2 — 164-165
- Estructura — 166-168
- Un poco más — 169-170
- Mi autobiografía — 171

Communication Activities Masters
- Palabras 1 — 96-97
- Palabras 2 — 98-99
- Estructura — 100-101

5 Bell Ringer Reviews — 36-37

Chapter Situation Cards A B C D

Chapter Quizzes
- Palabras 1 — 71
- Palabras 2 — 72
- Estructura — 73-74

Testing Program
- Listening Comprehension — 87
- Reading and Writing — 88-90
- Proficiency — 132
- Speaking — 153

Unit Test: Chapters 13-16
- Listening Comprehension — 91
- Reading and Writing — 92-94
- Speaking — 154
- Performance Assessment

Nosotros y Nuestro Mundo
- Nuestro Conocimiento Académico *La ecología y el medio ambiente*
- Nuestro Idioma *Palabras homófonas*
- Nuestra Cultura *Una leyenda mexicano-americana*
- Nuestra Literatura *"Coplas"* de Jorge Manrique
- Nuestra Creatividad
- Nuestras Diversiones

CAPÍTULO 16
Multimedia Resources

CD-ROM Interactive Textbook Disc 4

Chapter 16 Student Edition
- Palabras 1
- Palabras 2
- Estructura
- Conversación
- Lectura y cultura
- Hispanoparlantes
- Realidades
- Culminación
- Prueba

Review: Chapters 13-16
- Nuestro mundo
- Repaso: Chapters 13-16
- Fondo Académico
- Game: El laberinto del lenguaje

Audio Cassette Program with Student Tape Manual

Cassette	**Pages**
9B Palabras 1	273-274
9B Palabras 2	274-275
9B Estructura	275
9B Conversación	275
9B Pronunciación	276
9B Segunda parte	276-277

Compact Disc Program with Student Tape Manual

CD 9 Palabras 1	273-274
CD 9 Palabras 2	274-275
CD 9 Estructura	275
CD 9 Conversación	275
CD 9 Pronunciación	276
CD 9 Segunda parte	276-277

Overhead Transparencies Binder

- Vocabulary 16.1 (A&B); 16.2 (A&B)
- Pronunciation P-16
- Grammar G-16
- Communication C-16
- Maps
- Fine Art (with Blackline Master Activities)

Video Program

- Videocassette
- Video Activities Booklet — 47-48
- Videodisc
- Video Activities Booklet — 47-48

Computer Software (Macintosh, IBM, Apple)

- Practice Disk
  - Palabras 1 y 2
  - Estructura
- Test Generator Disk
  - Chapter Test
  - Customized Test

CHAPTER OVERVIEW

In this chapter students will learn to discuss some aspects of their daily routine and personal hygiene. In order to do this they will learn the reflexive verbs.

The cultural focus of the chapter is on outdoor living and the popularity of camping, particularly in Spain.

CHAPTER OBJECTIVES

By the end of this chapter students will know:

1. vocabulary associated with one's everyday routine
2. vocabulary associated with personal hygiene and grooming
3. vocabulary needed when camping
4. regular reflexive verbs
5. stem-changing reflexive verbs

CHAPTER 16 RESOURCES

1. Workbook
2. Student Tape Manual
3. Audio Cassette 9B
4. Vocabulary Transparencies
5. Pronunciation Transparency P-16
6. Grammar Transparency G-16
7. Bell Ringer Review Blackline Masters
8. Communication Activities Masters
9. Computer Software: Practice and Test Generator
10. Video Cassette, Chapter 16
11. Video Activities Booklet, Chapter 16
12. Situation Cards
13. Chapter Quizzes
14. Testing Program

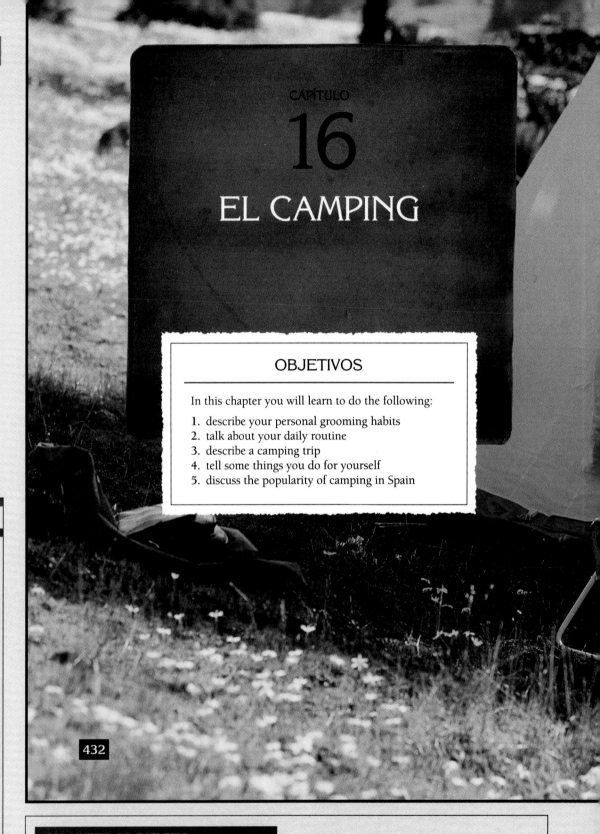

CAPÍTULO

16

EL CAMPING

OBJETIVOS

In this chapter you will learn to do the following:

1. describe your personal grooming habits
2. talk about your daily routine
3. describe a camping trip
4. tell some things you do for yourself
5. discuss the popularity of camping in Spain

432

CHAPTER PROJECTS

(optional)
1. Have students prepare a booklet on good hygiene. Have them make a list of do's and don'ts.
2. Have students prepare a brochure in Spanish advertising and describing a campsite.

Pacing

Chapter 16 will take eight to ten class sessions. Pacing will depend on the length of the class, the age of the students, and student aptitude.

433

LEARNING FROM PHOTOS

After you have presented all the vocabulary from the *Vocabulario* section, have students say all they can about the photo.

PRESENTATION
(pages 434–435)

A. Have students close their books. Model the new words using Vocabulary Transparencies 16.1 (A & B). Point to each illustration and have the class repeat the corresponding word or expression after you or the recording on Cassette 9B.

B. Now have students open their books and repeat the procedure as they read.

C. Act out the new words: *despertarse, levantarse, afeitarse, peinarse, lavarse, cepillarse, vestirse, ponerse la ropa, sentarse.*

D. As you present the new vocabulary, ask questions such as the following: *¿La muchacha se despierta por la mañana o por la noche? Entonces, ¿ella se levanta o se acuesta? ¿Se lava la cara y las manos? ¿Se cepilla los dientes? ¿Se viste en el cuarto de baño o en su dormitorio? ¿Ella se levanta o se acuesta a las diez de la noche?*

E. Call out the following verbs and have students pantomime each one: *despertarse, levantarse, lavarse, cepillarse los dientes, afeitarse.*

LA RUTINA

El muchacho se llama José.

la cama

El muchacho se acuesta. Él se duerme enseguida.

La muchacha se despierta.
Ella se levanta.

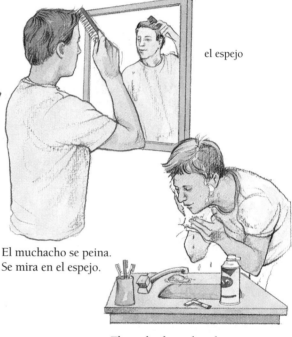

el espejo

El muchacho se peina.
Se mira en el espejo.

El muchacho se lava la cara.
Él se afeita. Se afeita con la navaja.

434 CAPÍTULO 16

TOTAL PHYSICAL RESPONSE

(following the Vocabulary presentation)

Getting ready

You may use a chair for a bed. Bring in an alarm clock or make a buzzing sound when you say *despertador.*

___, ven acá, por favor.
Son las siete de la mañana. Estás durmiendo.

Oyes el despertador. Te despiertas.
Te levantas. Vas al cuarto de baño.
Te lavas.
Te miras en el espejo.
Te cepillas los dientes.
Te peinas. Te vistes.
Sales para la escuela.
Gracias, ___. Y ahora puedes regresar a tu asiento.

La muchacha se lava las manos.

La muchacha se cepilla (se lava) los dientes.

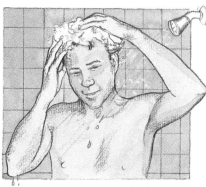

El muchacho se lava el pelo.

La muchacha se viste. Se pone la ropa.

La muchacha se sienta a la mesa.
Ella se desayuna.
Toma el desayuno.

1. *Dientes* are teeth and *muelas* are molars, both are often used as generic terms for teeth. A "toothache" is a *dolor de muelas*. You may wish to ask students to identify English cognates of *diente* and *muela*. You may wish to ask them to identify the *dientes caninos* and the *incisivos*.

2. The first meal of the day is "breakfast," to break a fast. The same concept applies to the Spanish word. Ask students what the word for "a fast" would be in Spanish (*ayuno*). You will hear both *desayunar* and *desayunarse*.

CROSS-CULTURAL CONNECTION

The breakfast the girl in the illustration is eating is typical of the U.S. and is becoming more common in many Hispanic countries. The usual breakfast in Spain and Latin America, however, continues to be *café con leche* with a great deal of *leche*, toast and, maybe juice or fruit. At mid-morning, a sandwich or snack is eaten to tide people over until the midday meal.

DID YOU KNOW?

In Hispanic countries it is considered unhealthy to bathe, even to shower, after eating. It is believed that bathing after eating will interrupt digestion and cause illness.

ANSWERS

Ejercicio A
1. El muchacho se llama José.
2. Sí, se levanta temprano.
3. Sí, se lava la cara en el cuarto de baño.
4. Sí, se lava las manos.
5. Sí, se cepilla (se lava) los dientes.
6. Sí, se peina.
7. Sí, baja al comedor donde se sienta a la mesa.
8. Se desayuna (toma el desayuno) en el comedor.
9. Se afeita antes del desayuno.
10. Se afeita con la navaja.
11. Sí, se pone la gabardina.

Ejercicio B
1. se levanta
2. se lava
3. se cepilla
4. se peina
5. se viste
6. se pone
7. se sienta
8. se desayuna

Ejercicios

A **Las actividades diarias de José.** Contesten.

1. ¿Cómo se llama el muchacho?
2. ¿Se levanta temprano el muchacho?
3. ¿Se lava la cara en el cuarto de baño?
4. ¿Se lava las manos?
5. ¿Se cepilla (se lava) los dientes?
6. ¿Se peina?
7. ¿Baja al comedor donde se sienta a la mesa?
8. ¿Dónde se desayuna (toma el desayuno)?
9. ¿Se afeita antes del desayuno o después?
10. ¿Con qué se afeita?
11. ¿Se pone la gabardina?

B **Las actividades de Elena.** Completen.

1. Elena ___ por la mañana.
2. Ella ___ la cara y las manos.
3. Ella ___ los dientes.
4. Ella ___ el pelo.
5. Ella se pone la ropa. Ella ___.
6. Esta mañana ella ___ una blusa y una falda.
7. Ella ___ a la mesa.
8. Ella ___ en la cocina.

436

C ¿Qué hace el muchacho? Describan.

1.

2.

3.

4.
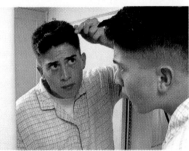

D ¿Qué hace la muchacha? Describan.

1.

2.

3.

4.

CAPÍTULO 16   **437**

Ejercicios C and D

After doing the exercises, have students say as much about each illustration as they can.

ABOUT THE LANGUAGE

Students will probably want to know the names of the objects in the photo on page 437. The *navaja* they know. The shaving brush is *la brocha de afeitar*, the shaving cream or soap is *la crema* or *el jabón de afeitar*.

ANSWERS

Ejercicio C

1. Se levanta.
2. Se lava la cara.
3. Se afeita
4. Se peina.

Ejercicio D

1. Se lava el pelo.
2. Se cepilla los dientes.
3. Se lava las manos.
4. Se desayuna.

LEARNING FROM PHOTOS

Additional questions you may wish to ask about the photos on page 437 are: *En la primera foto, ¿dónde está el muchacho? ¿Cómo es el pelo del muchacho? En la cuarta foto, ¿dónde está la muchacha? Describe todo lo que ves en la foto.*

INDEPENDENT PRACTICE

Assign any of the following:
1. Workbook, pages 163–164
2. Communication Activities Masters, pages 96-97, A & B
3. Exercises on student pages 436–437

Bell Ringer Review

Write the following on the board or use BRR Blackline Master 16-1: Write sentences using the following expressions.

1. ir a la playa
2. tomar el sol
3. nadar
4. usar una crema protectora
5. ir a un restaurante
6. pedir una paella

PRESENTATION
(pages 438–439)

A. Using Vocabulary Transparencies 16.2 (A & B), point to each item and have students repeat the corresponding word.
B. Students can open their books and read the words and expressions for additional reinforcement.
C. Bring to class as many of the items taught in *Palabras 2* as possible. Pass them around the class and have students identify each item.

Note If your students do not do much camping, you may wish to have them only be able to recognize the following words: *la carpa, la tienda de campaña, la linterna, la cantimplora.*

VOCABULARIO

PALABRAS 2

EL CAMPING

el campamento

el hornillo   la linterna

la carpa

la cantimplora

el botiquín

la tienda de campaña

el saco de dormir

acampar

el tubo
la pasta dentífrica

el champú

la navaja

la crema de afeitar

el papel higiénico
el rollo

el desodorante

una barra de jabón
el jabón   (la pastilla)

el peine   el cepillo

438 CAPÍTULO 16

TOTAL PHYSICAL RESPONSE

(following the Vocabulary presentation)
___, levántate y ven acá, por favor.
Estás en el cuarto de baño.
Abre el botiquín.
Busca la pasta dentífrica.
Destapa el tubo.
Saca el cepillo para los dientes del botiquín.

Pon pasta en el cepillo.
Lávate los dientes.
Y ahora tapa el tubo.
Pon el tubo de pasta dentífrica y el cepillo en el botiquín.
Cierra el botiquín.
Gracias, ___. Y ahora puedes sentarte.

la colina

el albergue juvenil

el bosque

las orillas del río

dar una caminata

Los jóvenes levantan (arman)
una tienda de campaña.

Los amigos dan una caminata.
Se divierten mucho.
Lo pasan muy bien.

la ducha

Los jóvenes se bañan en el mar.
Luego, toman una ducha.

ABOUT THE LANGUAGE

Point out to students that *dar una caminata* is "to go hiking." *Dar un paseo* is "to take a walk."

Ejercicios

PRESENTATION *(page 440)*

You may wish to follow some of the suggestions given in previous chapters.

ANSWERS

Ejercicio A

1. Sí, los amigos van de camping.
2. Sí, levantan una tienda de campaña.
3. Sí, preparan la comida en el hornillo.
4. Sí, se acuestan en un saco de dormir.
5. Sí, duermen en la carpa.
6. Sí, cuando se levantan, se visten.
7. Se ponen el traje de baño.
8. Sí, se desayunan.
9. Sí, dan una caminata por el bosque.
10. Sí, lo pasan bien.

Ejercicio B

1. pasta dentífrica
2. champú
3. desodorante
4. jabón
5. cepillo

Ejercicio C

1. jabón
2. una navaja
3. peine
4. el cepillo
5. tubo
6. barra
7. champú

A **De camping.** Contesten.

1. ¿Van de camping los amigos?
2. ¿Levantan una tienda de campaña?
3. ¿Preparan la comida en el hornillo?
4. ¿Se acuestan en un saco de dormir?
5. ¿Duermen en la carpa?
6. Cuando se levantan, ¿se visten?
7. ¿Qué se ponen?
8. ¿Se desayunan?
9. Luego, ¿dan una caminata por el bosque?
10. ¿Se divierten? ¿Lo pasan bien?

B **La mochila.** Contesten según la foto.

¿Qué ponen en la mochila?

1.
2.
3.
4.
5.

C **En el cuarto de baño.** Completen.

1. La muchacha va a tomar una ducha. Necesita una barra de ___.
2. El muchacho va a afeitarse. Necesita ___.
3. La muchacha quiere peinarse, pero ¿dónde está el ___?
4. Juanito quiere lavarse los dientes. ¿Dónde está ___?
5. No hay más pasta dentífrica. Tengo que comprar otro ___.
6. No hay más jabón. Tengo que comprar otra ___.
7. Siempre uso ___ para lavarme el pelo.

Ask students what flavor the toothpaste is (mint). Ask students to tell as much as they can from reading the labels. For example: Camay: *suave* (soft/gentle); *forma anatómica* (body shaped); *más consistente* (more solid). Rexona: *desodorante* (deodorant). Colgate: *anticaries* (anti-cavity), etc.

Assign any of the following:

1. Workbook, pages 164–165
2. Communication Activities Masters, pages 98-99, *C & D*
3. Exercises on student page 440

Comunicación

Palabras 1 y 2

A **De camping.** You and a Spanish friend (your partner) are getting ready for a camping trip in the Pyrenees. Make up a list of things you think you need to pack. Then while one reads the items on the list, the other has to decide which ones you should or shouldn't take and why.

B **La rutina diaria.** With your group, develop a series of questions about people's daily routines from morning until night. Ask what they do and at what time. After you have made up your questions, polish them and exchange your list with another group. Answer the questions given to you. When everyone has answered, get your list back and report to the class the typical time for each routine, and the "oddest" time.

C **De vacaciones.** Work with a classmate. Ask one another questions to find out what types of things you like to do on vacation. Decide if you think you would like to take a vacation together.

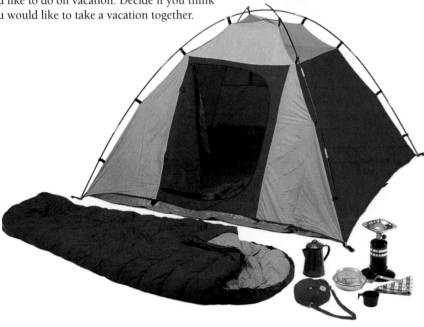

CAPÍTULO 16 **441**

Comunicación

(*Palabras 1* and 2)

ANSWERS

Actividad A

Answers will vary.

Actividad B

Answers will vary but may include the following.

¿Qué haces cuando te levantas?

¿Te desayunas temprano?

¿Te bañas al mediodía o en la noche?

¿A qué hora tomas el almuerzo?

Si cenas en un restaurante, ¿a qué hora vas a cenar?

Actividad C

Answers will vary.

441

ESTRUCTURA

Structure Teaching Resources

1. Workbook, pages 166–168
2. Student Tape Manual, page 275
3. Audio Cassette 9B
4. Grammar Transparency G-16
5. Communication Activities Masters, pages 100-101, A & B
6. Computer Software, *Estructura*
7. Chapter Quizzes, pages 73-74, *Estructura*

Bell Ringer Review

Write the following on the board or use BRR Blackline Master 16-2: Answer.

1. ¿A qué hora sales de casa por la mañana?
2. ¿Cómo vas a la escuela?
3. ¿A qué hora llegas a la escuela?
4. ¿Qué haces en la escuela?
5. ¿Dónde tomas el almuerzo?
6. ¿Qué haces después de las clases?

Los verbos reflexivos

PRESENTATION
(pages 442–443)

A. Have students open their books to page 442 and look at the illustrations. You may also wish to use Grammar Transparency G-16.
B. Ask students in which illustrations someone is doing something to himself (herself) and in which illustrations the person is doing something to someone else.
C. Then ask what additional word is used when the person is doing something to himself/herself. (*se*)
D. Explain to them that *se* is a reflexive pronoun and refers to the subject.

442

Los verbos reflexivos

Telling What People Do for Themselves

1. Compare the following pairs of sentences.

Elena baña al bebé.

Elena se baña.

Elena peina al bebé.

Elena se peina.

Elena mira al bebé.

Elena se mira.

In the sentences on the left, Elena performs the action. The baby receives it. In the sentences on the right, Elena both performs and receives the action of the verb. For this reason the pronoun *se* must be used. *Se* refers to Elena and is called a reflexive pronoun. It indicates that the action of the verb is reflected back to the subject.

442 CAPÍTULO 16

---

2. Each subject pronoun has its corresponding reflexive pronoun. Study the following.

INFINITIVE	LAVARSE	LEVANTARSE
yo	me lavo	me levanto
tú	te lavas	te levantas
él, ella, Ud.	se lava	se levanta
nosotros(as)	nos lavamos	nos levantamos
vosotros(as)	*os laváis*	*os levantáis*
ellos, ellas, Uds.	se lavan	se levantan

3. In the negative form, *no* is placed before the reflexive pronoun.

> Tú *no* te lavas las manos.
> La familia Martínez *no* se desayuna en el comedor.
> *No* nos cepillamos los dientes con esa pasta dentífrica.

4. In Spanish when you refer to parts of the body and articles of clothing, you use the definite article, not the possessive adjective.

> Él se lava *la* cara.
> Me lavo *los* dientes.
> Ella se pone *la* ropa.

PRESENTATION (continued)
E. Then read the explanation that follows on page 442.
F. Call on students to read the example sentences under each illustration or have the class read them in unison.
G. Write the verbs *lavarse* and *levantarse* on the board. After you say *me lavo*, have students supply *me levanto*. Do the same with each subject.
H. Read steps 3 and 4 and have the class read the example sentences aloud.

LEARNING FROM REALIA

You may wish to ask the following questions about the advertisement: *¿Para qué es el anuncio? ¿Quiénes son las personas? ¿Cómo llama la niña a su mamá? ¿Qué le pregunta la niña a su mamá? ¿Qué le dice su mamá? ¿De qué país es el producto?* Ask students to describe all they can in the child's room.

PRESENTATION

(page 444)

Ejercicios A and B can be done orally with books closed.

Ejercicio C

Have students refer to the illustrations as they do this exercise.

PAIRED ACTIVITY

Exercise C can also be done as a paired activity.

ANSWERS

Ejercicio A

Some answers will vary.

1. Madela se levanta a las (siete).
2. Sí, se baña por la mañana.
3. Sí, se desayuna en casa.
4. Sí, se lava los dientes.
5. Sí, se pone una gabardina cuando llueve.

Ejercicio B

Some answers will vary.

1. Me levanto a las (siete y media).
2. Me baño (tomo una ducha) por la mañana.
3. Sí, me lavo los dientes.
4. Sí, me peino.
5. Sí, me miro en el espejo cuando me peino.
6. Sí, me desayuno en casa.

Ejercicio C

1. ¿Te afeitas?
   Sí, me afeito.
2. ¿Te lavas la cara?
   Sí, me lavo la cara.
3. ¿Te peinas?
   Sí, me peino.
4. ¿Te lavas el pelo?
   Sí, me lavo el pelo.
5. ¿Te despiertas?
   Sí, me despierto.

Ejercicios

A **¿A qué hora se levanta?** Contesten.

1. ¿A qué hora se levanta Madela?
2. ¿Se baña por la mañana?
3. ¿Se desayuna en casa?
4. ¿Se lava los dientes?
5. ¿Se pone una gabardina cuando llueve?

B **El aseo.** Preguntas personales.

1. ¿A qué hora te levantas?
2. ¿Te bañas por la mañana o tomas una ducha?
3. ¿Te lavas los dientes?
4. ¿Te peinas?
5. ¿Te miras en el espejo cuando te peinas?
6. ¿Te desayunas en casa?

C **¿Y tú?** Formen una mini-conversación según el modelo.

¿Te lavas los dientes?
Sí, me lavo los dientes.

1.

2.

3.

4.

5.

444 CAPÍTULO 16

INDEPENDENT PRACTICE

Assign any of the following:

1. Workbook, page 166
2. Communication Activities Masters, page 100, *A*
3. Exercises on student pages 444–445

D **¿Y Uds.?** Preparen una mini-conversación según el modelo.

> **Ellos se levantan a las siete.**
> *Ah, sí. ¿Y a qué hora se levantan Uds. ?*
> *Nos levantamos a las siete también.*

1. Ellos se levantan a las siete.
2. Ellos se desayunan a las siete y media.
3. Ellos se bañan a las nueve.

E **¿Cómo se llaman todos?** Contesten.

1. ¿Cómo te llamas?
2. Y tu hermano(a), ¿cómo se llama?
3. ¿Cómo se llama tu profesor(a) de español?
4. ¿Y cómo se llaman tus abuelos?
5. Una vez más, ¿cómo te llamas?

F **La apariencia.** Completen según las fotos.

1. Yo
   Él
   Tú
   Ud.
2. Nosotros
   Ellos
   Uds.
   Él y yo

PRESENTATION (*page 445*)

Ejercicios D and E
  Exercises D and E can be done with books closed or open.

Extension of *Ejercicio E*
  Have one student ask his or her neighbor's name (*¿Cómo te llamas?*). The student who responds then asks the next student and so on.

Ejercicio F
  Have students look at the photos as they make up their sentences.

ANSWERS
Ejercicio D
  Answers will vary according to the model.

Ejercicio E
  Answers will vary.
1. Me llamo ___
2. Mi hermano(a) se llama ___.
3. Mi profesor(a) de español se llama ___.
4. Mis abuelos se llaman ___ y ___.
5. Me llamo ___.

Ejercicio F
1. Yo me lavo la cara.
   Él se lava la cara.
   Tú te lavas la cara.
   Ud. se lava la cara.
2. Nosotros nos peinamos.
   Ellos se peinan.
   Uds. se peinan.
   Él y yo nos peinamos.

LEARNING FROM PHOTOS

You may wish to ask the following questions about the photos on page 445. *¿Dónde está ella? ¿Se lava la cara o el pelo? ¿Se lava la cara con las manos? ¿Cuántos muchachos hay en la foto? ¿En qué se miran ellos? ¿Se peinan? ¿Cómo tienen el pelo?*

Los verbos reflexivos de cambio radical

PRESENTATION
(pages 446–447)

Note There is actually no new concept here since students are already familiar with the stem-changing verbs and the reflexive pronouns.

1. The reflexive verbs *sentarse, acostarse,* and *despertarse* are stem-changing verbs. Study the following forms.

INFINITIVE	SENTARSE (E > IE)	ACOSTARSE (O > UE)	DESPERTARSE (E > IE)
yo	me siento	me acuesto	me despierto
tú	te sientas	te acuestas	te despiertas
él, ella, Ud.	se sienta	se acuesta	se despierta
nosotros(as)	nos sentamos	nos acostamos	nos despertamos
vosotros(as)	*os sentáis*	*os acostáis*	*os despertáis*
ellos, ellas, Uds.	se sientan	se acuestan	se despiertan

2. The verbs *dormirse, divertirse,* and *vestirse* are also stem-changing verbs. These verbs have a stem change in both the present and the preterite.

DORMIRSE (O > UE, U)	
me duermo	me dormí
te duermes	te dormiste
se duerme	se durmió
nos dormimos	nos dormimos
os dormís	*os dormisteis*
se duermen	se durmieron

DIVERTIRSE (E > IE, I)	
me divierto	me divertí
te diviertes	te divertiste
se divierte	se divirtió
nos divertimos	nos divertimos
os divertís	*os divertisteis*
se divierten	se divirtieron

VESTIRSE (E > I, I)	
me visto	me vestí
te vistes	te vestiste
se viste	se vistió
nos vestimos	nos vestimos
os vestís	*os vestisteis*
se visten	se vistieron

446   CAPÍTULO 16

3. Many verbs in Spanish can be used with a reflexive pronoun. Often the reflexive pronoun gives a different meaning to the verb. Study the following examples.

María pone la blusa en la mochila.	*Mary puts the blouse in the knapsack.*
María se pone la blusa.	*Mary puts on her blouse.*
María duerme ocho horas.	*Mary sleeps eight hours.*
María se duerme en seguida.	*Mary falls asleep immediately.*
María llama a Carlos.	*Mary calls Carlos.*
Ella se llama María.	*She calls herself Mary. (Her name is Mary.)*
María divierte a sus amigos.	*Mary amuses her friends.*
María se divierte.	*Mary amuses herself. (Mary has a good time.)*

Ejercicios

A **Me duermo en seguida.** Preguntas personales.

1. ¿Duermes en una cama o en un saco de dormir?
2. Cuando te acuestas, ¿te duermes en seguida?
3. Y cuando te despiertas, ¿te levantas en seguida?
4. ¿Te sientas a la mesa para tomar el desayuno?
5. Luego, ¿te vistes?
6. ¿Qué te pones?
7. ¿Te diviertes en la escuela?

B **Duermo ocho horas.** Completen.

1. Cuando yo ___, yo ___ en seguida. (acostarse, dormirse)
2. Cada noche yo ___ ocho horas. (dormir)
3. Yo ___ a las once y ___ a las siete de la mañana. (acostarse, levantarse)
4. Cuando yo ___, ___ en seguida. (despertarse, levantarse)
5. Pero cuando mi hermana ___, ella no ___ en seguida. (despertarse, levantarse)
6. Y mi hermano, cuando él ___, él no ___ en seguida. Él se pasa horas dando vueltas en la cama. (acostarse, dormirse)
7. Así él ___ solamente unas seis horas. (dormir)
8. Cuando nosotros ___, todos ___ en seguida. (levantarse, vestirse)

C **Anoche también.** Den el pretérito.

1. Él se viste elegantemente.
2. Ellos se divierten.
3. Nosotros nos divertimos también.
4. Yo me acuesto tarde.
5. Y yo me duermo en seguida.
6. ¿Te duermes en seguida cuando te acuestas?

CAPÍTULO 16 **447**

PRESENTATION *(page 447)*

Ejercicios A and C

Exercises A and C can be done with books closed or open.

Ejercicio B

Exercise B can be done with books open.

Expansion of *Ejercicio B*

Call on one student to retell all the information in Exercise B in his/her own words.

ANSWERS

Ejercicio A

Answers will vary.
1. Duermo en una cama (en un saco de dormir).
2. Sí (No), (no) me duermo en seguida.
3. Sí (No), (no) me levanto en seguida.
4. Sí, me siento para tomar el desayuno.
5. Sí, luego me visto.
6. Me pongo una blusa y una falda (un pantalón y una camisa).
7. Sí, me divierto en la escuela.

Ejercicio B
1. me acuesto, me duermo
2. duermo
3. me acuesto, me levanto
4. me despierto, me levanto
5. se despierta, se levanta
6. se acuesta, se duerme
7. duerme
8. nos levantamos, nos vestimos

Ejercicio C
1. se vistió
2. se divirtieron
3. nos divertimos
4. me acosté
5. me dormí
6. te dormiste, te acostaste

ADDITIONAL PRACTICE

Read the following conversation.

—¿A qué hora te levantas, Carlos?
—¿Quieres saber a qué hora me levanto o a qué hora me despierto?
—¿A qué hora te levantas?
—Me levanto a las seis y media.
—¿Y a qué hora sales de casa?
—Salgo a las siete. Me lavo, me cepillo los dientes, me afeito y tomo el desayuno en media hora.
—¿Y te vistes también?
—Claro que me visto.

Now, ask the following questions.

1. ¿Cómo se llama el muchacho?
2. ¿A qué hora se levanta?
3. ¿Se cepilla los dientes?
4. ¿Se afeita?
5. ¿A qué hora sale de casa?
6. ¿Dónde se desayuna?
7. ¿Se viste también?

CONVERSACIÓN

Bell Ringer Review

Write the following on the board or use BRR Blackline Master 16-4: Write three things you did this morning before leaving your house.

PRESENTATION *(page 448)*

A. Tell students they are going to hear a conversation between Carlos and Mariluz. Have students listen as you read the conversation or play Cassette 9B.

B. Now have students open their books to page 448 and read the conversation once silently.

C. Call on several pairs of students to read or act out the conversation for the class.

D. Go over the exercise that accompanies the *Conversación.* Call on individuals to answer the questions. Then call on one student to retell the conversation in his/her own words.

ANSWERS

1. Mariluz no dice a qué hora se despertó.
2. Se levantó tarde.
3. Sí, se vistió rápido.
4. No, no se desayunó antes de salir para la escuela.
5. Sí, se dio prisa.
6. Llegó a tiempo a la escuela.

Escenas de la vida   *¿A qué hora te despertaste?*

CARLOS: Mariluz, ¿a qué hora te despertaste esta mañana?
MARILUZ: ¿Quieres saber a qué hora me desperté o a qué hora me levanté?

CARLOS: Pues, ¿cuándo te levantaste?
MARILUZ: Me levanté tarde, a las siete y media. Me vestí y no me desayuné antes de salir para la escuela.

CARLOS: ¿Llegaste tarde a la escuela?
MARILUZ: No, llegué a tiempo porque me di mucha prisa.

 Me di prisa. Contesten.

1. ¿A qué hora se despertó Mariluz?
2. ¿Se levantó en seguida?
3. ¿Se vistió rápido?
4. ¿Se desayunó antes de salir para la escuela?
5. ¿Se dio prisa?
6. ¿Llegó a tiempo o tarde a la escuela?

448   CAPÍTULO 16

LEARNING FROM PHOTOS

Have students describe the alarm clock in as much detail as possible. You may wish to ask them questions such as: *Este despertador, ¿es nuevo o viejo? ¿Es eléctrico el reloj? ¿Es un reloj de doce o de veinticuatro horas? ¿Qué horas se indican con números romanos y qué horas con números arábigos?*

Pronunciación   *Los diptongos*

1. The vowels **a**, **e**, and **o** are considered strong vowels in Spanish; **u** and **i** (and **y**) are weak vowels. When two strong vowels occur together, they are pronounced separately as two syllables. Note the following.

real	re-al
paseo	pa-se-o
caer	ca-er
leer	le-er

2. When two weak vowels or one weak and one strong vowel occur together, they blend together and are pronounced as one syllable. These are called diphthongs. Repeat the following words.

a	e	i	o	u
aire	*veinte*	*media*	*hoy*	*cuatro*
aula	*Europa*	*diez*	*voy*	*pueblo*
hay		*cuidado*		
		ciudad		

Repeat the following sentences.

Hay *seis autores en el aula.*   Luis tiene miedo.
Julia pronuncia bien.   Luisa tiene cuidado cuando viaja por Europa.
Voy a la ciudad hoy.   Luego voy al pueblo antiguo.

Comunicación

A **¿Por qué no vas a…?** Tell your partner what you want to do. Your partner will suggest where you should go for each one. Reverse roles.

> ir de camping
> Estudiante 1: Quiero ir de camping.
> Estudiante 2: ¿Por qué no vas a un camping en las montañas?

1. comer pizza
2. ver una película
3. nadar
4. jugar tenis
5. ir de compras
6. hablar por teléfono

B **Todos los días.** You and your partner will each make a list of your daily activities. Then put them in a logical order. Compare your lists and see how many activities you do at the same time. Report to the class.

CAPÍTULO 16   **449**

FOR THE NATIVE SPEAKER

The diphthongs in *ciudad, Europa, veinte,* and similar words are often a problem in many areas. It is common to hear *suidad* for *ciudad,* *vente* for *veinte,* and *Uropa* for *Europa.* If this is a problem for the group, practice the correct pronunciation.

Pronunciación
PRESENTATION (*page 449*)
You may have students read the explanation silently or you may explain the information to them. Then have them repeat the words after you or the recording on Cassette 9B.

Comunicación
ANSWERS
Actividad A
Answers will vary according to the model and cues provided.
Actividad B
Answers will vary.

LECTURA Y CULTURA

Bell Ringer Review

Write the following on the board or use BRR Blackline Master 16-5: Write four sentences about your favorite vacation activities.

READING STRATEGIES
(page 450)

Reading

You may wish to use any of the various procedures suggested for the presentation of previous *Lecturas.*

Post-reading

A. After going over the *Lectura,* assign the exercises that follow it.

B. You may want to locate the places mentioned in the *Lectura* on the map of Spain on page 473.

GEOGRAPHY CONNECTION

The climate of Alicante is so mild that it attracts tourists even in the winter months, especially tourists from northern Europe.

Alicante has a lovely sandy beach. The weather is extremely hot in the summer. The *Esplanada* which parallels the sea is lined with date palms. Alicante's origins are ancient, dating back to the days of the *iberos,* the original inhabitants of the Iberian peninsula.

Have students locate Alicante on the map of Spain (page 473).

EN UN CAMPING DE ESPAÑA

¡Hola! Me llamo Eduardo Bastida Iglesias. Soy de Pamplona, en el norte de España. Hace frío en Pamplona en el invierno. Aun en el verano hace un poco de fresco. En agosto mis padres tienen vacaciones y como muchas familias españolas de la clase media vamos de camping. En comparación con las tarifas de los hoteles, el camping es bastante económico y divertido al mismo tiempo[1].

Para pasar las vacaciones nosotros vamos al sur donde hace más calor. Por todo lo largo de la costa del Mediterráneo hay campings o campamentos. Pero el camping es muy popular y es necesario hacer una reservación, sobre todo en agosto.

Cuando llegamos al camping cerca de Alicante en la costa oriental, levantamos una tienda de campaña. El camping está en una colina. Desde la colina hay una vista magnífica del mar, el cual no está muy lejos. Por la mañana me levanto temprano, me desayuno con una taza de chocolate y unos churros[2] que compramos en el "supermercado" del camping. Me pongo un T shirt, un pantalón corto y los tenis y salgo a dar una caminata por los pinares o bosques de pinos. A veces voy en mi bicicleta a Elche donde hay un bosque de palmeras que dan dátiles. Los dátiles de Elche son famosos en el mundo entero.

Por la tarde, cuando hace mucho calor me baño en el Mediterráneo. De noche me preparo una buena tortilla de gambas[3]. Luego voy a la plaza con mis amigos donde nos sentamos en la terraza de un café y miramos a la gente que pasa.

[1] al mismo tiempo *at the same time*
[2] churros *a type of doughnut*
[3] gambas *shrimp (in Spain)*

Churros y chocolate

Una playa en Alicante, España

LEARNING FROM PHOTOS

Have students look at the photo of the *churros* on page 450. Explain to them that they are a very popular breakfast food in Spain—either *churros y una taza de chocolate* or *churros y café con leche.*

FOR THE NATIVE SPEAKER

After reading the *Lectura* on page 450, have students identify each reflexive verb and its corresponding pronoun. You may also give them the following paragraph and ask them to do the same. *Uds. no quieren que nos vayamos, pero nosotros nunca nos preocupamos por lo que ordenan Uds. Nos fijamos primero en lo que es justo hacer. Así es que si nos vamos o no, no es cosa para que Uds. se preocupen.*

Estudio de palabras

A **¿Cuál es la palabra?** Busquen en la lectura la palabra que quiere decir lo siguiente.

1. ni mucho calor ni mucho frío
2. el precio de una habitación en un hotel
3. que le permite divertirse
4. las orillas del mar
5. del este
6. una elevación en la tierra
7. una fruta
8. un bosque de pinos

B **Lo contrario.** Busquen lo contrario.

1. hola
2. el verano
3. el frío
4. económico
5. el norte
6. occidental
7. cerca
8. temprano
9. ceno
10. nos levantamos

a. el sur
b. nos sentamos
c. el invierno
d. oriental
e. me desayuno
f. adiós
g. tarde
h. el calor
i. lejos
j. caro, costoso

CAMPING/CABAÑAS

LAS DUNAS DE GUANAQUEROS

22 CABAÑAS
CABAÑAS DE 6 A 10 PERSONAS
HABITACIONES EN SUITES
TELÉFONO DIRECTO, TV. COLOR
CON SISTEMA SATELITAL
COCINA, BARBACOA, PÉRGOLA,
TERRAZAS
SERVICIO DE CAMARERA
UBICADAS A 50 MTS. DEL MAR
ESTACIONAMIENTOS

27 SITIOS DE CAMPING
BAÑOS CON AGUA CALIENTE
MESAS, SILLAS, CORRIENTE ELÉCTRICA, BARBACOA
RESTAURANT, DISCOTECA
EMBARCADERO EN LA PLAYA JUNTO A 7 KMS.
DE PLAYA
SUPERMERCADO

RESERVA AL 391135 - 391282 - GUANAQUEROS
MENDOZA 290317 - AV. SAN MARTÍN 1035 - 2º PISO

Comprensión

A **Eduardo Bastida.** Contesten.

1. ¿Cómo se llama el muchacho que nos habla?
2. ¿De dónde es él?
3. ¿Qué tienen sus padres?
4. ¿Adónde van?
5. ¿Dónde está el camping?
6. ¿Cómo es el camping en España?
7. ¿Desde dónde hay una vista del mar?
8. ¿Qué toma Eduardo para el desayuno?
9. ¿Qué se pone?
10. Y luego, ¿qué hace?

B **Informes.** Identifiquen.

1. el nombre de una ciudad del norte y una ciudad del sur de España
2. el nombre de la familia del padre y de la madre de Eduardo
3. el nombre de una región de España famosa por sus dátiles
4. dos tipos de árboles

C **Un descubrimiento.** In this reading selection a very popular Spanish pastime is referred to. What is it?

Estudio de palabras

PRESENTATION (*page 451*)

After going over Exercise B, you may wish to have students use the words in original sentences.

ANSWERS

Ejercicio A
1. fresco
2. la tarifa
3. divertido
4. la costa
5. oriental
6. una colina
7. el dátil
8. los pinares

Ejercicio B
1. f
2. c
3. h
4. j
5. a
6. d
7. i
8. g
9. e
10. b

Comprensión

ANSWERS

Comprensión A
1. Eduardo Bastida Iglesias
2. Pamplona
3. vacaciones en agosto
4. van de camping
5. está cerca de Alicante
6. económico y divertido
7. desde el camping (la colina)
8. churros y una taza de chocolate
9. un T shirt, un pantalón corto y los tenis
10. da una caminata o va en bicicleta a Elche

Comprensión B
1. Pamplona, Alicante
2. Bastida, Iglesias
3. Elche
4. palmeras, pinos

Comprensión C
Ir de camping

COOPERATIVE LEARNING

Have students work in groups of three. Tell them *Cada uno(a) de Uds. tiene 1.500 dólares. Van a pasar un mes en España. Preparen su viaje. Entonces, comparen sus itinerarios. Decidan quién va a hacer el viaje más interesante. Expliquen por qué.*

LEARNING FROM REALIA

Ask the following questions about the ad on page 451: *¿Cómo se llama el camping? ¿Cuántas cabañas hay? ¿Cuántas personas pueden dormir en la cabaña más grande? ¿Dónde se puede comer? ¿Adónde pueden ir los veraneantes para bailar?*

PRESENTATION
(pages 452–453)

Note In this section we have
given students the vocabulary
they need to describe an American
breakfast. This is important
because people are often asked to
describe their own customs.

You may wish to have students
scan the passage quickly and read
only about those topics that are of
interest to them.

GEOGRAPHY CONNECTION

Have students locate the
city of Pamplona on the
map of Spain on page 473.
Pamplona is located in the
region of Navarra. The
province of Navarra was
once a part of France.

DESCUBRIMIENTO CULTURAL

*E*n los Estados Unidos, cuando
queremos comprar artículos de tocador o
cosméticos, por lo general, vamos a una
farmacia. En muchas farmacias de los
países hispanos, no venden cosméticos.
En la farmacia sólo venden o despachan
medicamentos. Para comprar desodorante, talco, jabón, perfume o agua de
colonia la gente va a una perfumería o
droguería. Pero hoy día, sobre todo
en las grandes ciudades, hay más y más
farmacias que venden artículos de tocador. Igual que nuestros *"drugstores"*
tienen también una sección farmacéutica.

En España hay más de 550 campings.
El camping es muy popular, sobre todo
entre familias con niños y entre los
jóvenes que viajan por el país con su
mochila o en bicicleta.

En España hay también albergues juveniles[1] donde pasan o pueden pasar la
noche los turistas jóvenes. Pero la verdad
es que los albergues juveniles son menos
populares en España que en otros países
europeos. ¿Por qué? Porque en España
hay muchas pensiones, casas de huéspedes[2] o pequeños hoteles que son
bastante económicos, es decir no muy
caros. Pero la verdad es que los precios
están subiendo mucho. Hoy en día
España no es un destino turístico muy
económico.

Eduardo nos dice que por la mañana
él se desayuna. Toma una taza de
chocolate y unos churros que son un
tipo de *"doughnut"* español frito. En
España, el desayuno no es una comida
grande—sólo se toma chocolate o
café con leche con pan y se come con

mermelada o churros. Para describir el
desayuno que tomamos muchos de
nosotros, los españoles dicen, "desayuno
americano o inglés". El desayuno americano incluye jugo, o como dicen en
España zumo de naranja, huevos, jamón
o tocino[3], pan tostado y café. Y los
huevos, ¿cómo? ¿Fritos, revueltos[4],
pasados por agua o duros?

**UTILIZA
LOS CAMPINGS
AUTORIZADOS**

**CUIDA TU ENTORNO
ES DE TODOS**

PROHIBIDO EL CAMPISMO LIBRE

CRITICAL THINKING ACTIVITY

(Thinking skills: making inferences)
   *"Cuando en Roma, haz lo que hacen los
romanos"*. "When in Rome, do as the Romans
do," is a well-known proverb. Have students
explain what this proverb means. Then, have
them imagine that they are in Spain, and ask:
*¿Qué deben hacer para seguir la filosofía o las
recomendaciones de este refrán?*

LEARNING FROM REALIA

Have students tell you about the basic
message of the brochure on page 452.

La fiesta de San Fermín

Y AQUÍ EN LOS ESTADOS UNIDOS

En los barrios latinos de los Estados Unidos mucha gente visita a los herbolarios. Los herbolarios son personas que hacen preparaciones de hierbas para curar una variedad de males o enfermedades. Para cada enfermedad preparan una hierba específica. La gente generalmente hace un tipo de té con las hierbas y lo toma. La palabra "herbolario" se refiere a la persona y a la tienda. A los herbolarios también se llaman botánicas.

Eduardo nos dice que es de Pamplona. Pamplona es una ciudad famosa de España. ¿Por qué? Porque sus ferias y fiestas de San Fermín tienen mucha fama. Los jóvenes corren delante de los toros por las calles de Pamplona. El día de San Fermín es el siete de julio. Ernest Hemingway escribió mucho sobre los "sanfermines". San Fermín es el santo patrón de la ciudad de Pamplona.

¹ albergues juveniles *youth hostels*
² casas de huéspedes *guest houses*
³ tocino *bacon*
⁴ revueltos *scrambled*

Botanica Perez
DRUG STORE
433-9001

CAPÍTULO 16   **453**

PRESENTATION
(*pages 454–455*)

The purpose of this section is to have students enjoy the photographs in a relaxed manner in order to gain an appreciation of Hispanic culture. After reading the captions on page 454, you may wish to share the following information regarding the photos:

Photo 1: Ask students to describe the campsite. You may wish to have them figure out where it is located. Some clues are: the trees and foliage (not the south of Spain); the name of the site, *Vall d' Aran*, (not Spanish); the flags (the yellow and red bars are from the old kingdom of *Aragón* including *Cataluña*). The campsite is in the *Valle de Arán* in the province of *Lérida* in *Cataluña*. *Vall d'Aran* is *catalán*. The flags are the provincial flags of *Lérida* (with blue fringe) and the regional flags of *Cataluña* (red and yellow bars).

Photo 2: The Republic of Venezuela is one of the largest countries in the Americas. It has three distinct geographic zones: the montainous Northwest, the plains south of the mountains, and the area south of the Orinoco river called the *macizo de las Guayanas* or Guiana Highlands. Venezuela covers almost a million square kilometers and has a population of over 20,000,000. Venezuela is one of the world's major oil producers and a founding member of OPEC, *OPEP* in Spanish (*Organización de Países Exportadores de Petróleo*). You may wish to assign research reports to groups on the following topics: *la geografía de Venezuela; la historia de Venezuela; la industria del petróleo en Venezuela.*

REALIDADES

Es un camping en España **1**. ¿Te gusta el camping? ¿Te diviertes cuando vas de camping?

El camino Tepui de Venezuela **2**. ¿Quieres dar una caminata por ese camino?

Es un hostal en España **3**. Los hostales son bastante económicos.

Estas palmeras de Elche dan unos dátiles deliciosos **4**.

La Dama de Elche es un famoso busto representativo del arte iberofenicio **5**. Lo encontraron en Elche en 1897.

454

5

4

Photo 3: Ask students where they think the Hostal Rembrandt is located. *(Cataluña)*

Photo 5: Ask students to locate Elche on a map. Let them know it's in the province of Alicante. The *Dama de Elche* was found in *La Alcudia* (Elche) on August 4, 1897. It is thought to be the work of a native Spanish artist influenced by Phoenician and Greek artists. It is probably from the 5th century B.C.

INDEPENDENT PRACTICE

Assign the following:
1. Workbook, *Un poco más*, pages 169–170

Comunicación oral

ANSWERS

Actividad A

Answers will vary.

Actividad B

Answers will vary along these lines.

Me despierto a las seis.

Tú te levantas a las seis y media.

Me desayuno a las siete.

Tú cenas a las ocho.

Yo tomo el almuerzo a las doce.

Tú das una caminata a las dos.

Estudio en la tarde.

Tú te acuestas temprano.

Actividad C

Answers will vary.

Comunicación escrita

ANSWERS

Actividad A

Answers will vary.

Comunicación oral

A **¿Siempre o nunca?** When or where do you always (or never) do these things? Tell your partner and then your partner will tell you.

> **lavarse las manos**
> **Siempre me lavo las manos antes de comer.**

1. mirarse en el espejo
2. cepillarse los dientes
3. ponerse el traje de baño
4. vestirse elegantemente
5. acostarse tarde
6. levantarse temprano

B **En el camping.** Discuss with a classmate the routine for a camping trip. Take turns deciding at what time the two of you will do the following.

> despertarse   tomar el almuerzo
> levantarse   dar una caminata
> desayunarse   estudiar
> cenar   acostarse

C **¡Ridículo!** Ask your partner why he or she did or did not do the following things. See who can come up with the wierdest reasons. Reverse roles.

> **vestirse elegantemente**
> Estudiante 1: ¿Por qué te vestiste elegantemente?
> Estudiante 2: Porque voy a jugar al fútbol.

1. levantarse tarde
2. cepillarse los dientes
3. mirarse en el espejo
4. sentarse a la mesa
5. desayunarse
6. lavarse las manos
7. acostarse temprano

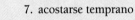

Hostal Maestre

✳ ✳

HABITACIONES CON Y SIN BAÑ

ROMERO BARROS, 16
(JUNTO A PLAZA DEL POTRO)
TELÉF. 475395

14003 CÓRDO

Comunicación escrita

A **Un anuncio.** Your group has been asked to do another radio ad. This time it's for a toy doll (*muñeca*) that can do all these things:

1. wake up in the morning
2. wash its face and hands
3. brush its teeth
4. dress itself
5. comb its own hair
6. say "mama"

In your ad give the price and say where the doll can be bought. Polish the ad and appoint an "announcer" to broadcast it to the class.

456 CAPÍTULO 16

FOR THE YOUNGER STUDENT

1. Have students draw scenes of a campsite. Have them label the items they draw. Then have them write a paragraph describing their drawing.
2. Have students write out a detailed daily schedule.

STUDENT PORTFOLIO

Written assignments that may be included in students' portfolios are the *Actividades escritas* on pages 456–457 and the *Mi autobiografía* section in the Workbook, page 171.

B **Una vez fui...** Did you ever go to camp or spend a night at a friend's house? Try to remember how you spent that one day or invent it. Write an entry for your diary telling in detail what you did from morning to night, and include the time that you did it.

> El sábado en casa de Daniel.
> A las siete de la mañana, Daniel me despertó.
> Nos cepillamos los dientes y nos vestimos.
> A las siete y media nos desayunamos.
> Comí huevos y pan. A las...

Este verano, lo tuyo es Zumosol
ZUMOSOL
ZUMO DE NARANJA

C **Fuimos de camping.** Susana and her friends love to take vacations. Once they went together to the beach, once they took a ski trip, and once they went camping. Write a paragraph about each one of their vacations.

Reintegración

En el coche-comedor. Contesten con sí.

1. ¿Hizo Elena un viaje en tren?
2. ¿Fue un viaje largo?
3. ¿Comió Elena en el tren?
4. ¿Fue al coche-comedor?
5. ¿Le dio el menú el mesero?
6. ¿Qué pidió Elena?
7. ¿Le sirvió el mesero?
8. ¿Le gustó la comida a Elena?
9. ¿Le dio buen servicio el mesero?
10. ¿Le dejó una propina Elena?

Vocabulario

SUSTANTIVOS
el botiquín
el tubo
la pasta dentífrica
la barra
la pastilla
el jabón
el champú
el desodorante
la crema de afeitar
la navaja
el rollo
el papel higiénico
el peine
el cepillo
el espejo

el cuarto de baño
la ducha
los dientes
el pelo
la cara
el camping
el campamento
la tienda de campaña
la carpa
el saco de dormir
la cama
el hornillo
la linterna
la cantimplora
el bosque
la colina

la orilla
el río
el mar
el albergue juvenil
la pensión

VERBOS
llamarse
despertarse (ie)
levantarse
lavarse
bañarse
afeitarse
peinarse
cepillarse
vestirse (i,i)
ponerse

sentarse (ie)
desayunarse
acostarse (ue)
dormirse (ue, u)
divertirse (ie, i)
mirarse
acampar

OTRAS PALABRAS Y
EXPRESIONES
ir de camping
armar una tienda
dar una caminata
tomar una ducha

ANSWERS
Actividad B
Answers will vary but should follow the model.
Actividad C
Answers will vary.

Reintegración
RECYCLING
This exercise reviews the preterite and vocabulary associated with trains and restaurants.

ANSWERS
1. Sí, Elena hizo un viaje en tren.
2. Sí, fue un viaje largo.
3. Sí, Elena comió en el tren.
4. Sí, fue al coche-comedor.
5. Sí, el mesero le dio el menú.
6. Elena pidió (un sándwich).
7. Sí, el mesero le sirvió.
8. Sí, a Elena le gustó la comida.
9. Sí, el mesero le dio buen servicio.
10. Sí, Elena le dejó una propina.

Vocabulario
There are approximately six cognates included in this *Vocabulario* list.

VIDEO
The video is intended to reinforce the vocabulary, structures, and cultural content in each chapter. It may be used here as a chapter wrap-up activity. See the *Video Activities Booklet* for additional suggestions on its use.

INTRODUCCIÓN   (1:04:36)

DANIEL Y SU MADRE   (1:05:56)

INDEPENDENT PRACTICE

Assign any of the following:
1. Exercises on student page 457
2. Workbook, *Mi autobiografía*, page 171
3. Chapter 16, Situation Cards

(optional material)

OVERVIEW

All the readings presented in the *Nuestro Mundo* section are authentic, uncut texts from publications of the Hispanic world. Students should be encouraged to read the text for overall meaning, but not intensively, word for word. Students should find satisfaction in their ability to derive meaning from "real" texts. Each reading is related to a theme or themes covered in the previous four chapters.

PRESENTATION *(page 458)*

Have students read the first selection silently for meaning.

Ejercicio

PRESENTATION

Ask students to respond orally to the ten questions on page 458.

ANSWERS

1. food or cooking
2. to parents
3. puré, molds, creams, pastas
4. They are more appetizing that way.
5. the children
6. tomato, carrot, cucumber
7. vegetable
8. Kids don't like them.
9. Answers will vary.
10. Answers will resemble the following: **Kids will eat vegetables if prepared in an appetizing way.**

NUESTRO MUNDO

This article comes from *MÁS*, a Spanish language magazine published in the United States.

SABOR

AL DIA CON Mas SABOR

TRUCOS CULINARIOS

Si a su hijo no le gustan los vegetales pruebe a convertirlos en puré. La zanahoria, las espinacas o los puerros son mucho más apetitosos si se convierten en cremas, mezclados con papas, y se colocan en moldecitos.

◆ Acostumbre a su hijo a beber jugos naturales de frutas y de vegetales. Además de la naranja, es saludable que aprenda a tomar jugo de tomate, zanahoria o pepino sin asombrarse.

◆ La pasta es ideal para engañar visualmente al niño, porque puede complementarla con alimentos que de otra forma no comería, como brócolis, zanahorias, guisantes, pimientos, etc.

Los trucos. Contesten.

1. What section of the magazine do you think this article comes from?
2. To whom is it directed?
3. The following words are almost the same in English: *puré, moldecitos (moldes), cremas, pastas.* What do you think they mean?
4. Why are they suggesting that you put *zanahorias y espinacas en cremas con papas, y en moldecitos?*
5. Whom are they trying to trick?
6. What are the less common juices that they suggest serving?
7. In what category do almost all the foods mentioned belong?
8. What do most of these foods have in common, aparently everywhere?
9. How many of the foods can you identify?
10. What is the main message of the article?

LEARNING FROM REALIA

You may wish to ask students the following questions about the realia on page 458: *¿De dónde viene el artículo? ¿Qué no les gusta comer a los niños? ¿Qué jugos prefieren tomar? ¿Qué jugos no les gustan? ¿Cuál es tu vegetal favorito? ¿Qué vegetales no te gustan?*

This article about railroads is from the Madrid newspaper *ABC*.

La estadounidense Amtrak interesada en la compra de varias unidades del Talgo pendular

La empresa estatal de ferrocarriles norteamericanos, Amtrak, está interesada en la compra de entre 10 y 20 unidades del Talgo pendular para realizar la conexión Boston-Nueva York, según informaron directivos de la compañía americana. En una prueba entre Boston y Nueva York un Talgo cubrió los 364 kilómetros de distancia en dos horas y cincuenta minutos, frente a las cuatro horas que se requieren actualmente.

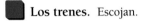 **Los trenes.** Escojan.

1. What is the name of the potential buyer?
   a. Talgo
   b. The Boston and New York Co.
   c. Amtrak

2. What is the company interested in buying?
   a. the entire Spanish railroad system
   b. 10-20 shares in Spanish railroads
   c. a number of special trains

3. How long does the Boston-New York run take at present?
   a. 2 hours and 50 minutes
   b. 3 hours and 14 minutes
   c. 4 hours

4. About how much time could be cut from the schedule with the new equipment?
   a. 24 minutes
   b. 1 hour and 10 minutes
   c. 3 hours and 14 minutes

5. What does *una empresa estatal* probably refer to?
   a. government pressure
   b. a state-owned corporation
   c. a stationary object

6. What is it most likely that the Talgo is?
   a. a railroad company
   b. a high-speed train
   c. an investment company

PRESENTATION (*page 459*)
Have students read the article on page 459 silently.

Ejercicio
PRESENTATION
Assign the questions as homework and go over the answers in class. You may wish to ask students to identify the place in the text where the questions were answered.

ANSWERS
1. c
2. c
3. c
4. b
5. b
6. b

CRITICAL THINKING ACTIVITY

(*Thinking skills: supporting statements with reasons*)

Write the following on the board or on an overhead transparency.

El tren de Boston a Nueva York toma cuatro horas. El avión toma una hora. El avión cuesta el doble del tren. Si tú vas a hacer un viaje de Boston a Nueva York, ¿vas a tomar el tren o el avión? ¿Qué factores tienes que considerar?

CAPÍTULOS 13–16

This section reviews key vocabulary and structure from Chapters 13–16. The topics were first presented on the following pages: the verbs *interesar, gustar, molestar,* and *encantar,* pages 368–369; the preterite of irregular verbs *hacer, querer,* and *venir,* page 394; the preterite of *estar, andar, tener, poder, poner,* and *saber,* page 396; the preterite of *pedir, servir, freír,* and *seguir,* page 418; *preferir* and *dormir,* page 420; reflexive verbs, pages 442–443.

REVIEW RESOURCES

1. Workbook, Self-Test 4
2. Computer Software
3. Testing Program, Unit Test 13-16

Conversación

PRESENTATION *(page 460)*

Have students repeat the lines of the conversation after you. Then call on two students to read the conversation aloud.

Ejercicio

ANSWERS

1. **Está en la tienda (en la ciudad).**
2. **Vive en un pueblo.**
3. **Hizo el viaje a la ciudad para comprar equipo de camping.**
4. **Estuvo el año pasado.**
5. **No le gusta perder el tiempo.**
6. **Tuvo que venir otra vez porque en su pueblo no pudo encontrar lo que necesita.**

Conversación   *De compras*

SEÑORITA: Hice este viaje a la ciudad para comprar equipo de camping. No me gusta perder el tiempo. Estuve aquí el año pasado y no pude encontrar nada.

VENDEDOR: Es verdad. Yo le serví.

SEÑORITA: Pues, tuve que venir otra vez porque en mi pueblo no pude encontrar lo que necesito.

■ **En la tienda.** Contesten.

1. ¿Dónde está la señorita?
2. ¿Dónde vive ella?
3. ¿Para qué hizo el viaje a la ciudad?
4. ¿Cuándo estuvo ella en la tienda?
5. ¿Qué no le gusta hacer?
6. ¿Por qué tuvo que venir otra vez?

CAMPING, EL _____

El Camping

Exposición, venta y alquiler
Equipos completos de camping
Remolques y tiendas - Accesorios
Taller de reparaciones

28020 MADRID
Bravo Murillo, 118
☎ 235 48 67 - 235 96 45
28002 - Francisco Campos, 25
☎ 260 03 93 - 260 61 33

Estructura

Los verbos *interesar, gustar, molestar, encantar*

1. Remember that the verbs *interesar, molestar,* and *enojar,* are usually used with an indirect object pronoun.

   Ese libro *me* interesa.
   Juan *nos* molesta.
   Esos vestidos *te* encantan, ¿verdad?

2. *Gustar* is also used with an indirect object pronoun.

   Me gusta la película. *The movie pleases me. (I like the movie.)*

A ¿Qué te gusta? Completen.

1. A mis amigos no ___ jugar golf. (gustar)
2. A ellos ___ más el tenis. (interesar)
3. Yo creo que el tenis es aburrido. ___ tener que jugar todos los días. (molestar)
4. A mi hermana y yo ___ la plancha de vela. (encantar)
5. ¿Cuál es tu deporte favorito? ¿ ___ más el tenis o el golf? (gustar)

COOPERATIVE LEARNING

Have students in groups of four create surveys of the likes and dislikes of the class. Some topics could be *deportes, clases, programas de televisión, personas famosas, música, comida, ropa.* Students can administer the surveys to their classmates and report the results to the class.

El pretérito de los verbos irregulares

Review the preterite forms of these irregular verbs.

hacer	hice, hiciste, hizo, hicimos, *hicisteis*, hicieron
querer	quise, quisiste, quiso, quisimos, *quisisteis*, quisieron
venir	vine, viniste, vino, vinimos, *vinisteis*, vinieron
estar	estuve, estuviste, estuvo, estuvimos, *estuvisteis*, estuvieron
andar	anduve, anduviste, anduvo, anduvimos, *anduvisteis*, anduvieron
tener	tuve, tuviste, tuvo, tuvimos, *tuvisteis*, tuvieron
poder	pude, pudiste, pudo, pudimos, *pudisteis*, pudieron
poner	puse, pusiste, puso, pusimos, *pusisteis*, pusieron
saber	supe, supiste, supo, supimos, *supisteis*, supieron

B **De viaje.** Completen.

Ramón y Teresa ___ (querer) venir anoche,
$\frac{}{1}$
pero no ___ (poder). Así es que Paco y
$\frac{}{2}$
yo ___ (hacer) el viaje al pueblo de Ramón
$\frac{}{3}$
y Teresa. No ___ (poder) viajar juntos.
$\frac{}{4}$
Yo ___ (tener) que viajar en tren y Paco
$\frac{}{5}$
___ (tener) que tomar un bus. Yo ___
$\frac{}{6}$ $\frac{}{7}$
(estar) en la estación muy temprano. Yo
me ___ (poner) un poco nervioso porque
$\frac{}{8}$
no vi a nadie en el andén. Pero el tren
llegó a tiempo.

Estructura

Los verbos interesar, gustar, molestar, encantar

PRESENTATION *(page 460)*

Go over the grammatical explanations with the class. Call on one student to read the example sentences with *me, nos,* and *te*. Have students ask each other questions like *¿Qué te gusta? ¿Qué no te gusta? ¿Qué te molesta? ¿Qué te interesa?*

ANSWERS

Ejercicio A
1. les gusta
2. les interesa
3. Me molesta
4. nos encanta
5. Te gusta

El pretérito de los verbos irregulares

PRESENTATION *(page 461)*

Have students review the paradigms on page 461 silently.

ANSWERS

Ejercicio B
1. quisieron
2. pudieron
3. hicimos
4. pudimos
5. tuve
6. tuvo
7. estuve
8. puse

El pretérito de los verbos con el cambio e > i y del verbo dormir

1. Certain verbs undergo a stem change *e > i*, *o > u* in the third person—*él/ella/Ud.* and *ellos/ellas/Uds.*—forms in the preterite.

pedir	pedí, pediste, pidió, pedimos, *pedisteis*, pidieron

dormir	dormí, dormiste, durmió, dormimos, *dormisteis*, durmieron

2. Other verbs like *pedir* are: *reír, repetir, servir, seguir,* and *preferir.*

C **Les servimos.** Cambien *yo* en *Ud.* y *nosotros* en *Uds.*

1. Yo pedí un biftec.
2. Yo freí el biftec.
3. Yo serví el biftec al cliente.
4. Nosotros les servimos a todos los clientes.
5. Seguimos trabajando en el comedor hasta las once.
6. Preferimos terminar temprano.

D **En el restaurante mexicano.** Contesten.

1. ¿Quién pidió tacos, tú o tu amigo?
2. ¿Quién pidió enchiladas?
3. ¿Sirvieron las enchiladas con mucho queso?
4. ¿Pediste arroz y frijoles también?
5. ¿Frió el cocinero los frijoles?
6. ¿Sirvió el mesero ensalada con la comida?
7. Después de comer, ¿dormiste?
8. ¿Durmió tu amigo?

PRESENTATION (page 462)

Review the concept of the verb stem. Have students study the paradigms silently. Call on students to provide the paradigms orally for *reír, repetir, servir, seguir,* and *preferir.* Select several students to write one or two of the paradigms on the board.

Ejercicios

PRESENTATION

Ejercicio C

This exercise can be a paired activity. One student reads the sentence, the other responds making the change.

ANSWERS

Ejercicio C

1. Ud. pidió un biftec.
2. Ud. frió el biftec.
3. Ud. sirvió el biftec al cliente.
4. Uds. les sirvieron a todos los clientes.
5. Uds. siguieron trabajando en el comedor hasta las once.
6. Uds. prefirieron terminar temprano.

Ejercicio D

1. Yo pedí (Mi amigo pidió) los tacos.
2. Yo pedí (Mi amigo pidió) las enchiladas.
3. Sí (No), (no) sirvieron las enchiladas con mucho queso.
4. Sí (No), (no) pedí arroz y frijoles también (tampoco).
5. Sí (No), el cocinero (no) frió los frijoles.
6. Sí (No), el cocinero (no) sirvió ensalada con la comida.
7. Sí (No), después de comer (no) dormí.
8. Sí (No), después de comer mi amigo (no) durmió.

PAIRED ACTIVITY

Have pairs of students create conversations about a meal they once had in a restaurant. They can be as imaginative as they wish.

462

LEARNING FROM PHOTOS

Have students say all they can about the photo on page 462. You may wish to ask questions such as: *¿Qué es el lugar? ¿Qué hace la gente allí? ¿Está el restaurante en el interior o el exterior? ¿Qué hay en las paredes? ¿Qué puedes ver en las mesas? ¿Hace mucho calor?*

Los verbos reflexivos

1. Remember, with reflexive verbs, the subject and the object are the same person.

      Yo me lavo.   **Ella se peina.**

2. Review the reflexive pronouns with their corresponding subject pronoun.

vestirse	me visto, tu te vistes, se viste, nos vestimos, *os vestís*, se visten
lavarse	me lavo, te lavas, se lava, nos lavamos, *os laváis*, se lavan

E **¿Cuándo se levantan?** Preguntas personales.

1. ¿A qué hora te levantas?
2. ¿Quién(es) en tu familia se afeita(n)?
3. ¿Cómo se llaman tus padres?
4. ¿Dónde te cepillas los dientes?
5. ¿A qué hora se desayunan Uds.?

F **La rutina.** Preguntas personales.

1. ¿Te acostaste tarde o temprano anoche?
2. ¿Te dormiste en seguida?
3. ¿A qué hora te despertaste esta mañana?
4. ¿Te vestiste antes de desayunar?
5. ¿Quiénes se sentaron a la mesa para comer?

Comunicación

A **De camping.** Tell the class what you prepared and ate on a camping trip, real or imagined. The class will ask you questions about your trip.

B **No tengo ropa.** You and a classmate play the roles of a clothing store clerk and a client in to buy a new wardrobe. Tell the clerk what items you want to buy, the color, and how much you want to spend.

C **¿Quién soy?** Divide the class in groups of four. Each of you has a turn pretending you are a world famous athlete. The rest of the group has to guess who you are. They will ask questions about what sport you played; where and when you played; your family; your education; your travels; other things you did. Take turns so that everyone has a chance to play "superstar."

INDEPENDENT PRACTICE

Assign any of the following:
1. Exercises and activities on pages 460–463
2. Workbook, Self-Test 4

Los verbos reflexivos

PRESENTATION *(page 463)*

A. Have students study the paradigms silently.
B. Have students repeat the forms after you.
C. Write these verbs on the board: *despertarse, levantarse, lavarse,* and *vestirse.* Call on individual students to ask a classmate at what time he/she wakes up, gets up, etc. After they have answered, ask a third student to tell the class at what time the person does each thing.

ANSWERS

Ejercicio E
  Answers will vary.
1. Me levanto a…
2. … y… se afeitan.
3. Mis padres se llaman… y…
4. Me cepillo los dientes en el baño.
5. Nosotros nos desayunamos a las…

Ejercicio F
  Answers will vary but should include the following:
1. Me acosté tarde (temprano).
2. Sí (No), (no) me dormí en seguida.
3. Me desperté a las…
4. Sí (No), (no) me vestí antes de desayunar.
5. … se sentaron (nos sentamos) a la mesa para comer.

Comunicación

PRESENTATION *(page 463)*

Actividades A and B
  Have students present what they are asked to do in the activities orally.

ANSWERS

Actividades A, B, and C
  Answers will vary.

FONDO ACADÉMICO

Las ciencias: La medicina
(optional material)

OVERVIEW

The three readings in this section deal with medicine, the sociology of youth and the epic poem *La Araucana*.

Antes de leer

PRESENTATION *(page 464)*

A. Prior to the reading, assign the *Antes de leer* exercise as homework.

B. Ask students to tell briefly, in Spanish if possible, who each of the three figures were and what the Hippocratic oath is.

C. Have students discuss the opening statement and tell whether they agree or disagree.

D. Ask students to skim the text for cognates. Among the less obvious cognates are *tratamientos, naturaleza, la linfa, la bilis*.

Lectura

PRESENTATION
(pages 464–465)

A. Have students read the selection silently.

B. Have students read the questions in *Después de leer* Exercise A and look for the answers in the text.

C. Ask students to develop three original questions based on the selection to ask in class.

LAS CIENCIAS: LA MEDICINA

Antes de leer

The advances in medical science in the last hundred years have resulted in a life expectancy and quality of life undreamed of before the 19th century. The study and practice of medicine, however, goes back thousands of years. In the reading that follows you will learn about some major figures in the early history of medicine. In preparation, please familiarize yourself with:

1. the Hippocratic oath
2. Claudius Galeno
3. William Harvey
4. André Vesalio

Lectura

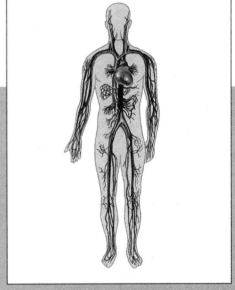

El sistema circulatorio

Hasta la Edad Media, la medicina se basaba casi exclusivamente sobre los preceptos de los médicos griegos Hipócrates y Galeno. Hoy, en español, es común referirse a un médico como un "galeno".

Hipócrates vivió entre 460 y 377 antes de Cristo. Él viajó por toda Grecia y Asia Menor, y finalmente se instaló en Cos. Él recomendaba los tratamientos simples que permiten obrar a la naturaleza. Él practicaba la cirugía, una de las ramas[1] de la medicina más avanzada en Grecia. La patología de Hipócrates se basaba en la alteración de los humores, teoría que subsistía hasta la Edad Media: el equilibrio entre la sangre, la linfa, la bilis amarilla y la bilis negra, constituía la salud; la falta o el exceso de una de ellas constituía la enfermedad. Hipócrates escribió el *Corpus Hippocraticum*. Hoy los médicos siguen tomando el juramento hipocrático que remonta siglos.

Claudio Galeno vivió en el siglo II antes de Cristo. Es un médico griego que ejerce la medicina en Pérgamo y en Roma. Él también, como Hipócrates, se subscribe a la teoría de los humores. Gracias a las disecciones de animales, él hace importantes hallazgos[2] en anatomía, en particular sobre el sistema nervioso y el corazón.

CRITICAL THINKING ACTIVITY

The Spaniard Miguel Servet conceived the theory of blood circulation. The Briton William Harvey fully explained and proved the circulation of blood. Most medical breakthroughs come from the combined efforts of many thinkers. Ask students for other examples. (AIDS research in France and the U.S.; Jonas Salk and Albert Sabin, polio vaccines).

La medicina moderna se debe a un anatomista belga, André Vesalio, médico de Carlos V y Felipe II. Vesalio estudia la medicina en Lovaina y en Italia. En 1544 pasa al servicio de Carlos V. Vesalio ataca las teorías de los antiguos en un tratado titulado *De Corporis Humani Fabrica, La estructura del cuerpo humano*. Lo acusaron de haber hecho una desección sobre un hombre agonizante y, por eso, lo obligaron a hacer un peregrinaje[3] a Tierra Santa. Murió durante una tempestad en el viaje de regreso. Es a Vesalio a quien se deben las ciencias de la anatomía—el estudio de la estructura del cuerpo humano—y de la fisiología—el estudio de las funciones del organismo humano, tales como la nutrición, la motricidad, la sensación y la percepción.

Un español, Miguel Servet, en el siglo XVI, expone la teoría de la circulación de la sangre[4]. En 1628, el médico británico William Harvey escribe un tratado en el que describe en detalle la circulación sistémica y la circulación pulmonar de la sangre. Más tarde, la anatomía y la fisiología progresan dramáticamente gracias a técnicas modernas, tales como el endoscopio, que permite examinar el cuerpo.

William Harvey

[1] ramas *branches*
[2] hallazgos *findings*
[3] peregrinaje *pilgrimage*
[4] sangre *blood*

Después de leer

A **Hipócrates.** Contesten.

1. ¿De dónde son Hipócrates y Galeno?
2. ¿Qué es un "galeno"?
3. ¿Qué clase de tratamientos recomendaba Hipócrates?
4. ¿Cuáles son tres funciones del organismo humano?

B **Los médicos.** Escojan.

1. Una de las especialidades de Hipócrates fue ___.
   a. la patología   b. la cirugía
   c. la bilis
2. En tiempos de Hipócrates la sangre, la linfa y la bilis se llamaban ___.
   a. humores   b. tratamientos
   c. enfermedades
3. El estudio de la estructura del cuerpo humano es ___.
   a. la disección   b. la anatomía
   c. enfermedades
4. El "padre" de la anatomía y fisiología modernas es ___.
   a. Hipócrates   b. Galeno
   c. Vesalio
5. El médico que expone, inicialmente, la idea de la circulación de la sangre es ___.
   a. español   b. griego   c. inglés
6. El que describió precisamente la circulación pulmonar de la sangre es ___.
   a. español   b. griego   c. inglés

C **Seguimiento.** Contesten.

1. ¿Qué dice el *Juramento hipocrático*?
2. Explique por qué Vesalio tuvo que ir a Tierra Santa.
3. Describa el "endoscopio" y lo que hace.

Después de leer

PRESENTATION *(page 465)*

A. Go over Exercises A, B, and C orally in class.
B. Have students ask the three questions they developed above in Exercise C.

ANSWERS

Ejercicio A
1. Grecia
2. médico
3. tratamientos simples
4. la nutrición, la motricidad, la sensación y la percepción

Ejercicio B
1. b
2. a
3. b
4. c
5. a
6. c

Ejercicio C
1. Answers will vary, but may include: **No hacer daño al paciente** (Do not harm the patient). **Ser honrado en su vida personal y profesional** (Lead an honorable personal and professional life). **Respetar la vida privada del paciente** (Respect the privacy of patients).
2. **Porque le acusaron de haber hecho una disección sobre un hombre agonizante.**
3. **El endoscopio es un instrumento médico moderno que permite examinar el cuerpo.**

DID YOU KNOW?

Many of the most important modern medicines were first used by the Indians of the Americas before being discovered by Europeans. Even today, researchers continue to look for new medicines among the indigenous peoples of the South American jungles. One of the first discoveries was quinine for the treatment of malaria. It was originally derived from the bark of the *Chinchona* tree, named for the *Marquesa de Chinchón*.

Las ciencias sociales: La sociología
Antes de leer

PRESENTATION *(page 466)*

A. Assign the definitions on page 466 as homework before the reading.

B. Ask students to identify some subcultures in the U.S.

Lectura

PRESENTATION *(page 466)*

A. Have students skim the passage for cognates.

B. Ask individual students to read a few sentences aloud.

C. Ask comprehension questions such as: *¿Qué es una subcultura? ¿Cuál es una cultura dominante? ¿Cuál es un ejemplo de comportamiento distinto y especial? ¿Por qué entran los adolescentes en el estado de adulto más tarde en los EE.UU. que en otros países? ¿Qué adoptan los adolescentes?*

LAS CIENCIAS SOCIALES: LA SOCIOLOGÍA

Antes de leer

Look up the definitions of culture and subculture.

Lectura

Los sociólogos identifican variedades dentro de una cultura. A estas variedades les damos el nombre de subcultura. Una subcultura es un segmento de la sociedad que tiene unas costumbres y unos valores diferentes de los de la sociedad mayor. Los miembros de una subcultura forman parte de la cultura dominante. Pero al mismo tiempo muestran un comportamiento distinto y especial.

Una de las subculturas más importantes es la subcultura de los adolescentes. En los EE.UU., por razones educacionales y económicas, los adolescentes no entran en el estado de adulto hasta más tarde que en otras sociedades. La sociedad segrega a los adolescentes en escuelas superiores y universidades. Como todo el mundo, ellos están buscando una identidad. Adoptan la última moda de su grupo: la música, los ídolos de la canción o del cine, una ropa particular, una forma de peinarse, un habla especial, hasta las preferencias en la comida. La moda "punk", que se vio en Europa igual que en América, es un ejemplo. Los T shirt, los jeans y las camisas de deporte, especialmente las que llevan emblemas de

universidades norteamericanas, son el uniforme de los jóvenes en todas partes. Nadie se pone zapatos. Los jóvenes se ponen tenis o zapatillas de baloncesto. El "rock", el "heavy metal" y el "rap" se oyen igual en Madrid que en Roma, Londres o Nueva York. Y allí también sirven pizza, hamburguesas, Coca Cola y papas fritas a los clientes jóvenes en restaurantes norteamericanos de comida rápida.

Otras subculturas se basan en la etnicidad, en la región geográfica, en la profesión, o en los intereses de los miembros.

CRITICAL THINKING ACTIVITY

(Thinking skills: supporting statements with reasons)

Ask students for their interpretation of and comments on these statements:

a. *"La sociedad segrega a los adolescentes en escuelas superiores y universidades."*

b. *"En los EE.UU., por razones educacionales y económicas, los adolescentes no entran en el estado de adulto hasta más tarde que en otras sociedades."*

¡Esta es tu página!
Anímate y cuéntanos
tus gustos y
opiniones. Tu carta
participará en el
sorteo

de tres cajitas de un
maravilloso
perfume,
creado
especialmente para
ti. ¡Suerte!

1. Escoge las 5 secciones que más te "molen" de TeEN:

Chicas TeEN — Los secretos del amor
Papel de carta — He tenido un sueño
Canciones para ti — Tablón de anuncios
Fotonovela — Tus versos
Pósters — Horóscopo TeEN
Te lo cuenta una fan — 8 fichas "Tú y él"

2. ¿Qué reportaje te ha gustado más de este TeEN?...........

3. Tus ídolos favoritos son:
Cantantes..........
Grupos..........
Actores..........
Y los más guapos..........
4. Los programas o series de televisión que nunca te pierdes son: ....
5. ¿Qué regalo te ha gustado más de TeEN?...........
6. ¿Compras otras revistas? NO ☐ SI ☐ ¿Cuáles?...........
7. Nombre.......... Edad..........
Apellidos..........
Dirección completa..........

Envía tu encuesta a: TeEN Encuesta nº 21.
Apartado de Correos nº 35. 227. 08080 Barcelona.

Después de leer

A **Los adolescentes.** Completen.

1. Una subcultura es un ___ de la cultura dominante.
2. Las costumbres de una subcultura son ___ de las del grupo dominante.
3. Los adolescentes entran en el mundo adulto más tarde en los EE.UU. por razones ___ y ___.
4. La sociedad segrega a los adolescentes y adultos jóvenes en ___ y ___.
5. Los jóvenes buscan una ___.
6. La moda "punk" existió en ___ y en ___.
7. Tres clases de música que escuchan los jóvenes son el ___, el ___ y el ___.
8. En lugar de zapatos, los jóvenes se ponen ___.
9. Algunas subculturas se basan en la ___ o la ___.

B **Seguimiento.** Contesten.

1. Describa la ropa y otras características de una subcultura de los EE.UU.
2. ¿Cuál es un ejemplo del habla especial de una subcultura?
3. ¿Cuál es un ejemplo de una cultura que se basa en una profesión u ocupación? Explique.

FONDO ACADÉMICO **467**

Después de leer

PRESENTATION *(page 467)*

A. Go over Exercise A orally in class. Ask students to identify where the information is given in the passage.
B. For Exercise B, have pairs of students work together to develop responses.

ANSWERS

Ejercicio A
1. segmento
2. diferentes
3. educacionales y económicas
4. escuelas superiores y universidades
5. identidad
6. Europa, América
7. rock, heavy metal, rap
8. zapatillas de baloncesto
9. etnicidad, la región geográfica, la profesión, los intereses de los miembros

Ejercicio B
Answers will vary.

LEARNING FROM REALIA

In this ad on page 467 there is another example of the use of English in ads and brands. Ask students the following questions about the ad: *¿Qué es TeEN? ¿Por qué dieron el nombre TeEN a la revista? ¿Qué regalo le van a dar a las personas que ganan? ¿Qué preguntas les hacen a los jóvenes?*

Have students try to answer the questions on the survey themselves.

Literatura
Antes de leer

PRESENTATION *(page 468)*

A. Assign the *Antes de leer* exercise as homework.

B. Go over the introductory material in *Antes de leer*. Find out if anyone has read any epics or parts of epics, and have them comment. Ask why they think the authors of many early epics are unknown.

C. As follow-up to the homework, assign one student to ask biographical questions about the author. The student should ask questions such as: *¿De dónde es? ¿Dónde nació? ¿Cuándo nació? ¿Dónde murió? ¿Dónde sirvió de soldado?*

Lectura

PRESENTATION
(pages 468–469)

A. Have students read the first paragraph silently.

B. You might ask questions such as the following about the content: *¿Cuáles son algunos poemas épicos europeos? ¿Quién escribió La Araucana? ¿Dónde luchó él? ¿Contra quiénes lucharon los españoles? Describan a los araucanos.*

C. Select individual students to read the speech by Colocolo and the paragraphs that follow. Call on students to orally summarize, each of the paragraphs.

LA LITERATURA: LA ARAUCANA

Antes de leer

Epic poetry deals with the adventures, conquests, and exploits of national heroes. Epic poems constitute the first European literature: Homer's *Iliad* and *Odyssey*, the *Sagas* of the Norse peoples, England's *Beowulf*, the *Chanson de Roland* of France. The authors of most of the early epic poems are unknown. Not so with *La Araucana*, the epic of Spanish America. In preparation, please read a brief biography of Alonso de Ercilla y Zúñiga, and the major events in the conquest of Chile by Pedro de Valdivia.

Lectura

El poema épico de la literatura hispano-americana es *La Araucana*. Ya sabemos que la mayoría de los autores de los poemas épicos europeos son anónimos. No es así con *La Araucana*. Lo escribió Alonso de Ercilla, un soldado español que luchó en la conquista de Chile durante el siglo XVI contra los araucanos, una raza de indios fuerte y valiente. Al principio los españoles fueron victoriosos, pero los araucanos no quisieron aceptar la idea de vivir bajo el dominio de un poder extranjero[1].

Un día habló Colocolo, su jefe[2]:
—Soy un hombre viejo. La lucha contra los españoles es difícil. Necesitamos otro jefe, no un viejo como yo. Necesitamos un joven fuerte. Aquí tengo el tronco de un árbol. El hombre que por más tiempo soporte el tronco en los hombros va a ser nuestro nuevo jefe.

Se levantaron algunos jóvenes. Cada uno levantó el tronco y lo puso en sus hombros. Luego se levantó Lincoya. Él soportó el tronco por veinte y cuatro horas. ¡Tiene que ser Lincoya el nuevo jefe! Pero después se presentó Caupolicán, un joven fuerte y severo. Levantó el tronco. Anduvo, anduvo, anduvo. Pasaron más de veinte y cuatro horas, y finalmente tiró el tronco al suelo con gran ceremonia. Todos vinieron a recibir a su nuevo jefe.

Alonso de Ercilla

CRITICAL THINKING ACTIVITY

(Thinking skills: supporting ideas; drawing conclusions)

Write the following on the board or on an overhead transparency.

Alonso de Ercilla fought against the Araucanos by day and wrote an epic praising them by night. Comment on this and contrast it with the traditional epics that glorify national heroes.

Empezó de nuevo la batalla con los españoles. Los campos verdes se pusieron rojos. Los araucanos ganaron una gran victoria. Capturaron a Valdivia, el capitán español. Pero continuaron las batallas, y por fin los españoles capturaron a Caupolicán y también a su esposa, Fresia. Fresia, con su infante en los brazos, le gritó a su marido que no quería ser la esposa de un hombre cautivo[3]. Así el gran jefe de los indios sufrió un insulto severo. Unos días después, los españoles lo torturaron, y por fin lo mataron. Así terminó otra guerra cruel.

[1] extranjero   *foreign power*
[2] jefe   *leader*
[3] cautivo   *captured*

Después de leer

A   Los araucanos.   Contesten.

1. ¿Quién fue el viejo jefe de los araucanos?
2. Describa a los araucanos.
3. ¿Qué no quisieron aceptar los araucanos?
4. ¿En qué consistió la prueba para elegir un nuevo jefe?
5. ¿Por cuánto tiempo llevó el tronco Lincoya?
6. ¿Quién llevó el tronco por más tiempo?
7. ¿A quién capturaron los araucanos?
8. ¿Quiénes capturaron a Caupolicán?
9. ¿Qué le hicieron a Caupolicán?
10. ¿Qué no quería Fresia?

B   Seguimiento.   Escriban.

1. Write, in Spanish, a biographical sketch of Pedro de Valdivia.
2. Tests of strength or valor are common in epics. What others can you think of?
3. Describe the "severe insult" suffered by Caupolicán.
4. Discuss the treatment of Caupolicán by his captors.

AMÉRICA DEL SUR

CHILE

Después de leer

PRESENTATION *(page 469)*

A. You may wish to have students ask and answer the questions in Exercise A orally, or you might assign this exercise as written homework.
B. For Exercise B have students do number 1 as written homework. Numbers 2, 3, and 4 are appropriate for class discussion.

Ejercicios

ANSWERS

Ejercicio A
1. Colocolo
2. Son fuertes y valientes.
3. la idea de vivir bajo el dominio de un poder extranjero
4. soportar un tronco
5. 24 horas
6. Caupolicán
7. Valdivia
8. los españoles
9. lo torturaron y lo mataron
10. ser la esposa de un hombre cautivo

Ejercicio B
Answers will vary.

ABOUT THE LANGUAGE

Remind students that in literature words often have a meaning beyond their literal one. Ask the meaning of *"Los campos verdes se pusieron rojos."*

GEOGRAPHY CONNECTION

Have students use a map of Chile to describe the campaigns of Pedro de Valdivia against the Araucanos. One of Chile's major cities is Valdivia. Have them locate it on a map.

DID YOU KNOW?

The Araucanians destroyed Spanish settlements south to the Bío Bío river in 1598. They continued to fight against the Spanish in the 17th and 18th centuries. Many captured horses and escaped across the Andes into Argentina. They were not fully subjugated in Chile until 1883. There are over 200,000 Araucanians in Chile today.

APÉNDICES

470

471

MAPAS

ESPAÑA

FRANCIA

ANDORRA

PIRINEOS

Mar Cantábrico

Golfo de Vizcaya

San Sebastián
Pamplona
Bilbao
Santander
Oviedo
León
Burgos
Zaragoza
CORDILLERA CANTÁBRICA
Santiago de Compostela
Valladolid
Salamanca
Segovia
Ávila
Madrid
SIERRA DE GUADARRAMA
Barcelona

Ebro
Río
Duero

PORTUGAL

ESPAÑA

Río Tajo
Río Guadiana

Toledo
Sierra Morena
SIERRA MORENA

Valencia
Alicante
Murcia

Granada
SIERRA NEVADA
Córdoba
Málaga
Sevilla
Río Guadalquivir
Jerez de la Frontera
Cádiz
Gibraltar (R.U.)
Ceuta (Esp.)
Tánger

Océano Atlántico

Lisboa

ISLAS BALEARES

Menorca
Mallorca
Palma de Mallorca
Ibiza
Formentera

Mar Mediterráneo

ÁFRICA

Penón de Alhucemas (Esp.)
Melilla (Esp.)
Islas Chafarinas (Esp.)
Peñón de Vélez de la Gomera (Esp.)
MARRUECOS

ARGELIA

N
O — E
S

0   100   200
Kilómetros

ISLAS CANARIAS

Lanzarote
Fuerteventura
Santa Cruz de Tenerife
Las Palmas
Gran Canaria
La Palma
Gomera
Tenerife
Hierro

ÁFRICA

473

LA AMÉRICA DEL SUR

Mar Caribe

Maracaibo ⊕ Caracas
VENEZUELA GUYANA
Georgetown SURINAM
Medellín Paramaribo Cayena
Bogotá GUAYANA
COLOMBIA FRANCESA

Islas
Galápagos
(Ecuador)

Quito ⊕
ECUADOR
Guayaquil Iquitos
Río Amazonas

PERÚ BRASIL
Lima Cuzco
BOLIVIA Brasilia
La Paz
Sucre

CORDILLERA DE LOS ANDES

PARAGUAY São Paulo
Asunción Río de Janeiro

Océano
Pacífico

Córdoba
Rosario URUGUAY
Valparaíso Buenos Aires Montevideo
Santiago
ARGENTINA Mar del Plata
CHILE

Puerto Montt Bariloche

Océano
Atlántico

Islas
Malvinas
(R.U.)

N
O E
S

0 500 1000
Kilómetros

Punta Arenas

474

110° 100° 90° 80° 70° 60° 50° 40° 30° 20°

MÉXICO, LA AMÉRICA CENTRAL Y EL CARIBE

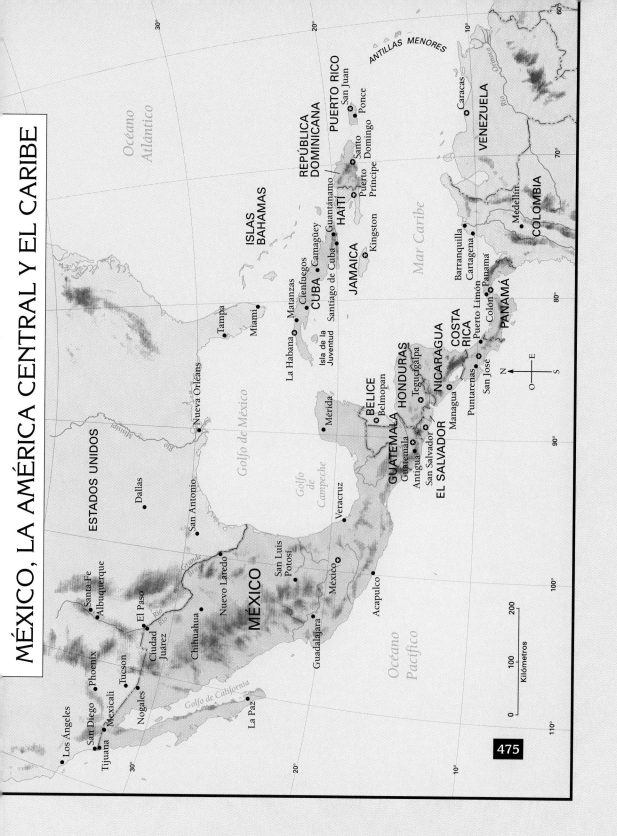

Océano Atlántico

ANTILLAS MENORES

PUERTO RICO
San Juan
Ponce

REPÚBLICA DOMINICANA

Caracas

VENEZUELA

Río Orinoco

Santo Domingo

HAITÍ
Puerto Príncipe

COLOMBIA
Medellín

ISLAS BAHAMAS

Guantánamo

Kingston

JAMAICA

Mar Caribe

CUBA
Matanzas
Cienfuegos
Camagüey
Santiago de Cuba

La Habana
Isla de la Juventud

Barranquilla
Cartagena
Puerto Limón
Colón
Panamá

Tampa
Miami

NICARAGUA
COSTA RICA
PANAMÁ

HONDURAS
Tegucigalpa

Managua
Puntarenas
San José

N
E
S
O

BELICE
Belmopan

Mérida

GUATEMALA
Guatemala
Antigua
San Salvador
EL SALVADOR

ESTADOS UNIDOS

Golfo de México

Golfo de Campeche

Veracruz

Dallas

San Antonio

Nueva Orleans

Misisipi

Río Grande

MÉXICO
San Luis Potosí
México

Acapulco

Santa Fe
Albuquerque

El Paso
Ciudad Juárez
Chihuahua
Nuevo Laredo

Río Grande / Río Bravo

Guadalajara

Phoenix
Tucson

Los Ángeles
San Diego
Tijuana
Mexicali
Nogales

Golfo de California

La Paz

Océano Pacífico

200

100

Kilómetros

0

475

30°
20°
60°
10°
70°
80°
90°
100°
110°
20°
30°
10°

VERBOS

A. Verbos regulares

INFINITIVO	**hablar** _to speak_	**comer** _to eat_	**vivir** _to live_
PRESENTE PROGRESIVO	estar hablando	estar comiendo	estar viviendo
PRESENTE	yo hablo tú hablas él, ella, Ud. habla nosotros(as) hablamos _vosotros(as) habláis_ ellos, ellas, Uds. hablan	yo como tú comes él, ella, Ud. come nosotros(as) comemos _vosotros(as) coméis_ ellos, ellas, Uds. comen	yo vivo tú vives él, ella, Ud. vive nosotros(as) vivimos _vosotros(as) vivís_ ellos, ellas, Uds. viven
PRETÉRITO	yo hablé tú hablaste él, ella, Ud. habló nosotros(as) hablamos _vosotros(as) hablasteis_ ellos, ellas, Uds. hablaron	yo comí tú comiste él, ella, Ud. comió nosotros(as) comimos _vosotros(as) comisteis_ ellos, ellas, Uds. comieron	yo viví tú viviste él, ella, Ud. vivió nosotros(as) vivimos _vosotros(as) vivisteis_ ellos, ellas, Uds. vivieron

B. Verbos regulares con cambio en la primera persona singular
(Regular verbs with stem change in the first person singular)

INFINITIVO	**conocer** _to know_	**salir** _to leave_	**ver** _to see_
PRESENTE PROGRESIVO	estar conociendo	estar saliendo	estar viendo
PRESENTE	yo conozco	yo salgo	yo veo

C. Verbos con cambio radical
(Stem-changing verbs)

INFINITIVO	**preferir**[1] **(e>ie)** *to prefer*	**volver**[2] **(o>ue)** *to return*	**pedir**[3] **(e>i)** *to ask for*
PRESENTE PROGRESIVO	estar prefiriendo	estar volviendo	estar pidiendo
PRESENTE	yo prefiero tú prefieres él, ella, Ud. prefiere nosotros(as) preferimos *vosotros(as) preferís* ellos, ellas, Uds. prefieren	yo vuelvo tú vuelves él, ella, Ud. vuelve nosotros(as) volvemos *vosotros(as) volvéis* ellos, ellas, Uds. vuelven	yo pido tú pides él, ella, Ud. pide nosotros(as) pedimos *vosotros(as) pedís* ellos, ellas, Uds. piden
PRETÉRITO	yo preferí tú preferiste él, ella, Ud. prefirió nosotros(as) preferimos *vosotros(as) preferisteis* ellos, ellas, Uds. prefirieron	yo volví tú volviste él, ella, Ud. volvió nosotros(as) volvimos *vosotros(as) volvisteis* ellos, ellas, Uds. volvieron	yo pedí tú pediste él, ella, Ud. pidió nosotros(as) pedimos *vosotros(as) pedisteis* ellos, ellas, Uds. pidieron

D. Verbos irregulares

INFINITIVO	**andar** *to walk*	**dar** *to give*	**decir** *to tell, to say*
PRESENTE PROGRESIVO	estar andando	estar dando	estar diciendo
PRESENTE	yo ando tú andas él, ella, Ud. anda nosotros(as) andamos *vosotros(as) andáis* ellos, ellas, Uds. andan	yo doy tú das él, ella, Ud. da nosotros(as) damos *vosotros(as) dais* ellos, ellas, Uds. dan	yo digo tú dices él, ella, Ud. dice nosotros(as) decimos *vosotros(as) decís* ellos, ellas, Uds. dicen
PRETÉRITO	yo anduve tú anduviste él, ella, Ud. anduvo nosotros(as) anduvimos *vosotros(as) anduvisteis* ellos, ellas, Uds. anduvieron	yo di tú diste él, ella, Ud. dio nosotros(as) dimos *vosotros(as) disteis* ellos, ellas, Uds. dieron	yo dije tú dijiste él, ella, Ud. dijo nosotros(as) dijimos *vosotros(as) dijisteis* ellos, ellas, Uds. dijeron

[1] Verbos similares: *sugerir*

[2] Verbos similares: *morir, jugar*

[3] Verbos similares: *freír, repetir, seguir, servir*

Verbos irregulares

INFINITIVO	**empezar** *to begin*	**estar** *to be*	**hacer** *to do*
PRESENTE PROGRESIVO	estar empezando		estar haciendo
PRESENTE	yo empiezo tú empiezas él, ella, Ud. empieza nosotros(as) empezamos *vosotros(as) empezáis* ellos, ellas, Uds. empiezan	yo estoy tú estás él, ella, Ud. está nosotros(as) estamos *vosotros(as) estáis* ellos, ellas, Uds. están	yo hago tú haces él, ella, Ud. hace nosotros(as) hacemos *vosotros(as) hacéis* ellos, ellas, Uds. hacen
PRETÉRITO	yo empecé tú empezaste él, ella, Ud. empezó nosotros(as) empezamos *vosotros(as) empezasteis* ellos, ellas, Uds. empezaron	yo estuve tú estuviste él, ella, Ud. estuvo nosotros(as) estuvimos *vosotros(as) estuvisteis* ellos, ellas, Uds. estuvieron	yo hice tú hiciste él, ella, Ud. hizo nosotros(as) hicimos *vosotros(as) hicisteis* ellos, ellas, Uds. hicieron
INFINITIVO	**ir** *to go*	**poder** *to be able*	**poner** *to put*
PRESENTE PROGRESIVO	estar yendo	estar pudiendo	estar poniendo
PRESENTE	yo voy tú vas él, ella, Ud. va nosotros(as) vamos *vosotros(as) vais* ellos, ellas, Uds. van	yo puedo tú puedes él, ella, Ud. puede nosotros(as) podemos *vosotros(as) podéis* ellos, ellas, Uds. pueden	yo pongo tú pones él, ella, Ud. pone nosotros(as) ponemos *vosotros(as) ponéis* ellos, ellas, Uds. ponen
PRETÉRITO	yo fui tú fuiste él, ella, Ud. fue nosotros(as) fuimos *vosotros(as) fuisteis* ellos, ellas, Uds. fueron	yo pude tú pudiste él, ella, Ud. pudo nosotros(as) pudimos *vosotros(as) pudisteis* ellos, ellas, Uds. pudieron	yo puse tú pusiste él, ella, Ud. puso nosotros(as) pusimos *vosotros(as) pusisteis* ellos, ellas, Uds. pusieron

Verbos irregulares

INFINITIVO	**querer** *to want*	**saber** *to know*	**ser** *to be*
PRESENTE PROGRESIVO	estar queriendo	estar sabiendo	estar siendo
PRESENTE	yo quiero tú quieres él, ella, Ud. quiere nosotros(as) queremos *vosotros(as) queréis* ellos, ellas, Uds. quieren	yo sé tú sabes él, ella, Ud. sabe nosotros(as) sabemos *vosotros(as) sabéis* ellos, ellas, Uds. saben	yo soy tú eres él, ella, Ud. es nosotros(as) somos *vosotros(as) sois* ellos, ellas, Uds. son
PRETÉRITO	yo quise tú quisiste él, ella, Ud. quiso nosotros(as) quisimos *vosotros(as) quisisteis* ellos, ellas, Uds. quisieron	yo supe tú supiste él, ella, Ud. supo nosotros(as) supimos *vosotros(as) supisteis* ellos, ellas, Uds. supieron	yo fui tú fuiste él, ella, Ud. fue nosotros(as) fuimos *vosotros(as) fuisteis* ellos, ellas, Uds. fueron
INFINITIVO	**tener** *to have*	**traer** *to bring*	**venir** *to come*
PRESENTE PROGRESIVO	estar teniendo	estar trayendo	estar viniendo
PRESENTE	yo tengo tú tienes él, ella, Ud. tiene nosotros(as) tenemos *vosotros(as) tenéis* ellos, ellas, Uds. tienen	yo traigo tú traes él, ella, Ud. trae nosotros(as) traemos *vosotros(as) traéis* ellos, ellas, Uds. traen	yo vengo tú vienes él, ella, Ud. viene nosotros(as) venimos *vosotros(as) venís* ellos, ellas, Uds. vienen
PRETÉRITO	yo tuve tú tuviste él, ella, Ud. tuvo nosotros(as) tuvimos *vosotros(as) tuvisteis* ellos, ellas, Uds. tuvieron	yo traje tú trajiste él, ella, Ud. trajo nosotros(as) trajimos *vosotros(as) trajisteis* ellos, ellas, Uds. trajeron	yo vine tú viniste él, ella, Ud. vino nosotros(as) vinimos *vosotros(as) vinisteis* ellos, ellas, Uds. vinieron

E. Verbos reflexivos

INFINITIVO	**lavarse** *to wash oneself*		
PRESENTE PROGRESIVO	estar lavándose		
PRESENTE	yo me lavo tú te lavas él, ella, Ud. se lava nosotros(as) nos lavamos *vosotros(as) os laváis* ellos, ellas, Uds. se lavan		
PRETÉRITO	yo me lavé tú te lavaste él, ella, Ud. se lavó nosotros(as) nos lavamos *vosotros(as) os lavasteis* ellos, ellas, Uds. se lavaron		

F. Verbos reflexivos con cambio radical

INFINITIVO	**acostarse (o>ue)** *to go to bed*	**despertarse (e>ie)** *to wake up*	**dormirse (o>ue, u)** *to fall asleep*
PRESENTE PROGRESIVO	estar acostándose	estar despertándose	estar durmiéndose
PRESENTE	yo me acuesto tú te acuestas él, ella, Ud. se acuesta nosotros(as) nos acostamos *vosotros(as) os acostáis* ellos, ellas, Uds. se acuestan	yo me despierto tú te despiertas él, ella, Ud. se despierta nosotros(as) nos despertamos *vosotros(as) os despertáis* ellos, ellas, Uds. se despiertan	yo me duermo tú te duermes él, ella, Ud. se duerme nosotros(as) nos dormimos *vosotros(as) os dormís* ellos, ellas, Uds. se duermen
PRETÉRITO	yo me acosté tú te acostaste él, ella, Ud. se acostó nosotros(as) nos acostamos *vosotros(as) os acostasteis* ellos, ellas, Uds. se acostaron	yo me desperté tú te despertaste él, ella, Ud. se despertó nosotros(as) nos despertamos *vosotros(as) os despertasteis* ellos, ellas, Uds. se despertaron	yo me dormí tú te dormiste él, ella, Ud. se durmió nosotros(as) nos dormimos *vosotros(as) os dormisteis* ellos, ellas, Uds. se durmieron

Verbos reflexivos con cambio radical			
INFINITIVO	**divertirse (e>ie, i)** *to enjoy oneself*	**sentarse** *to sit down*	**vestirse (e>i, i)** *to dress oneself*
PRESENTE PROGRESIVO	estar divirtiéndose	estar sentándose	estar vistiéndose
PRESENTE	yo me divierto tú te diviertes él, ella, Ud. se divierte nosotros(as) nos divertimos *vosotros(as) os divertís* ellos, ellas, Uds. se divierten	yo me siento tú te sientas él, ella, Ud. se sienta nosotros(as) nos sentamos *vosotros(as) os sentáis* ellos, ellas, Uds. se sientan	yo me visto tú te vistes él, ella, Ud. se viste nosotros(as) nos vestimos *vosotros(as) os vestís* ellos, ellas, Uds. se visten

PRETÉRITO	yo me divertí
	tú te divertiste
	él, ella, Ud. se divirtió
	nosotros(as) nos divertimos
	vosotros(as) os divertisteis
	ellos, ellas, Uds. se
	    divirtieron
		yo me senté
		tú te sentaste
		él, ella, Ud. se sentó
		nosotros(as) nos sentamos
		vosotros(as) os sentasteis
		ellos, ellas, Uds. se
		    sentaron
			yo me vestí
			tú te vestiste
			él, ella, Ud. se vistió
			nosotros(as) nos vestimos
			vosotros(as) os vestistéis
			ellos, ellas, Uds. se
			    vistieron

VOCABULARIO
ESPAÑOL-INGLÉS

The *Vocabulario español-inglés* contains all productive and receptive vocabulary from the text.

The reference numbers following each productive entry indicate the chapter and vocabulary section in which the word is introduced. For example **3.2** means that the word first appeared in *Capítulo 3, Palabras 2.* **BV** refers to the introductory *Bienvenidos* lesson.

Words without a chapter reference indicate receptive vocabulary (not taught in the *Palabras* sections).

A

abordar to get on, board, 8.1
  el pase de abordar boarding pass, 8.1
abotonado(a) buttoned
abotonar to button
la abreviatura abbreviation
el abrigo overcoat, 13.1
abril April, BV
abrir to open, 8.2
la abuela grandmother, 6.1
el abuelo grandfather, 6.1
los abuelos grandparents, 6.1
abundante abundant
aburrido(a) boring, 1.1
aburrir to bore, 13
el abuso abuse
la academia academy
académico(a) academic
acampar to camp, 16.2
el aceite oil, 15.2
aceptar accept
acompañar to accompany
acostarse (ue) to go to bed, 16.1
la actividad activity, 5.2
el actor actor, 12.2
la actriz actress, 12.2
la actualidad present time
actualmente at present
acuático(a): el esquí acuático, water skiing, 11.1
acudir to go; to attend
el acueducto aqueduct
acuerdo: de acuerdo OK, all right
acusar to accuse
adecuado(a) adequate
la adicción addiction
adiós good-bye, BV
la adivinanza riddle, puzzle
adivinar to guess
el/la adolescente adolescent
¿adónde? (to) where?, 4
adoptar to adopt
la aduana customs, 8.2
aeróbico(a) aerobic, 10.2
el aeropuerto airport, 8.1
afeitarse to shave, 16.1
  la crema de afeitar shaving cream, 16.2
las afueras outskirts, 5.1
el/la agente agent, 8.1
la aglomeración collection
agonizante dying
agosto August (m), BV
agotador(a) exhausting

agradable pleasant
la agricultura agriculture
el agua (f.) water, 11.1
  el agua de colonia cologne
  el agua mineral mineral water
  esquiar en el agua to water ski, 11.1
ahora now
aislado(a) isolated
al (a + el) to the
  al aire libre outdoors, 9.2
la alberca swimming pool, 11.2
el albergue juvenil youth hostel, 16.2
el alcohol alcohol
el alcoholismo alchoholism
alegre happy
alemán (alemana) German
la alergia allergy, 10.2
el alga seaweed
el álgebra algebra, 2.2
algo something, 9.1
alguien somebody, 13
algún, alguno(a) some, any
la alimentación food
alimentar to feed
alimentario (a) nourishing
el almacén department store
la almeja clam
el almuerzo lunch, 5.2
alquilar to rent, 11.1
alrededor de around, 6.2
la alteración alteration
alto(a) tall, 1.1; high, 3.2
la altura height
el/la alumno(a) student, 1.1
allá there
allí there
amable kind, 2.1
amarillo(a) yellow, 13.2
amazonas: el Río Amazonas Amazon River
amazónico(a) Amazon, Amazonian
la ameba amoeba
la América del Sur South America, 8.1
americano(a) American, 1.2
el/la amigo(a) friend, 1.1
amplio(a) large, roomy
el análisis analysis
analizar to analyze
anaranjado(a) orange (color), 13.2
el/la anatomista anatomist
ancho(a) wide, 13.2
la anchura width

andar to walk
  andar en monopatín to skateboard, 9
el andén railway platform, 14.1
andino(a) Andean
el animal animal
anoche last night, 11.2
anónimo(a) anonymous
el anorak anorak, 9.1
anotar una carrera to score a run (baseball)
antártico(a) antarctic
anteayer the day before yesterday, 11.2
los anteojos de (para el) sol sunglasses, 11.1
antes before
los antibióticos antibiotics, 10
antiguo(a) ancient
antipático(a) unpleasant (person), 1.1
la antropología anthropology
el/la antropólogo(a) anthropologist
el anuncio advertisement, announcement
el año year, 11.2
  el año pasado last year, 11.2
  este año this year, 11.2
  hace muchos años it's been many years
aparecer (zc) to appear
el apartamento apartment, 5.1
aparte separate
el apellido last name
aplaudir to applaud, 12.2
el aplauso applause
el apodo nickname
aprender to learn, 5.2
el aprendizaje learning
apretar to pinch, 13.2
  Me aprieta(n). It (They) pinch(es) me., 13.2
aprobado(a) passing
aproximadamente approximately
los apuntes notes, 3.2
  tomar apuntes to take notes, 3.2
aquel, aquella that, 9.2
aquí here
el/la árbitro(a) referee, 7.1
el árbol tree, 6.2
  el árbol genealógico family tree
el área (f.) area
la arena sand, 11.1
argentino(a) Argentinian, 2.1
la aritmética arithmetic, 2.2

armar una tienda to put up a tent, 16.2
arqueológico(a) archeological
el **aro** hoop, 7.2
el **arroz** rice, 15.2
el **arte** (f.) art, 2.2
  las bellas artes fine arts
el **artefacto** artifact
el **artículo** article
  el artículo de tocador toiletry item
el/la **artista** artist, 12.2
  artístico: el patínaje artístico figure skating, 12
  asado(a) roast
la **ascendencia** ancestry
el **ascensor** elevator, 5.1
  así thus
el **asiento** seat, 8.1
  el número del asiento seat number, 8.1
la **asignatura** subject, 2.2
el **asistente, la asistenta de vuelo** flight attendant, 8.2
  asistir to attend, to assist, 5.2
el **asombro** amazement
el **asunto** subject
  atacar to attack
el **aterrizaje** landing
  aterrizar to land, 8.2
  Atlántico: Océano Atlántico Atlantic Ocean
el/la **atleta** athelete
  atractivo(a) attractive, 1.2
  atrapar to catch, 7.2
  atravesar to cross
  aun even
  aunque although
  austral southern
el **autobús** bus, 3.1
  perder el autobús to miss the bus, 12.1
el **automóvil** car
el/la **autor(a)** author, 12.2
  avanzado(a) advanced
la **avenida** avenue, 5.1
el/la **aventurero** adventurer
el **avión** airplane, 8.1
  en avión by plane, 8.1
la **avioneta** small airplane
el **aviso** warning
  ayer yesterday, 11.1
  ayer por la mañana yesterday morning, 11.2
  ayer por la tarde yesterday afternoon, 11.2
la **ayuda** help
  ayudar to help

azul blue, 13.2
  azul marino navy blue

B

la **bacteria** bacterium
bailar to dance, 4.2
el **baile** dance
  bajar to go down, 9.1
  bajar del tren to get off the train, 14.2
  bajo below, 9.1
  bajo cero below zero, 9.1
  bajo(a) short (person), 1.1; low, 3.2
el **balcón** balcony, 6.2
el **balneario** beach resort, 11.1
el **baloncesto** basketball, 7.2
el **balón** ball, 7.1
la **ballena** whale
el **banco** bench, seat, BV; bank
la **banda** (music) band
la **bandera** flag
el **bañador** bathing suit, swimsuit, 11.1
  bañarse to go for a swim; to take a bath, 16.2
  baño: el traje de baño bathing suit, 11.1
  el cuarto de baño bathroom, 5.1
  barato(a) cheap, 13.1
el **barquito** small boat, 11.1
la **barra** bar (of soap), 16.2
el **barrio** neighborhood
  basar to base
  basarse to be based
la **báscula** scale, 8.1
la **base** base, 7.2
  básico(a) basic
el **básquetbol** basketball, 7.2
  bastante rather, quite, 1.1
el **bastón** pole, 9.1; club (golf), 11.2
la **batalla** battle
el **bate** bat, 7.2
el/la **bateador(a)** batter, 7.2
  batear to hit (baseball), 7.2
el **bautizo** baptism
  beber to drink, 5.2
el **béisbol** baseball, 7.2
  belga Belgian
la **belleza** beauty
  bello(a) beautiful
la **biblioteca** library, 4.1
la **bicicleta** bicycle, 6.2
  bien fine, well, BV
  bien cocido (hecho) well done (meat), 15.2
el **biftec** steak, 15.2

bilingüe bilingual
la **bilis** bile
el **billete** ticket, 8.1
  el billete de ida y vuelta round-trip ticket, 14.1
  el billete sencillo one-way ticket, 14.1
la **biología** biology, 2.2
el/la **biólogo(a)** biologist
  blanco(a) white, 13.2
el **bloc** writing pad, 3.2
  bloquear to block, 7.1
el **blue jean** blue jeans, 13.1
la **blusa** blouse, 13.1
  la blusa de cuello sin espalda halter, 13
el **blusón** jacket, 13.1
la **boca** mouth, 10.2
el **bocadillo** sandwich, 5.2
la **boda** wedding
la **bola** (golf) ball, 11.2
la **boletería** ticket window, 9.1
el **boleto** ticket, 8.1
el **bolígrafo** ballpoint pen, BV
  bonito(a) pretty, 6.2
  borde: al borde de on the brink of
  borde: a bordo (de) aboard, on board
el **bosque** forest, 16.2
la **bota** boot, 9.1
la **botánica** botany; herbalist's shop
la **botella** bottle
el **botiquín** first aid kit, 16.2
el **botón** button, 13.2
  brasileño(a) Brazilian
el **brazo** arm
  brillar to shine, 11.1
  brincar to bounce
  británico(a) British
  bronceadora: la crema bronceadora suntan lotion, 11.1
  bucear to skindive, 11.1
el **buceo** skindiving, 11.1
  bueno(a) good, 1.2
  buenas noches good evening, good night, BV
  buenas tardes good afternoon, BV
  buenos días hello, good morning, BV
el **burro** donkey
el **bus** bus, 3.1
  busca: en busca de searching for
  buscar to look for
la **butaca** orchestra seat, 12.1

C

el **caballero** man, gentleman, **13.1**
la **cabeza** head, **7.1**
    el **dolor de cabeza** headache, **10.1**
    cabotaje: de cabotaje domestic, **8**
cada each
la **cadena** chain
el **café** coffee, **5.2**; café
la **cafetería** cafeteria
la **caja** cash register, **13.1**
los **calcetines** socks, **13.1**
la **calculadora** calculator, **BV**
el **calendario** calendar
la **calificación** grade, **3**
la **calistenia** calisthenics
el **calor** heat, **11.1**
    Hace calor. It's hot., **11.1**
la **caloría** calorie, **10.2**
la **calle** street, **5.1**
la **callejuela** side street; alley
la **cama** bed, **10.1**
la **cámara: de cámara** court, royal
el **camarón** shrimp
    cambiar to change, exchange
el **cambio** change
    caminar to walk
la **caminata** hike, **16.2**
    dar una caminata to take a hike, **16.2**
el **camino** trail, path
la **camisa** shirt, **13.1**
    la camisa de deporte sports shirt
la **camiseta** undershirt, **13.1**
el **campamento** camp, **16.2**
la **campaña** campaign
el **campeonato** championship
el **camping** camping, **16.2**; campgrounds
    ir de camping to go camping
el **campo** country, **5.1**; field, **7.1**
    el campo de fútbol soccer field, **7.1**
    canadiense, canadiensa Canadian
el **canal** channel
el **canasto** basket, **7.2**
el **cáncer** cancer
la **canción** song
la **cancha** court (sports), **7.2**
    la cancha de tenis tennis court, **11.2**
    cansado(a) tired, **10.1**
el/la **cantante** singer
    cantar to sing, **4.2**

la **cantidad** quantity
la **cantimplora** canteen, **16.2**
la **cantina** lunchroom
el **cañón** canyon
la **capital** capital
    capturar to capture
la **cara** face, **16.1**
el **carácter** character
la **característica** characteristic
el **carbohidrato** carbohydrate, **10.2**
el **Caribe** Caribbean
la **carne** meat, **5.2**
    la carne de res beef
    carnívoro(a) carnivorous
    caro(a) expensive, **13.1**
la **carpa** tent, **16.2**
la **carretera** trail
el **carrito** (shopping) cart
el **carro** car, **3.1**
la **carta** letter, **5.2**
la **casa** house, **4.1**
    la casa de huéspedes guest house
    la casa particular private house
    en casa at home
    ir a casa to go home, **4.1**
    casi almost
    casi crudo rare (meat), **15.2**
el **casino** casino
el **caso** case
el **castigo** punishment
    castizo(a) real, legitimate, genuine
el **catarro** cold (medical), **10.1**
    tener catarro to have a cold, **10.1**
el **catálogo** catalogue
el/la **cátcher** catcher, **7.2**
    cate failing (grade)
la **catedral** cathedral
la **categoría** category
    católico(a) Catholic
la **causa** cause
    a causa de because of
    causar to cause
    cautivo(a) captured
    cazar to hunt
la **cebolla** onion
la **celebración** celebration
    celebrar to celebrate
la **célula** cell
la **cena** dinner, **5.2**
    cenar to dine
el **centígrado** centigrade, **9.1**
el **centro** center
    el centro comercial

    shopping center, **4.1**
Centroamérica Central America
    cepillarse to brush one's hair, **16.1**
el **cepillo** brush, **16.2**
    cerca de near
las **cercanías** outskirts
la **ceremonia** ceremony
    cero zero, **BV**
el **cesto** basket, **7.2**
la **chabola** shack
el **champú** shampoo, **16.2**
    chao good-bye, **BV**
la **chaqueta** jacket, **13.1**
el/la **chico(a)** boy (girl)
el **chimpancé** chimpanzee
    chino(a) Chinese
la **choza** shack
el **churro** a type of doughnut
el **ciclomotor** motorbike, **6.2**
el **cielo** sky, **11.1**
    cien(to) one hundred, **BV**
la **ciencia** science, **2.2**
    la ciencia política political science
    las ciencias naturales natural sciences
    las ciencias sociales social sciences, **2.2**
    de ciencia ficción science fiction (book, movie, etc.)
el/la **científico(a)** scientist
    científico(a) scientific
    cinco five, **BV**
    cincuenta fifty, **BV**
el **cine** movie theater, **12.1**
    cinematográfico(a) cinematographic
la **cinta** tape, **4.1**
el **cinturón** belt, **13.1**
la **circulación** circulation
el **círculo** circle
la **cirugía** surgery
el/la **cirujano(a)** surgeon
la **ciudad** city, **5.1**
el/la **ciudadano(a)** citizen
la **civilización** civilization
el **círculo** circle
    claro (que sí) of course
la **clase** class, **2.1**; type
    la clase media middle class
    clásico(a) classical, **4**
el/la **cliente** customer, **5.2**
el **clima** climate
    climático(a) climatic
la **clínica** clinic, **10.2**
    cocido(a) cooked, **15.2**

bien cocido (hecho) well done (meat), **15.2**
la **cocina** kitchen, **4.1**
el/la **cocinero(a)** cook, **15.1**
el **cóctel** cocktail
el **coche** car, **3.1**; train car, **14.2**
el **coche-cama** sleeping car, **14.2**
el **coche-comedor** dining car, **14.2**
el **cochinillo: el cochinillo asado** roast pork
coeducacional coeducational
la **cola** line (of people), **12.1**
  hacer cola to wait on line
la **colección** collection
el **colegio** high school, **1.1**
la **colina** hill, **16.2**
colombiano(a) Colombian, **1**
el **color** color, **13.2**
  de color crema, vino, café, oliva, marrón, turquesa cream-, wine-, coffee-, olive-, brown-, turquoise-colored, **13.2**
el/la **comandante** captain, **8.2**
combinar to combine
la **comedia** comedy
el **comedor** dining room, **5.1**
el **comentario** commentary
comenzar (ie) to begin, **7**
comer to eat, **5.2**
la **comida** meal, **5.2**
  la comida rápida fast food
como as, like
¿cómo? what?; how?, **1.1**
  ¿Cómo estás? How are you?
la **compañía** company
el/la **compañero(a)** friend, companion
la **comparación** comparison
comparar to compare
el **compartimiento** compartment, **14.2**
la **competencia** competition
competir to compete
completamente completely
completo(a) full
el **comportamiento** behavior; comportment
comprar to buy, **5.2**
compras: de compras shopping, **13.1**
comprender to understand, **5.2**
el **comprimido** pill, **10.2**
el **compuesto** compound
la **computadora** computer, **BV**
común common
comunicar to communicate
la **comunidad** community

con with
  con retraso late, **14.2**
  con una demora late, **14.2**
el **concierto** concert, **12.2**
el **concurso** contest
el **condominio** condominium
conducir to drive
la **conducta** conduct
el/la **conductor(a)** driver
la **conexión** connection
confrontar to confront
el **conjunto** outfit
conocer to know (a person), **9.1**
la **conquista** conquest
el **consejo** advice
conservar to conserve
considerar to consider
la **construcción** construction
construir to build, construct
la **consulta del médico** doctor's office, **10.2**
el **consultorio del médico** doctor's office, **10.2**
el/la **consumidor(a)** consumer
contemporáneo(a) contemporary
contar to count
contener to contain
contento(a) happy, **10.1**
contestar to answer
el **continente** continent
continuar to continue
contra against
contraer: contraer matrimonio to get married
contrario(a) opposite
  lo contrario the opposite
la **contribución** contribution
el **control** inspection, **8.1**
  el control de seguridad security inspection, **8.1**
  el control de pasaportes passport inspection, **8.2**
controlado(a) controlled
el **convento** convent
la **conversación** conversation
convertir to convert
la **copa** cup
  la Copa Mundial World Cup
el/la **copiloto** copilot, **8.2**
el **corazón** heart
la **corbata** necktie, **13.1**
corregir to correct
correr to run, **7.2**
corto(a) short, **13.2**
  el pantalón corto shorts
la **cosa** thing

los **cosméticos** cosmetics
la **costa** coast
  costar to cost, **13.1**
  costarricense, costarricensa Costa Rican
la **costumbre** custom
creer to believe
la **crema: la crema bronceadora** suntan lotion, **11.1**
  la crema de afeitar shaving cream, **16.2**
  la crema protectora suntan lotion, **11.1**
la **cremallera** zipper, **13.2**
criar to raise
cristalino(a) crystalline, transparent
la **crítica** criticism
crudo(a) raw, **15.2**
  casi crudo rare (meat), **15.2**
cruel cruel
cruzar to cross
el **cuaderno** notebook, **BV**
cuadrado(a) square
el **cuadrante** quadrant
el **cuadro** painting, picture, **12.2**
  cuadros: a cuadros plaid, **13.2**
¿cuál? what?, which?, **BV**
  ¿Cuál es la fecha de hoy? What is today's date?, **BV**
cualquier any
cuando when
¿cuándo? when?, **3.1**
¿cuánto(a)? how much?, **BV**
  ¿Cuánto cuesta? How much does it cost?, **13.1**
  ¿Cuánto es? How much is it?, **BV**
cuarenta forty, **BV**
cuarto(a) fourth, **5.1**
  menos cuarto a quarter to (the hour), **2**
  y cuarto a quarter after (the hour), **2**
el **cuarto** room, **5.1**; quart
  el cuarto de baño bathroom, **5.1**
  el cuarto de dormir bedroom, **5.1**
cuatro four, **BV**
cubano(a) Cuban, **1**
cubierto(a) covered, **9.2**
cubrir to cover
la **cuchara** spoon, **15.1**
la **cucharita** teaspoon, **15.1**
la **cuchilla** blade, **9.2**
el **cuchillo** knife, **15.1**
la **cuenta** bill, **12.2**

el **cuentagotas** eyedropper
el **cuerpo** body
la **cuesta** slope, **9.1**
  cuesta(n): ¿Cuánto
    cuesta(n)____? How much
    do(es)____cost?
  cuidado be careful
  cuidar to take care of
  cultivar to grow
  culto(a) cultured
la **cultura** culture
el **cumpleaños** birthday, **6.2**
  cumplir to be (so many years)
    old
  curar to cure
  curioso(a) curious
el **curso** course, **2.1**

D

la **dama** woman, lady, **13.1**
  dar to give, **4.2**
    darse prisa to rush, hurry
    dar (presentar) una
      representacíon to put on
      a performance, **12.2**
    dar una caminata to take a
      hike, **16.2**
el **dátil** date (fruit)
el **dato** fact
  de of, from, for, **1.1**
    de equipo (adj.) team, **7**
    de jazz jazz, **4**
    De nada. You're welcome.,
      BV
    de rock rock, **4**
    de vez en cuando now and
      then
  deber to owe; (+ infinitive)
    should, ought
  debido a due to
  decidir to decide
  decimal decimal
  décimo(a) tenth, **5.1**
  decir to say, tell, **9**
la **definición** definition
  dejar to leave (something
    behind), **12.2**
    dejar una propina to leave a
      tip, **12.2**
  del (de + el) from the, of the
  delante de in front of
  delicioso(a) delicious, **15.2**
  demasiado too, too much, **13.2**
la **demografía** demography
la **demora** delay, **14.2**
  con una demora late, **14.2**
  denso(a) thick

  dentro de in; inside, within
  depender to depend
el/la **dependiente** salesperson, **13.1**
el **deporte** sport, **2.2**
  deportivo(a) related to sports
  depredador(a) plunderer
la **derecha** right, **5.1**
  a la derecha to the right, **5.1**
  derrotar to defeat
  desaparecer (zc) to disappear
  desaprobado(a) failing
  desayunarse to eat breakfast,
    16.1
el **desayuno** breakfast, **5.2**
  descansar to rest
el **descanso** rest
  descender to descend
el/la **descendiente** descendant
  describir to describe
el **descubrimiento** discovery
  descubrir to discover
  desde from; since
  desgraciadamente
    unfortunately
el **desierto** desert
el **desodorante** deodorant, **16.2**
  despachar to dispense, to sell,
    10.2
  despegar to take off (airplane),
    8.2
  despertarse (ie) to wake up,
    16.1
  después de after, **4.1**
el **destino** destination, **8.1**
  con destino a to, **8**
la **detalle** detail
  determinar to determine
  devolver (ue) to return, **7.2**
el **día** day
la **diagnosis** diagnosis, **10.2**
  diario(a) daily; diary
  dibujar to sketch
el **díbujo** drawing, sketch
  diciembre December, **BV**
el **diente** tooth, **16.1**
la **dieta** diet, **10.2**
  diez ten, **BV**
la **diferencia** difference
  diferente different
  difícil difficult, **2.1**
  dinámico(a) dynamic
el **dinero** money
  ¡Dios mio! Gosh!
la **dirección** address
el **directivo** board of directors,
    management
el/la **director(a)** conductor, **12.2**;
    director

la **disciplina** subject, **2.2**
el **disco** record, **4.1**
la **discoteca** discotheque
la **disección** dissection
el/la **diseñador(a)** designer
  diseñar to design
  disfrutar to enjoy
la **distancia** distance
  distinto(a) distinct
el **distrito** district
la **diversión** amusement
  divertido(a) fun, **1.1**
  divertirse (ie, i) to enjoy
    oneself, **16.2**
  dividir to divide
el **divorcio** divorce
  doblado(a) dubbed
  doler to hurt, ache, **10.2**
    Me duele____. My____(part
      of body) hurts, aches., **10**
el **dolor** ache, pain, **10.1**
    el dolor de cabeza headache,
      10.1
    el dolor de estómago
      stomachache, **10.1**
    el dolor de garganta sore
      throat, **10.1**
  dominante dominant
el **domingo** Sunday, **BV**
  dominicano(a) Dominican
el **dominio** power
  ¿dónde? where?, **1.2**
  dormir (ue, u) to sleep, **7**
    dormirse (ue, u) to fall
      asleep, **16.1**
el **dormitorio** bedroom, **5.1**
  dos two, **BV**
la **dosis** dose, **10.2**
  dramáticamente dramatically
  dramático(a) dramatic
  driblar con to dribble, **7.2**
la **droga** drug, **10.2**
la **drogadicción** drug addiction
la **droguería** drugstore
la **ducha** shower, **16.2**
    tomar una ducha to take a
      shower, **16.2**
la **duda** doubt
    no hay duda there is no
      doubt
    duele: Me duele____.
      My____ (part of body)
      hurts, aches., **10**
  durante during, **4.2**
  duro(a) hard

E

echar to throw
  echar una siesta to take a nap, **11.1**
la **economía** economy
  la economía doméstica home economics, **2.2**
económico(a) economical
ecuatorial equatorial
ecuatoriano(a) Ecuadorean
la **Edad Media** Middle Ages
el **edificio** building, **5.1**
educacional educational
la **educación** education
  la educación cívica social studies, **2.2**
  la educación física physical education, **2.2**
educar to educate
el **efecto** effect
el **ejemplo** example
  por ejemplo for example
ejercer to practice (a profession)
el **ejercicio** exercise, **10.2**
  el ejercicio aeróbico aerobic exercise, **10.2**
  el ejercicio físico physical exercise, **10.2**
el **the** (m. sing.), **1.1**
él he, **1.1**
el **elefante** elephant
elegante elegant
el **elemento** element
ella she, her, **1.2**
ellos(as) they, them
el **embarque** boarding, **8**
el **emblema** emblem
el/la **emigrante** emigrant
la **emisión deportiva** sports broadcast, **5.2**
la **emoción** emotion; excitement
empatado(a) tied, **7**
empezar (ie) to begin, **7.1**
el/la **empleado(a)** employee
emplear to employ, use
la **empresa** business; company
en in, **1.1**
  en autobús by bus, **3.1**
  en avión by plane, **8**
  en carro (coche) by car, **3.1**
  en este momento right now, **8.1**
  en seguida at once, immediately, **16**
  en todas partes everywhere
encantador delightful

encantar to love, **13**
encestar to make a basket (basketball), **7.2**
encontrar to find
la **energía** energy
enero January, **BV**
enfadar to annoy, anger, **13**
la **enfermedad** sickness
el/la **enfermero(a)** nurse, **10.2**
el/la **enfermo(a)** sick person, **10.1**
enfermo(a) sick, **10.1**
enlazar to join, connect
enojar to annoy, anger, **13**
enorme enormous
la **ensalada** salad, **5.2**
la **enseñanza** teaching
enseñar to teach, **3.2**
entero(a) whole
el **entierro** burial
la **entrada** entrance, **6.2**; inning, **7.2**; admission ticket, **12.1**
entrar to enter, **3.1**
  entrar en escena to come on stage, **12.2**
entre between, among
el **entremés** appetizer
la **entrevista** interview
épico(a) epic
el **época** epoch, age
el **equilibrio** equilibrium
el **equipaje** baggage, luggage, **8.1**
  el equipaje de mano carry-on luggage, **8.1**
  el reclamo de equipaje baggage claim, **8.2**
el **equipo** team, **7.1**; equipment
equivalente equivalent
eres you (sing. fam.) are
es he/she/it is, **1.1**
la **escalera** stairway, **5.1**
los **escalofríos** chills, **10.1**
escandinavo(a) Scandinavian
escaparse to escape
el **escaparate** shop window, **13.1**
la **escena** scene; stage, **12.2**
  entrar en escena to come on stage, **12.2**
escoger to choose
escolar school (adj.), **3.1**
escribir to write, **5.2**
escrito(a) written
escuchar to listen, **4.1**
la **escuela** school, **1.1**
  la escuela intermedia junior high, middle school
  la escuela primaria elementary school
  la escuela secundaria high

school, **1.1**
  la escuela superior high school
  la escuela vocacional vocational school
el/la **escultor(a)** sculptor, **12.2**
la **escultura** sculpture
  eso: a eso de about, **3.1**
España Spain
el **español** Spanish (language), **2.2**
español(a) Spanish (adj.)
la **especialidad** specialty
el/la **especialista** specialist
especialmente especially
específico(a) specific
espectacular spectacular
el **espectáculo** show, performance, **12.2**
el/la **espectador(a)** spectator, **7**
el **espejo** mirror, **16.1**
esperar to wait for
la **espinaca** spinach
la **esposa** wife, **6.1**
el **esposo** husband, **6.1**
el **esquí** ski, **9.1**
el **esquí** skiing, **9.1**
  el esquí alpino downhill skiing, **9.1**
  el esquí acuático water skiing, **11.1**
  el esquí de descenso downhill skiing, **9.1**
  el esquí de fondo cross-country skiing, **9.1**
  el esquí nórdico cross-country skiing, **9.1**
el/la **esquiador(a)** skier, **9.1**
esquiar to ski, **9.1**
  esquiar en el agua to water ski, **11.1**
establecer to establish
la **estación** season; station; resort
  la estación de esquí ski resort, **9.1**
  la estación de ferrocarril train station, **14.1**
el **estadio** stadium, **7.1**
el **estado** state
  el estado libre asociado commonwealth
los **Estados Unidos** United States
estadounidense from the United States
están they/you (pl. form.) are, **4.1**
estar to be, **4.1**
  estar enfermo(a) to be sick
  estar en onda to be in vogue

estás you (sing. fam.) are
estatal of the state
la **estatua** statue, 12.2
el **este** east
este(a) this, 9
el **estilo** style
el **estómago** stomach, 10.1
  el dolor de estómago
    stomachache, 10.1
estornudar to sneeze, 10.1
estoy I am
estrecho(a) tight, 13.2; narrow
la **estrella** star
la **estructura** structure
el/la **estudiante** student
estudiantil student (adj.)
estudiar to study, 3.2
el **estudio** study
estupendo(a) terrific
la **etnicidad** ethnicity
el **eucalipto** eucalyptus tree
la **Europa** Europe
europeo(a) European
la **evaluación** evaluation
exacto(a) exact
el **examen** exam, test, 3.2
examinar to examine, 10.2
la **excepción** exception
el **exceso** excess
exclusivamente exclusively
la **excursión** excursion
existir to exist
exótico(a) exotic
el **experimento** experiment
experto(a) expert, 9.1
explicar to explain
el/la **explorador(a)** explorer
exponer to explain, expound
la **exposición** exhibition, 12.2
la **expresión** expression
extender (ie) to extend
extranjero(a) foreign
extraordinario(a) extraordinary
extremo(a) extreme

F

fabuloso(a) fabulous
fácil easy, 2.1
facturar to check (luggage), 8.1
facultativo(a) optional
la **falda** skirt, 13.1
falso(a) false
la **falta** lack
faltar to lack
la **fama** fame
la **familia** family, 5.1
familiar of the family

famoso(a) famous
fanfarrón(a) boastful, 9.1
fantástico(a) fantastic, 1.2
el/la **farmacéutico(a)** pharmacist, 10.2
la **farmacia** pharmacy, 10.2
fascinante fascinating
febrero February, BV
la **fecha** date, BV
    ¿Cuál es la fecha de hoy?
      What is today's date?, BV
feliz happy
el **fenómeno** phenomenon
la **feria** fair
el **ferrocarril** railway, railroad, 14.1
festejar to celebrate
la **fibra** fiber, 10.2
la **fiebre** fever, 10.1
la **fiesta** party, 4.2
la **fila** row, 8; line, 12.1
el **film(e)** film, 12.1
el **fin** end
    el fin de semana weekend
    en fin finally
el **final** end
el **fiordo** fiord
la **física** physics, 2.2
el/la **físico** physicist
físico(a) physical, 10.2
la **fisiología** physiology
flamenco(a) Flemish
la **flexibilidad** flexibility
la **flor** flower, 6.2
la **formación** formation
formal formal
formar to form, make
la **formulación** formation
el **formulario** form
la **foto** photo
francés (francesa) French, 2.2
la **frecuencia** frequency
    con frecuencia frequently
frecuentar to frequent
frecuentemente frequently
freír (i, i) to fry, 15.1
frente: en frente de in front of
    frente a facing, opposite
fresco(a) fresh, cool
    Hace fresco. It's cool.
el **frijol** bean, 15.2
el **frío** cold (weather), 9.1
    Hace frío. It's cold., 9.1
frito(a) fried
la **frontera** border
la **fruta** fruit, 15.2
fuerte strong
la **función** function
funcionar to function

el/la **fundador(a)** founder
fundir to found
el **fútbol** soccer, 7.1
    el campo de fútbol soccer
      field, 7.1

G

la **gabardina** raincoat, 13.1
las **gafas** glasses, goggles, 9.1
el **galón** gallon
gallego(a) Galician
la **gamba** shrimp (Spain)
el **ganado** cattle
el/la **ganador(a)** winner
ganar to win, 7.1; to earn
la **ganga** bargain
el **garaje** garage, 6.2
la **garganta** throat, 10.1
    el dolor de garganta sore
      throat, 10.1
gas: con gas carbonated
la **gaseosa** soft drink, soda, 5.2
la **gasolinera** gas station
el **gato** cat, 6.1
la **generación** generation
el **general: por lo general** in
      general
generalizar to generalize
el **género** kind, sort, genre
la **gente** people
la **geografía** geography, 2.2
geográfico(a) geographic
la **geometría** geometry, 2.2
gigantesco(a) gigantic, huge
el **gimnasio** gymnasium
el **glaciar** glacier
el **gobierno** government
el **gol** goal (soccer), 7.1
    meter un gol to score a goal
      (soccer), 7.1
el **golf** golf, 11.2
    el campo de golf golf course,
      11.2
    el juego de golf golf game,
      11.2
    la bolsa de golf golf bag,
      11.2
golpear to hit, 11.2
la **goma** eraser, BV
el **gorro** cap, 9.1
gozar to enjoy
gracias thank you, BV
el **grado** degree, 9.1
    gran, grande big, 2.1
    Las Grandes Ligas Major
      Leagues
el **grano** grain

grave serious, grave
el **green** green (golf), **11.2**
griego(a) Greek
la **gripe** flu, cold, **10.1**
gris grey, **13.2**
gritar to shout
el **grupo** group
el **guante** glove, **7.2**
guardar to guard, **7**
guardar cama to stay in bed,
  10.1
guatemalteco(a) Guatemalan
la **guerra** war
guerrero(a) war-like
la **guitarra** guitar, **4.2**
gustar to like, **13.1**

H

la **habichuela** bean, **15.2**
la **habitación** room, **5.1**
el/la **habitante** inhabitant
habla: de habla española
  Spanish-speaking
hablar to speak, **3.1**
hace: Hace calor. It's hot., **11.1**
Hace frío it's cold, **9.1**
hace mucho tiempo a long
  time ago
Hace muchos años que...
  For many years
hacer to do; to make, **8.1**
hacer un viaje to take a trip,
  8.1
hacer juego con to go with,
  match, **13.2**
hacer la maleta to pack one's
  suitcase, **8**
hacia toward
el **hallazgo** finding
la **hamaca** hammock, **11.1**
la **hambre** hunger, **15.1**
tener hambre to be hungry,
  15.1
la **hamburguesa** hamburger
hasta until, **BV**
Hasta la vista. See you later.,
Hasta luego. See you later.,
  BV
Hasta mañana. See you
  tomorrow., **BV**
Hasta pronto. See you soon.,
  BV
hay there is, there are, **5.1**
Hay sol. It's sunny., **11.1**
el **helado** ice cream, **5.2**
el **hemisferio** hemisphere
herbívoro(a) herbivorous

el/la **herbolario(a)** herbalist
heredar to inherit
el/la **hermanastro(a)** stepbrother
  (stepsister)
el/la **hermano(a)** brother (sister),
  2.1
el/la **héroe** hero
la **hibridación** hybridization
el **hielo: el patinaje sobre hielo**
  ice skating, **9.2**
la **hierba** herb
el/la **hijastro(a)** stepson
  (stepdaughter)
el/la **hijo(a)** son (daughter), **6.1**
los **hijos** children (sons and
  daughters), **6.1**
el **hipopótamo** hippopotamus
hispánico(a) Hispanic
hispano(a) Hispanic
la **historia** history, **2.2**; story
el/la **historiador(a)** historian
histórico(a) historic
el **hit** hit (baseball), **7.2**
la **hoja** sheet, **BV**; blade, **9.2**
la hoja de papel sheet of
  paper, **BV**
hola hello, **BV**
holandés (holandesa) Dutch
el **hombre** man
el **hombro** shoulder
honesto(a) honest, **1.2**
el **honor** honor
la **hora** hour; time
el **horario** schedule, **14.1**
el **hornillo** portable stove, **16.2**
el **hospital** hospital, **10.2**
el **hotel** hotel
hoy today, **11.2**
hoy en día nowadays
¿Cuál es la fecha de hoy?
  What is today's date?, **BV**
el **hoyo** hole, **11.2**
el **huevo** egg, **15.2**
los huevos duros hardboiled
  eggs
los huevos pasados por agua
  poached eggs
los huevos revueltos
  scrambled eggs
el/la **humanista** humanist
el **humano** human being
humano(a) human
humilde humble
el **humor: de buen humor** in a
  good mood, **10**
de mal humor in a bad
  mood, **10**
el **huso horario** time zone

I

la **idea** idea
idéntico(a) identical
la **identidad** identity
identificar to identify
el **idioma** language
el/la **ídolo(a)** idol
la **iglesia** church
igual equal; the same
el **imperio** empire
la **importancia** importance
importante important
imposible impossible
impresionado(a) impressed
impresionante amazing,
  impressive
incainco(a) Inca (adj.)
incluso including
increíble incredible
independiente independent
indígena native
individual individual (adj.), **7**
el/la **individuo** individual
la **industria** industry
industrializado(a)
  industrialized
la **infanta** Infanta (princess)
inferior inferior; lower
el **infierno** hell
la **influencia** influence
la **información** information
informal informal
informar to inform
el **informe** report
el **inglés** English (language), **2.2**
inglés (inglesa) English (adj.)
inhóspito(a) inhospitable
inmenso(a) immense
el/la **inquilino(a)** tenant
inspeccionar to inspect, **8.2**
inspirar to inspire
instalarse to establish oneself
la **institución** institution
el **instituto** institute
las **instrucciones** instructions, **5.2**
el **instrumento** instrument
insuficiente incompetent
el **insulto** insult
íntegro(a) integral
inteligente intelligent, **2.1**
intercambio exchange
el **interés** interest
interesante interesting, **2.1**
interesar to interest, **13.1**
internacional international
el/la **intérprete** interpreter
interrogativo(a) interrogative

la **investigación** investigation
el **invierno** winter, 9.1
la **invitación** invitation, 5.2
invitar to invite, 4.2
la **inyección** injection, shot
ir to go, 4.1
   ir a (+infinitive) to be going
     to (plus infinitive), 6
   ir de camping to go
     camping, 16
irlandés (irlandesa) Irish
la **isla** island
el **istmo** isthmus
el **italiano** Italian (language), 2.2
la **izquierda** left, 5.1
   a la izquierda to the left, 5.1

J

el **jabón** soap, 16.2
el **jamón** ham, 15.2
japonés (japonesa) Japanese
el **jarabe** syrup
el **jardín** garden, 6.2
el/la **jardinero(a)** outfielder
   (baseball), 7.2
el/la **jefe(a)** leader, chief
el **jersey** sweater, 13.1
el **jonrón** home run, 7.2
el/la **joven** young person
   joven young, 6.1
las **joyas** jewelry
el **juego** game
   hacer juego con to go with,
     coordinate with, 13.2
el **jueves** Thursday, BV
el/la **jugador(a)** player, 7.1
   jugar (ue) to play, 7.1
el **jugo** juice
julio July, BV
la **jungla** jungle
junio June, BV
juntos(as) together
el **juramento** oath

K

el **kilogramo** kilogram
el **kilómetro** kilometer

L

la the (f. sing.), 1.1
el **laboratorio** laboratory
el **lado** side
el **lago** lake
la **lana** wool
la **langosta** lobster
la **lanza** spear

el/la **lanzador(a)** pitcher, 7.2
   lanzar to throw, 7.1
el **lápiz** pencil, 5.2
   largo(a) long, 13.2
   largo: a lo largo de along
las the (f. pl.)
la **lástima** pity
la **lata** can
   lateral side (adj.)
el **latín** Latin, 2.2
   latino(a) Hispanic, Latino
la **Latinoamérica** Latin America
   latinoamericano(a) Latin
     American
la **latitud** latitude
   lavarse to wash oneself, 16.1
   le (pron.) him, her, you (form.)
la **lección** lesson, 3.2
la **lectura** reading
la **leche** milk, 5.2
el **lechón** suckling pig
la **lechuga** lettuce, 15.2
   leer to read, 5.2
la **legumbre** vegetable, 15.2
   lejano(a) distant, far away
la **lengua** language, 2.2
    la lengua materna native
     language
   les (pron.) them, you (form.)
   levantarse to get up, 16.1
la **ley** law
la **leyenda** legend
la **libra** pound
   libre free, 14.2
la **libreta** notebook, 3.2
el **libro** book, BV
el **liceo** primary school in México,
   but high school in most places
   ligero(a) light
el **límite** limit; boundary
la **limonada** lemonade, BV
   limpio(a) clean
la **línea** line
    la línea aérea airline, 8.1
la **linfa** lymph
la **linterna** flashlight, 16.2
la **liquidación** sale
el **líquido** liquid
la **litera** berth, 14.2
la **literatura** literature
el **litro** liter
   llamarse to be called, named,
    16.1
la **llegada** arrival, 8.1
    el tablero de llegadas y
     salidas arrival and
     departure board, 8.1
   llegar to arrive, 3.1

   llevar to carry, 3.2; to wear; to
    bear (the name)
   llueve it is raining, 11.2
   lo: lo que what
el **lobo de mar** sea lion
la **localidad** seat (in theater), 12.1
la **longitud** longitude
   los the (m. pl.)
la **lucha** fight
   luchar to fight
   luego then
    Hasta luego. See you later., BV
el **lugar** place
    tener lugar to take place
   lujo: de lujo deluxe
el **lunes** Monday, BV
la **luz** light

M

la **madastre** step-mother
la **madera** wood
la **madre** mother, 6.1
el/la **madrileño(a)** native of Madrid
la **madrina** godmother
   maestro(a) teacher, master
   magnífico(a) magnificent
el **maíz** corn
la **mal** ailment, illness
la **maleta** suitcase, 8.1
    hacer la maleta to pack one's
     suitcase, 8
el/la **maletero(a)** trunk (of a car),
   8.1; porter, 14-1
   malo(a) bad, 1
la **mamá** mom, 5.2
   manejar to drive
   manera way, manner, 1.1
    de ninguna manera by no
     means, 1.1
la **manga** sleeve, 13.2
el **mango** handle, 11.2
la **manía** mania
la **mano** hand, 7.1
    el equipaje de mano hand
     (carry-on) luggage, 8.1
la **mansión** mansion
el **mantel** tablecloth, 15.1
   mantener maintain
el **mantenimiento** maintenance
la **mañana** morning, 2
    esta mañana this morning,
     11.2
   mañana tomorrow
el **mapa** map
el **mar** sea, 11.1
    el Mar Caribe Carribbean Sea
   maravilloso(a) marvelous,

wonderful

marcar to score (sports), **7.1**

el **marido** husband, **6.1**

el **marisco** shellfish, **15.2**

marrón brown, **13.2**

el **martes** Tuesday, **BV**

marzo March, **BV**

más more, most

la **masa** mass

la **mascota** pet

matar to kill

las **matemáticas** mathematics, **2.2**

la **materia** subject matter, **2.2**; matter

materno(a) maternal

la **lengua materna** native language

el **matrimonio** wedding; marriage

el/la **maya** Maya, Mayan

mayo May, **BV**

mayor great, greater, greatest

la **mayoría** majority

mayormente principally, mainly

me (to, for) me

las **medias** stockings, pantihose, **13.1**

media: y media half past the hour, **2**

la **medianoche** midnight, **2**

el **medicamento** medication, **10.2**

la **medicina** medicine, **10**

el/la **médico(a)** doctor, **10.2**

la **medida** measurement

medieval medieval

el **medio** mean, way

el **medio de transporte** means of transportation

medio(a) middle

la clase media middle class

medio: a término medio medium (meat), **15.2**

el **mediodía** midday, noon, **2**

medir (i, i) to measure

el **mejillón** mussel

menos less

menos cuarto a quarter to (the hour), **2**

menos de less than

mental mental

la **mentira** lie

el **menú** menu, **12.2**

el **mercado** market

el **meridiano** meridian

la **merienda** snack, **4.1**

la **mermelada** marmalade

el **mes** month

la **mesa** table, **12.2**

el/la **mesero(a)** waiter (waitress), **12.2**

meter to put in, **7**

meter en el cesto to make a basket, **7.2**

meter un gol to score a goal, **7.1**

meter la pata to put one's foot in it

métrico(a) metric

el **metro** meter; subway, **12.1**

mexicano(a) Mexican, **1.1**

mezclar to mix

mi my

el **microscopio** microscope

microscópico(a) microscopic

el/la **miembro(a)** member

mientras while

el **miércoles** Wednesday, **BV**

la **migración** migration

mil (one) thousand, **BV**

la **milla** mile

el **millón (de)** million

el/la **millonario(a)** millonaire

el **minuto** minute

mirar to look at, **3.2**

mirarse to look at oneself, **16.1**

mismo(a) same

mixto(a) mixed

la **mochila** backpack, knapsack, **BV**

la **moda** style

de moda in style

el **modelo** model

moderno(a) modern

modesto(a) of modest means

el/la **modisto(a)** designer (clothes)

molestar to bother, **13**

el **momento** moment

en este momento right now, **8.1**

el **monopatín** skateboard, **9.2**

andar en monopatín to skateboard, **9**

la **montaña** mountain, **9.1**

montañoso(a) mountainous

el **monton** heap, pile, mountain

moreno(a) dark, **1.1**

morir (ue, u) to die, **15**

el **mostrador** counter, **8.1**

mostrar (ue) to show

el **motor** motor

la **motricidad** motor function

el/la **mozo(a)** porter, **14.1**

la **muchacha** girl, **BV**

el **muchacho** boy, **BV**

muchísmo very, extremely

mucho(a) a lot; many, **5**

Mucho gusto. Nice to meet you., **BV**

la **mujer** wife, **6.1**

múltiple multiple

mundial worldwide

la Copa Mundial World Cup

la Serie Mundial World Series

el **mundo** world

el **mural** mural, **12.2**

el **muralla** wall

el **museo** museum, **12.2**

la **música** music, **2.2**

musical musical, **12.2**

el/la **músico** musician, **12.2**

muy very, **BV**

N

nacer to be born

el **nacimiento** birth

nacional national

la **nacionalidad** nationality, **1**

nada nothing, **13.1**

nadar to swim, **11.1**

nadie no one, nobody, **13**

los **narcóticos** narcotics

natural natural

la **naturaleza** nature

el/la **naturalista** naturalist

la **navaja** razor, **16.1**

necesario(a) necessary

necesitar to need

negro(a) black, **13.2**

nervioso(a) nervous, **10.1**

la **nevada** snowfall, **9.1**

nevar (ie) to snow, **9.1**

Nieva. It is snowing., **9**

ni... ni neither... nor

ni yo tampoco me neither, **13**

nicaragüense Nicaraguan

el/la **nieto(a)** grandchild, **6.1**

los **nietos** grandchildren, **6.1**

la **nieve** snow, **9.1**

la **niña** girl

ninguno(a): de ninguna manera by no means, **1.1**

el **nivel: el nivel del mar** sea level

no no

No hay de qué. You're welcome., **BV**

el **noble** noble

nocturno(a) night (adj.)

la **noche** night, **2**

esta noche tonight, **11.2**

el **nombre** name

el **norte** north
   norteamericano(a) North
   American
la **Noruega** Norway
   nos us (pron.)
   nosotros(as) we, **2.2**
la **nota** grade, **3.2**
   notable outstanding
las **noticias** news, **5.2**
la **novela** novel, **5.2**
   noveno(a) ninth, **5.1**
   noventa ninety, **BV**
   noviembre November, **BV**
el/la **novio(a)** boyfriend (girlfriend);
   fiancé(e)
la **nube** cloud, **11.1**
   nublado(a) cloudy, **11.1**
      Está nublado. It's cloudy.,
      11.1
   nuestro(a) our
   nueve nine, **BV**
   nuevo(a) new, **6.2**
el **número** number, **8.1**
   el número del vuelo flight
      number, **8.1**
   el número del asiento seat
      number, **8.1**
   nunca never, **13.1**
la **nutrición** nutrition

O

   o or
el **objetivo** objective
el **objeto** object
   obligar to force
   obligatorio(a) required
la **obra** work, **12.2**
   obrar to work
   observar to observe
   obvio(a) obvious
   occidental western
el **océano** ocean
      el Océano Atlántico Atlantic
      Ocean
      el Océano Pacífico Pacific
      Ocean
   octavo(a) eighth, **5.1**
   octubre October, **BV**
   ocupado(a) occupied, **14.2**
   ocupar to occupy
   ochenta eighty, **BV**
   ocho eight, **BV**
el **oeste** west
      del oeste western (movie, etc.)
la **oferta** offer
   ofrecer to offer
   oír to hear

la **ola** wave, **11.1**
la **oliva** olive
   omnívoro(a) omnivorous
la **onza** ounce
la **opción** option
   opcional optional
la **opereta** operetta
   opinar to think
la **oración** sentence
el **orangután** orangutan
   orgánico(a) organic
el **organismo** organism
   oriental eastern
el **origen** origin
   original original
   originario(a) originating;
      native, descendant
la **orilla** bank (of a river), **16.2**
el **oro** gold
la **orquesta** orchestra, **12.2**
el **otoño** autumn, **7.1**
   otro(a) other, **2.2**
el **out** out (baseball), **7.2**
la **ovación** ovation
   ovalado(a) oval
la **oveja** sheep
   oye listen

P

el **padastro** step-father
el **padre** father, **6.1**
los **padres** parents, **6.1**
el/la **padrino(a)** godfather,
      godmother
los **padrinos** godparents
   pagar to pay, **13.1**
el **pago** pay
el **país** country
el **paisaje** countryside
la **palabra** word
el **palacio** palace
la **paella** paella (seafood dish)
la **palmera** palm tree
el **palo** (golf) club, **11.2**
el **pan** bread, **15.2**
   el pan tostado toast
   panameño(a) Panamanian
el **panqueque** pancake
los **pantalones** pants, **13.1**
   el pantalón corto shorts
   el traje pantalón pantsuit
la **pantalla** screen, **8.1**
el **papá** dad, **5.2**
la **papa** potato, **5.2**
   las papas fritas French fries
el **papel** paper, **BV**
   la hoja de papel sheet of

paper, **BV**
el **papel higiénico** toilet
   paper, **16.2**
   para for; to
la **parada** stop, **14.2**
el **paramecio** paramecium
   parar to block, **7.1**
el **parasol** parasol, **11.1**
   parecer to seem
la **pareja** couple
el/la **pariente** relative
el **parque** park, **6.2**
la **parte** part
      tomar parte to take part
   particular private; particular, **5.1**
el **partido** game, **7.1**
el **pasado** past
   pasado(a) last
      el año pasado last year
      la semana pasada last week
el/la **pasajero(a)** passenger, **8.1**
el **pasaporte** passport, **8.2**
      el control de pasaportes
      passport inspection, **8.2**
   pasar to pass, **7.2**; to happen
el **pasatiempo** pastime, hobby
el **pase de abordar** boarding
      pass,.**8.1**
el **paseo** stroll, walk
el **pasillo** corridor, **14.2**
la **pasta dentífrica** toothpaste,
      16.2
la **pastelería** pastry shop
la **pastilla** pill, **10.2**; bar (of soap),
      16.2
el/la **pastor** shepherd
      el pastor vasco Basque
      shepherd
la **pata: meter la pata** to put one's
      foot in it
la **patata** potato
   paterno(a) paternal
el **patín** skate, **9.2**
el **patinadero** skating rink, **9.2**
el/la **patinador(a)** skater, **9.2**
el **patinaje** skating, **9.2**
      el patinaje artístico figure
      skating, **9.2**
      el patinaje sobre hielo ice-
      skating, **9.2**
      el patinaje sobre ruedas
      roller skating, **9.2**
      la pista de patinaje skating
      rink, **9.2**
   patinar to skate, **9**
el **patio** patio, courtyard
la **patología** pathology

la **patria** homeland, native land
patrón (patrona) patron,
    patron saint
el **pecho** chest, 10.2
    pedir (i, i) to ask for, 15.1
    pegar un fly to hit a fly
    peinarse to comb one's hair,
    16.1
el **peine** comb, 16.2
la **película** movie, film, 5.2
    dar una película to show a
        movie, 12
el **peligro** danger
el **pelo** hair, 16.1
    tomar el pelo a alguien to
        pull someone's leg
la **pelota** ball, 7.2
la **península** peninsula
    pensar to think
la **pensión** boarding house, 16.2
    pequeño(a) small, 2.1
la **percepción** perception
    perder (ie) to lose, 7.1
        perder el autobús to miss
            the bus, 12.1
    perdón excuse me
el **peregrinaje** pilgrimage
el **perfume** perfume
la **perfumería** perfume shop
el **periódico** newspaper, 5.2
    perjudicial harmful
    permanente permanent
    permitir to permit
    pero but
el **perro** dog, 6.1
la **persona** person
    personal personal
    peruano(a) Peruvian
el **pescado** fish, 15.2
el/la **pescador(a)** fisherman/woman
    pescar to fish
el **peso** weight; monetary unit of
        several Latin American
        Countries
el/la **pianista** pianist
el **piano** piano, 4.2
el **pico** peak
el/la **pícher** pitcher, 7.2
el **pie** foot, 7.1
    a pie on foot, 3.1
    de pie standing
la **piel** skin
la **píldora** pill, 10.2
el/la **piloto** pilot, 8.2
la **pimienta** pepper, 15.1
el **pinar** pine grove
el **pino** pine tree
la **pinta** pint

pintar to paint
el/la **pintor(a)** painter
    pintoresco(a) picturesque
la **pintura** painting
la **piscina** swimming pool, 11.2
el **piso** floor, 5.1
la **pista** ski trail, 9.1
    la pista de patinaje skating
        rink, 9.2
la **pizarra** chalkboard, BV
el **pizarrón** chalkboard, 3.2
el **plan** plan
la **plancha de vela** windsurf
        board, 11.1
la **planta** floor, 5.1; plant, 6.2
    la planta baja ground floor,
        5.1
    plástico(a) plastic
la **plata** silver
el **plátano** plantain
el **platillo** home plate (baseball),
        7.2; saucer, 15.1
el **platino** platinum
el **plato** plate, dish, 15.1
la **playa** beach, 11.1
    playero(a) beach (adj.), 11.1
    la toalla playera beach
        towel, 11.1
    plegable: la silla plegable,
        folding chair, 11.1
la **población** population
    pobre poor
    poco(a) little, small (amount)
    poder (ue) to be able, 7.1
el **poder extranjero** foreign power
el **poema** poem
    polar polar
    policíaco(a) detective (adj.)
        novelas policíacas mysteries,
            detective fiction
    político(a) political
los **políticos (parientes)** in-laws, 6
el **pollo** chicken, 15.2
el **poncho** poncho, cape
    poner to put, to place, 8.1
        ponerse to put on, 16.1
        poner la mesa to set the
            table
    popular popular, 2.1
la **popularidad** popularity
    poquito más a little more
    por about, for, by
        por consiguiente
            consequently
        por ejemplo for example
        por encima over, 7.2
        por eso therefore
        por favor please, BV

por lo menos at least
¿por qué? why?
porque because
la **portada** cover (of magazine,
    book, etc.)
la **portería** goal, 7.1
el/la **portero(a)** goalkeeper, goalie,
    7.1
posible possible
el **postre** dessert, 5.2
practicar to practice
el **precepto** precept
el **precio** price, 13.1
precioso(a) beautiful, 6.2
la **preferencia** preference
preferir (ie, i) to prefer, 7
el **prefijo** prefix
preguntar to ask
el **premio** prize
la **prenda** garment, article of
    clothing
la **preparación** preparation
preparar to prepare, 4.1
el **presente** present
el/la **presidente(a)** president
primario(a) elementary
la **primavera** spring, 7.2
primer, primero(a) first, BV
el/la **primo(a)** cousin, 6.1
principal main
el/la **principiante** beginner, 9.1
principio: al principio in the
    beginning
la **prisa** haste, hurry
    darse prisa to rush, hurry
privado(a) private, 5.1
probable probable
probar (ue) to try; to taste
el **problema** problem
el **proceso** process
producir to produce
el **producto** product
el/la **productor(a)** producer
la **profesión** profession
profesional professional
el/la **profesor(a)** teacher, 2.1
profundo(a) profound
el **programa** program
el/la **propietario(a)** owner
la **propina** tip, 12.2
propio(a) one's own
protectora: la crema protectora
    suntan lotion, 11.1
la **proteína** protein, 10.2
protestante Protestant
próximo(a) next, 14.2
la **prueba** test
publicado(a) published

el **público** public; audience, **12.2**
público(a) public (adj.)
el **pueblo** town, **5.1**; people
el **puente** bridge
el **puerco** pork
la **puerta** gate, **8.1**
    la **puerta de salida** departure gate, **8.1**
el **puerto** port
  puertorriqueño(a) Puerto Rican, **2**
pues well
la **pulgada** inch
pulmonar pulmonary
punto: en punto on the dot, **3.1**

Q

que that
qué what; how, **BV**
  ¿Qué es? What is it?, **BV**
  ¿Qué tal? How are you?, **BV**
  ¿Qué tal la vista? How do you like the view?
  ¿Qué tal le gusta esta camisa? How do you like this shirt?
  ¿Qué hora es? What time is it?, **2**
  ¿Qué tiempo hace? What's the weather like?, **9.1**
queda: quedar empatado(a) to be tied (sports), **7.1**
  Me queda bien. It fits me., **13.2**
querer (ie) to want, **7**
  querer decir to mean
el **queso** cheese, **15.2**
¿quién? who?, **BV**
  ¿Quién es? Who is it (he, she)?, **BV**
la **química** chemistry, **2.2**
el/la **químico** chemist
la **quinceañera** young woman's fifteenth birthday
quinientos five hundred
quinto(a) fifth, **5.1**
el **quiosco** newsstand, **14.1**
Quisiera ... I would like ...
quizás perhaps

R

la **rama** branch
rápidamente quickly
rápido fast, **9.1**
la **raqueta** racquet, **11.2**

el **rasgo** feature
el **ratón** rat
rayas: a rayas striped, **13.2**
el **rayo** ray
la **razón** reason
razonable reasonable
realizar to carry out, put into effect
realmente really; actually
la **rebaja** reduction
la **rebanada** slice
el/la **receptor(a)** catcher (baseball), **7.2**
la **receta** prescription, **10.2**
recetar to prescribe, **10**
recibir to receive, **5.2**
reciente recent
reclamar to claim, **8.2**
el **reclamo de equipaje** baggage claim, **8.2**
recoger to pick up, collect, **8.2**
la **recomendación** recommendation
recomendar to recommend
recordar to remember
el **recorrido** distance traveled, trip
  de largo recorrido long-distance
la **red** net, **7.2**
redondo(a) round
reducido(a) reduced
referir (ie, i) to refer
reflejar to reflect
el **refrán** proverb
el **refresco** soft drink, **4.1**
el **refugio** refuge
el **regalo** gift, **6.2**
el **régimen** regimen
la **región** region
regresar to return
el **regreso** return
regular fair, passing (grade)
reinar to reign
la **relación** relationship
relativamente relatively
religioso(a) religious
rellenar to fill
remontar to go back (to some date in time)
repetir (i, i) to repeat, **15**
la **representación** performance, **12.2**
  dar una representacíon to put on a performance, **12.2**
representar to represent
la **reproducción** reproduction
la **república** republic
requerir (ie, i) to require

la **reserva** reserve
reservado(a) reserved, **14.2**
residencial residential
resolver (ue) to resolve
el **restaurante** restaurant, **12.2**
el **resultado** result
resultar to result
el **retraso** delay, **14.2**
  con retraso late, **14.2**
revisar to inspect, **8**
el/la **revisor(a)** (train) conductor, **14.2**
la **revista** magazine, **5.2**
revolucionario(a) revolutionary
revueltos scrambled (eggs)
el **rey** king
rico(a) rich; tasty, **15.2**
riguroso(a) rigorous
el **río** river, **16.2**
riquisimo very rich
robar to steal, **7.2**
rodar (ue) to shoot a movie
rojo(a) red, **13.2**
el **rollo** roll (of paper), **16.2**
romántico(a) romantic
la **ropa** clothes, **8.2**
  poner la ropa en la maleta to pack (a suitcase)
rubio(a) blond(e), **1.1**
la **rueda** wheel, roller, **9.2**
el **ruido** noise
la **ruina** ruin

S

el **sábado** Saturday, **BV**
saber to know how, **9.1**
sacar to get, receive, **3.2**
  sacar notas buenas (malas) to get good (bad) grades, **3.2**
el **sacerdote** priest
el **saco** sport jacket, **13.1**
el **saco de dormir** sleeping bag, **16.2**
la **sal** salt, **15.1**
la **sala** living room, **4.1**
  la sala de clase classroom, **3.1**
  la sala de espera waiting room, **14.1**
el **saldo** sale
la **salida** departure, **8.1**
  la puerta de salida departure gate, **8.1**
  el tablero de llegadas y salidas arrival and departure board, **8.1**
salir to leave, **8.1**; to go out

el **salón** health club
el **salón de clase** classroom, **3.1**
　saltar to jump out
la **salud** health, **10**
　　estar de buena salud to be in good health
　saludable healthy
las **sandalias** sandals, **13.1**
el **sándwich** sandwich, **5.2**
la **sangre** blood
el/la **santo(a)** saint, saint's day
la **sección de no fumar** no smoking section, **8.1**
el **sector** section
　secundario(a) secondary, **1.1**
　　la escuela secundaria high school, **1.1**
　secuoya: árboles secuoyas sequoia trees
la **sed** thirst, **15.1**
　　tener sed to be thirsty, **15.1**
el **segmento** segment
　segregar to segregate
　seguida: en seguida at once, immediately
　seguir (i, i) to follow, **15**
　segundo(a) second, **5.1**
la **seguridad** security, **8.1**
　　el control de seguridad security control, **8.1**
　según according to
　seis six, **BV**
la **selva** rainforest
la **semana** week, **11.2**
　　la semana pasada last week, **11.2**
el **semestre** semester
el/la **senador(a)** senator
　sencillo(a) one-way, **14.1**
la **sensación** sensation
　sentarse (ie) to sit down, **16.1**
　　Me sienta(n) bien. It (They) suit(s) me well. **13.1**
el **señor** Mr., sir, **BV**; lord
la **señora** Mrs., Ms., ma'am, **BV**
la **señorita** Miss, Ms., **BV**
　separado(a) separated
　septiembre September, **BV**
el **ser: el ser vivo** living being
　ser to be, **1**
la **serie: la Serie Mundial** World Series
　serio(a) serious, **1.2**
el **servicio** service; tip
la **servilleta** napkin, **15.1**
　servir (i, i) to serve, **15.1**
　sesenta sixty, **BV**
la **sesión** show (movies), **12.1**

　setenta seventy, **BV**
　severo(a) severe
　sexto(a) sixth, **5.1**
　séptimo(a) seventh, **5.1**
　si if
　sí yes; used for emphasis
el **SIDA** AIDS
　siempre always, **5.2**
　　siempre no not always
la **sierra** mountain range
la **siesta** nap, **11.1**
　　echar (tomar) una siesta to take a nap, **11.1**
　siete seven, **BV**
el **siglo** century
　significar to mean
　siguiente following
la **silla** chair, **BV**
　　la silla plegable folding chair, **11.1**
　simple simple
　simplemente simply
　sin without
　　sin embargo nevertheless
　　sin escala nonstop
la **sinagoga** synagogue
　sincero(a) sincere, **1.2**
el **síntoma** symptom, **10.2**
el **sistema** system
　　el sistema nervioso nervous system
la **situación** situation
el **slálom** slalom, **9.1**
　sobre above, over; about
　　sobre todo especially, above all
　sobresaliente outstanding
　sobrevolar (ue) to fly over
el/la **sobrino(a)** nephew (niece), **6.1**
los **sobrinos** niece(s) and nephew(s), **6.1**
　social social
la **sociedad** society
　sociología sociology, **2.2**
el/la **sociólogo(a)** sociologist
　sofisticado(a) sophisticated
el **sol** sun, **11.1**
　　Hay sol. It's sunny., **11.1**
　　tomar el sol to sunbathe, **11.1**
　solamente only
el/la **soldado** soldier
　soler (ue) to tend to, to be accustomed
　solo(a) alone
　sólo only
el **sombrero** hat, **13.1**
la **sombrilla** umbrella, **11.1**

　somos we are, **2.2**
　son they/you (pl. form.) are, **2.1**
la **sopa** soup, **5.2**
　soportar to support
　sorprender to surprise, **13**
　soy I am, **1.2**
　su his, her, your (form.), their
la **subcultura** subculture
　subir to go up, **5.1**
　　subir a to get on, to board, **8.1**
　subscribir to subscribe
　subsistir to continue to exist
la **substancia** substance
　subterráneo(a) underground, **12**
el **subtítulo** subtitle
los **suburbios** suburbs, **5.1**
　sucesivo(a) successive
　sudamericano(a) South American
el **suelo** ground, **7**
　　tocar el suelo to touch the ground
el **sueño** dream
la **suerte: tener suerte** to be lucky
el **suéter** sweater, **13.1**
　sufrir to suffer
la **superficie** surface
　superior superior; higher
el **supermercado** supermarket
el **sur** south
　　La America del Sur South America, **8.1**
el **suroeste** southwest
　suspenso(a) failing (grade)
la **sustancia** substance

T

el **T shirt** T-shirt, **13.1**
la **tabla hawaiiana** surfing
el **tablero** backboard (basketball), **7.2**
　　el tablero de llegadas y salidas arrival and departure board, **8.1**
　　el tablero indicador scoreboard, **7.1**
el **tacón** heel, **13.2**
　tal such
el **talco** talcum powder
el **talento** talent
el **talón** luggage claims ticket, **8.1**
la **talla** size, **13.1**
el **tamaño** size, **13.1**
　también also, too, **1.1**
　tampoco neither, either

(Ni) yo tampoco. Me neither., **13**

tan so

el **tanto** score; point, **7.1**

la **taquilla** ticket office, **12.1**

la **tarde** afternoon

    esta tarde this afternoon, **11.2**

tarde late, **8.1**

la **tarifa** fare, rate

la **tarjeta** card, **5.2**

    la tarjeta de crédito credit card, **13.1**

    la tarjeta de embarque boarding pass, **8.1**

    la tarjeta postal postcard, **5.2**

el **taxi** taxi, **8.1**

la **taza** cup, **15.1**

te you (fam. pron.)

el **té** tea

teatral theatrical, **12.2**

el **teatro** theater, **12.2**

la **técnica** technique

técnico(a) technical

el **teléfono** telephone, **4.1**

    por teléfono on the phone, **4.1**

la **telenovela** soap opera, **5.2**

el **telesilla** chair lift, **9.1**

el **telesquí** ski lift, **9.1**

la **televisión** television, **4.1**

el **televisor** television (set)

el **telón** curtain, **12.2**

el **tema** theme, subject

la **temperatura** temperature, **9.1**

la **tempestad** storm

temprano early

el **templo** temple

el **tenedor** fork, **15.1**

tener to have, **6.1**

    tener... años to be... years old, **6.1**

    tener hambre to be hungry, **15.1**

    tener que to have to, **6**

    tener sed to be thirsty, **15.1**

    tener tos to have a cough, **10.1**

el **tenis** tennis, **11.2**

    la cancha de tenis tennis court, **11.2**

    el juego de tenis tennis game, **11.2**

los **tenis** tennis shoes, **13.1**

la **teoría** theory

tercer(o) (a) third, **5.1**

terminar to end

el **término** term, word

    a término medio medium (meat)

la **terraza** terrace

el **terreno: el terreno de juego** playing field

el **territorio** territory

el/la **testigo(a)** witness

la **tía** aunt, **6.1**

el **tiempo** half (of a soccer game), **7.1**; time, weather

    a tiempo on time, **8.1**

    a tiempo completo full-time

    a tiempo parcial part-time

    al mismo tiempo at the same time

    hace mucho tiempo a long time ago

la **tienda** store, **4.1**; tent

    armar una tienda to put up a tent, **16.2**

    la tienda de campaña tent, **16.2**

    la tienda de departamentos department store

    la tienda de ropa para caballeros (señores) men's clothing store, **13.1**

    la tienda de ropa para damas (señoras) women's clothing store, **13.1**

la **tierra** Earth

    la Tierra Santa Holy Land

el **tigre** tiger

tímido(a) timid, shy, **1.2**

tinto(a) red

el **tío** uncle, **6.1**; guy

los **tíos** aunt(s) and uncle(s), **6.1**

típicamente typically

típico(a) typical

el **tipo** type

tirar to throw, **7.2**

    tirar con el pie to kick

titulado(a) entitled

el **título** degree

la **tiza** chalk, **BV**

la **toalla playera** beach towel, **11.1**

tocar to play (an instrument), **4.2**; to touch, **7**

el **tocino** bacon

todavía yet, still

todo everything

todo(a) every, all, **4.2**

    en todas partes everywhere

    sobre todo especially

    todo el mundo everybody

todos everyone

tomar to take, **3.2**; to drink, **4.1**

    tomar el sol to sunbathe, **11.1**

    tomar una ducha to take a shower, **16.2**

la **tonelada** ton

el **toro** bull

tórrido(a) torrid

la **torta** cake

la **tortilla** tortilla, **15.2**

torturar to torture

la **tos** cough, **10.1**

    tener tos to have a cough, **10.1**

tostadito(a) tanned

el **tostón** fried plantain slice

totalmente totally

trabajar to work, **4.1**

el **trabajo** work, job

    el trabajo a tiempo parcial part-time work

la **tradición** tradition

tradicional traditional

la **traducción** translation

traer to bring, **8**

el **tráfico** traffic

el **tragedia** tragedy

el **traje** suit, **13.1**

    el traje de baño bathing suit, swimsuit, **11.1**

    el traje pantalón pantsuit

tranquilo calm, quiet

transbordar to transfer, **14.2**

transmitir to transmit

el **transporte** transportation, **12**

el **tratado** treatise

el **tratamiento** treatment

tratar to deal with

    tratar de to be about

treinta thirty, **BV**

el **tren** train, **14.1**

    el tren de vía estrecha narrow gauge train

    subir al tren to get on the train, **14.2**

tres three, **BV**

la **trigonometría** trigonometry, **2.2**

la **tripulación** crew, **8.2**

triste sad, **10.1**

triunfante triumphant

triunfar to win, triumph

la **trompeta** trumpet, **4.2**

el **tronco** trunk

tropical tropical

el **truco** trick, device

tu your (sing. fam.)

tú you (sing. fam.)

el **tubo** tube, **16.2**

la **turbulencia** turbulence
turbulento(a) turbulent
el/la **turista** tourist, **12.2**
turquesa turquoise

U

u or (used instead of **o** before words beginning with **o** or **ho**)
Uds., ustedes you (pl. form.), **2.2**
último(a) last
un(a) a, an, **BV**
único(a) only
la **unidad** unit
el **uniforme** uniform
llevar uniforme to wear a uniform
unir to unite
la **universidad** university
uno(a) one, **BV**
uruguayo(a) Uruguayan
usar to use, **11.1**
el **uso** use

V

va he/she/it goes, is going
las **vacaciones** vacation
el **vacío** vacuum
el **vagón** train car, **14.1**
valer to be worth
valiente brave, valient
el **valor** value
el **valle** valley
vamos we go, we are going
van they/you (pl. form.) go, are going, **4.1**
la **variación** variation
variar to vary
la **variedad** variety
varios(as) several
vas you (sing. fam.) go, you are going
el **vaso** (drinking) glass, **5.2**
veces: a veces sometimes, **5.2**
la **vegetación** vegetation
el **vegetal** vegetable, **15.2**
el/la **vegetariano(a)** vegetarian
veinte twenty, **BV**
vencer to overcome, conquer
vender to sell, **5.2**
venezolano(a) Venezuelan
venir to come, **8**
venta: en venta for sale
la **ventanilla** ticket window, **9.1**
ver to see, to watch, **5.2**

el **verano** summer, **11.1**
el **verbo** verb
la **verdad** truth, **1.1**
¿no es verdad? isn't it true?, **1.1**
¿verdad? right?, **1.1**
verdadero(a) real
verde green, **13.2**
la **verdura** vegetable, **15.2**
verificar to check
versátil versatile
la **versión** version
el **vestido** dress, **13.1**
el vestido de boda wedding dress
vestirse (i, i) to get dressed, **16.1**
la **vez** time
de vez en cuando now and then
en vez de instead of
la **vía** track, **14.1**
de vía estrecha narrow-gauge (train)
viajar to travel
el **viaje** trip, **8.1**
hacer un viaje to take a trip, **8.1**
la **víbora** snake
la **victoria** victory
victorioso(a) victorious
la **vida** life
viejo(a) old, **6.1**
el **viento** wind, **11.1**
Hace viento. It's windy., **11.1**
el **viernes** Friday, **BV**
el **vinagre** vinegar
el **vino** wine
el **violín** violin, **4.2**
la **vista** view, **6.2**
la **vitamina** vitamin, **10.2**
la **vitrina** shop window, **13.1**
la **vivienda** housing
vivir to live, **5.1**
vivo(a) living
el ser vivo living being
el **vocabulario** vocabulary
volar (ue) to fly
el **volcán** volcano
el **vólibol** volleyball, **7.2**
volver (ue) to go back, **7.1**
vosotros(as) you (pl. fam.)
voy I go, I am going
el **vuelo** flight, **8.1**
el asistente (la asistenta) de vuelo flight attendant, **8.2**
el número del vuelo flight number, **8.1**

vuestro(a) your (pl. fam.)

Y

y and, **1.2**
ya already
el **yate** yacht
yo I, **1.2**

Z

la **zanahoria** carrot
los **zapatos** shoes, **13.1**
el **zíper** zipper, **13.2**
la **zona** district, zone
la zona postal postal (zip) code
la **zoología** zoology
el **zumo de naranja** orange juice

VOCABULARIO
INGLÉS-ESPAÑOL

501

The *Vocabulario inglés-español* contains all productive vocabulary from the text.

The reference numbers following each entry indicate the chapter and vocabulary section in which the word is introduced. For example **2.2** means that the word first appeared actively in *Capítulo 2, Palabras 2*. Boldface numbers without a *Palabras* reference indicate vocabulary introduced in the grammar section of the given chapter. **BV** refers to the introductory *Bienvenidos* lesson.

A

a, an un(a), **BV**
about a eso de, **3.1**
ache el dolor, **10.1**
to **ache** doler, **10.2**
    My____(part of body) aches.
    Me duele____., **10**
activity la actividad, **5.2**
actor el actor, **12.2**
actress la actriz, **12.2**
admission ticket la entrada, **12.1**
aerobic aeróbico(a), **10.2**
after después de, **4.1**
afternoon la tarde
    good afternoon buenas tardes, **BV**
    this afternoon esta tarde, **11.2**
agent el/la agente, **8.1**
airline la línea aérea, **8.1**
airplane el avión, **8.1**
    by plane en avión, **8.1**
airport el aeropuerto, **8.1**
algebra el álgebra, **2.2**
allergy la alergia, **10.2**
also también, **1.1**
always siempre, **5.2**
    not always siempre no
am soy, **1.2**
American americano(a), **1.2**
and y, **1.2**
to **anger** enojar, enfadar, **13**
to **annoy** enojar, enfadar, **13**
anorak el anorak, **9.1**
apartment el apartamento, **5.1**
to **applaud** aplaudir, **12.2**
April abril (m.), **BV**
are son, **2.1**; están, **4.1**
Argentinian argentino(a), **2.1**
arithmetic la aritmética, **2.2**
around alrededor de, **6.2**; a eso de (time), **3.1**
arrival la llegada, **8.1**
    arrival and departure board el tablero de llegadas y salidas, **8.1**
to **arrive** llegar, **3.1**
art el arte, **2.2**
artist el/la artista, **12.2**
to **ask for** pedir (i, i), **15.1**
to **assist** asistir, **5.2**
    at once en seguida, **16.1**
to **attend** asistir, **5.2**
    attractive atractivo(a), **1.2**
    audience el público, **12.2**
    August agosto (m.), **BV**

aunt la tía, **6.1**
aunt(s) and uncle(s) los tíos, **6.1**
author el/la autor(a), **12.2**
autumn el otoño, **7.1**
avenue la avenida, **5.1**

B

backboard (basketball) el tablero, **7.2**
backpack la mochila, **BV**
bad malo(a), **1**
baggage el equipaje, **8.1**
    baggage claim el reclamo de equipaje, **8.2**
balcony el balcón, **6.2**
ball el balón, **7.1**; la pelota, **7.2**; la bola, **11.2**
ballpoint pen el bolígrafo, **BV**
bank (of a river) la orilla, **16.2**
bar (of soap) la barra, la pastilla, **16.2**
base el base, el platillo, **7.2**
baseball el béisbol, **7.2**
basket el cesto, el canasto, **7.2**
    to make a basket encestar, meter en el cesto, **7.2**
basketball el baloncesto, el básquetbol, **7.2**
bat el bate, **7.2**
bathing suit el traje de baño, el bañador, **11.1**
bathroom el cuarto de baño, **5.1**
batter el/la bateador(a) **7.2**
to **be** ser, **1**; estar, **4.1**
    to be... years old tener... años, **6.1**
    to be hungry tener hambre, **15.1**
    to be thirsty tener sed, **15.1**
    to be tied (score) quedar empatado(a), **7.1**
to **be able** poder (ue), **7.1**
to **be called** llamarse, **16.1**
to **be going to** ir a, **6**
to **be named** llamarse, **16.1**
    beach la playa, **11.1**; playero(a) (adj), **11.1**
    beach resort el balneario, **11.1**
    beach towel la toalla playera, **11.1**
    bean el frijol, la habichuela, **15.2**
to **bear (the name)** llevar (el nombre)
    beautiful precioso(a), **6.2**
    bed la cama, **10.1**
    bedroom el cuarto de dormir, el

dormitorio, **5.1**
to **begin** empezar (ie), **7.1**; comenzar (ie)
beginner el/la principiante, **9.1**
below bajo, **9.1**
    below zero bajo cero, **9.1**
belt el cinturón, **13.1**
bench el banco, **BV**
berth la litera, **14.2**
bicycle la bicicleta, **6.2**
big grande, **2.1**
bill la cuenta, **12.2**
biologist el/la biólogo(a)
biology la biología, **2.2**
birthday el cumpleaños, **6.2**
black negro(a), **13.2**
blade la cuchilla, la hoja, **9.2**
to **block** bloquear, parar, **7.1**
blond(e) rubio(a), **1.1**
blouse la blusa, **13.1**
blue azul, **13.2**
blue jeans el blue jean, **13.1**
to **board** abordar, subir a, **8.1**
    board el tablero, **8.1**
    arrival and departure board el tablero de llegadas y salidas, **8.1**
boarding house la pensión, **16.2**
boarding el embarque, **8**
boarding pass la tarjeta de embarque, el pase de abordar, **8.1**
boastful fanfarrón (fanfarrona), **9.1**
boat el barco
    small boat el barquito, **11.1**
book el libro, **BV**
bookbag la mochila, **BV**
boot la bota, **9.1**
to **bore** aburrir, **13**
boring aburrido(a), **1.1**
to **bother** molestar, **13**
boy el muchacho, **BV**
bread el pan, **15.2**
breakfast el desayuno, **5.2**
    to eat breakfast desayunarse, **16.1**
to **bring** traer, **8**
brother el hermano, **2.1**
brown marrón, **13.2**
to **brush one's hair** cepillarse, **16.1**
brush el cepillo, **16.2**
building el edificio, **5.1**
bus el autobús, el bus, **3.1**
    to miss the bus perder el autobús, **12.1**
button el botón, **13.2**

to **buy** comprar, **5.2**
by (plane, car, bus, etc.) en

C

calculator la calculadora, **BV**
calorie la caloría, **10.2**
to **camp** acampar, **16.2;** ir de camping
camp el campamento, **16.2**
camping el camping, **16.2**
  to go camping acampar, **16.2;** ir de camping,
canteen la cantimplora, **16.2**
cap el gorro, **9.1**
captain el/la comandante, **8.2**
car el coche, el carro, **3.1;** (train) el vagón, **14.1;** el coche, **14.2**
carbohydrate el carbohidrato, **10.2**
card la tarjeta, **13.1**
  credit card la tarjeta de crédito, **13.1**
to **carry** llevar, **3.2**
carry-on luggage el equipaje de mano, **8.1**
cash register la caja, **13.1**
cat el/la gato(a), **6.1**
to **catch** atrapar, **7.2**
catcher el/la cátcher, el/la receptor(a), **7.2**
centigrade el centígrado, **9.1**
chair la silla, **BV**
  folding chair la silla plegable, **11.1**
chair lift el telesilla, **9.1**
chalk la tiza, **BV**
chalkboard la pizarra, **BV;** el pizarrón, **3.2**
cheap barato(a), **13.1**
to **check (luggage)** facturar, **8.1**
cheese el queso, **15.2**
chemistry la química, **2.2**
chest el pecho, **10.2**
chicken el pollo, **15.2**
children los hijos, **6.1**
chills los escalofríos, **10.1**
city la ciudad, **5.1**
civic education la educación cívica, **2.2**
to **claim** reclamar, **8.2**
class la clase, **2.1**
classical clásico(a), **4**
classroom la sala de clase, el salón de clase, **3.1**
clinic la clínica, **10.2**
clothes la ropa, **8.2**

clothing store la tienda de ropa, **13.1**
cloud la nube, **11.1**
cloudy nublado(a), **11.1**
  It's cloudy. Está nublado., **11.1**
club (golf) el palo, el bastón, **11.2**
coffee el café, **5.2**
cold (medical) el catarro, la gripe, **10.1**
  to have a cold tener catarro, **10.1**
cold (weather) el frío, **9.1**
  It's cold. Hace frío., **9.1**
to **collect** recoger, **8.2**
Colombian colombiano(a), **1**
color el color, **13.2**
  cream-, wine-, coffee-, olive-, maroon-, turquoise-colored de color crema, vino, café, oliva, marrón, turquesa, **13.2**
comb el peine, **16.2**
to **comb one's hair** peinarse, **16.1**
to **come on stage** entrar en escena, **12.2**
compartment el compartimiento, **14.2**
computer la computadora, **BV**
concert el concierto, **12.2**
conductor el/la director(a), **12.2;** (train) el/la revisor(a), **14.2**
cook el/la cocinero(a), **15.1**
co-pilot el/la copiloto, **8.2**
corridor el pasillo, **14.2**
to **cost** costar, **13.1**
cough la tos, **10.1**
  to have a cough tener tos, **10.1**
counter el mostrador, **8.1**
country el campo, **5.1**
course el curso, **2.1**
court (sports) la cancha, **7.2**
  tennis court la cancha de tenis, **11.2**
cousin el/la primo(a), **6.1**
covered cubierto(a), **9.2**
crew la tripulación, **8.2**
cup la taza, **15.1**
curtain el telón, **12.2**
customer el/la cliente, **5.2**
customs la aduana, **8.2**

D

dad el papá, **5.2**
to **dance** bailar, **4.2**
dark moreno(a), **1.1**
date la fecha, **BV**
  What is today's date? ¿Cuál es

la fecha de hoy? **BV**
daughter la hija, **6.1**
day el día
  the day before yesterday anteayer, **11.2**
December diciembre (m.), **BV**
degree el grado, **9.1**
delay el retraso, la demora, **14.2**
delicious delicioso(a), **15.2**
to **delight** encantar, **13**
deodorant el desodorante, **16.2**
departure la salida, **8.1**
  arrival and departure board el tablero de llegadas y salidas, **8.1**
  departure gate la puerta de salida, **8.1**
dessert el postre, **5.2**
destination el destino, **8.1**
diagnosis la diagnosis, **10.2**
to **die** morir (ue, u), **15**
diet la dieta, **10.2**
difficult difícil, **2.1**
dining car el coche-comedor, **14.2**
dining room el comedor, **5.1**
dinner la cena, **5.2**
  to have dinner cenar
to **dispense** despachar, **10.2**
doctor el/la médico(a), **10.2**
doctor's office la consulta del médico, el consultorio del médico, **10.2**
dog el perro, **6.1**
domestic de cabotaje, **8**
dose la dosis, **10.2**
dot: on the dot en punto, **3.1**
dress el vestido, **13.1**
to **dribble** driblar con, **7.2**
to **drink** tomar, **4.1;** beber, **5.2**
drug la droga, **10.2**
during durante, **4.2**

E

early temprano
easy fácil, **2.1**
to **eat** comer, **5.2**
  to eat breakfast desayunarse, **16.1**
egg el huevo, **15.2**
eight ocho, **BV**
eighth octavo, **5.1**
eighty ochenta, **BV**
elevator el ascensor, **5.1**
English el inglés, **2.2;** inglés (inglesa) (adj.)
to **enjoy oneself** divertirse (ie, i),

16.2
to **enter** entrar, **3.1**
  entrance la entrada, **6.2**
  eraser la goma, **BV**
  evening la noche
    good evening buenas noches,
    BV
  everyone todos, **4.2**
  examination el examen, **3.2**
to **examine** examinar, **10.2**
  exercise el ejercicio, **10.2**
    aerobic exercise el ejercicio
    aeróbico, **10.2**
    physical exercise el ejercicio
    físico, **10.2**
  exhibition la exposición, **12.2**
  expensive caro(a), **13.1**
  expert experto(a), **9.1**

F

  face la cara, **16.1**
to **fall asleep** dormirse (ue, u), **16.1**
  family la familia, **5.1**
  fantastic fantástico(a), **1.2**
  fast rápido, **9.1**
  father el padre, **6.1**
  February febrero (m.), **BV**
  fever la fiebre, **10.1**
  fiber la fibra, **10.2**
  field el campo, **7.1**
    soccer field el campo de
    fútbol, **7.1**
  fifth quinto(a), **5.1**
  fifty cincuenta, **BV**
  figure skating el patinaje
    artístico, **9.2**
  film la película, el film(e), **12.1**
  fine bien, **BV**
  first primer, primero(a), **BV**
  first aid kit el botiquín, **16.2**
to **fit** sentar bien a, **13.1**
    It fits me. Me sienta bien., **13.1**
  five cinco, **BV**
  flashlight la linterna, **16.2**
  flight el vuelo, **8.1**
    flight attendant el asistente (la
    asistenta) de vuelo, **8.2**
    flight number el número del
    vuelo, **8.1**
  floor el piso, **5.1**
  flower la flor, **6.2**
  flu la gripe, **10.1**
  folding plegable, **11.1**
    folding chair la silla plegable,
    11.1

to **follow** seguir (i, i), **15**
  foot el pie, **7.1**
    on foot a pie, **3.1**
  for de, **1.1**
  forest el bosque, **16.2**
  fork el tenedor, **15.1**
  forty cuarenta, **BV**
  four cuatro, **BV**
  fourth cuarto(a), **5.1**
  free libre, **14.2**
  French francés (francesa), **2.2**
  Friday el viernes, **BV**
  friend el/la amigo(a), **1.1**
  from de, **1.1**
  fruit la fruta, **15.2**
to **fry** freír (i, i), **15.1**
  fun divertido(a), **1.1**

G

  game el partido, **7.1**; el juego,
    11.2
    tennis game el juego de tenis,
    11.2
  garage el garaje, **6.2**
  garden el jardín, **6.2**
  gate la puerta, **8.1**
    departure gate la puerta de
    salida, **8.1**
  geography la geografía, **2.2**
  geometry la geometría, **2.2**
to **get** sacar, **3.2**
    to get good (bad) grades sacar
    notas buenas (malas), **3.2**
to **get dressed** vestirse (i, i), **16.1**
to **get off the train** bajar del tren,
    14.2
to **get on** subir a, **8.1**
    to get on the train subir al
    tren, **14.2**
to **get up** levantarse, **16.1**
  gift el regalo, **6.2**
  girl la muchacha, **BV**
to **give** dar, **4.2**
    glass (drinking) el vaso, **5.2**
    glasses (eye) las gafas, **9.1**
    glove el guante, **7.2**
to **go** ir, **4.1**
    they go van, **4.1**
    to go camping ir de camping,
    16.2
    to go home ir a casa, **4.2**
to **go back** volver (ue), **7.1**
to **go down** bajar, **9.1**
to **go for a swim** bañarse, **16.2**
to **go to bed** acostarse (ue), **16.1**
to **go up** subir, **5.1**

to **go with** hacer juego con, **13.2**
  goal el gol, la portería, **7.1**
  goalkeeper el/la portero(a), **7.1**
  golf el golf, **11.2**
    golf club el bastón, **11.2**
    golf course el campo de golf,
    11.2
    golf game el juego de golf,
    11.2
    golf bag la bolsa de golf, **11.2**
  good bueno(a), **1.2**
    good evening, good night
    buenas noches, **BV**
    good afternoon buenas tardes,
    BV
    good morning buenos días, **BV**
  good-bye adiós, chao, **BV**
  grade la nota, **3.2**; la calificacíon
  grandchild el/la nieto(a), **6.1**
  grandfather el abuelo, **6.1**
  grandmother la abuela, **6.1**
  grandparents los abuelos, **6.1**
  green el green (golf), **11.2**; verde
    (color), **13.2**
  grey gris, **13.2**
  ground el suelo, **7**
    ground floor la planta baja, **5.1**
to **guard** guardar, **7**
  guitar la guitarra, **4.2**

H

  hair el pelo, **16.1**
  half el tiempo (soccer), **7.1**
  ham el jamón, **15.2**
  hammock la hamaca, **11.1**
  hand la mano, **7.1**
  handle el mango, **11.2**
  happy contento(a), **10.1**
  hat el sombrero, **13.1**
to **have** tener, **6.1**
    to have to tener que, **6**
  he él, **1.1**
  head la cabeza, **7.1**
  headache el dolor de cabeza,
    10.1
  health la salud, **10**
  heat el calor, **11.1**
  heel el tacón, **13.2**
  hello hola, buenos dias, **BV**
  hi hola, **BV**
  high alto(a), **3.2**
  high school el colegio, la escuela
    secundaria, **1.1**
  hike la caminata, **16.2**
    to take a hike dar una
    caminata, **16.2**

hill la colina, **16.2**
history la historia, **2.2**
to **hit** golpear, **11.2;** batear (baseball), **7.2**
to **hit (baseball)** batear, **7.2**
hit (baseball) el hit, **7.2**
hole el hoyo, **11.2**
home casa, **4.2**
  at home en casa, **4.2**
home economics la economía domestica, **2.2**
home plate el platillo, **7.2**
home run el jonrón, **7.2**
honest honesto(a), **1.2**
hoop el aro, **7.2**
hospital el hospital, la clínica, **10.2**
hot: It's hot. Hace calor., **11.1**
house la casa, **4.1**
How much? ¿Cuánto(a)?, **BV**
  How much does it cost? ¿Cuánto cuesta?, **13.1**
  How much is it? ¿Cuánto es?, **BV**
how? ¿qué?, **BV;** ¿cómo?, **1.1**
  How are you? ¿Qué tal?, **BV;** ¿Cómo estás?
hunger el hambre, **15.1**
  to be hungry tener hambre, **15.1**
to **hurt** doler, **10.2**
  My___(part of body) hurts, aches. Me duele___., **10**
husband el marido, el esposo, **6.1**

I

I yo, **1.2**
ice el hielo, **9.2**
ice cream el helado, **5.2**
ice-skating el patinaje sobre hielo, **9.2**
immediately en seguida, **16**
in en, **1.1**
individual individuo, **7**
inning la entrada, **7.2**
to **inspect** revisar, **8;** inspeccionar, **8.2**
inspection el control, **8.1**
  passport inspection el control de pasaportes, **8.1**
  security inspection el control de seguridad, **8.1**
instructions las instrucciones, **5.2**
intelligent inteligente, **2.1**
to **interest** interesar, **13.1**

interesting interesante, **2.1**
invitation la invitación, **5.2**
to **invite** invitar (a), **4.2**
is es, **1.1**
It looks good on me. Me queda bien. **13.2**
Italian italiano(a), **2.2**

J

jacket la chaqueta, el saco, el blusón, **13.1**
January enero (m.), **BV**
jazz (adj.) de jazz, **4**
July julio (m.), **BV**
June junio (m.), **BV**

K

kind amable, **2.1**
kitchen la cocina, **4.1**
knapsack la mochila, **BV**
knife el cuchillo, **15.1**
to **know (a person)** conocer (a), **9.1**
to **know how** saber, **9.1**

L

lady la dama, **13.1**
to **land** aterrizar, **8.2**
language la lengua, **2.2**
large gran, grande, **2.1**
last: last night anoche, **11.2**
  last week la semana pasada, **11.2**
  last year el año pasado, **11.2**
late tarde, **8.1;** con retraso, con una demora, **14.2**
Latin el latín, **2.2**
to **learn** aprender, **5.2**
to **leave (something behind)** dejar, **12.2**
to **leave** salir, **8.1**
  left la izquierda, **5.1**
    to the left a la izquierda, **5.1**
lemonade la limonada, **BV**
lesson la lección, **3.2**
letter la carta, **5.2**
lettuce la lechuga, **15.2**
library la biblioteca, **4.1**
to **like** gustar, **13.1**
line (of people) la cola, la fila, **12.1**
to **listen** escuchar, **4.1**
  little poco(a), **5.2**
to **live** vivir, **5.1**
  living room la sala, **4.1**
  long largo(a), **13.2**

to **look at** mirar, **3.2**
  to look at oneself mirarse, **16.1**
to **lose** perder (ie), **7.1**
  low bajo, **3.2**
to **love** encantar, **13**
  luggage el equipaje, **8.1**
    carry-on (hand) luggage el equipaje de mano, **8.1**
  lunch el almuerzo, **5.2**

M

ma'am señora, **BV**
magazine la revista, **5.2**
to **make** hacer, **8.1**
  to make a basket encestar meter en el cesto, **7.2**
man el caballero, el señor, **13.1**
manner la manera, **1.1**
many muchos(as), **5**
March marzo (m.), **BV**
to **match** hacer juego con, **13.2**
mathematics las matemáticas, **2.2**
May mayo (m.), **BV**
Me neither. Ni yo tampoco., **13**
meal la comida, **5.2**
means: by no means de ninguna manera, **1.1**
meat la carne, **5.2**
medication el medicamento, **10.2**
medicine la medicina, **10**
medium (meat) a término medio, **15.2**
menu el menú, **12.2**
Mexican mexicano(a), **1.1**
midday el mediodía, **2**
midnight la medianoche, **2**
milk la leche, **5.2**
mirror el espejo, **16.1**
Miss señorita, **BV**
to **miss the bus** perder el autobús, **12.1**
mom la mamá, **5.2**
moment momento, **8.1**
Monday el lunes, **BV**
mood humor, **10**
  in a good mood de buen humor, **10**
  in a bad mood de mal humor, **10**
morning la mañana
  good morning buenos días, **BV**
  this morning esta mañana, **11.2**
mother la madre, **6.1**
motorbike el ciclomotor, **6.2**

mountain la montaña, 9.1
mouth la boca, 10.2
movie la película, 5.2; el film (e),
  12.1
    to show a movie dar
    (presentar) una película
movie theater el cine, 12.1
Mr. señor, BV
Mrs. señora, BV
mural el mural, 12.2
museum el museo, 12.2
music la música, 2.2
musical musical, 12.2
musician el/la músico, 12.2

N

nap la siesta, 11.1
    to take a nap echar (tomar)
    una siesta, 11.1
napkin la servilleta, 15.1
narrow estrecho(a), 13.2
nationality la nacionalidad, 1
necktie la corbata, 13.1
neither: Me neither. (Ni) yo
  tampoco., 13
nephew el sobrino, 6.1
nervous nervioso(a), 10.1
net la red, 7.2
never nunca, 13.1
new nuevo(a), 6.2
news las noticias, 5.2
newspaper el periódico, 5.2
newsstand el quiosco, 14.1
next próximo(a), 14.2
Nice to meet you. Mucho gusto.,
  BV
niece la sobrina, 6.1
niece(s) and nephew(s) los
  sobrinos, 6.1
night la noche
    good night buenas noches, BV
    last night anoche, 11.2
nine nueve, BV
ninety noventa, BV
ninth noveno, 5.1
no: by no means de ninguna
  manera, 1.1
no one, nobody nadie, 13
noncarbonated soft drink el
  refresco, 4.1
no smoking section la sección de
  no fumar, 8.1
noon el mediodía, 2
notebook el cuaderno, BV; la
  libreta, 3.2
notes los apuntes, 3.2

    to take notes tomar apuntes, 3.2
nothing nada, 13.1
novel la novela, 5.2
November noviembre (m.), BV
number el número, 8.1
    flight number el número del
    vuelo, 8.1
    seat number el número del
    asiento, 8.1
nurse el/la enfermero(a), 10.2

O

occupied ocupado(a), 14.2
October octubre (m.), BV
of de, 1.1
oil el aceite, 15.2
old viejo(a), 6.1
one uno, BV
one hundred cien(to), BV
one thousand mil, BV
one-way sencillo, 14.1
to open abrir, 8.2
opposite contrario(a), 7
orange (color) anaranjado(a), 13.2
orchestra la orquesta, 12.2
orchestra seat la butaca, 12.1
other otro(a), 2.2
out (baseball) el out, 7.2
outdoors al aire libre, 9.2
outfielder (baseball) el/la
  jardinero(a), 7.2
outskirts las afueras, 5.1
over por encima, 7.2
overcoat el abrigo, 13.1

P

to pack one's suitcase hacer la
  maleta, 8
painting el cuadro, 12.2
pantihose las medias, 13.1
pants los pantalones, 13.1
paper el papel, BV
    sheet of paper la hoja de
    papel, BV
parasol el parasol, 11.1
parents los padres, 6.1
park el parque, 6.2
party la fiesta, 4.2
to pass pasar, 7.2
passenger el/la pasajero(a), 8.1
passport el pasaporte, 8.1
    passport inspection el control
    de pasaportes, 8.1
patient el/la enfermo(a), 10.1
to pay pagar, 13.1

pencil el lápiz, 5.2
pepper la pimienta, 15.1
performance la representación, el
  espectáculo, 12.2
pharmacist el/la farmacéutico(a),
  10.2
pharmacy la farmacia, 10.2
physical físico(a), 10.2
    physical education la
    educación física, 2.2
physics la física, 2.2
piano el piano, 4.2
to pick up recoger, 8.2
picture el cuadro, 12.2
pill la pastilla, la píldora, el
  comprimido, 10.2
pilot el/la piloto, 8.2
to pinch apretar (ie), 13.2
    It (They) pinch(es) me. Me
    aprieta(n)., 13.2
pitcher el/la pícher, el/la
  lanzador(a), 7.2
plaid a cuadros, 13.2
plane el avión, 8
    by plane en avión, 8
plant la planta, 6.2
plate el plato, 15.1
    home plate el platillo, 7.1
to play (an instrument) tocar, 4.2
to play jugar (ue), 7.1
    player el/la jugador(a), 7.1
    please por favor, BV
point (score) el tanto, 7.1
pole el bastón, 9.1
pool la piscina, la alberca, 11.2
popular popular, 2.1
portable stove el hornillo, 16.2
porter el/la maletero(a), el/la
  mozo(a), 14.1
postcard la tarjeta postal, 5.2
potato la papa, 5.2
to prefer preferir (ie, i), 7
to prepare preparar, 4.1
to prescribe recetar, 10
    prescription la receta, 10.2
    pretty bonito(a), 6.2
    price el precio, 13.1
    private particular, privado(a), 5.1
    protein la proteína, 10.2
Puerto Rican puertorriqueño(a), 2
to put poner, 8.1
to put in meter, 7.1
to put on (clothes) ponerse, 16.1
to put on a performance dar una
  representación, 12.2
to put up a tent armar una tienda,
  16.2

Q

quarter: a quarter to, a quarter
  past menos cuarto, y cuarto, 2
quite bastante, 1.1

R

racquet la raqueta, 11.2
railroad el ferrocarril, 14.2
railway platform el andén, 14.1
railway track la vía, 14.1
to rain llover, 11.1
  It is raining. Llueve, 11.1
raincoat la gabardina, 13.1
rare (meat) casi crudo, 15.2
rather bastante, 1.1
raw crudo(a), 15.2
razor la navaja, 16.1
to read leer, 5.2
to receive sacar, 3.2; recibir, 6
record el disco, 4.1
red rojo(a), 13.2
referee el/la árbitro(a), 7.1
to rent alquilar, 11.1
to repeat repetir (i, i), 15
reserved reservado(a), 14.2
restaurant el restaurante, 12.2
to return (something) devolver
  (ue), 7.2
rice el arroz, 15.2
right la derecha, 5.1
  to the right a la derecha, 5.1
Right? ¿Verdad?, 1.1
right now en este momento, 8.1
rink la pista de patinaje, el
  patinadero, 9.2
river el río, 16.2
rock (music) (adj.) de rock, 4
roll (of paper) el rollo, 16.2
roller la rueda, 9.2
  roller skating el patinaje sobre
  ruedas, 9.2
room el cuarto, la habitación, 5.1
  classroom la sala de clase, el
  salón de clase, 3.1
  waiting room la sala de espera,
  14.1
round-trip de ida y vuelta, 14.1
row la fila, 8
to run correr, 7.2

S

sad triste, 10.1
salad la ensalada, 5.2
salesperson el/la dependiente,
  13.1

salt la sal, 15.1
sand la arena, 11.1
sandals las sandalias, 13.1
sandwich el sándwich, el
  bocadillo, 5.2
Saturday el sábado, BV
saucer el platillo, 15.1
to say decir, 9
scale la báscula, 8.1
schedule el horario, 14.1
school el colegio (high-school), la
  escuela, 1.1
  high school la escuela
  secundaria, el colegio, 1.1
school (adj.) escolar, 3.1
science la ciencia, 2.2
to score (sports) marcar, 7.1
scoreboard el tablero indicador,
  7.1
screen la pantalla, 8.1
sculptor el/la escultor(a), 12.2
sea el mar, 11.1
seat (in theater) la localidad,
  12.1
seat el asiento, 8.1; (movie
  theater) la butaca, 12.1
  seat number el número del
  asiento, 8.1
second segundo(a), 5.1
secondary secundario(a), 1.1
security la seguridad, 8.1
  security control el control de
  seguridad, 8.1
to see ver, 5.2
  See you later. Hasta luego., BV
  See you tomorrow. Hasta
  mañana., BV
  See you soon. Hasta pronto., BV
to sell vender, 5.2; despachar, 10.2
September septiembre (m.), BV
serious serio(a), 1.2
to serve servir (i, i), 15.1
seven siete, BV
seventh séptimo(a), 5.1
seventy setenta, BV
shampoo el champú, 16.2
to shave afeitarse, 16.1
  shaving cream la crema de
  afeitar, 16.2
she ella, 1.2
sheet la hoja, BV
  sheet of paper la hoja de
  papel, BV
shellfish el marisco, 15.2
to shine brillar, 11.1
shirt la camisa, 13.1
shoes los zapatos, 13.1

shop window el escaparate, la
  vitrina, 13.1
shopping de compras, 13.1
shopping center el centro
  comercial, 4.1
short (person) bajo(a), 1.1;
  (length) corto(a), 13.2
show el espectáculo, 12.2;
  (movies) la sesión, 12.1
to show a movie dar (presentar) una
  película, 12
shower la ducha, 16.2
  to take a shower tomar una
  ducha, 16.2
shy tímido(a), 1.2
sick enfermo(a), 10.1
sick person el/la enfermo(a),
  10.2
sincere sincero(a), 1.2
to sing cantar, 4.2
sir el señor, BV
sister la hermana, 2.1
to sit down sentarse (ie), 16.1
six seis, BV
sixth sexto(a), 5.1
sixty sesenta, BV
size el tamaño, la talla, 13.1
skate el patín, 9.2
to skate patinar, 9
skateboard el monopatín, 9.2
  to skateboard andar en
  monopatín, 9
skater el/la patinador(a), 9.2
skating el patinaje, 9.2
  figure skating el patinaje
  artístico, 9.2
  ice skating el patinaje sobre
  hielo, 9.2
  roller skating el patinaje sobre
  ruedas, 9.2
skating rink el patinadero, la
  pista de patinaje, 9.2
ski el esquí, 9.1
to ski esquiar, 9.1
  ski lift el telesquí, 9.1
  ski pole el bastón, 9.1
  ski resort la estación de esquí,
  9.1
  ski trail la pista, 9.1
skier el/la esquiador(a), 9.1
skiing el esquí, 9.1
  cross-country skiing el esquí
  nordico, el esquí de fondo, 9.1
  downhill skiing el esquí de
  descenso, el esqui alpino, 9.1
to skindive bucear, 11.1
  skindiving el buceo, 11.1

skirt la falda, 13.1
sky el cielo, 11.1
slalom el slálom, 9.1
to sleep dormir (ue, u), 7
sleeping bag el saco de dormir, 16.2
sleeping car el coche-cama, 14.2
sleeve la manga, 13.2
long-sleeved de manga larga, 13.2
short-sleeved de manga corta, 13.2
slope la cuesta, 9.1
small pequeño(a), 2.1; (amount) poco(a), 5.2
smoking (no smoking) section la sección de (no) fumar, 8.1
snack la merienda, 4.1
to sneeze estornudar, 10.1
snow la nieve, 9.1
to snow nevar (ie), 9.1
It's snowing. Nieva., 9
snowfall la nevada, 9.1
soap el jabón, 16.2
soap opera la telenovela, 5.2
soccer el fútbol, 7.1
soccer field el campo de fútbol, 7.1
social science las ciencias sociales, 2.2
social studies la educación cívica, 2.2
sociology la sociología, 2.2
socks los calcetines, 13.1
soda la gaseosa, 5.2
soft drink la gaseosa, 5.2
somebody alguien, 13
something algo, 9.1
sometimes a veces, 5.2
son el hijo, 6.1
sore throat el dolor de garganta, 10.1
soup la sopa, 5.2
South America la América del Sur, 8.1
Spanish el español (language), 2.2; español(a)
to speak hablar, 3.1
spectator el/la espectador(a), 7
spoon la cuchara, 15.1
sport el deporte, 2.2
sports broadcast la emisión deportiva, 5.2
spring la primavera, 7.2
stadium el estadio, 7.1
stage la escena, 12.2
to come on stage entrar en

escena, 12.2
stairway la escalera, 5.1
station la estación, 12.1
train station la estación de ferrocarril, 14.1
statue la estatua, 12.2
to stay in bed guardar cama, 10.1
steak el biftec, 15.2
to steal robar, 7.2
stockings las medias, 13.1
stomach el estómago, 10.1
stomachache el dolor de estómago, 10.1
stop la parada, 14.2
to stop parar, 7.1
store la tienda, 4.1 ·
men's clothing store la tienda de ropa para caballeros (señores), 13.1
women's clothing store la tienda de ropa para damas (señoras), 13.1
street la calle, 5.1
striped a rayas, 13.2
student el/la alumno(a), 1.1
to study estudiar, 3.2
subject la asignatura, la disciplina, 2.2
suburbs los suburbios, 5.1
subway el metro, 12.1
suit el traje, 13.1
suitcase la maleta, 8.1
to pack one's suitcase hacer la maleta, 8
summer el verano, 11.1
sun el sol, 11.1
It's sunny Hay sol, 11.1
suntan lotion la crema protectora (bronceadora), 11.1
to sunbathe tomar el sol, 11.1
Sunday el domingo, BV
sunglasses los anteojos de (para el) sol, 11.1
to surprise sorprender, 13
sweater el suéter, el jersey, 13.1
to swim nadar, 11.1
swimsuit el traje de baño, el bañador, 11.1
swimming pool la piscina, la alberca, 11.2
symptom el síntoma, 10.2

T

T-shirt el T shirt, 13.1
table la mesa, 12.2

tablecloth el mantel, 15.1
tablet la pastilla, 16.2
to take tomar, 3.2
to take a bath bañarse, 16
to take a hike dar una caminata,16.2
to take a nap echar (tomar) una siesta, 11.1
to take a shower tomar una ducha, 16.2
to take a trip hacer un viaje, 8.1
to take off (airplane) despegar, 8.2
tall alto(a), 1.1
tape la cinta, 4.1
taxi el taxi, 8.1
to teach enseñar, 3.2
teacher el/la profesor(a), 2.1
team el equipo; de equipo (adj.), 7.1
teaspoon la cucharita, 15.1
telephone el teléfono, 4.1
on the phone por teléfono, 4.1
television la televisión, 4.1
to tell decir, 9
temperature la temperatura, 9.1
ten diez, BV
tennis el tenis, 11.2
tennis court la cancha de tenis, 11.2
tennis game el juego de tenis, 11.2
tennis shoes los tenis, 13.1
tent la tienda de campaña, la carpa, 16.2
to put up a tent armar una tienda, 16.2
tenth décimo(a), 5.1
test el examen, 3.2
thank you gracias, BV
that eso, 3.1; aquel, aquella, 9.2
the el, la, 1.1
theater el teatro, 12.2
theatrical teatral, 12.2
there is/are hay, 5.1
third tercer(o)(a), 5.1
thirst la sed, 15.1
to be thirsty tener sed, 15.1
thirty treinta, BV
this este (esta), 9
thousand mil, BV
three tres, BV
throat la garganta, 10.2
sore throat el dolor de garganta, 10.1
to have a sore throat tener dolor de garganta, 10.1
to throw tirar, lanzar, 7.1; echar
Thursday el jueves, BV

ticket el boleto, el billete **8.1**
  one-way ticket el billete sencillo, **14.1**
  round-trip ticket el billete de ida y vuelta, **14.1**
  ticket window la ventanilla, la boletería, **9.1**; la taquilla, **12.1**
tied empatado(a), **7**
tight estrecho(a), **13.2**
time tiempo, **7.1**
  on time a tiempo, **8.1**
  At what time? ¿A qué hora?, **2**
timid tímido(a), **1.2**
tip la propina, **12.2**
tired cansado(a), **10.1**
to a; con destino a, **8**
today hoy, **BV**
toilet paper el papel higiénico, **16.2**
tonight esta noche, **11.2**
too también, **1.1**
too (much) demasiado, **13.2**
tooth el diente, **16.1**
toothpaste la pasta dentífrica, **16.2**
tortilla la tortilla, **15.2**
to **touch** tocar, **7**
tourist el/la turista, **12.2**
towel la toalla, **11.1**
  beach towel la toalla playera, **11.1**
town el pueblo, **5.1**
trail la pista, **9.1**
train el tren, **14.1**
  train station la estación de ferrocarril, **14.1**
to **transfer** transbordar, **14.2**
transportation el transporte, **12**
tree el árbol, **6.2**
trigonometry la trigonometría, **2.2**
trip el viaje, **8.1**
  to take a trip hacer el viaje, **8.1**
trumpet la trompeta, **4.2**
trunk (of car) el/la maletero(a), **8.1**
truth la verdad, **1.1**
  Isn't it true? ¿No es verdad?, **1.1**
tube el tubo, **16.2**
Tuesday el martes, **BV**
twenty veinte, **BV**
two dos, **BV**

U

umbrella la sombrilla, **11.1**

uncle el tío, **6.1**
underground subterráneo(a), **12**
undershirt la camiseta, **13.1**
to **understand** comprender, **5.2**
unpleasant antipático(a), **1.1**
until hasta, **BV**
to **use** usar, **11.1**

V

vegetable la legumbre, la verdura, el vegetal, **15.2**
very muy, **BV**
view la vista, **6.2**
violin el violín, **4.2**
vitamin la vitamina, **10.2**
volleyball el vólibol, **7.2**

W

to **wait for** esperar
  waiter el mesero, **12.2**
  waitress la mesera, **12.2**
to **wake up** despertarse (ie), **16.1**
to **want** querer (ie), **7**
to **wash oneself** lavarse, **16.1**
to **watch** ver, **5.2**
  water el agua, **11.1**
  water skiing el esquí acuático, **11.1**
    to go water skiing esquiar en el agua, **11.1**
  wave la ola, **11.1**
  way la manera, **1.1**
we nosotros(as), **2.2**
we are somos, **2.2**; estamos, **4**
to **wear** llevar
Wednesday el miércoles, **BV**
week la semana, **11.2**
  last week la semana pasada, **11.2**
  this week esta semana, **11.2**
well bien, **BV**
well done (meat) bien cocido (hecho), **15.2**
what? ¿cuál?, ¿qué?, **BV**; ¿cómo?, **1.1**
  What is it? ¿Qué es?, **BV**
  What is today's date? ¿Cuál es la fecha de hoy?, **BV**
  What time is it? ¿Qué hora es?, **2**
  What's the weather like? ¿Qué tiempo hace?, **9.1**
wheel la rueda, **9.2**
when? ¿cuándo?, **3.1**
where? ¿dónde?, **1.2**; ¿adónde?, **4**

which? ¿cuál?, **BV**
white blanco(a), **13.2**
who? ¿quién?, **BV**
  who is it (she, he)? ¿quién es?, **BV**
wide ancho(a), **13.2**
wife la esposa, la mujer, **6.1**
to **win** ganar, **7.1**
wind el viento, **11.1**
  It's windy. Hace viento., **11.1**
windsurfboard la plancha de vela, **11.1**
winter el invierno, **9.1**
work la obra, **12.2**
to **work** trabajar, **4.1**
to **write** escribir, **5.2**
  writing pad el bloc, **3.2**

Y

year el año, **11.2**
  last year el año pasado, **11.2**
  this year este año, **11.2**
yellow amarillo(a), **13.2**
yesterday ayer, **11.1**
  the day before yesterday anteayer, **11.2**
  yesterday afternoon ayer por la tarde, **11.2**
  yesterday morning ayer por la mañana, **11.2**
you Uds., ustedes (pl. form.), **2.2**
you are son (pl. form.), **2.1**; están (pl. form.), **4.1**
you go van (pl. form.), **4.1**
You're welcome. De nada, No hay de qué, **BV**
young joven, **6.1**
youth hostel el albergue juvenil, **16.2**

Z

zero cero, **BV**
zipper la cremallera, el zíper, **13.2**

ÍNDICE
GRAMATICAL

511